BARBARY CAPTIVES

Barbary Captives

AN ANTHOLOGY OF EARLY MODERN
SLAVE MEMOIRS BY EUROPEANS
IN NORTH AFRICA

Mario Klarer

Columbia University Press
New York

Columbia University Press
Publishers Since 1893
New York   Chichester, West Sussex
cup.columbia.edu

Copyright © 2022 Columbia University Press
All rights reserved

Library of Congress Cataloging-in-Publication Data
Names: Klarer, Mario, 1962– editor.
Title: Barbary captives : an anthology of early modern slave memoirs by Europeans in North Africa / Mario Klarer.
Description: New York : Columbia University Press, [2022] | Includes bibliographical references and index.
Identifiers: LCCN 2021033280 (print) | LCCN 2021033281 (ebook) | ISBN 9780231175241 (hardback) | ISBN 9780231175258 (trade paperback) | ISBN 9780231555128 (ebook)
Subjects: LCSH: Slavery—Africa, North—History—Sources. | Captivity narratives—Africa, North. | Slaves—Africa, North—Biography—Sources.
Classification: LCC HT1345 .B37 2022 (print) | LCC HT1345 (ebook) | DDC 306.3/620961—dc23
LC record available at https://lccn.loc.gov/2021033280
LC ebook record available at https://lccn.loc.gov/2021033281

Cover design: Milenda Nan Ok Lee
Cover image: Engraving of early modern Tunis. Georg Braun and Frans Hogenberg, *Civitates Orbis Terrarum*, vol. 2 (Cologne, 1575), Mario Klarer, private collection.

For Marjorie Perloff

Contents

Preface ix
Acknowledgments xiii

Introduction 1

Narratives

I Balthasar Sturmer, *Account of the Travels of Mister Balthasar Sturmer* (1558 German manuscript; captivity in Tunis 1534–1535; complete text) 51

II Antonio de Sosa, *Topography of Algiers*: Attempted Escape of Miguel de Cervantes (1612 Spanish print edition; captivity in Algiers 1577; selection) 91

III Ólafur Egilsson, *The Travels of Reverend Ólafur Egilsson* (undated Icelandic manuscripts; Icelandic raid and captivity in Algiers 1627–1628; selection) 101

IV Emanuel d'Aranda, *Short Story of My Unfortunate Journey* (undated Dutch manuscript; captivity in Algiers 1640–1641; complete captivity narrative) 117

V Antoine Quartier, *The Religious Slave and His Adventures* (1690 French print edition; captivity in Tripoli 1660–1668; selection) 161

VI   Andreas Matthäus and Johann Georg Wolffgang, *Travels and Wonderful Fortunes of Two Brothers in Algerian Bondage* (1767 German print edition; captivity in Algiers 1684–1688; complete text)   187

VII   Isaac Brassard, *The Tale of Mr. Brassard's Captivity in Algiers* (1878 French print edition; captivity in Algiers 1687–1688; complete captivity narrative)   201

VIII   Thomas Pellow, *The History of the Long Captivity and Adventures of Thomas Pellow* ([1740?] British print edition; captivity in Morocco 1715–1738; selection)   211

IX   Hark Olufs, *The Remarkable Adventures of Hark Olufs* (1747 Danish print edition; captivity in Constantine 1724–1735; complete text)   233

X   Maria ter Meetelen, *Miraculous and Remarkable Events of Twelve Years of Slavery* (1748 Dutch print edition; captivity in Morocco 1731–1743; selection)   255

XI   Marcus Berg, *Description of the Barbaric Slavery in the Kingdom of Fez and Morocco* (1757 Swedish print edition; captivity in Morocco 1754–1756; selection)   281

XII   Elizabeth Marsh, *Narrative of Elizabeth Marsh's Captivity in Barbary* (undated British manuscript; captivity in Morocco 1756; complete captivity narrative)   307

XIII   Felice Caronni, *The Account of an Amateur Antiquarian's Short Journey* (1805 Italian print edition; captivity in Tunis 1804; selection)   339

Appendix: Selection of European and American Barbary Captivity Narratives   357
List of Works Cited and General Works on North African Piracy and Captivity   369
Index of Persons and Locations   389

Preface

Abducted by pirates,[1] sold on the slave market, and enslaved in North Africa—such was the fate of hundreds of thousands of Europeans, both male and female, in the early modern period. A large number of returnees from Muslim captivity on the "Barbary Coast," as the North African shore was called, wrote and published accounts of their experiences.[2] This anthology brings together, for the very first time, English translations of a selection of Barbary captivity narratives from nine different European regions and languages. The linguistic and geographic spectrum of these texts includes narratives in Spanish, Italian, French, German, Dutch, English, Danish, Swedish, and Icelandic. The diverse European national specimens of the Barbary captivity narrative also span three centuries, from the mid-sixteenth to the early nineteenth century, during which these texts assumed

---

1. *pirate*: in this anthology, the terms "corsair," "pirate," and "privateer" are used in a broad sense. While "corsair" and "privateer" usually refer to pirates operating with state sanction, it should be noted that the distinctions between these terms are often blurred by the authors of the early modern narratives in this anthology.

2. *Muslim captivity*: in this anthology, the terms "Muslim captivity" and "North African captivity" are used in a broad sense and encompass persons who were captured by North African pirates, those who were sold in North African slave markets, those who were held for ransom (without necessarily having to work as slaves), and those who were forced into slave labor, among other things. For more on terminological aspects of captives and slaves, see Peter Mark, "'Free, Unfree, Captive, Slave': António de Saldanha, a Late Sixteenth-Century Captive in Marrakesh," in *Piracy and Captivity in the Mediterranean*, ed. Mario Klarer (London: Routledge, 2019), 99–110.

a genre-like status.[3] These narratives greatly influenced the development of the modern novel and autobiography—an impact that this anthology helps unearth by making the various manifestations of this early modern text type accessible to international readers, scholars, and students.

The thirteen texts in this selection bear witness to the different facets of Barbary captivity narratives, documenting the fates of male and female European slaves in Algiers, Tunis, Tripoli, and Morocco, thus representing the major settings of Barbary corsairing and slavery. The selected narratives cover a wide range of experiences, including those of Christian pirates, Christian rowers on Muslim galleys, and house slaves in the palaces of rulers, as well as simple domestic servants, agricultural slaves, renegades (Christians who had converted to Islam), social climbers in captivity, entrepreneurial slaves, and female captives who found themselves objects of a sultan's desire. The texts also reflect the various ways in which Europeans fell into the hands of corsairs, including the capture of vessels on the high seas and land raids for human bounty. In addition, the narratives illustrate different possibilities of being liberated from slavery, including forms of ransom and exchange, escape, and religious conversion. Despite their North African setting, the texts also demonstrate a variety of political and religious tensions at work in early modern Europe, above all, the antagonism between Catholicism and Protestantism. Finally, the selected narratives in the anthology also cover early modern dissemination practices of this particular text type, ranging from uniquely preserved handwritten manuscripts and multiple print editions to historical translations that bridged linguistic and cultural divides. The aim of this collection is to highlight the diverse nature of the Barbary captivity narrative as a genre, while simultaneously pointing out its common features.

Each of the thirteen texts in this anthology is preceded by a short headnote that places the narrative in its larger context and historical background. The English translations deliberately remain as close as possible to the originals with respect to syntax, wording, and structure. However, all translations use modern English and do not try to mimic the historicity of the original language. To enhance readability, the translations at times provide information in square brackets that was not part of the original text.

3. *national*: the terms "nation," "national," and "nationality" are used loosely in this anthology to indicate the origins of persons as well as regions. It should be noted that several of the early modern authors also use these terms to refer to their own backgrounds and those of others, rather than to what are considered nation-states today.

Footnotes explain terminology, proper and geographic names, and historical context where necessary. Whenever possible, the testimonies in this anthology are included in full length. Some of the longer narratives had to be shortened to stay within the framework of a concise and usable collection. If a text has been cut, this is clearly indicated in the table of contents and in the headnote, as well as in the text itself.

All texts have been arranged in chronological order with regard to the events depicted in the narratives. In some cases, this might lead to a substantial discrepancy between the date of the print publication and the temporal setting of the original narrative.

Acknowledgments

I am indebted to a number of organizations and individuals who contributed to this collection in a variety of ways. The Austrian Science Fund granted the five-year research project ESCAPE (www.uibk.ac.at/projects/escape) from 2014 to 2019. The project made it possible to host two conferences on piracy and captivity in the early modern Mediterranean in 2015 and 2016 and to organize the large summer exhibition *Pirates and Slaves in the Mediterranean* in Schloss Ambras, Innsbruck, from 20 June to 6 October 2019—an event that assembled many original artifacts and attracted international scholars as well as sixty thousand interested visitors. The Austrian Federal Ministry of Education, Science and Research granted the Sparkling Science project SLAVES (www.uibk.ac.at/projects/slaves) from 2017 to 2019 to allow high school students to participate in the organization of the museum exhibition. These different events brought together contributors to two collections of essays on Barbary captivity for a fruitful exchange of ideas and perspectives that greatly impacted this anthology.

I wish to thank Julia Ott, Robert Spindler, and Bernadette Rangger for their support over the years in putting together this anthology. In addition to his general input, Robert Spindler also retrieved all images and permissions for illustrations. I would also like to express my gratitude to the following individuals for giving their valuable time and expertise to assist with providing explanations and clarifying cases of doubt in the following languages: Mark Cruse and Renaud Tschirner for French; Erica Autelli for Italian;

Diana de Armas Wilson, Alfonso Merello Astigarraga, and Camila Torres Carrillo for Spanish; Devin Stewart, Stephan Procházka, and Ercan Akyol for Arabic and Ottoman Turkish; Frederiek ten Broeke and Lisa Kattenberg for Dutch; Klaus Amann and Hubert Alisade for early modern German. Wolfgang Kaiser and Magnus Ressel have supported me with their knowledge of various aspects of early modern captivity and ransom. I am very indebted to Gillian Weiss for reading through the entire manuscript and for improving it with her great expertise on piracy and slavery in the Mediterranean.

Most of the translations in this anthology are collaborative works by a number of individuals who will be credited separately for their input in the respective sections. As the editor, I provided all the headnotes that precede the narratives, edited all translations, and created most of the explanatory footnotes. Footnotes in Egilsson's narrative were, for the most part, kindly provided by Karl Smári Hreinsson and Adam Nichols. Particular thanks go to Almiria Wilhelm for assisting with editing the translations, copyediting and proofreading this volume, compiling the index, as well as for her help in seeing the anthology through the final stages of production.

I dedicate this anthology to my dear friend Marjorie Perloff, whose life story has always reminded me of the narratives by Barbary captives in the early modern era. At the age of six, she was forced to leave her hometown of Vienna for New York to escape the Nazi terror and consequently had to come to terms with a completely new language and culture. For the past thirty years, I have been able to follow Marjorie's gradual re-embracing of her Austrian background, both academically, with books on the Austrian philosopher Ludwig Wittgenstein and major Austrian writers between the two world wars, as well as on a personal level, by publishing her memoir *The Vienna Paradox* (2004) about her flight from a hometown that had ceased to be home.

BARBARY CAPTIVES

Introduction

Captivity Narratives as an Early Modern Genre

When considering "historical slave narratives," we almost reflexively equate them with the autobiographical accounts of slaves of African descent in the Americas. These narratives are commonly regarded as the oldest examples of a tradition-rich text type that gave voice to an oppressed and unfree group. However, even experts focusing on slavery in the United States or the Caribbean often overlook the fact that this autobiographical genre of African American self-expression harks back structurally and in content to a series of narrative predecessors. Among these textual forerunners are the testimonies of Europeans who fell into North African captivity during the early modern period.[1] Between the early sixteenth and the early nineteenth century, it is estimated that several hundred thousand European sailors, passengers, and inhabitants of coastal regions were captured, sold, and held as slaves in the North African cities Tunis, Algiers, Tripoli, and Salé

---

1. Two essay collections deal with this early modern phenomenon from a multinational perspective: Mario Klarer, ed., *Piracy and Captivity in the Mediterranean: 1550–1810* (London: Routledge, 2019); and Mario Klarer, ed., *Mediterranean Slavery and World Literature: Captivity Genres from Cervantes to Rousseau* (London: Routledge, 2020). In addition, the museum catalogue from the 2019 international exhibition in Schloss Ambras, Innsbruck, Austria, provides a concise overview of the topic with ample visual material: Mario Klarer, Sabine Haag, and Veronika Sandbichler, eds., *Piraten und Sklaven im Mittelmeer: Eine Ausstellung in Schloss Ambras Innsbruck 20. Juni bis 6. Oktober 2019* (Vienna: Kunsthistorisches Museum, 2019).

Figure I.1 Schematic map of the Mediterranean showing major places mentioned in the narratives
Source: Moritz Klarer

(see fig. I.1).[2] Many of these captives on the so-called Barbary Coast served primarily as a means to demand ransom from Europe. Such ransom activities appear to have been an important part of North Africa's economy at the time (see fig. I.2).

Naturally, Mediterranean piracy and the enslavement of people that resulted from it was not a phenomenon that originated only in North Africa. There were analogous structures on the European side as well. The Knights of Malta and the Order of Saint Stephen, in particular, played leading roles in European Christian piracy and privateering. Most likely, a similar or even larger number of North African Muslim individuals fell into European hands and were traded at slave markets such as those in Malta, Livorno, Málaga,

---

2. Robert C. Davis, "Counting European Slaves on the Barbary Coast," *Past & Present* 172, no. 1 (2001): 87–124; Robert C. Davis, *Christian Slaves, Muslim Masters: White Slavery in the Mediterranean, the Barbary Coast, and Italy, 1500–1800* (Basingstoke, UK: Palgrave Macmillan, 2003); Gerald MacLean, "Slavery and Sensibility: A Historical Dilemma," in *Slavery and the Cultures of Abolition: Essays Marking the Bicentennial of the British Abolition Act of 1807*, ed. Brycchan Carey and Peter J. Kitson (Cambridge: Brewer, 2007), 173–94; Salvatore Bono, *Schiavi Musulmani Nell'Italia Moderna: Galeotti, vu' Cumpra', Domestici* (Perugia: Universitá degli Studii, 1999); Salvatore Bono, *Schiavi. Una storia mediterranea (XVI–XIX secolo)* (Bologna: Société Editrice il mulino, 2016).

Figure I.2 Frontispiece depicting a monk redeeming a Christian slave
Source: Pierre Dan, *Historie van Barbaryen, En des zelfs Zee-Roovers* (Amsterdam, 1684); Mario Klarer, private collection.

and Marseille.³ This bilateral phenomenon dominated Mediterranean history for three centuries. The involvement of the young United States during the so-called Barbary Wars at the beginning of the nineteenth century and the colonial politics of France, with the conquest of Algiers in 1830, finally marked the end of Mediterranean piracy and slavery.⁴

During the three centuries of corsairing and human trafficking in the Mediterranean, a large number of returnees—mostly Europeans, as well as some Americans—published accounts of their experiences in North African captivity.⁵ These testimonies were much in demand from printers and publishers due to their exotic settings and their dramatic and adventurous content. Like the early novel, these authentic narratives captured the imagination of a large target audience in Europe. Several of these captivity narratives, such as that of Emanuel d'Aranda, included in this anthology, went through many print runs or were translated into several major European languages.

Because of their popularity, these captivity reports took on an almost literary or genre-like character and shaped the rise of the novel substantially. For instance, the major examples of the modern novel, *Don Quixote* (1605) and *Robinson Crusoe* (1719), are strongly influenced by North African slavery:

---

3. Salvatore Bono gives one of the highest estimates of Muslim slaves in European captivity. He believes that between the sixteenth and nineteenth centuries, as many as two million Muslim slaves from the Mediterranean region may have been held in Europe. See Salvatore Bono, "Slave Histories and Memoirs in the Mediterranean World: A Study of the Sources (Sixteenth–Eighteenth Centuries)," in *Trade and Cultural Exchange in the Early Modern Mediterranean, Braudel's Maritime Legacy*, ed. Maria Fusaro, Colin Heywood, and Mohamed-Salah Omro (New York: Tauris, 2010), 105; Bono, *Schiavi*, 72. See also Daniel Hershenzon, " '[P]ara que me saque cabesa por cabesa . . .': Exchanging Muslim and Christian Slaves Across the Western Mediterranean," *African Economic History* 42 (2014): 11–36. For more detailed estimates for specific regions, see also Alessandro Stella, *Histoires d'Esclaves dans la Péninsule Ibérique* (Paris: Éditions EHESS, 2000), 78–79; Raffaella Sarti, "Bolognesi schiavi dei 'turchi' e schiavi 'turchi' a Bologna tra cinque e settecento: alterità etnico-religiosa e riduzione in schiavitù," *Quaderni Storici* 107 (2001): 450; Michel Fontenay, "Il mercato maltese degli schiavi al tempo dei Cavalieri di San Giobanni," *Quaderni Storici* 107 (2001): 397.

4. For more on the Barbary Wars, see Robert J. Allison, *The Crescent Obscured: The United States and the Muslim World, 1776–1815* (New York: Oxford University Press, 1995); Frederic C. Leiner, *The End of Barbary Terror, America's 1815 War Against the Pirates of North Africa* (New York: Oxford University Press, 2007); Brett Goodin, *From Captives to Consuls: Three Sailors in Barbary and Their Self-Making Across the Early American Republic, 1770–1840* (Johns Hopkins University Press, 2020).

5. For British Barbary captivity narratives, see the anthology by Daniel Vitkus, ed., *Piracy, Slavery, and Redemption: Barbary Captivity Narratives from Early Modern England* (New York: Columbia University Press, 2001); for American narratives, see Paul M. Baepler, ed., *White Slaves, African Masters: An Anthology of American Barbary Captivity Narratives* (Chicago, IL: University of Chicago Press, 1999); for a German selection, see Mario Klarer, ed., *Verschleppt, Verkauft, Versklavt: Deutschsprachige Sklavenberichte aus Nordafrika (1550–1800)* (Vienna: Böhlau, 2019); for a selection of narratives by female slaves, see Khalid Bekkaoui, ed., *White Women Captives in North Africa: Narrative of Enslavement, 1735–1830* (Basingstoke, UK: Palgrave Macmillan, 2011).

The author Miguel de Cervantes, who was a captive in Algiers for five years in the 1570s, incorporated personal slave experiences into his literary works including *Don Quixote*;[6] Daniel Defoe's *Robinson Crusoe* (see fig. I.3) was shaped by authentic captivity narratives published in England in the sixteenth century.[7] Through Cervantes and Defoe as pivotal authors, captivity and narratives of captivity set in North Africa can be causatively connected to the evolution of the genre of the novel in the early modern era. Barbary narratives also served as models for captivity narratives in general, starting with Mary Rowlandson's seventeenth-century account of captivity among Native Americans (1682). Thus, the Barbary captivity narrative influenced both the rise of the European novel and various forms of the modern autobiography.

Naturally, Barbary captivity narratives also had an impact on the genre of African American slave accounts, which emerged much later and, in turn, indirectly impacted the abolition of slavery in the nineteenth century.[8] Even one of the first Puritan texts criticizing slavery in North America, Samuel Sewall's *The Selling of Joseph* (1700), made recourse to white slavery in North Africa to facilitate identification with the victims of slavery in America. Despite being a serious religious text, Sewall's essay structurally anticipated Benjamin Franklin's satirical diatribe "Sidi Mehemet Ibrahim on the Slave Trade." In this 1790 attack on slavery, Franklin adopted the voice of an Algerian beneficiary of white slavery who uses economic, religious, and cultural arguments analogous to those of the proponents of slavery in the United States.[9] About half a century later, before the American Civil War,

---

6. Michael Ross Gordon, "Cervantes' Algerian Swan Song: The Birth of *Los baños de Argel* and Its Positive Portrayal of Jews," in *Mediterranean Slavery and World Literature: Captivity Genres from Cervantes to Rousseau*, ed. Mario Klarer (London: Routledge, 2020), 96–110; María A. Garcés, *Cervantes in Algiers: A Captive's Tale* (Nashville, TN: Vanderbilt University Press, 2002).

7. G. A. Starr, "Defoe, Slavery, and Barbary," in *Mediterranean Slavery and World Literature: Captivity Genres from Cervantes to Rousseau*, ed. Mario Klarer (London: Routledge, 2020), 277–93; G. A. Starr, "Escape from Barbary: A Seventeenth-Century Genre," *Huntington Library Quarterly* 29 (1965): 35–52.

8. European captivity narratives from North Africa influenced the content and structure of, among others, American captivity narratives like *A Narrative of the Captivity and Restoration of Mrs. Mary Rowlandson* (1682)—a "best seller" about the kidnapping and abduction of a white woman by North American indigenous inhabitants—as well as African American slave accounts such as *The Interesting Narrative of the Life of Olaudah Equiano, Or Gustavus Vassa, The African* (1789).

9. Carsten Junker, "Of Cross and Crescent: Analogies of Violence and the Topos of 'Barbary Captivity' in Samuel Sewall's *The Selling of Joseph* (1700), with a Postscript on Benjamin Franklin," in *Mediterranean Slavery and World Literature: Captivity Genres from Cervantes to Rousseau*, ed. Mario Klarer (London: Routledge, 2020), 259–76.

Figure I.3 Frontispiece and title page of the first edition of *Robinson Crusoe*
Source: Daniel Defoe, *Robinson Crusoe* (London, 1719); frontispiece: Don. e. 442; title page: Don. e. 442; Bodleian Library, University of Oxford, UK.

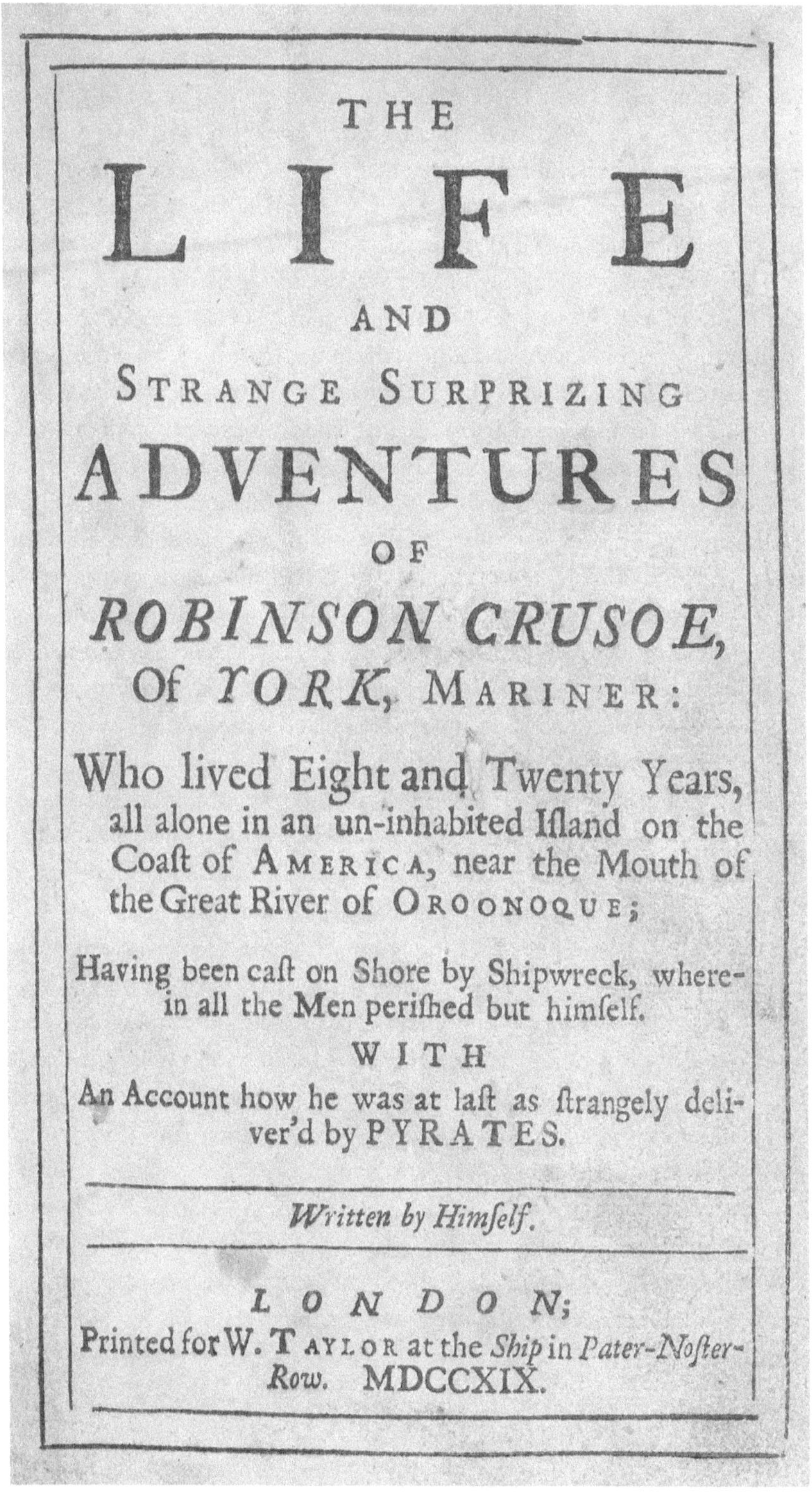

THE
LIFE
AND

STRANGE SURPRIZING

ADVENTURES

OF

ROBINSON CRUSOE,
Of *YORK,* MARINER:

Who lived Eight and Twenty Years,
all alone in an un-inhabited Island on the
Coast of AMERICA, near the Mouth of
the Great River of OROONOQUE;

Having been cast on Shore by Shipwreck, wherein all the Men perished but himself.

WITH

An Account how he was at last as strangely deliver'd by PYRATES.

Written by Himself.

LONDON;
Printed for W. TAYLOR at the *Ship* in *Pater-Noster-Row.* MDCCXIX.

Figure I.3 (Continued)

Charles Sumner, a U.S. senator from Massachusetts known for his abolitionist stance, published a short history of Barbary captivity entitled *White Slavery in the Barbary States* (1853). By depicting white slavery in North Africa in the early modern period and thus indirectly drawing a parallel with the enslavement of persons of African descent in the United States, he made it easier for his readers to identify and sympathize with the fate of American slaves.

However, the large number of white slaves affected by Barbary captivity has also been instrumentalized to serve non-humanitarian positions. Captivity narratives by Europeans and Americans in particular have provided handy representations of Otherness that have lent themselves to exploitation for xenophobic and white supremacist agendas. The narratives' leitmotif of North African masters exerting power over European or American captives, together with often gruesome depictions of violence and torture, seemingly legitimize stereotyping and political sanctions along an alleged Muslim–Christian binary (see figs. I.15, I.16, I.17). On closer inspection, the narratives turn out to be very complex negotiations of power that escape such simplistic Muslim–Christian antagonism. Very often, the actors in this theater of power cannot be assigned to clear-cut religious positions. Renegades, in particular, are key figures in this oscillation between domination and subjugation.

Barbary captivity narratives are set in the multicultural metropolises of North Africa, making the genre an ideal testing ground for key terminologies of contemporary cultural and postcolonial theory. Concepts including "third space," "mimicry," "hybridity," and "ambivalence" come into play in the representations of indigenous populations, the Ottoman and Arabic ruling classes, Jewish communities, Muslim refugees from the Iberian Peninsula, the international mix of European and sub-Saharan slaves, as well as renegades with diverse religious and linguistic backgrounds.[10] Not many other early modern geographic areas are able to provide more significant multicultural settings than the Barbary coast as represented in more than three centuries of European captivity narratives. Edward Said's claim that Western Orientalist discourses employ the Orient primarily as a foil to negotiate concerns that shed more light on Europe than on the "exotic" country also largely holds true for European Barbary captivity narratives.[11] Intra-Christian religious friction, open political conflicts, and national tensions among Europeans characterize many of the narratives, including those in this volume.

---

10. Homi K. Bhabha, *The Location of Culture* (London: Routledge, 1994).
11. Edward W. Said, *Orientalism* (New York: Random House, 1979), 6.

The present selection of North African captivity narratives assembles a cross section of this prolific genre in a number of European languages, spanning geographic regions from the southern Mediterranean to the North Atlantic. The anthology includes texts in Spanish, Italian, French, German, Dutch, English, Danish, Swedish, and Icelandic. In addition to accounts that have survived only as handwritten manuscripts, a large number of texts appeared in print, some of which went through multiple editions and translations into several languages. Even the small sample of texts assembled in this anthology shows how international and cross-national this early modern genre was. In addition to language barriers, many of these texts also bridged Christian denominational boundaries. This was quite remarkable at a time when the Thirty Years' War (1618–1648) was exposing Europe's intra-Christian antagonisms. The Barbary captivity narratives are representations of very personal experiences that also reflect larger political affairs, both domestic and foreign. The texts in this selection are contemporary eyewitness accounts of major historical developments in the early modern period. They are also specimens of a text type that decisively shaped the evolution of modern literature and the novel in particular—an influence that has yet to be explored fully in scholarship.

The opening text in the collection, namely the eyewitness account of the German merchant's son Balthasar Sturmer from the mid-sixteenth century, constitutes the first recorded North African captivity narrative in the early modern era.[12] With Balthasar Sturmer's account, the genre made a dramatic entrance. Despite being the first of its kind, Sturmer's text also represents a high point of the genre, with the structure and style of his narrative barely inferior to the that of the early picaresque novel. Indeed, a general affinity with the novel characterizes North African captivity narratives, as in the account of the Wolffgang brothers (also included in this anthology). In spite of its authenticity, the narrative of the two copper engravers from Augsburg who were kept as house slaves by the ruler of Algiers orients itself to the popular novel *Robinson Crusoe*, which was available in German translations as early as 1720.[13] Thus, a pattern emerges: First,

---

12. Mario Klarer, "Trading Identities: Balthasar Sturmer's *Verzeichnis der Reise* (1558) and the Making of the European Barbary Captivity Narrative," in *Piracy and Captivity in the Mediterranean: 1550–1810*, ed. Mario Klarer (London: Routledge, 2019), 25–55.

13. Ernstpeter Ruhe, "Images from the Dey's Court: The Artist as Slave in Algiers (1684–88)," in *Mediterranean Slavery and World Literature: Captivity Genres from Cervantes to Rousseau*, ed. Mario Klarer (London: Routledge, 2020), 212–40.

North African captivity narratives (as in the case of Sturmer) anticipate the early novel, then the early novel (including *Robinson Crusoe*) borrows heavily from Barbary captivity narratives, and finally, later slave accounts from the middle of the eighteenth century onward (such as the testimony of the Wolffgang brothers) integrate elements of the early novel into their authentic Barbary reports.

These mechanisms also reveal one of the most important questions relating to this genre, namely that of the veracity of the texts. As in all autobiographical writings, the transition between fact and fiction is fluid. The genre of North African captivity narratives especially makes it difficult for us to differentiate between truth and narrative liberty. Frequently, the respective authors' North African experiences, which are in many cases verifiable and thus authentic, meld with the use of novelistic elements. Only by placing individual texts within the larger context of the European and American tradition of authentic *and* fictional Barbary captivity narratives will it be possible to gauge the degree of authenticity of individual texts. For example, the English-language narrative by Maria Martin (1807), allegedly a translation from the Italian, turns out, on closer inspection, to be a purely fictional text with a plethora of plagiarized passages from various older Barbary narratives and literary texts. The Robinsonade by the Austrian Leonhard Eisenschmidt (1807), on the other hand, despite its exuberantly Robinsonesque elements, proves to be, at its core, the authentic testimony of a captive in Algiers. This means that there are authentic Barbary narratives that are "disguised" as fiction and that historical scholarship has consequently not yet taken into consideration. The Robinsonade "genre," in particular, is a promising starting point, as its influence spread to so many national contexts.[14]

Naturally, the large number of recorded captivity narratives by Europeans in North African captivity should not belie the fact that Mediterranean piracy and slavery represented a two-way phenomenon. It is likely that a similarly large number of North African persons were captured by Christian forces and traded at European slave markets such as those in Malta, Livorno, Málaga, and Marseille. However, if one were to judge merely on the basis of the large volume of recorded European captivity narratives, Mediterranean slavery would appear to be a phenomenon carried out primarily by the

---

14. Robert Spindler, *Corsairs, Captives, Converts in Early Modernity: Narrating Barbary Captivity in German-Speaking Europe and the World, 1558–1807* (Würzburg: Königshausen & Neumann, 2020).

North African, that is, Muslim, side. While more than one hundred captivity narratives were handed down in various European languages from the beginning of the sixteenth to the early nineteenth century, the number of *longer* personal reports from the North African side amounts to only a handful of texts and a number of letters.[15] This lack of documentation means that we have hardly any longer autobiographical testimonies of the fates of North African slaves in European hands, although their number from the early sixteenth to the late eighteenth century would nevertheless have been in the hundreds of thousands.

This unequal distribution of surviving narratives might stem from a dissimilar attitude toward texts and an idiosyncratic valence attached to the captivity experience in the respective cultures. For example, in Muslim North Africa during the early modern period, there was no dissemination of texts comparable with that of the European printing industry. This means that North African testimonies of captivity were almost exclusively written by hand, while European captivity narratives appeared on the market in great number and in many editions. Thus, the likelihood of accounts being preserved was much lower in the Muslim cultures of North Africa than in the European context with its widespread early modern printing industry.

In addition to the differing culture of text dissemination, a different stance toward personal suffering seems to be at work in Muslim accounts of captivity. Where Christian slaves typically portrayed their individual experiences in line with a Christ-like Passion, Muslim captives in the hands of Europeans, after a successful return home, emphasized their theological superiority over their Christian adversaries. North African returnees did not depict themselves as humiliated persons but stressed the Europeans' respectful treatment of them.[16] Thus, the two cultures seem to differ fundamentally in how they represent or exploit personal captivity experiences for their respective religious and cultural agendas. The present collection, therefore, provides a representative cross section of the rich tradition of historical

---

15. In the five-year Austrian Science Fund project ESCAPE: European Slaves: Christians in African Pirate Encounters. Barbary Coast Captivity Narratives (1550–1780) (project leader: Mario Klarer; www.uibk.ac.at/projects/escape), more than one hundred captivity narratives in all major European languages were collected and studied. For the North African perspective, see Nabil Matar, *Mediterranean Captivity Through Arab Eyes, 1517–1798* (Boston: Brill, 2020).

16. Nabil Matar, "Two Arabic Accounts of Captivity in Malta: Texts and Contexts," in *Piracy and Captivity in the Mediterranean: 1550–1810*, ed. Mario Klarer (London: Routledge, 2019), 235–76.

European captivity narratives set in Northern Africa from over three centuries and from nine different European linguistic and geographic regions.[17]

Selection of European Barbary Captivity Narratives

1. Balthasar Sturmer, Account of the Travels of Mister Balthasar Sturmer *(1558): A German pirate's and captive's narrative set in Tunis in 1534–1535, preserved in a handwritten manuscript from 1558*

The European Barbary captivity narrative as a genre emerges with the testimony by the German merchant, pirate, and slave Balthasar Sturmer. After squandering his father's money as a merchant in Lisbon, Sturmer found himself penniless and decided to become a Christian pirate before falling into the hands of Muslim corsairs and being forced to labor as an Ottoman galley slave. During his captivity, Sturmer experienced the siege and conquest of Tunis by Emperor Charles V in 1535. Sturmer's account provides a unique, nonofficial record of this major geopolitical event. It also paints a multifaceted picture of the evolving Mediterranean corsairing and slavery industry in the early sixteenth century, including a rare firsthand depiction

---

17. For some of the most notable recent book-length publications of the last decade on North African piracy, slavery, and redemption, see Gillian L. Weiss, *Captives and Corsairs: France and Slavery in the Early Modern Mediterranean* (Stanford, CA: Stanford University Press, 2011); Magnus Ressel, *Zwischen Sklavenkassen und Türkenpässen. Nordeuropa und die Barbaresken in der Frühen Neuzeit* (Berlin: de Gruyter, 2012); Lisa Voigt, *Writing Captivity in the Early Modern Atlantic: Circulations of Knowledge and Authority in the Iberian and English Imperial Worlds* (Chapel Hill: University of North Carolina Press, 2012); Elizabeth Watzka-Pauli, *Triumph der Barmherzigkeit: Die Befreiung christlicher Gefangener aus muslimisch dominierten Ländern durch den österreichischen Trinitarierorden 1690–1783* (Göttingen: V&R Unipress, 2016); Joshua White, *Piracy and Law in the Ottoman Mediterranean* (Stanford, CA: Stanford University Press, 2017); Will Smiley, *From Slaves to Prisoners of War: The Ottoman Empire, Russia, and International Law* (Oxford: Oxford University Press, 2018); Helgason Þorsteinn, *The Corsairs' Longest Voyage: The Turkish Raid in Iceland 1627* (Boston: Brill, 2018); Daniel Hershenzon, *The Captive Sea: Slavery, Communication, and Commerce in Early Modern Spain and the Mediterranean* (Philadelphia: University of Pennsylvania Press, 2018); Erica Heinsen-Roach, *Consuls and Captives: Dutch–North African Diplomacy in the Early Modern Mediterranean* (Rochester, NY: University of Rochester Press, 2019); Ernstpeter Ruhe, *Aus Barbareÿen Erlösett* (Würzburg, Germany: Königshausen & Neumann, 2020); Matar, *Mediterranean Captivity Through Arab Eyes*. Meredith Martin and Gillian Weiss's *The Sun King at Sea: Maritime Art and Galley Slavery in Louis XIV's France* (Los Angeles: Getty Publications, forthcoming 2022) provides a valuable perspective on the enslavement of Muslims in France, paying special attention to the repercussions of this phenomenon in the visual arts.

of Christian piracy. Balthasar Sturmer's mutable character anticipates, in many ways, the protagonists of the Spanish picaro novels of the sixteenth and seventeenth centuries.

2. Antonio de Sosa, Topography of Algiers *(1612)*: *An encyclopedic Spanish compilation of knowledge about Algiers from the latter part of the sixteenth century with a biographical note on Miguel de Cervantes*

Picaresque figures are the staple of early novels such as Miguel de Cervantes's *Don Quijote* (1605). However, the author Cervantes himself appears to have adopted these character traits at times, as illustrated by a short excerpt from the Spanish multivolume *Topography of Algiers* (1612) by Antonio de Sosa. The passage selected for this volume recounts one of Cervantes's four futile attempts to escape from Algerian captivity before he was ransomed by the Trinitarian Order in 1580, after five years in captivity. This glimpse of an episode from Cervantes's life is embedded in an encyclopedic compilation of information on Algiers that was typical for Iberian print publications on North Africa at the time. The section from Antonio de Sosa's multivolume work is included here to illustrate specifically this Iberian manifestation of the Barbary captivity text type, which goes beyond the first-person captivity narratives typical of northern European returnees from Barbary.

3. Ólafur Egilsson, The Travels of Reverend Ólafur Egilsson *(undated): An Icelandic account of the 1627 raids of Iceland by Barbary pirates and the ensuing captivity of civilians in Algiers*

Barbary corsairing and captivity were not restricted to southern Europe or the Mediterranean basin alone. The seventeenth-century Icelandic report by Reverend Ólafur Egilsson demonstrates how far Barbary pirates were able to venture into the northern Atlantic. Reverend Ólafur records one of the most impressive feats of North African piracy—the 1627 land raid by Moroccan and Algerian corsairs that resulted in the abduction and enslavement of around four hundred civilians from Iceland. As a consequence, Reverend Ólafur, together with his wife and two children, was sold into slavery in Algiers. He was later released in order to embark on an unsuccessful mission to raise ransom money from the king of Denmark for his family and compatriots. The "Turkish" raid of Iceland, as it is preserved in Reverend Ólafur's narrative, is still a central part of Icelandic cultural memory. It stands out among other European Barbary captivity narratives for its detailed account of the otherwise little-documented Atlantic land raids for human bounty, which include similar attacks in Madeira in 1617 and Ireland in 1631.

4. Emanuel d'Aranda, Short Story of My Unfortunate Journey *(undated): A Flemish nobleman's handwritten account of his Algerian captivity from 1640 to 1641*

Much like Barbary corsairs, who were able to affect even the remotest parts of Europe, specific Barbary captivity narratives could sometimes also reach diverse audiences across Europe. The Dutch account by Emanuel d'Aranda from the mid-seventeenth century is one of the most popular exemplars of the European Barbary captivity genre. D'Aranda's narrative appeared in a number of editions and was translated into French, German, and English. All these print versions go back to d'Aranda's original handwritten account in Dutch, which was recently discovered at an auction. This volume presents, for the very first time, an English translation of the Dutch autograph manuscript in d'Aranda's own hand. It documents the original intention of a returnee from Barbary captivity before the editorial interventions by printers, editors, and translators could appropriate the narrative for their respective marketing purposes. D'Aranda's text, which was as well received in Catholic France as in Protestant England and Germany, is a testimony to the success of the Barbary captivity genre across cultural and religious divides.

5. Antoine Quartier, The Religious Slave and His Adventures *(1690): French printed slave narrative by a Catholic captive in Tripoli in the 1660s*

Christian denominational frictions are also only of minor importance in the late seventeenth-century French narrative by Antoine Quartier, who, as a Catholic, was part of the state-licensed religious mainstream in France. In contrast to the numerous reports depicting Moroccan, Algerian, and

Tunisian captivity, the Tripolitan setting of Quartier's text is exceptionally rare. Equally fascinating is Quartier's vivid description of agricultural slave work in North Africa. These sections stand out because most other Barbary accounts depict the experiences of galley rowers, house slaves, or economically "self-reliant" captives who are forced to earn their fare through entrepreneurial endeavors such as running taverns or trading.

6. Andreas Matthäus Wolffgang and Johann Georg Wolffgang,
Travels and Wonderful Fortunes of Two Brothers in
Algerian Bondage *(1767): German printed narrative of two Bavarian copper engravers who were house slaves at the court of the dey of Algiers from 1684 to 1688*

Two engravers from Augsburg, Andreas Matthäus Wolffgang and Johann Georg Wolffgang, were house slaves in North Africa, like countless other Europeans. However, the experiences of the two German brothers stand out, because they spent their four-year tenure in Algiers as captives in the privileged setting of the palace of the dey of Algiers. Also, in addition to their printed captivity narrative, images documenting their experiences that were executed by the older brother, Andreas, have survived (see fig. I.4). These engravings are the only known visual representations carried out by a Barbary captive. Both brothers were sent to Holland by their father as part of their training as engravers. They disregarded their father's explicit instructions not to visit England and were taken captive by Algerian pirates in the English Channel on their return trip in 1684. The report of the Wolffgang brothers is highly intertextual, containing not only religious motifs, including references to the parable of the prodigal son, but also, more importantly, to the German translation of Daniel Defoe's *Robinson Crusoe*. Similar to the Wolffgang brothers, Defoe's protagonist goes to sea against his father's wishes, and his subsequent misfortune is considered to be the punishment for this sin. The posthumously published text of the Wolffgang brothers—eighty years after their actual captivity—documents a popular trend in eighteenth-century Barbary captivity accounts, where authentic North African slave experiences were clad in narrative structures reminiscent of Daniel Defoe's successful novel *Robinson Crusoe*.

Figure I.4 Engraving by Andreas Matthäus Wolffgang: "Portrait of Mezzomorto, formerly the Dey of Algiers and now Kapudan Pasha of the Sultan's fleet"
Source: Jeremias Wolf, *Trachtenbuch, Sammlung von 142 teilw. kolorierten Trachtenbildern* [Augsburg etc., ca. 1700–1750], Chalc. 116, fol. 40; Bayerische Staatsbibliothek München.

7. *Isaac Brassard*, The Tale of Mr. Brassard's Captivity in Algiers *(1878): Account of a French Huguenot captive in Algiers in 1687–1688*

While popular printed captivity narratives such as those by Emanuel d'Aranda and Antoine Quartier deliberately toned down denominational differences in favor of cross-national marketability, the late seventeenth-century account of the French Huguenot captive Isaac Brassard inevitably lacks this ability to bridge religious boundaries. As a self-proclaimed Protestant victim of Catholic persecution in France in the 1680s, Brassard stressed his identity as a steadfast Huguenot through his Barbary captivity account. In Brassard's testimony, the issue of conversion to Islam, which is so prominent in most Barbary narratives, gives way to a different form of enticing apostasy in the shape of leaving Protestantism in favor of Catholicism. Renouncing his Huguenot belief would have made Brassard eligible for ransom efforts by the French official agencies. What becomes apparent in Brassard's account is the extent to which the Barbary genre served as a forum in which to negotiate regional or national concerns of a religious and political nature that go far beyond the superficial stereotype of Christianity versus Islam.

8. *Thomas Pellow,* The History of the Long Captivity and Adventures of Thomas Pellow *(1740?): British printed narrative by a slave who was abducted at the age of eleven and spent twenty-three years in Morocco from 1715 to 1738*

Falling into the hands of Moroccan pirates as an English boy at the age of eleven and returning to England almost a quarter of a century later produced a peculiar psychological dynamic in Thomas Pellow. Pellow is one of the few former captives who openly admits to having converted to Islam, albeit purportedly as a result of extreme physical and psychological pressure. The returnee Pellow appears to experience some displacement upon his arrival in England in 1738, after having spent two-thirds of his life in Muslim North Africa. Hints at Pellow's difficulty in coming to terms with his native English culture, from which he had become thoroughly estranged, are revealed toward the end of his narrative, when the reader accompanies Pellow on a meeting with the Moroccan consul in London. Only there, when he is offered couscous, the Moroccan dish he got so accustomed to during his long captivity, does Pellow "feel at home" for the first time after his return to England.

9. *Hark Olufs,* The Remarkable Adventures of Hark Olufs *(1747): Printed Danish account of a Dane captured in 1724 at the age of fifteen, who became a chief military officer in Constantine before returning home in 1735*

Hark Olufs's Danish account is another story of teenage captivity and of a problematic reacculturation process. The fifteen-year-old captive Hark Olufs most likely chose to embrace Islam and thus climbed the North African career ladder to become chief military commander of the bey of Constantine in Algeria. The bey eventually restored Olufs's liberty in return for his fourteen years of loyal service. Hark Olufs's Danish eyewitness report from the mid-eighteenth century is, on the one hand, an example of the successful acculturation process of an adolescent Christian into Muslim North Africa. On the other hand, it is also a testimony to the problematic reintegration of a slave after his return home. Apparently, Olufs continued wearing his North African outfit and behaved in an outlandish manner long after his return home to the small island of Amrum in the North Sea.

10. *Maria ter Meetelen,* Miraculous and Remarkable Events of Twelve Years of Slavery *(1748): Printed Dutch narrative of a female captive in Morocco from 1731 to 1743, whose friendship with the ruler became life-threatening after a revolution*

Closeness to the emperor while in North African captivity was not automatically beneficial for the captive. For the Dutch female slave Maria ter Meetelen, one of the few authentic female captivity authors, the interest of the king of Morocco posed a twofold danger. Ter Meetelen, along with her husband, was captured on the high seas in 1731 and abducted to Morocco. After her husband's death, Maria had to look for a new Christian husband to protect herself from the advances of Muslim men, among them the Moroccan king himself. Nevertheless, through intelligence and wisdom, she succeeded in establishing a friendly relationship with the king. However, this close connection to the ruler was almost her downfall. When chaos broke out in Morocco over a change of power, Ter Meetelen was associated with the old regime and escaped persecution only by a hair's breadth. Maria ter Meetelen's detailed descriptions of her entrepreneurial endeavors, such as running a tavern to make a living as a captive, provide deep insights into the economic and structural logic of slavery in North Africa.

11. Marcus Berg, Description of the Barbaric Slavery in the Kingdom of Fez and Morocco (1757): Printed Swedish narrative of a captive in Fez from 1754 to 1756 with a description of the most devastating earthquake of the eighteenth century

The Swedish captive Marcus Berg provides us with yet another depiction of Morocco and its ruler around the middle of the eighteenth century. As one of thirteen Swedish crew members, Berg spent two years in captivity in Fez from 1754 to 1756, when Swedish authorities paid for his ransom. His narrative paints a gloomy picture of the emperor as a sadistic tyrant whose uncontrollable wrath could turn against anyone, regardless of nationality or religion. Marcus Berg's printed narrative is extraordinary because of his detailed, firsthand description of one of the deadliest earthquakes in history. In 1755, an earthquake of immense magnitude destroyed the city of Lisbon and killed up to one hundred thousand people. Its epicenter was off the coast of Morocco, and Berg experienced the apocalyptic force of this event from the roof of his prison in Morocco. Berg's narrative is also the only authentic printed Swedish Barbary captivity narrative.

12. Elizabeth Marsh, Narrative of Elizabeth Marsh's Captivity in Barbary (undated): Manuscript of the first British Barbary captivity narrative, written by a woman held in Morocco and printed in 1756

Elizabeth Marsh fell captive to a Salé rover in 1755 and spent four months in Moroccan captivity before she was able to return home to England. Similar to Maria ter Meetelen, Elizabeth Marsh had to ward off the advances of the Moroccan ruler, who expressed his interest in her during personal meetings. After her return to England, this proximity to the sultan led to suspicions about whether she had maintained her chastity during her captivity in Morocco. Elizabeth Marsh is one of the few female returnees who directly addresses the sexual insinuations that were leveled against her in her home country. To what extent the publication of her captivity narrative was part of a strategy to fend off these allegations is hard to determine. It is, however, very likely that framing herself as an unwavering, self-confident, and self-reliant female captive who was strong enough to stand up to the Moroccan ruler was an attempt to improve her reputation. Like Emanuel d'Aranda's narrative, Marsh's text in this anthology follows the manuscript version rather than the published edition. The manuscript text provides a firsthand account of the author's intention before publishers could adorn her narrative in the tradition of sentimental plots featuring female characters in distress that so beguiled eighteenth-century readers.

13. Felice Caronni, The Account of an Amateur Antiquarian's Short Journey *(1805): One of the latest North African slavery accounts by a captive in Tunis in 1804 and a rare instance of an Italian Barbary narrative*

Felice Caronni's account is one of the very few Italian testimonies that have survived and made it into print. Because of the geographic proximity between Italy and North Africa, inhabitants of the peninsula had been the prey of Barbary pirates for centuries. Given the high number of Italian returnees, it is most surprising that we have hardly any fully fledged Italian testimonies of these slaves' experiences in North Africa. Select parts of Caronni's two-volume narrative are included in this anthology to give a voice to this underrepresented group. Caronni's relatively short captivity experience of four months is also unique, as this Barnabite priest, amateur classical scholar, and art collector had a deep interest in the classical heritage of Tunisia. In his account, he provides a firsthand description of numerous Tunisian archeological sites and artifacts. Caronni's narrative was published in 1805, thus making it one of the last descriptions of Barbary corsairing and slavery before the decline of the industry due to the Barbary Wars with the United States (1801–1805; 1815) and the subsequent European colonial activities in North Africa in the early nineteenth century. Despite the end of North African piracy, Barbary captivity narratives continued to be published for a number of years. However, unlike Caronni's text, on closer inspection, many of the captives' tales from the early nineteenth century turn out to be fictitious, riding the last wave of a once-popular genre of authentic life writing.

This cross section of European-language captivity narratives from "Barbary" or the "Barbary Coast" deliberately excludes obviously fictional specimens in favor of verifiably authentic testimonies by European slaves. Thus, the texts in this selection reflect, albeit indirectly, a cataclysmic geopolitical phenomenon that is no longer part of today's cultural memory. The selection of diverse narratives, which spans three centuries and nine different languages, allows the largely forgotten early modern conflict between Europe and North Africa to be accessed anew by contemporary readers.

Piracy in the Mediterranean

The phenomenon of piracy in the Mediterranean is as old as seafaring in the Mediterranean itself, appearing in the first literary documents from the ancient world. In Homer's *Odyssey*, for example, there is an account of how Odysseus and the companions on his ship seized a city and carried its population into slavery.[18] Later, during the Roman Empire, there were spectacular incidents involving pirates. For example, the young Julius Caesar was captured by Cilician pirates on the way to Rhodes and revenged himself savagely upon them after his release.[19] Gnaeus Pompeius also achieved great fame in the first century before Christ when he succeeded in fighting the pirates in the eastern Mediterranean. After the fall of the Roman Empire at the end of the ancient world, as well as during the Middle Ages, piracy underwent a revival, especially under Muslim captains.

How widespread piracy must have been in the Middle Ages is demonstrated by legislation introduced by Frederick II (1194–1250), who, as the newly enthroned emperor of the Holy Roman Empire, passed a law concerning stranded goods, pirates, and "enemies of Christendom" in 1220.[20]

---

18. *Odyssey* 9.39–61.

19. This incident is recorded by a number of Roman historians, including Velleius Paterculus 2.41.3–42.3; Sueton, *Caesar* 4.1–2 and 74.1; and Plutarch, *Caesar* 1.8–2.7.

20. Georg Heinrich Pertz, *Monumenta Germaniae Historica, inde ab anno Christi quingentesimo usque ad annum millesimum et quingentesimum*, vol. 16, *Annales aevi Suevici* (Stuttgart, 1859), 109, lines 18–25.

Pirates also feature in medieval literature, as in the story "The Pirate's Daughter," which is part of the highly popular *Gesta Romanorum* (ca. 1300), an anonymous Latin collection of diverse exempla-like narratives.[21] In this text, a pirate's beautiful daughter is willing to help a prisoner escape from her own father's prison if the captive is willing to marry her in return. Another literary example that foreshadows early modern Barbary captivity narratives in an almost uncanny way is Rudolf von Ems's Middle High German verse narrative *The Good Gerhard* (ca. 1220). The story revolves around a group of European noblemen and noblewomen who are ransomed out of Moroccan captivity by a German merchant.[22] Of course, plots like these were inspired by actual ransoms of Christians from Muslim captivity in the Holy Land during the Crusades.[23] Nevertheless, *The Good Gerhard* and similar fictional texts anticipate the major structural elements of later Barbary captivity narratives as they emerge in the sixteenth century, including their typical amalgamation of religious and economic features.

In the first decades of the sixteenth century, the corsair and later Ottoman admiral Hayreddin Barbarossa (ca. 1478–1546) (see fig. I.5) took piracy to an entirely new level. Hayreddin and his older brother Oruç (ca. 1473–1518) succeeded in bringing the major coastal cities of North Africa—Algiers, Tripoli, and Tunis—under their rule. These regions, as well as the independent Kingdom of Morocco, were subsequently labeled the "Barbary Coast" in reference to the Berber tribes who lived there. Barbarossa proceeded very astutely by placing himself nominally under the protection of the Ottoman Empire. From his strongholds—first and foremost from Algiers—Hayreddin Barbarossa controlled most of the trade and a large part of the shipping in the Mediterranean (see fig. I.6). Consequently, he came into conflict with the Christian sea powers and the Habsburgs in particular.

Emperor Charles V (1500–1558) tried to take control of the situation in a number of confrontations, resulting in clashes between Hayreddin Barbarossa

---

21. *Gesta Romanorum: Lateinisch/Deutsch*, ed. and trans. Rainer Nickel (Stuttgart: Reclam, 2003), 7–19.

22. For more on *The Good Gerhard*, the *Gesta Romanorum*, and the pirate law of Frederick II, see Mario Klarer, "Before Barbary Captivity Narratives: Slavery, Ransom, and the Economy of Christian Virtue in *The Good Gerhard* (c. 1220) by Rudolf of Ems," in *Mediterranean Slavery and World Literature: Captivity Genres from Cervantes to Rousseau*, ed. Mario Klarer (London: Routledge, 2020), 23–48.

23. For the complex history of human exchanges during the Crusades, see Philippe Goridis, *Gefangen im Heiligen Land: Verarbeitung und Bewältigung christlicher Gefangenschaft zur Zeit der Kreuzzüge* (Ostfildern: Thorbecke, 2015).

Figure I.5 Portrait of the naval commander and privateer Hayreddin Barbarossa
Source: Schloss Ambras Innsbruck; KHM-Museumsverband, Vienna.

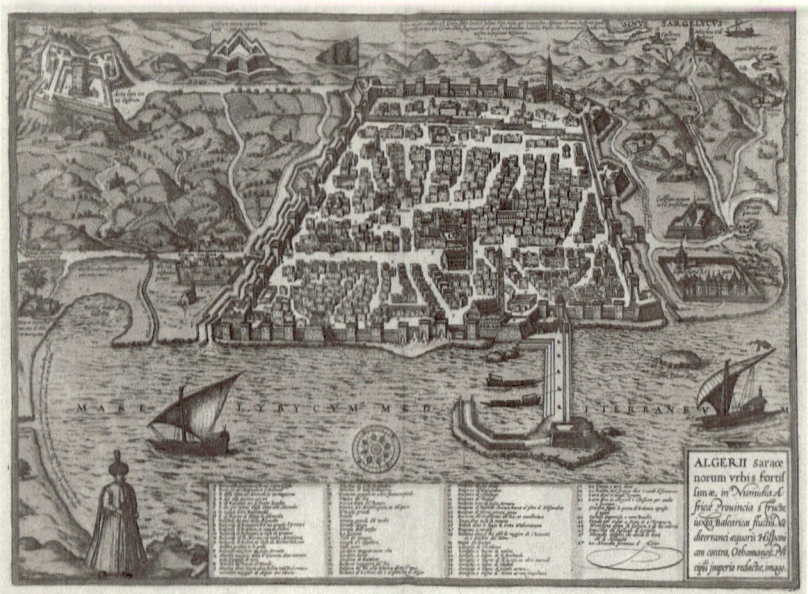

Figure I.6 Engraving of early modern Algiers
Source: Georg Braun and Frans Hogenberg, *Civitates Orbis Terrarum*, vol. 2 (Cologne, 1575); Mario Klarer, private collection.

and Andrea Doria, the fleet commander of the Christian Habsburg forces. Charles V undertook two major attacks against North African strongholds. The first was his successful siege and conquest of the city of Tunis in 1535—an event that is at the center of Balthasar Sturmer's account (included in this anthology as the first European Barbary captivity narrative). A subsequent attempt to take over the city of Algiers in 1541 was thwarted by adverse weather conditions and turned the entire expedition into a complete disaster for the Habsburg emperor. However, in the largest sea battle between Muslim and Christian fleets at the Greek island of Lepanto in 1571, Christian forces celebrated victory (see fig. I.7). This tipped the scale of power in the Mediterranean in favor of European forces for only a short time. Within a few years, the Ottoman navy recovered and the galleys of North African corsairs resumed their major role in the race for booty in the Mediterranean.

When early modern texts refer to pirates, corsairs, or privateers, they typically do so in a very loose manner. Authors of early modern narratives

Figure I.7 The victors of the naval Battle of Lepanto, 1571
Source: Schloss Ambras Innsbruck; KHM-Museumsverband, Vienna.

frequently blur the boundaries between these terms, regardless of whether these forces acted on their own or were under the protection of a nation or city-state in return for a portion of their booty. To acquire their loot, corsairs practiced two kinds of assault. The majority of the attacks took place on the high seas. Vessels of nations that had no contractual agreements with the Barbary states were attacked and goods, ships, and, above all, people were taken as booty. Naturally, there were also land incursions. For this reason, major parts of the southern Italian coastal region as well as the islands off the coast of the peninsula were depopulated during the early modern era out of fear of these pirate raids. Today, the surviving signs of the dangers of that time are, for example, the more than one hundred watchtowers along the coast of the island of Corsica (see fig. I.8). The inhabitants of entire villages or regions could be enslaved in such raids. In 1627, Algerian and Moroccan corsairs advanced all the way to Iceland in a venture during which four hundred locals were captured and abducted to North Africa—an incident described in the narrative by Ólafur Egilsson included in this volume.

Figure I.8 Genoese tower at Cap Corse
Source: Mario Klarer, private collection.

Piracy or corsairing in the early modern period was in no way practiced exclusively by the Muslim side. European pirates also preyed on Ottoman ships and territories. In particular, the Knights of Malta and the Knights of Saint Stephen were active in this regard. Christian powers undertook raids into surrounding Muslim territories, especially from early modern European colonies in North Africa like Oran, whereby entire village communities were carried into European slavery. For example, in 1607, the Knights of Saint Stephen abducted and enslaved two thousand civilians, including women and children, from the Algerian town Bone (Annaba), an event that the Jesuit scribe Fulvio Fontana called "the most glorious undertaking the Order of Saint Stephen has ever done."[24]

Despite their cruelty, privateering and corsairing did not take place in a completely lawless sphere. Numerous treaties that both North African city-states and European nations forged throughout the early modern period testify to this. Felice Caronni's Italian account of 1805, which is included here, is a prime example of such contractual agreements between North African city-states and European powers. After falling into the hands of Tunisian corsairs, Caronni is able to leave Tunis as soon as his identity as a Milanese citizen is confirmed. These treaties led to situations in which passengers whose home countries had no bilateral agreements with the corsairs' city base would be singled out for captivity. Other passengers or crew members who benefited from existing treaties could leave unharmed and keep their possessions and commodities. Also, ransomed slaves received documents that identified them as liberated slaves in order to guarantee them free passage in case of another pirate attack on their journey home.[25]

In addition to bilateral diplomatic agreements that regulated corsairing and human trafficking, various European legislations and international laws also defined the legal status of pirates. Barbary corsairs received the status of state enemies (*hostes*) or thieves (*piratae, latrones*), who were then situated

---

24. "L'espugnazione di Bona è l'impresa più gloriosa, che habbia mai fatto la Religione di Santo Stefano." See Fulvio Fontana, *I pregi della Toscana nell'imprese più segnalate de' cavalieri di Santo Stefano: opera data in luce da Fulvio Fontana della compagnia di Gesù dedicata all'altezza reale di Cosimo III, gran duca di Toscana e gran maestro dell'ordine* (Firenze: Per Pier Mattia Miccioni, e Michele Nestenus, 1701), 138. See also Ariel Salzmann, "Migrants in Chains: On the Enslavement of Muslims in Renaissance and Enlightenment Europe," *Religions* 4, no. 3 (2013): 396.

25. The German captive Michael Kühn mentions a "Frey-Zeddul" ("free paper") in *Johann Michael Kühns merckwürdige Lebens- und Reise-Beschreibung* (Gotha: Mevius, 1741), 391.

outside international legal standards.[26] These distinctions were absolutely necessary to facilitate trading of goods that had passed through the hands of pirates and resolved pressing questions such as: Who is the rightful owner of goods that were captured *from* pirates? Are these commodities still the possession of the initial owner from whom the pirates originally took them? Problems like these could be regulated through domestic legislation concerning the status of pirates or corsairs. Sometimes, political powers, such as the fledgling United States in the Barbary Wars, used specific legal argumentation to engage in military conflicts with North African corsairs on the grounds of their lack of equal standing in terms of international law.

Piracy in North Africa came to an end at the beginning of the nineteenth century. Military intervention by the United States was one deciding factor. After the Declaration of Independence from England, the United States had to pay—in some instances—up to 20 percent of its yearly revenue to North African states to protect its trade ships and their crews. In spite of these high sums, American ships and seamen continued to be seized and taken captive.[27] Thus, Thomas Jefferson, the third president, decided to establish the U.S. Navy and to approach the conflict militarily in the Barbary Wars (1801–1805; 1815).[28] European colonial politics in North Africa in the nineteenth century, such as the French annexation of Algiers in 1830, furthered the demise of piracy and human trafficking in the Mediterranean.

North African Slavery

Estimates suggest that up to one million European Christian victims of Muslim corsairs were held as slaves in North Africa in the early modern

---

26. Walter Rech, "Ambivalences of Recognition: The Position of the Barbary Corsairs in Early Modern International Law and International Politics," in *Piracy and Captivity in the Mediterranean: 1550–1810*, ed. Mario Klarer (London: Routledge, 2019), 76–98. See also Joshua M. White, "Slavery, Manumission, and Freedom Suits in the Early Modern Ottoman Empire," in Slaves and Slave Agency in the Ottoman Empire, ed. Stephan Conermann and Gül Şen (Göttingen: V&R Unipress for Bonn University Press, 2020), 283–318; White, *Piracy and Law in the Ottoman Mediterranean*.

27. Lotfi Ben Rejeb, "Jonathan Cowdery's *American Captives in Tripoli* (1806): Experience of the Frigate *Philadelphia* Officers (1803–05)," in *Mediterranean Slavery and World Literature: Captivity Genres from Cervantes to Rousseau*, ed. Mario Klarer (London: Routledge, 2020), 241–56.

28. For more on the role of the Barbary corsairs in the awareness of a young United States, see Junker, "Of Cross and Crescent," 259–76.

era between around 1550 and 1800.[29] While a furious debate has flared up about the exact figure, there is general consensus that many hundreds of thousands of individuals were captured on both sides.[30] In his 1694 German translation of Emanuel d'Aranda's captivity narrative, Johann Frisch claims that Algiers had a population of 48,000 European slaves.[31] Most likely this number is exaggerated, but it still drives home the extent of slavery in the early modern Mediterranean. More reliable demographic figures from Livorno in the early seventeenth century document that one out of twelve residents was a slave, that is, approximately 3,000 individuals of a total of 37,000 people living in the city in 1616 were unfree.[32]

In addition to the debate on the number of slaves in North Africa during this time, there is also the question whether the term "slavery" can be applied to this specific form of unfreedom in the early modern Mediterranean. Part of the controversy is based on the fundamental difference between the North African situation and, for example, slavery in the Americas with respect to ransom possibilities and the economic status of individuals. Slaves of African origin in the Americas had no real options to end or change their unfree status. Peter Mark, for example, suggests that one should define "'captives' as those prisoners who were held primarily for their ransom value and 'slaves' as those used primarily for their work value."[33] Even if we accept this commonsense definition, it would not coincide with historical usage. Throughout the early modern period, the terms "captive" or "captivity" and "slave" or "slavery" were used almost synonymously, particularly in Barbary narratives.

One should also bear in mind that, unlike today, early modern European notions of slavery were largely modeled on North African bondage

---

29. Davis, "Counting European Slaves on the Barbary Coast," 87–124; Davis, *Christian Slaves, Muslim Masters*.

30. MacLean, "Slavery and Sensibility," 173–94.

31. Johann Frisch, *Schauplatz Barbarischer Sclaverey: Worauff unter Beschreibung der 4 vornehmsten Raub-Städte: Algiers, Thunis, Tripoli und Salee. Derselben Regierung, Raubereyen, Sitten, Gewohnheiten und andere seltzame Begebenheiten und Zufälle vorgestellet warden* (Hamburg: Thomas von Wiering, 1694), 31.

32. Molly Greene, *Catholic Pirates and Greek Merchants: A Maritime History of the Mediterranean* (Princeton, NJ: Princeton University Press, 2010), 93. Similar numbers exist for other Christian ports in the Mediterranean: Trapani in Sicily had 5,000 Muslim slaves in 1569; in Naples, 10,000 to 20,000 of its 270,000 inhabitants in the early seventeenth century were slaves. See Bono, *Schiavi Musulmani Nell'Italia Moderna*, 24–31.

33. Peter Mark, "'Free, Unfree, Captive, Slave': António de Saldanha, a Late Sixteenth-Century Captive in Marrakesh," in *Piracy and Captivity in the Mediterranean: 1550–1810*, ed. Mario Klarer (London: Routledge, 2019), 99.

Figure I.9 "Barbarian galleys"
Source: Pierre Dan, *Historie van Barbaryen, En des zelfs Zee-Roovers* (Amsterdam, 1684), fol. 299; Mario Klarer, private collection.

of Europeans and only to a much lesser extent on enslaved Africans of the Americas. Also, the entire basis of the slave economy in the Americas differed from that of North African captives, many of whom had to make their own living through business endeavors while in bondage. Maria ter Meetelen's early eighteenth-century Dutch narrative, parts of which are contained in this anthology, is a striking example of entrepreneurial strategies required for survival by a European slave in North Africa. In some cases, especially with respect to renegades, that is, converts to Islam, it becomes increasingly difficult to maintain a clear distinction between unfree versus free labor. Rather than trying to apply modern terminology, it might help to look at some of the different manifestations of captivity or slavery in early modern North Africa.

Mostly, people fell captive to corsairs either on the high seas or during land raids, and the captives' eventual fates were largely dependent on their social rank. Poor people like ordinary seamen, for whom there were few ransom prospects, were often deployed as galley slaves. Because of the harsh conditions on warships, this could amount to a death sentence (see fig. I.9). Balthasar Sturmer's account in this collection provides one of the few descriptions of forced labor on an Ottoman corsair galley. Although we have no direct longer testimonies of North African captives on European galleys, some of their letters as well as European accounts give us an indirect understanding of the harsh conditions to which North Africans were subjected. The European legal system sometimes sentenced criminals to labor on galleys alongside Muslim captives. Therefore, testimonies of European convicts, such as the French Huguenot Jean Marteilhe in the early eighteenth century, allow us to gauge, by analogy, the conditions that unfree rowers of Ottoman origin experienced on European warships.[34] Also, eighteenth-century descriptions of cursory encounters in harbors between non-Christian rowers and European travelers shed indirect light on their lot. For example, in 1770, an English female traveler in Genoa observed the Muslim galley slaves' "poor legs, which were naked, almost black, and, of some, the flesh had partly grown over their fetters."[35]

Europeans in North African captivity who came from better circumstances were much more likely to be ransomed with funds from Europe than those from poorer backgrounds. Nevertheless, slaves sometimes tried to lower their ransom price by not disclosing their true identity. Emanuel d'Aranda's narrative, included in this selection, gives testimony to the nobleman's attempt to pass as a common soldier to reduce his ransom. While in Algerian captivity, Miguel de Cervantes was mistaken for a high-level state official, which made his ransom price skyrocket and postponed his release for years. In his account of 1741, the German Michael Kühn explains how North African masters bribed their Christian slaves to trick newly arrived European captives into disclosing their true background, that is, their actual "market value."[36]

A third possibility that existed for captives, in addition to ransom or escape, was conversion to Islam. Renegades or converts could then lead relatively normal lives in the city-states of North Africa and could even hold very high offices. These options were especially attractive for individuals with highly specialized skills, such as carpenters, gunsmiths, or sea captains. Anthony Jansen, a native of Holland, was among the most illustrious of

---

34. Jean Marteilhe, *The Huguenot Galley-Slave: Being the Autobiography of a French Protestant Condemned to the Galleys for the Sake of his Religion* (New York: Leypoldt and Holt, 1867). On Marteilhe, see also Gillian Weiss, "Infidels at the Oar: A Mediterranean Exception to France's Free Soil Principle," *Slavery & Abolition* 32, no. 3 (2011): 397–412. For a good survey of the European galley slave economy, see Salzmann, "Migrants in Chains," 391–411. For Muslim slaves on French galleys, see Meredith Martin and Gillian Weiss, *The Sun King at Sea*.

35. *Letters from Italy describing the Manners, Customs, Antiquities, Painting, etc. of that Country in the Years MDCCLXX and MDCCLXXI by an English Woman to a Friend Residing in France* (London: Edward and Charles Dilly, 1776), 1: 308–09. See also Salzmann, "Migrants in Chains," 391–92.

36. Kühn, *Merckwürdige Lebens- und Reise-Beschreibung*, 144.

the seventeenth-century renegades. He voluntarily turned his back on his home country and converted to Islam in order to pursue a career in North Africa as Admiral Murat Reis. The major land raids of Iceland in 1627 and Ireland in 1631, during which many hundreds of civilians were captured and enslaved, can be credited to Murat Reis.[37] Also, Hark Olufs, whose Danish account is part of this anthology, could hardly have advanced to the position of a military leader in Constantine without converting. However, the major disadvantage of "taking the turban" or "turning Turk," as conversion to Islam was commonly referred to, was that renegades had to renounce their faith and thus forfeited the possibility of ransom through Christian funds. The narrative of the English convert Thomas Pellow, included in this anthology, gives testimony to this disadvantage when he laments the fact that, as a renegade, he cannot be among a group of approximately three hundred liberated British captives.[38] Conversion thus usually entailed a conscious decision to remain in North Africa for the rest of one's life.[39]

Many of the slaves could move relatively freely through the city during the day (see fig. I.10) but were locked up at night in so-called *bagnios* or prisons (see fig. I.11). North African slavery was remarkable in that slaves could manage businesses with relative independence. For example, the Englishman William Okeley, who was enslaved in Algiers in the mid-seventeenth century, reported that he ran a rather lucrative import–export business.[40] In exchange for this, he had to hand over a monthly sum to his master. Okeley writes, and this is particularly noteworthy, that he fared better financially as a slave in Algiers than as a free man in England. Nevertheless, William Okeley decided to flee. He undertook a week-long escape with several companions, during which he rowed more than two hundred miles from Algiers to Mallorca in a tiny collapsible boat, suffering great deprivations (see fig. I.12).

---

37. Murat Reis's sons purchased property on the peninsula of Manhattan and Humphrey Bogart and Jackie Kennedy number among their descendants. See Khalid El Abdaoui, "Murat Reis," in *Piraten und Sklaven im Mittelmeer: Eine Ausstellung in Schloss Ambras Innsbruck 20. Juni bis 6. Oktober 2019*, ed. Mario Klarer, Sabine Haag, and Veronika Sandbichler (Vienna: Kunsthistorisches Museum, 2019), 37–9.

38. Thomas Pellow, *The History of the Long Captivity and Adventures of Thomas Pellow, in South Barbary [. . .]* (London: R. Goadby, 1740 [?]), 71.

39. For more on conversion to Islam in the early modern period, see Bartolomé Bennassar and Lucile Bennassar, *Les chrétiens d'Allah. L'histoire extraordinaire des renégats XVIe–XVIIe siècles* (Paris: Perrin, 2006).

40. For a modern edition of William Okeley's *Ebenezer*, see Vitkus, *Piracy, Slavery, and Redemption*, 124–92. For more on William Okeley, see Starr, "Escape from Barbary," 35–52; and Spindler, *Corsairs, Captives, Converts in Early Modernity*, 133–42.

Figure I.10 "How the slaves walk with chains on their feet"
Source: Pierre Dan, *Historie van Barbaryen, En des zelfs Zee-Roovers* (Amsterdam, 1684), fol. 390; Mario Klarer, private collection.

Figure I.11 Depiction of a *bagnio*
Source: Leonard Eisenschmieds, eines Österreichischen Unterthans Merkwürdige Land- und Seereisen durch Europa, Africa und Asien, part 1 (Grätz, 1807), 196.

Figure I.12 William Okeley's sensational escape in a folding boat
Source: Pierre Dan, *Historie van Barbaryen, En des zelfs Zee-Roovers* (Amsterdam, 1684), fol. 147; Mario Klarer, private collection.

Miguel de Cervantes also attempted four futile escapes during his five-year enslavement in Algiers, one of which is the subject of a passage in Antonio de Sosa's narrative included in this volume.

The Ransom of Slaves

In addition to flight, there was also the possibility for captives to be ransomed or exchanged. Emanuel d'Aranda's narrative, which is also part of this collection, is a prominent example of an exchange of prisoners.[41] For d'Aranda's release, Ottoman captives in Europe were brought back to North Africa. Nevertheless, ransom was by far the more common practice. In Catholic countries, the Trinitarian monastic order specialized in ransoming slaves out of Muslim captivity.[42] Their detailed lists, in particular from the late eighteenth century, provide complete itemizations of the ransoms carried out and document the demographics of the captives by gender, age, provenance, and ransom price.[43] The Trinitarians held parades in European cities, during which former slaves had to appear once again in slaves' clothing and chains (see fig. I.13). These spectacles generated donations for future ransoms by the order.

In Protestant countries, first and foremost in Hanseatic cities like Hamburg, ransom was undertaken by the so-called *Sklavenkassen* ("slave banks"), institutions set up to purchase the freedom of sailors captured by pirates.[44] These were insurances entered into by shipowners so that the crews who fell into the hands of North African corsairs could be ransomed. This represents the first kind of social security system in a German-speaking region and was introduced as early as the seventeenth century. This insurance was also the reason why German captains frequently offered little resistance

---

41. For more on the economy of ransom, see Wolfgang Kaiser, "Sprechende Ware. Gefangenenfreikauf und Sklavenhandel im frühneuzeitlichen Mittelmeerraum," *Zeitschrift für Ideengeschichte* 3, no. 2 (2009): 29–39; Wolfgang Kaiser, *Le commerce des captifs: Les intermédiaires dans l'échange et le rachat des prisonniers en Méditerraneé, XVe–XVIIIe siècle* (Rome: École française de Rome, 2008). For the reciprocal nature of ransoms, see Daniel Hershenzon, "The Political Economy of Ransom in the Early Modern Mediterranean," *Past & Present* 231, no. 1 (2016): 61–95; Hershenzon, *The Captive Sea.*

42. Andrea Pelizza, "Confraternity Models in the 'Redemption of Slaves' in Europe: The *Broederschap der alderheylighste Dryvuldigheyt* of Bruges (Brugge) and the *Scuola della Santissima Trinità* of Venice," in *Piracy and Captivity in the Mediterranean: 1550–1810*, ed. Mario Klarer (London: Routledge, 2019), 199–219.

43. Watzka-Pauli, *Triumph der Barmherzigkeit.*

44. Ressel, *Zwischen Sklavenkassen und Türkenpässen.*

Figure I.13 "Procession of the freed slaves"
Source: Pierre Dan, *Historie Van Barbaryen, En des zelfs Zee-Roovers* (Amsterdam, 1684), fol. 059; Mario Klarer, private collection.

during pirate attacks, knowing that the Sklavenkasse would eventually come up with their ransom.

Ransoms were not organized only by the Europeans. Since a large number of North Africans also fell into Christian hands, the Muslim side also ransomed slaves time and again. There is, for example, a Moroccan text from the late eighteenth century that reports that six hundred to one thousand slaves were bought out of Spanish captivity in one year. One should not forget that large slave markets and bagnios (slave prisons) also existed in European cities like Livorno, Málaga, and Marseille. In the 1780s, Muhammad III, the sultan of Morocco, undertook one of the largest ransom initiatives to liberate Muslim slaves, freeing one thousand subjects of North African states from captivity in Malta.[45]

While sailors and coastal populations were most at risk of capture, people from astonishingly far-removed areas such as remote Alpine valleys could fall into North African slavery. The case of the Tyrolean farmer

---

45. Godfrey Wettinger, *Slavery in the Islands of Malta and Gozo, ca. 1000–1812* (Valletta: Publishers Enterprises Group, 2002), 577–83.

Georg Kleubenschedl illustrates this. It shows how ransoms from North Africa were transacted and, more specifically, the lengthy periods of time these transactions could require.[46] While on a pilgrimage to the Holy Land in 1612, the Tyrolean farmer from the district of Stams in the Oberinntal Valley was abducted to Tunis and held there for almost two decades. Georg Kleubenschedl emerged from the shadows of history toward the end of the 1620s when he attempted to end his enslavement by trying to organize the sale of his farm in the Tyrol to raise the demanded ransom.[47] Through middlemen at home—among whom were numbered abbots at the monastery in Stams and burghers in Innsbruck and Petersberg—Georg Kleubenschedl contacted businessmen in Innsbruck, Venice, and Genoa, and Jews in Innsbruck and Tunis, as well as potential Tyrolean moneylenders. After half a decade, Georg Kleubenschedl finally succeeded in selling his house and farm from Tunis in order to be able to raise half of the ransom payment demanded.[48]

On the basis of documents like the ones regarding Georg Kleubenschedl's enslavement, it is possible to determine how various institutions and groups of people cooperated for such ransoms in the early modern era and the expenditures of time and complex logistical issues connected to such transactions. In Kleubenschedl's case, it is also possible to determine the immense ransom sums involved: One can assume that his ransom amounted to double the worth of a sizable farm in the Tyrolean uplands or, more specifically, that Kleubenschedl could only finance half of his release with the possessions of a well-to-do farmer. The fact that Kleubenschedl could go on a trip to the Holy Land in the first place indicates that he came from relatively well-off circumstances and thus must have owned a valuable farm. Georg Kleubenschedl is one of only a handful of examples of Austrian captives whose fate we can reconstruct relatively precisely. Most others remain in the dark recesses of history. This includes the fates of female Austrian captives such

---

46. Mario Klarer, "Regionale Verflechtungen transmediterraner Piraterie und Sklaverei: Tunis, Danzig und Innsbruck," in *Piraten und Sklaven im Mittelmeer. Eine Ausstellung in Schloss Ambras Innsbruck 20. Juni bis 6. Oktober 2019*, ed. Mario Klarer, Sabine Haag, and Veronika Sandbichler (Vienna: Kunsthistorisches Museum, 2019), 49–55.

47. In the 1920s, more than a dozen letters completely documenting Kleubenschedl's release were still preserved in the Tyrolean archives. Unfortunately, the majority of these documents are no longer traceable in spite of intense research and can only be reconstructed thanks to a short essay from 1928 by the Tyrolean state archivist Karl Klaar. See Karl Klaar, "Georg Kleubenschedl von Stams, Sklave in Tunis und seine Befreiung 1612–1636," *Tiroler Heimat* 1 (1928): 182–85.

48. *Oberösterreichische Regierung, Kopialbücher, Parteibücher 1636*, vol. 94, fol. 387v, last paragraph (Innsbruck, Tiroler Landesarchiv).

as a Tyrolean mother and her sons of whom we know only that they were abducted to Tripoli in the seventeenth century, according to archival entries in the Tyrolean State Archive.[49] Unfortunately, relatively few Barbary captivity accounts by women have survived, at least when compared with the number of narratives by male slaves. The few extant female accounts are in Dutch and English, selections of which are also included in this anthology.

Female Slaves

The majority of European Christian slaves in early modern North Africa were men. However, time and again, women also fell into the hands of Muslim pirates.[50] Women were sometimes captured from ships on which they were passengers or, alternatively, could fall into slavery during land raids, in which large numbers of children were also frequently taken. For example, in his eighteenth-century German account, Michael Kühn writes that "[t]he Turks had also taken 132 Spaniards, including many *officers* and *officer's wives* as prisoners."[51]

One of the most prominent authentic female captivity accounts is that of Maria ter Meetelen, a Dutch woman who was abducted to Morocco in the first half of the eighteenth century. What especially distinguishes Maria ter Meetelen's account, excerpts of which are included in this volume, is the strong realism and insight that her notes on the day-to-day life of a female slave in North Africa provide. Like her fellow male slaves, she had to struggle for her very survival by, for example, keeping a tavern to earn money for her living and to keep a roof over her head. Moreover, her account makes it particularly clear that this European exile community in North Africa was greatly marked by domestic tensions. The individual communities of captives operated relatively separately from each other and had their own leaders. Everyday life also seems to have been marked by conflict between the female slaves. Maria ter Meetelen was eventually ransomed and was able to return to Holland after twelve years of captivity. From there, she eventually emigrated to South Africa, where her trail is lost.

The lives of female slaves in Muslim North Africa could take quite a different path from that of someone like ter Meetelen, as shown by the example

---

49. *Von der fürstlichen Durchlaucht*, vol. 99, ff. 252r–254r (Innsbruck, Tiroler Landesarchiv).
50. Bekkaoui, *White Women Captives in North Africa*.
51. Kühn, *Merckwürdige Lebens- und Reise-Beschreibung*, 385–86.

of several *renegadas*, female converts to Islam. We know of many so-called renegada-queens who, upon adopting Islam, rose from enslavement to being rulers' wives.[52] They include the Englishwoman Janet, who became the Moroccan queen named Lalla Belkis in the early eighteenth century. The Scottish captive Helen Gloag became the wife of the Moroccan ruler Sidi Muhammed in the second half of the eighteenth century.[53] As queens, these women played important roles in diplomatic exchanges, because they were often engaged by both sides for the release of slaves in North Africa and Europe.

Gender-specific components of North African slavery could produce strange situations, as a document from 1636 demonstrates. In a letter, a gunner called for the English king to exchange English prostitutes for male captives in North Africa at a ratio of one to six—that is to say, one female English prostitute for six enslaved men.[54] That this suggestion was ever put into practice, however, is doubtful, as there are no further sources on that matter.

European slaves who managed to return home from North Africa were under great pressure to prove that they had not converted to Islam while in captivity. This burden affected men as well as women, but women had to face an additional, complicating factor. Very often they were subjected to the latent accusation that they had had sexual relations with Muslim men during their captivity. Elizabeth Marsh's narrative, which is part of this selection, is a case in point.[55]

The sexual purity of female prisoners occupied a dominant position in mainstream European imagination.[56] For example, Wolfgang Amadeus Mozart's 1782 opera *The Abduction from the Seraglio* revolves around the sexual steadfastness of European captives in a North African Muslim court.[57] Therefore, in the early nineteenth century especially, female captivity

52. Khalid Bekkaoui, "Piracy, Diplomacy, and Cultural Circulations in the Mediterranean," in *Piracy and Captivity in the Mediterranean: 1550–1810*, ed. Mario Klarer (London: Routledge, 2019), 186–98.

53. Elizabeth Ewan, Rosemary J. Pipes, Jane Rendall, and Siân Reynolds, *The New Biographical Dictionary of Scottish Women* (Edinburgh: Edinburgh University Press, 2018).

54. Bekkaoui, *White Women Captives in North Africa*, 19.

55. On Elizabeth Marsh, see Linda Colley, *The Ordeal of Elizabeth Marsh: How a Remarkable Woman Crossed Seas and Empires to Become a Part of World History* (London: Harper Perennial, 2014).

56. See, for example, Charles Sabatos, *Frontier Orientalism and the Turkish Image in Central European Literature* (Lanham, MD: Lexington, 2020).

57. Kurt Palm, "Mozart, Islam, and the Hangman of Salzburg," in *Mediterranean Slavery and World Literature: Captivity Genres from Cervantes to Rousseau*, ed. Mario Klarer (London: Routledge, 2020), 197–211. For more on depictions of the Ottoman Empire in opera, see Larry Wolff, *The Singing Turk: Ottoman Power and Operatic Emotions on the European Stage from the Siege of Vienna to the Age of Napoleon* (Stanford, CA: Stanford University Press, 2016).

narratives were often driven by this focus on sexual danger for women and thus sold very well.[58] Admittedly, in most cases, these accounts were pure fiction—novels that only purported to be authentic reports. The most striking example of this is the narrative by Maria Martin published in the United States in 1807, allegedly a translation from Italian.[59] On closer inspection it becomes clear that this early nineteenth-century female Barbary captivity narrative only pretends to be an authentic account. In reality the text is composed of plagiarized passages derived from numerous other slave narratives and historical works on North Africa. The frontispiece of one of the editions of Martin's text, showing a scantily clad female in shackles, is indicative of the sales value of plots with female slaves threatened by the sexual violence of their Muslim captors (see fig. I.14). The image thus graphically renders the title of the narrative: *History of the Captivity and Sufferings of Mrs. Maria Martin: Who Was Six Years a Slave in Algiers, Two of Which She Was Confined in a Dark and Dismal Dungeon, Loaded with Irons for Refusing to Comply with the Brutal Request of a Turkish Officer.* The case of Maria Martin is a perfect example of how Barbary captivity narratives, authentic or fictional, are interwoven with literary trends in the early modern period.

Captivity Narratives and World Literature

As we have seen, a large number of Christians who had been enslaved by North African pirates between the early sixteenth and the early nineteenth century published eyewitness accounts after their flight or ransom. These captivity narratives were very successful, often going through several editions. For Europeans in the early modern period, these eyewitness reports represented one of the most important sources on Islam in general and North Africa in particular, while at the same time quenching their readers' thirst for gripping plots in exotic settings.

For the five-year research project ESCAPE at the University of Innsbruck, more than one hundred accounts were collected in all major European languages from the early sixteenth to the early nineteenth century. These early

---

58. Stefanie Fricke, "Female Captivity in Penelope Aubin's *The Noble Slaves* (1722) and Elizabeth Marsh's *The Female Captive* (1769)," in *Mediterranean Slavery and World Literature: Captivity Genres from Cervantes to Rousseau*, ed. Mario Klarer (London: Routledge, 2020), 111–31.

59. *History of the Captivity and Sufferings of Mrs. Maria Martin: Who Was Six Years a Slave in Algiers, Two of Which She Was Confined in a Dark and Dismal Dungeon, Loaded with Irons for Refusing to Comply with the Brutal Request of a Turkish Officer* (Boston: Crary, 1807).

Figure I.14 Frontispiece of Maria Martin's narrative
Source: *History of the Captivity and Sufferings of Mrs. Maria Martin* (Boston, 1807), image ID: psnypl_rbk_1101; Rare Book Division, Digital Public Library of America, New York Public Library.

Figure I.15 Various torture methods
Source: Pierre Dan, *Historie Van Barbaryen, En des zelfs Zee-Roovers* (Amsterdam, 1684), fol. 324; Mario Klarer, private collection.

modern testimonies were published for a variety of reasons, including arousing sympathy in readers, thus indirectly increasing their willingness to make donations for the ransom of captives still trapped in North Africa. Consequently, these accounts often included detailed descriptions or representations of torture and atrocities to generate sympathy and donations for the captives. The 1684 Dutch edition of Pierre Dan's *Histoire de Barbarie* (*History of Barbary*) provides especially striking visual representations of physical abuses.[60] Three large images—each with three triptych-like illustrations of various methods of torture, punishment, and execution—are prime examples of this voyeuristic display of violence in the captivity genre (see figs. I.15, I.16, I.17).

Naturally, besides eliciting sympathy, self-preservation also influenced these reports. After their return, many slaves had to counter accusations that they had converted to Islam during their captivity. Thus, a narrative that emphasized religious steadfastness was, of course, of great personal advantage. Despite frequent, graphic representations of violence, the narratives themselves often feature understanding and benevolent North

60. Pierre Dan, S. Vries, and G. Broekhuizen, *Historie van Barbaryen, En des zelfs Zee-Roovers: Behelzende een beschrijving van de Koningrijken en Steden Algiers, Tunis, Salé, en Tripoli* (Amsterdam: Jan ten Hoorn, 1684). This text was originally published in French: Pierre Dan, *Histoire de Barbarie et de ses corsaires, des royaumes, et des villes d'Alger, de Tunis, de Salé & de Tripoly* (Paris: P. Rocolet, 1637).

Figure I.16 Crucifixion of a slave
Source: Pierre Dan, *Historie van Barbaryen, En des zelfs Zee-Roovers* (Amsterdam, 1684), fol. 54; Mario Klarer, private collection.

Figure I.17 "Terrible punishments which the Turks inflict on the slaves"
Source: Pierre Dan, *Historie van Barbaryen, En des zelfs Zee-Roovers* (Amsterdam, 1684), fol. 407; Mario Klarer, private collection.

African slaveholders. These Muslim masters, despite tempting their captives with voluntary conversion, were nevertheless understanding when Christian slaves chose to remain true to their own religion. Depictions of such benevolent masters may, at times, have served as literary tropes to legitimize the narrators' claims that they did not convert.

Numerous elements of these authentic eyewitness accounts anticipate the early novel. Above all, the thrilling scenes of capture and flight, the successful deception of the pursuer, as well as the frequently prankster-like aspects of the first-person narrators foreshadow and parallel the picaresque novel of the sixteenth century in many ways. When we read early modern texts, many of us overlook the fact that the early novel is heavily influenced by piracy and, more particularly, by slavery in North Africa.[61] For example, Miguel de Cervantes's aforementioned experiences in North African captivity during the 1570s strongly shaped his work, with a number of his dramas revolving around the theme of slavery. Cervantes also incorporated the tale of a European slave in North Africa in *Don Quixote* in chapters 38–41 (see fig. I.18).

The first major English novel, Daniel Defoe's *Robinson Crusoe* (1719), was also influenced by authentic captivity narratives from North Africa. Before his more famous adventures on the deserted island, the protagonist Robinson Crusoe is captured by Muslim pirates and is only able to free himself after two years of captivity in Morocco. Many elements in *Robinson Crusoe* can be traced back to early Barbary captivity narratives, including the motif of taking to sea against the father's wishes and the styling of former slaves' return to their native society as a reclamation from purgatory, in which they were purified. Defoe's novel also engages with various attempts to flee from captivity in a manner reminiscent of North African captivity narratives like that of the Englishman William Okeley (1675)—an account with striking parallels to *Robinson Crusoe* and most likely known to Defoe.

Interestingly, the captivity narrative's impact on the genre of the novel is not a one-way phenomenon. It also worked the other way around. After the publication of *Robinson Crusoe*, a reciprocal mechanism kicked in, where *Robinson Crusoe* influenced later, authentic captivity narratives set in North Africa with respect to style, narrative technique, and content. This became a many-layered interchange, with older captivity narratives shaping the development of the early novel. The novel, in turn, influenced subsequent captivity narratives of the late eighteenth and early nineteenth centuries.

61. The essay collection edited by Mario Klarer, *Mediterranean Slavery and World Literature*, takes an in-depth look at the literary components of slave narratives set in North Africa.

EL INGENIOSO
HIDALGO DON QVI-
XOTE DE LA MANCHA,

Compuesto por Miguel de Ceruantes Saauedra.

DIRIGIDO AL DVQVE DE BEIAR,
Marques de Gibraleon, Conde de Benalcaçar, y Bañares, Vizconde de la Puebla de Alcozer, Señor de las villas de Capilla, Curiel, y Burguillos.

Año, 1605.

CON PRIVILEGIO,
EN MADRID, Por Iuan de la Cuesta.

Vendese en casa de Francisco de Robles, librero del Rey nro señor.

Figure I.18 Title page of the first edition of *Don Quixote*
Source: Miguel de Cervantes, *Don Quijote* (Madrid, 1605); Sig. 207.629; © Universitäts- und Landesbibliothek Innsbruck.

The most curious amalgamation of authentic Barbary captivity experiences and fiction is found in the popular genre of the Robinsonade, with a multitude of novels riding the wave of success experienced by Defoe's popular work.[62] Among many other things, Robinsonades served as a vehicle for communicating authentic North African captivity experiences in the late eighteenth century. Leonhard Eisenschmied's authentic Austrian Barbary captivity account, for instance, demonstrates indebtedness to Defoe's novel.[63] In Eisenschmied's case, the Barbary captivity of the protagonist is embedded in an array of Robinson-like adventures, such as piracy, shipwreck, and being stranded for years on a deserted island. However, despite these numerous derivative fictional episodes, external evidence proves that the core of the narrative describing Eisenschmied's captivity in Algiers is authentic.

In general, borrowing and intertextuality are recurrent themes in Barbary captivity narratives, thus making it difficult to differentiate unequivocally between fictional embellishment and authentic elements. For example, Michael Kühn's eighteenth-century German captivity narrative exhibits strong fantastical elements, such that one would designate it as pure fiction at first glance. However, archival documents unearthed by the historian Magnus Ressel indicate that Michael Kühn really appears to have been in North Africa and was ransomed. Nevertheless, Kühn utilized content from a variety of other texts in a way that would be called plagiarism today. This was common practice in the early modern publishing world and does not put the authentic nature of his account into question.

In addition to many instances of authentic life writing with the odd fictional "interferences," the Barbary genre could, however, also emancipate itself completely from true-to-life experiences. Jean-Jacques Rousseau's continuation of his novel *Émile* (1762) in the late eighteenth century shows that piracy and slavery themes found their way into pure fiction. In the short fragment *Émile et Sophie, ou les solitaires*, Émile falls into North African captivity and resigns himself to slavery.[64] Rousseau uses the captivity plot for fictional purposes, while at the same time probing larger philosophical questions. What is most surprising is that the character Émile does not revolt against his fate but accepts captivity as a metaphor for life. Rousseau employs North African enslavement as an allegory for the unavoidable confinements

62. Robert Spindler, "The Robinsonade as a Literary Avatar of Early Nineteenth-Century Barbary Captivity Narration," in *Mediterranean Slavery and World Literature: Captivity Genres from Cervantes to Rousseau*, ed. Mario Klarer (London: Routledge, 2020), 175–94.

63. For a German edition of Eisenschmied's narrative, see Klarer, *Verschleppt, Verkauft, Versklavt*, 210–34.

of human existence. With Rousseau's *Émile et Sophie*, the Barbary captivity genre fully liberates itself from its roots in authentic, true-to-life writing and metamorphoses into pure fiction. At the same time, Rousseau's fragment problematizes the implications of captivity and slavery against the backdrop of Enlightenment philosophy.

One of the latest examples of how Barbary captivity influenced world literature—although almost imperceptibly—is Annette von Droste-Hülshoff's 1842 German novella *The Jews' Beech Tree* (*Die Judenbuche*). The core of the book is based on the authentic North African captivity of a young murderer from rural Westphalia in Germany, who, after fleeing from the region in the 1780s to avoid persecution for killing a Jew, fell into the hands of corsairs.[65] After his return from his decades-long slavery, broken in body and spirit, he is unsuccessful at reintegrating into his native society. Despite his harrowing experiences as a captive in North Africa, the fact that he once committed murder means he is no longer assimilable into village life and eventually takes his own life.

What is most interesting about the novella is that, on the surface, it has no obvious connection to Barbary captivity. Droste-Hülshoff devotes only one sentence to the protagonist's extended "Turkish" slavery. Her use of an authentic case of a forgotten Barbary captivity experience during the mid-nineteenth century no longer exploits the full potential of the captivity genre as older works of fiction did. Since the threat of Barbary piracy and slavery was losing its prominence in the 1840s, older narrative patterns had to give way to strategies that could accommodate the waning awareness of Mediterranean corsairing and slavery in cultural memory. Thus, *The Jews' Beech Tree*, despite being indebted to the long tradition of Barbary captivity narratives, silences the central North African slavery experience in favor of other plot elements.

Despite the declining awareness of Barbary captivity in cultural memory, it may, nevertheless, have affected world literature as late as the mid-twentieth century with Albert Camus's *The Plague* (1947). In 2020, more than half a century after its original publication, Camus's classic novel once again made it onto international best seller lists. Camus's fictitious text describes the lockdown of the North African city of Oran during the outbreak of the plague, which explains the renewed interest in the book during the COVID-19

---

64. Jeremy D. Popkin, "*Émile* in Chains: A New Perspective on Rousseau, Slavery, and Hegel's Phenomenology," in *Mediterranean Slavery and World Literature: Captivity Genres from Cervantes to Rousseau*, ed. Mario Klarer (London: Routledge, 2020), 294–310.

65. Magnus Ressel, "A Dystopia as Utopia: The Algerian City of Oran and Annette von Droste-Hülshoff's *The Jew's Beech Tree* (*Die Judenbuche*)," in *Mediterranean Slavery and World Literature: Captivity Genres from Cervantes to Rousseau*, ed. Mario Klarer (London: Routledge, 2020), 132–50.

crisis. However, very few readers of *The Plague* would likely be aware of the fact that both the setting and plotlines of Camus's novel resemble those of the early modern Barbary captivity narrative, albeit with a postcolonial twist. Born in colonial Algeria, Camus must have been aware that the Algerian town of Oran was one of the most important European enclaves and first colonial outposts in North Africa in the early modern period. At times, the situation described in Camus's novel comes very close to the historical circumstances in Oran. For centuries, Oran attracted opportunists and mercenaries with dubious backgrounds from all over Europe, similar to the modern Foreign Legion. Surrounded by "enemy territory," the historical enclave of Oran resembled a quarantined city at the best of times, cut off from outside contact. Frequent supply shortages, famines, and epidemics turned the European garrison of early modern Oran into a community of quasi-captives. These deplorable living conditions led many soldiers from Christian Oran to give up their alleged "freedom" in favor of deserting into Muslim captivity in Algiers, hoping to improve their precarious fate. The description of the quarantined characters in Camus's novel also resembles the situation of slaves in numerous historical Barbary captivity narratives: The early modern European slave communities in North Africa exhibited similar modes of coping with their situation, oscillating between adapting to the system and attempting to escape from it.

The plot of Camus's postcolonial novel unfolds before the background of the Algerian War of Independence, during which the colonial French population of Algerian cities found itself cut off from their homeland. Resistance against the French colonizer spread like an epidemic and increased the pressure on colonial communities. In the 1940s, near the end of the French colonial experiment in Algeria, the threat for Europeans in North Africa started to resemble the pressure on the first colonial forces in the enclave of Oran. Camus, so it seems, deliberately referenced the genre of the Barbary captivity narrative for his plot, which gravitates around the larger philosophical concept of confinement.

This anthology consciously excludes purely fictional literary works and contains solely authentic or verifiable North African slave narratives. Despite their factuality, however, these eyewitness accounts, which span a period from the early sixteenth to the early nineteenth century, clearly demonstrate that they are in a state of constant exchange with fictional literature. Thus, the genre of the Barbary captivity narrative, as it is presented in this cross-national anthology, reveals its full complexity only when viewed within larger historical *and* literary contexts.

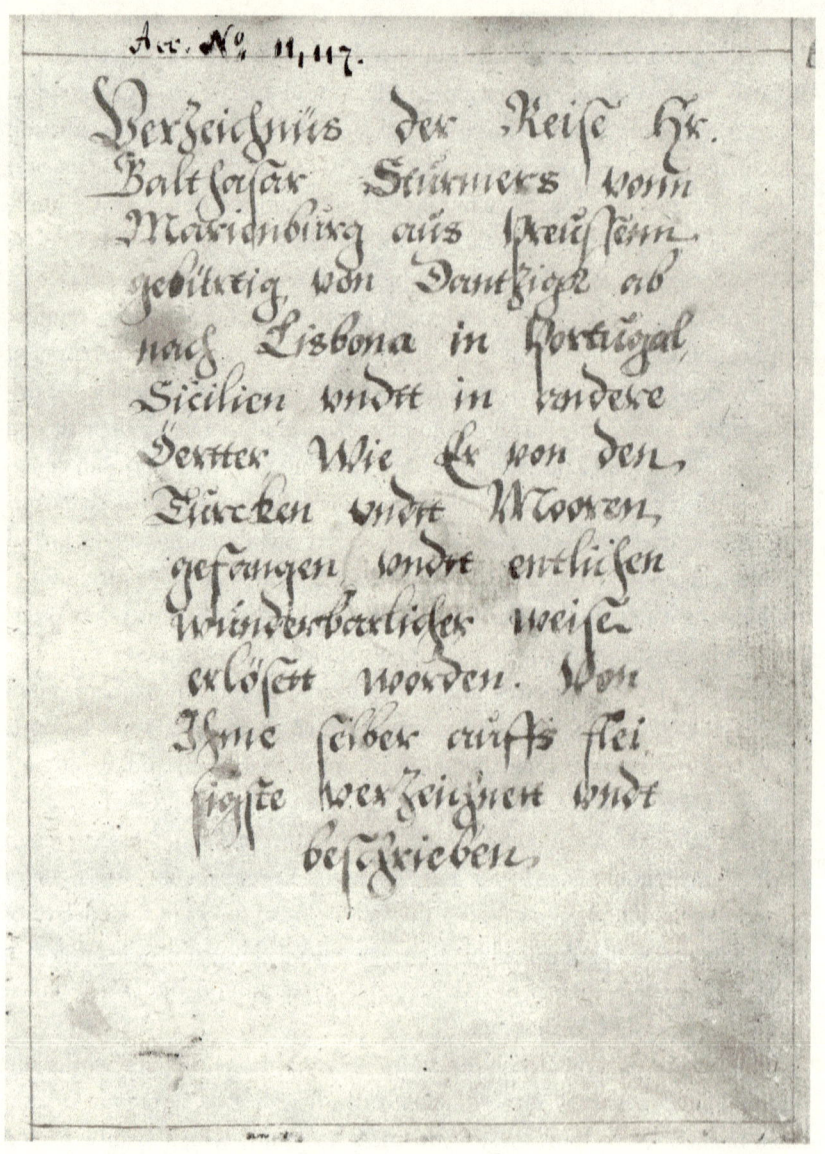

Figure 1.1 Title page of Balthasar Sturmer's narrative
Source: Balthasar Sturmer, *Verzeichnüs der Reise* (1558); © bpk-Bildagentur; MS germ.qu. 1014, f. 1r; Staatsbibliothek zu Berlin, Manuscript Department.

CHAPTER I

BALTHASAR STURMER, *ACCOUNT OF THE TRAVELS OF MISTER BALTHASAR STURMER*

1558 German manuscript; complete text

Captivity in Tunis 1534–1535

The first text in this anthology, the handwritten account of the German merchant's son Balthasar Sturmer, is most probably also the first recorded North African captivity narrative by a European in the early modern era.[1] It chronicles Sturmer's adventures as a Christian pirate and as an Ottoman galley slave during major geopolitical events in the Mediterranean in the 1530s. Despite being the first representative text of a genre that would achieve great popularity in the following decades, this narrative also marks a high point of the genre. Balthasar Sturmer's testimony exhibits an astonishing narrative variety, individualistic and psychologically insightful depiction of the first-person narrator, and a self-reflexive religious framing of the captivity. The religious context in particular would later become a standard characteristic of Barbary captivity accounts as well as of the early novel.

As a young man, Balthasar Sturmer accompanies a shipload of his father's wheat from Gdańsk to Lisbon. There, he successfully sells the grain but, in accordance with his character, squanders the entire proceeds of the sale.

---

1. On Balthasar Sturmer, see Mario Klarer, "Trading Identities: Balthasar Sturmer's *Verzeichnis der Reise* (1558) and the Making of the European Barbary Captivity Narrative," in *Piracy and Captivity in the Mediterranean: 1550–1810*, ed. Mario Klarer (London, New York: Routledge, 2019), 25–55; Robert Spindler, "An Early 'Schelmenroman': The Picaresque Elements in the German Barbary Narrative 'Verzeichnis der Reise' (1558) by Balthasar Sturmer," *Germanisch-Romanische Monatsschrift* 69, no. 1 (2019): 1–20; Anne-Barbara Ritter, "Ein deutscher Sklave als Augenzeuge bei der Eroberung von Tunis (1535). Untersuchung und Edition eines unbekannten Reiseberichts aus dem Jahr 1558," in *Europas islamische Nachbarn. Studien zur Literatur und Geschichte des Maghreb*, ed. Ernstpeter Ruhe (Würzburg: Königshausen & Neumann, 1993), 187–231.

To earn money for the trip home, he has to enter service on a Christian ship that preys on Ottoman merchant vessels, thus becoming a European pirate. As illustrated by Sturmer's text, slavery and piracy in the Mediterranean were not only carried out by corsairs from the North African side but were also engaged in by Europeans. Balthasar Sturmer's testimony thus distinguishes itself from other captivity accounts by addressing *Christian* piracy and also by describing it in great detail.

The pirate ship on which Balthasar Sturmer hires himself out is so successful that the ship's crew become rich men within a few weeks. The crew, in turn, plan to set themselves up as "self-employed" pirates by acquiring their own galley. While in this state of euphoria over their success, Balthasar Sturmer and his fellows are attacked by Ottoman pirate ships. Half of the men are killed during the attack and the other half, including the severely wounded Sturmer, are taken into captivity.

Sturmer's precise financial records of wages, booty, the proceeds from slaves, and the estimated cost of the construction of a galley provide an in-depth look at the economy of piracy and slavery in the Mediterranean in the first half of the sixteenth century. For example, due to financial difficulties, Sturmer had to hire himself out for two ducats[2] a month as a gunsmith's assistant on the aforementioned Christian pirate ship. Within a few weeks, Sturmer's personal cut of the booty amounted to two thousand ducats—vastly more than his yearly salary of twenty-four ducats as a "normal" crew member. Enticed by financial success, Balthasar Sturmer wanted to establish an independent pirate operation with his companions and to have a galley built for 150,000 ducats, but this plan was abruptly thwarted by the Ottoman pirate attack. He was sold to the highest bidder for forty ducats and had to serve on the Ottoman side as a galley slave in the fleet of Hayreddin Barbarossa, the most important Ottoman admiral in North Africa during the sixteenth century.[3]

Sturmer's "Turkish" captivity coincided with major geopolitical events in the Mediterranean in the 1530s, during which time Balthasar Sturmer took part in two sieges of the city of Tunis. The first was the conquest of Tunis by Hayreddin Barbarossa, who brought all of North Africa (with the exception of the Kingdom of Morocco) under the control and influence

---

2. *ducat*: a widely used coin, usually of gold.

3. For more on Hayreddin Barbarossa, see Jacques Heers, *Les Barbaresques: La course et la guerre en Méditerranée, XIVe–XVIe siècle* (Paris: Perrin, 2001); Diana de Armas Wilson, "Khayr al-Din Barbarossa: Clashing Portraits of a Corsair-King," in *Piracy and Captivity in the Mediterranean: 1550–1810*, ed. Mario Klarer (London: Routledge, 2019), 223–33.

Figure 1.2 Engraving of early modern Tunis
Source: Georg Braun and Frans Hogenberg, *Civitates Orbis Terrarum*, vol. 2 (Cologne, 1575); Mario Klarer, private collection.

of the Ottoman Empire during the first half of the sixteenth century. The second siege was the historically well-documented capture of the fortress La Goulette and the city of Tunis (see fig. 1.2) by Emperor Charles V in 1535.

To capitalize adequately on the political PR opportunities that the conquest of the city of Tunis would provide, Charles V hired prominent painters such as Jan Cornelisz Vermeyen and Cornelis Anthonisz to participate in the venture and to execute visual representations of the event. These men created numerous scenes of the siege and capture of the city of Tunis that

4. For the Tunis tapestries, see Katja Schmitz-von Ledebur, "Emperor Charles V Captures Tunis: A Unique Set of Tapestry Cartoons," *Studia Bruxellae* 13, no. 1 (2019): 387–404; Katja Schmitz-von Ledebur, "Der Tunis-Kriegszug Kaiser Karls V. Eine Dokumentation in Kartons und Tapisserien," in *Piraten und Sklaven im Mittelmeer: Eine Ausstellung in Schloss Ambras Innsbruck 20. Juni bis 6. Oktober 2019*, ed. Mario Klarer, Sabine Haag, and Veronika Sandbichler (Vienna: Kunsthistorisches Museum, 2019), 57–63; Katja Schmitz-von Ledebur and Sabine Haag, *Fäden der Macht: Tapisserien des 16. Jahrhunderts aus dem Kunsthistorischen Museum Wien: Eine Ausstellung des Kunsthistorischen Museums Wien 14. Juli bis 20. September 2015* (Vienna: Kunsthistorisches Museum, 2015).

Figure 1.3 "The emperor was [. . .] surrounded by the Moors [. . .]"
Source: Franz Hogenberg, *Geschichtsblätter* [ca. 1574]; Mario Klarer, private collection.

then served as templates for tapestry designs.[4] The wall hangings could be used as a portable instrument of propaganda, creating a tent that featured a three-dimensional panorama and that styled Charles V as the conqueror of the Muslim opponent. Additionally, copper engravings of the designs were produced by Frans Hogenberg (see fig. 1.3). Balthasar Sturmer's narrative is one of the few "unofficial" documents about the events surrounding the capture of Tunis in 1535.

As a slave, Balthasar Sturmer had to operate on the Ottoman side. This gives his account a unique perspective on this violent cross-cultural contact between Christian Europe and Muslim North Africa in the 1530s. Thus, Balthasar Sturmer's text not only records the historic siege of Tunis from the worm's-eye view of a simple galley slave on the "wrong" side of the European attack but, beyond that, also astonishes with its numerous literary and narrative merits. Sturmer's unusually fresh, gripping, and exciting narration is outstanding. One could go so far as to suggest that the narrative style and the lengthy personal reflection of Sturmer's eyewitness account makes it seem like the first European novel, despite the fact that it was written fifty years before Miguel de

Cervantes's landmark novel *Don Quixote*. Naturally, Sturmer's narrative is not a fictional or literary text but rather an autobiographical eyewitness account. However, authenticity, or the pretense thereof, was quite conducive to the success of the early novel, as in the case of Daniel Defoe's *Robinson Crusoe*. Nevertheless, in his testimony, Sturmer develops techniques and elements that make his account seem like a novel. He anticipates the early Spanish picaresque novel à la Lazarillo de Tormes, as well as the narrative elements that we find, for example, in Cervantes's *Don Quixote* or in Defoe's *Robinson Crusoe*. In particular, the religious frame story of an old and penitent Balthasar Sturmer, into which are embedded the youthful first-person narrator's picaresque-like escapades, places this memoir in a larger religious context and thus anticipates the connection between adventure and religion in Defoe's *Robinson Crusoe*.

Balthasar Sturmer's account opens a new chapter in Europe's literary history in the form of the Barbary captivity narrative. Furthermore, instead of making a modest first appearance, as one might expect, Sturmer produced a formidable text in this first exemplar of a genre that would shape the literary landscape of early modern Europe like no other.

Notes on the Present Translation of Balthasar Sturmer's *Account of the Travels of Mister Balthasar Sturmer*

This translation is based on the only surviving manuscript from 1558: Balthasar Sturmer, *Verzeichnüs der Reise Herrn Balthasar Sturmers. Vonn Marienburg aus Preussenn gebürtig, von Dantzigk ab nach Lisbona in Portugal, Sicilien vndtt in andere Oertter. Wie er von den Turcken vndtt Mooren gefangen vndtt entlichen wunderbarlicher Weise erlösett worden. Von ihme selber auffs fleisigste verzeichnett vndt beschrieben* (1558, MS germ. Quart. 1014, Berlin State Library),[5] and the recent German transcription in Mario Klarer (ed.), *Verschleppt, Verkauft, Versklavt: Deutschsprachige Sklavenberichte aus Nordafrika (1550–1800)* (Vienna: Böhlau, 2019), 49–80.

The numbers in brackets {} in the text always indicate the beginning of a page and refer to the original page numbers of the manuscript. The translation introduces additional paragraph breaks to enhance the readability of the narrative. Place names that could be identified clearly have been

---

5. Digitized collection: http://digital.staatsbibliothek-berlin.de/werkansicht?PPN=PPN737576820&PHYSID=P HYS_0001.

updated to their modern versions throughout the text. In cases of doubt, the original spelling has been retained and annotated with a footnote. Camila Torres Carrillo and Ashley Nissler assisted with the preparation of this final translation. Special thanks go to Stephan Procházka, Devin Stewart, and Ercan Akyol for their invaluable assistance with regard to Arabic and Ottoman Turkish, as well as to Klaus Amann and Hubert Alisade for clarifying cases of doubt with regard to antiquated German.

Balthasar Sturmer, *Account of the Travels of Mister Balthasar Sturmer, Native of Marienburg in Prussia, from Dantzigk to Lisbon in Portugal, Sicily, and Many Other Places. How He Was Captured by the Turks and Moors, and Finally Released in a Wondrous Manner. Assiduously Chronicled and Described by Himself* (Manuscript 1558, MS germ. Quart. 1014, Berlin State Library)

Translated by Robert Spindler and Almiria Wilhelm

The grace of God, through our Lord and Savior Jesus Christ, be with us all. Amen.

Dear Honorable Mr. Frantz,[6] since Your Honor recently informed me that you would like to hear from me about how I was captured and released, I could not refrain from communicating my experiences to Your Honor in writing.

However, before I begin, I have to report to Your Honor the circumstances through which I fell into captivity. Your Honor will see how, in times of woe, our good Lord can save His own very wondrously and [in a manner] beyond rational comprehension, and how many times my faithful God elevated and humbled me, all of which oftentimes happened for my own good. He, our good Father, knows well what is good for us and {2v} therefore chastises us frequently. In the beginning, we might think we are not being treated properly, but when we look at our record, we realize that we actually deserved a harsher punishment than the one we have endured, whereby we come to true insight and repentance. Our good Lord also wants to forgive the misdeeds of men when they show repentance for their sins, but His punishment never fails to come, for the Lord disciplines those whom He loves.[7] Even the good David, who clothed himself

---

6. *Mr. Frantz*: the addressee of the account. There is no extratextual evidence of his existence.

in sackcloth and repented for his sin, was punished soon after.[8] There have been so many such instances that it is unnecessary to recount them all.

I would also like to speak further of the trade [in which I took part]. {3r} In 1532, I sailed from Gdańsk[9] to Lisbon on a ship with a considerable load of wheat. When we arrived there, we suffered great losses, for the freight cost of each load was twelve ducats, and the wheat was not worth more than fourteen ducats. Here I also encountered a citizen of Gdańsk by the name of Otto Meyer, from the city of Niederhoffe.[10]

It was there, too, that I befriended a German gunsmith, for I did not know the [local] language well. He helped me sell my wheat, for which I remunerated him, but shortly after the wheat had been sold, the money ran out almost entirely as well, for victuals are very expensive there.

After the money had vanished, I thought to myself, "How can I return home empty-handed?" I therefore asked this gunsmith where I might find a master, so that I might try my luck in a foreign country, whereupon he answered {3v} that there was a ship bound for Sicily, and the skipper seemed to require two gunsmiths, so he would try to take me onto the ship with him as his assistant,[11] since he wanted to go along himself.

And so it came about that he was taken on as a gunsmith and I as his apprentice.[12] His salary was four ducats a month and I received two ducats a month. We were bound for three harbors or ports: Genoa in Italy,[13] Livorno,[14] which is not far from Rome, and Naples, so we sailed from Lisbon and came to Cádiz[15] and Andalusia. There we collected our cargo

---

7. *the Lord disciplines those whom He loves*: Sturmer could be referring either to Prov. 3:12: "For whom the Lord loveth he correcteth [. . .]" (King James Version [KJV hereafter]) or to Heb. 12:6: "For whom the Lord loveth he chasteneth [. . .]" (KJV).

8. *Even the good David [. . .] soon after*: "and David lifted up his eyes, and saw the angel of the Lord stand between the earth and the heaven, having a drawn sword in his hand stretched out over Jerusalem. Then David and the elders of Israel, who were clothed in sackcloth, fell upon their faces" (1 Chron. 21:16, KJV).

9. *Gdańsk*: a city in Poland, also formerly known as Danzig. "Dantzigk" in the 1558 German manuscript.

10. *Niederhoffe*: probably Księży Dwór, Poland, called Niederhof in German until 1920.

11. *assistant*: "für einen halben Man" in the 1558 German manuscript. Literally: "for [the pay of] half a man."

12. *apprentice*: "Diener" in the 1558 German manuscript. Literally: "servant."

13. *Italy*: it appears in the 1558 German manuscript as "Welschlandtt," a term used in the past by different Germanic communities to refer to regions inhabited by Romance language speakers.

14. *Livorno*: a port city on the Ligurian sea in western Tuscany, Italy.

15. *Cádiz*: a port city in southwestern Spain. "Cales" in the 1558 German manuscript. Ritter, "Ein deutscher Sklave als Augenzeuge bei der Eroberung von Tunis," identifies it as Calais (195n34), but this makes little sense geographically.

and in the name of God sailed to Livorno, where we unloaded what was destined [for Livorno]. From there we went to Genoa and Naples. Thus the voyage was over and we received our payment.

I parted ways with my companions and sailed to Sicily to {4r} find work. I had not been in Messina for long when an armada was assembled and loaded by order of His Imperial Majesty[16] to sail to Koroni.[17] His Imperial Majesty had taken this city from the Turks the year before; it is situated in Greece and had previously belonged to the Venetians. I would also like to speak of the reasons why His Imperial Majesty took the city.

At that time, the Venetians had broken the peace with the Turks at His Imperial Majesty's behest, so he intended to sail [from Koroni] to Constantinople with a large armada. However, the empress died around this time[18] and the armada was dissolved. To make peace with the Turks again, the Venetians were forced to give them two islands and several tons of gold and were therefore far from pleased with His Imperial Majesty. Indeed, the Venetian trade was in a situation where they had to keep the {4v} peace with the Turk[19] for the sake of commerce. Otherwise, they would have had to be powerful enough to hold out against the Turks for the sake of the trading they do in Turkey. Moreover, they routinely get the majority of their grain from Thessaloniki.[20]

Returning to my subject, the Turk had besieged the city of Koroni by land and sea by positioning 1,200 men on land before the city and seventy galleys at sea. [Our] armada had been arrayed—as previously planned—in Messina, Sicily, to break the siege of Koroni. Andreas Doria[21] of Genoa had arrived with twenty-four of his galleys and about thirty other large ships,

---

16. *His Imperial Majesty*: Charles V (1500–1558), Holy Roman Emperor from 1519 to 1556.

17. *Koroni*: a town on the peninsula of the Peloponnese in southern Greece. "Coron" in the 1558 German manuscript. Ritter, "Ein deutscher Sklave als Augenzeuge bei der Eroberung von Tunis," identifies this as the Greek town Koroneia (196n37). However, based on Sturmer's observations about the city's history, Koroni seems more likely. See Hans H. A. Hötte, *Atlas of Southeast Europe. Geopolitics and History*, vol. 1, *1521–1699* (Leiden: Koninklijke Brill NV, 2014), 47–48.

18. *the empress died around this time*: Sturmer seems to misremember the circumstances under which the armada was dissolved, given that Isabella of Portugal, Charles V's wife, died four years after the conquest of Tunis. See Peter G. Bietenholz and Thomas B. Deutscher, *Contemporaries of Erasmus: A Bibliographical Register of the Renaissance and Reformation* (Toronto: University of Toronto Press, 1985), 257.

19. *the Turk*: Suleiman I (1494–1566), also known as Suleiman the Magnificent, sultan of the Ottoman Empire from 1520 to 1566. Sturmer also uses the term "Turk" to refer to the Ottoman forces in general.

20. *Thessaloniki*: a port city in Greece. "Salynitiken" in the 1558 German manuscript.

21. *Andreas Doria*: Andrea Doria (1466–1560), a Genoese admiral and the biggest adversary of the Ottoman admiral Barbarossa.

well equipped with arms and victuals, and I was there as well, working as a gunsmith. Once our whole armada was ready, we sailed to Koroni in the name of God. First, we reached Corfu, an island belonging to the Venetians. Then, we went to Sento,[22] which is also an island under {5r} Venetian rule. It was there that we learned how strong the Turk's position was; we were no more than six miles away from him.

At midnight, we awoke early to sail to Koroni with our armada. When we came into view, the Turks decided to wait for us and lay near the shore with their galleys. As we sailed past them, they quickly shot at us while at the same time keeping their distance. [This they did] because their supreme commander Ibrakim Bahsa[23] had ordered it so, as he had seen in their horoscope that they would have no luck that day. Therefore, they intended to stay on land, unless we engaged them, in which case they would face us, their enemies, like heroes. Thus, we thanked God for this turn of events and managed to bring our ships, ammunition, and victuals into port.

However, not far from the port, two ships that had stayed behind were captured by the Turks, but only one of them [was taken completely]. The other {5v} had only been [boarded] on the upper deck, [since] the ship carried three hundred Spanish riflemen with arquebuses,[24] who had all gathered below deck and fired upward in such a manner that no Turk succeeded in entering until the other ships had managed to make it safely to port.

We then sailed back and put the Turkish galleys to flight toward Methoni,[25] which is only nine Italian miles[26] away from Koroni. As we approached [our besieged] ship, which had not yet surrendered, a German gunsmith yelled at us to hold our fire, as they still held the ship below. Well, this we did, and we regained control of both ships shortly after and sailed triumphantly into the harbor.

---

22. *Sento*: probably the (now Greek) island of Zakynthos in the Ionian Sea (Ritter, "Ein deutscher Sklave als Augenzeuge bei der Eroberung von Tunis," 197n45).

23. *Ibrakim Bahsa*: Sturmer may be referring to Ibrahim Pasha (1493–1536), grand vizier of the Ottoman Empire. However, it seems unlikely that he would have been personally involved in the siege of Koroni. See Hester D. Jenkins, *Ibrahim Pasha, Grand Vizir of Suleiman the Magnificent* (New York: Columbia University Press, 1911), 103–05.

24. *riflemen with arquebuses*: "Hacken Schützen" in the 1558 German manuscript. Literally: "riflemen armed with 'hook guns.'" The arquebus is an early type of long gun.

25. *Methoni*: a former Greek municipality. "Modon" in the 1558 German manuscript.

26. *Italian miles*: at the time, one Italian mile was roughly equivalent to a kilometer.

Once there, we discovered that all the ammunition of the fortress,[27] as well as the galleys, had been exhausted. The Spaniards had been deprived of any real food for so long that they resembled ghosts. Indeed, their victuals had run out several weeks before, and {6r} they had been feeding on cats and rats since.

The 1,200 Turks [who had been positioned] on land also fled to Methoni after burying their arms, which we appropriated. We subsequently garrisoned the fortress with fresh men and sailed toward Sicily. First we came to Aistol,[28] a town in Calabria opposite Messina, where [we found] twenty Spanish galleys which were supposed to be part of our armada but had come too late. They welcomed us by firing *kartouwes*[29] and other cannons, and we did the same.

Next, we sailed to Messina, where [our victory] was celebrated once more, and from there we went to Naples, where we brought all of our armada's cannonry to three castles. It was there that we received our salaries and were put on leave.

A year later the Turk had once again laid siege to the city of Koroni. Due to the fact that the troops from Constantinople had returned, His Imperial Majesty had a difficult time relieving the city on a yearly basis. {6v} Therefore, an exchange was arranged between Ferdinand[30] and the Turk. Ferdinand would gain a city in Hungary, and the city of Koroni [would be ceded to] the Turk. Then, the Turk withdrew and we were called back to Sicily with our ships, where we were put on leave.

In the meantime, in Messina, a Rhodian[31] by the name of Frey Lison announced that whoever wanted to sail in search of adventure or against the Turks should present himself at the church on the Feast of St. Francis. I was afraid of being late, so I hurried there, but to my misfortune,[32] I was taken on as a gunsmith and was promised three pays, that is to say, three

---

27. *the fortress*: the Spanish fortress of Koroni in Greece (Ritter, "Ein deutscher Sklave als Augenzeuge bei der Eroberung von Tunis," 198n48). "Schloss" in the 1558 German manuscript. Literally: "castle."

28. *Aistol*: probably the coastal city Reggio Calabria, Italy (Ritter, "Ein deutscher Sklave als Augenzeuge bei der Eroberung von Tunis," 198n49).

29. *kartouwes*: large-caliber cannons.

30. *Ferdinand*: Ferdinand I (1503–1564) was Charles V's younger brother and became Holy Roman Emperor (1558–1564) after Charles's abdication. "Ferdinandus" in the 1558 German manuscript.

31. *Rhodian*: possibly a Knight Hospitaller. The Hospitallers were also known as the Knights of Rhodes. See also note 41.

32. *misfortune*: Sturmer foreshadows the unlucky events to come.

parts of the future booty.³³ And, indeed, we received the amount promised soon enough, but we did not get to enjoy it for long, as I will now explain.

Once we had readied our galleys, we sailed from Messina and out of Sicily. We came to a city by the name of Taranto,³⁴ where we collected victuals and necessities, and then {7r} we sailed to Constantinople. Along the way, we came to an island called Sapientza.³⁵ We had been there no longer than four days when two Turkish ships³⁶—they were rough sails³⁷ from Alexandria—approached us on the way to Constantinople. When they reached us, [we realized that] their little ships were small and highly maneuverable. Had the wind not been so strong, we would have caught them both. Believing that the wind would eventually abate, we chased them for a whole day until we were almost fourteen miles from Constantinople. They got away.

We therefore decided to seek our fortune elsewhere and sailed to an island called Ciffoloniam,³⁸ which belongs to the Venetians. There we received tidings that a ship would sail from Venice to Constantinople with Turkish and Indian goods, and that it would have to sail past us.

We had been there for no longer than sixteen days when a ship escaped a {7v} great storm at sea. Due to the inordinate gales and thunder, it came into the port where we were moored. It was not the ship we had been waiting for, but its cargo was almost the same. After they had anchored, our captain inquired of the ship whence they came, where they were headed, and what goods they had on board. They answered that they were Venetians who had also loaded [their ship] in Venice with both Venetian and Florentine goods and that they wanted to sail to Constantinople. Our commander, however, was not satisfied with their answer and once again sent [a message] to the ship demanding that the ship's clerk come on board and bring their clearance certificates. This did not suit them and they replied that they were not obliged to give us any documents.

Our commander therefore ordered us to prepare our cannons and fire at them with two half kartouwes,³⁹ which happened {8r} soon thereafter.

33. *three parts of the future booty*: the exact amount is unclear, but it seems to indicate that Stumer's share of the booty as a gunsmith was three times that of a regular crew member.
34. *Taranto*: a city in southern Italy. "Tarantum" in the 1558 German manuscript.
35. *Sapientza*: a Greek island. "Sapenta" in the 1558 German manuscript. For this identification, see Ritter, "Ein deutscher Sklave als Augenzeuge bei der Eroberung von Tunis," 198n53.
36. *ships*: "Schÿrachen" in the 1558 German manuscript. It is unclear what type of ship he is referring to.
37. *rough sails*: possibly a type of ship; "rohe Siegell" in the 1558 German manuscript.
38. *Ciffoloniam*: most likely Kephalonia, an island in the Ionian Sea, Greece.
39. *half kartouwes*: a siege gun. "Half" refers to a size standard.

Nonetheless, they refused to produce the certificates. In short, the largest cannon was prepared and the commander ordered us to actually hit the ship, [as we] had been purposefully missing so far. This time, the ship was hit from the back, so that the missile exited through the front but, praise God, no person was hit.

Immediately after, they signaled that they wanted to come on board. The ship's clerk came and protested much, saying that there were no goods on the ship other than those of the Venetians and the Florentines. Since we did not trust him, the maiden[40] was fetched, and he was lightly screwed down. He soon confessed what the Turks and Indians had stored in the ship, just as the Master of Rhodes[41] had informed us. Although [I have been speaking] of Rhodes, which belongs to the Turks, [the inhabitants] are also called Rhodians. However, they are actually based on an island called Malta,[42] which is close to {8v} Africa.

The ship had to forgo her cargo and bring the goods on board. These consisted of valuable bundles of Venetian sheets and a small casket with pearls, which was estimated at more than forty thousand ducats. When we had stowed our cargo—we could not load everything that belonged to the Turks—our captain gave the skipper his complete freight [costs], as though [the skipper] had brought the goods to Constantinople, and also gave him proof that he had taken [the goods] from him. We sailed from there and swiftly came to Sicily, to a port called Palermo. They did not want us there, for we came from plague-stricken places. Due to the manner in which we had been refused, our commander, who was from Nice, informed us that he wanted us to sail home with him if we were willing. With heavy hearts, we agreed.

{9r} [It was at this time that] the Turks set sail hoping to find their fortune on Italian soil, just as we had done on Turkish soil. After sailing out of Palermo, on the way to Nice, we passed an island called Vulcano,[43] which burned day and night, producing a large amount of sulfur.

---

40. *the maiden*: although this is a reference to a method of torture, it is unclear whether Sturmer means an actual iron maiden. "Maiden" could also refer to a deadeye, an item used for rigging the sails.

41. *the Master of Rhodes*: possibly Philippe Villiers de L'Isle-Adam (1464–1534), grand master of the Knights Hospitaller and a prominent opponent of the North African pirates and privateers. See Whitworth Porter, *Malta and Its Knights* (London: Pardon and Son, 1871), 38, 65.

42. *actually based on [. . .] Malta*: the Order of Knights of the Hospital of Saint John of Jerusalem was known by various names, including the Knights Hospitaller, and the Order of Saint John. This Catholic military order was established in Jerusalem in the eleventh century. Their base was moved first to Rhodes (1310–1522) and then to Malta (1530–1798).

43. *Vulcano*: an Aeolian island north of Sicily. "Bulcani" in the 1558 German manuscript. For this identification, see Ritter, "Ein deutscher Sklave als Augenzeuge bei der Eroberung von Tunis," 200n61.

As we sailed past it, we spotted three galleys about three miles away from us. We did not know whether they were friends or foes, so, after taking counsel among ourselves, [we decided to] return to Sicily. However, the wind was against us and, unfortunately for us, in their favor. To make matters worse, we had overloaded the galley, so she was poorly protected. As they came closer, we realized that they were Turkish galleys, and we all became disheartened because they outnumbered us. But we called out to God that He might help us escape and deliver us from them. Quickly, our cannons were put in order and {9v} each of us was assigned one to attend to. Our trumpets sounded, the banners were raised, and we [steered] quickly toward them and fired. God had mercy on us the first time around, for we drove them back. One galley was hit, so that the crew had to careen it to close the hole.

In the meantime, we charged our cannons again. God allowed us to hit them again, which drove them back once more, but many of us were wounded and several were already dead. They all came on board together the third time around. They assailed us and captured our ship with everything she contained.

The day before,[44] I had taken counsel with my companions about what we wanted to do with the great sum of money we were to receive in Nice. They decided among themselves to take it to Antwerp[45] with a bill of exchange, since each would receive two thousand ducats at least, given that the booty itself was worth over {10r} 150,000 ducats.[46] To this I replied, "Why would we want to go home already? We should first try our luck once more and sail to Sicily again, buy a galley there or have one built, and be on our way and amass even more booty. Then we can return home in triumph!" They were willing, and so it was decided, but the tables were about to turn: "Homo proponit, Deus disponit,"[47] as they say.

By now, approximately sixty Turks from three ships and about twenty-three of our men lay slain. Those who were still alive but had been wounded

---

44. *The day before*: this is an example of Sturmer's curious use of analepsis, jumping back in narrated time during a moment of suspense.

45. *Antwerp*: the city of Antwerp was part of the Habsburg Netherlands at the time. "Antorffen" in the 1558 German manuscript.

46. *150,000 ducats*: compare this sum to the two ducats per month Sturmer was paid as an apprentice to the gunsmith shortly before.

47. *Homo proponit, Deus disponit*: "Man proposes, God disposes." Sturmer references a proverb taken from a popular Christian devotional book by Thomas à Kempis. See Thomas à Kempis, *The Imitation of Christ*, trans. Richard Challoner (Rockford, IL: Tan Books and Publishers, 1989), 46.

were thrown overboard, along with seventeen corpses.[48] I was badly wounded myself but pretended to be in better condition than I actually was. I would have hated to be thrown in *aquam*[49] as well.

The following day, they sailed with us to a desert island whose name I have forgotten. There, we were brought ashore and sold among them as a portion of their share [of the booty]. I was sold for forty ducats.

{10v} We then sailed to an island called Djerba,[50] where, due to the fact that my first master had to depart for Constantinople at once, I was sold for thirty-two ducats. Djerba is not far from Tripoli,[51] where the Rhodians had previously been headquartered. However, the Turks later also conquered it. There, they divided the booty they had taken from us.

Soon after that, I was chained to a Turkish galley, where I had to pull the long feather.[52] We then sailed again in search of adventure and God smiled upon the Turks, for they took fifteen Christian ships within three weeks, after which we sailed back to the island of Djerba, where I was sold a third time. Neither rye[53] nor wheat grows there, only barley, wine, and many dates. In the meantime, winter drew near, although there is not much winter to speak of. Yet, despite the fact that it never gets very cold, [the Turks] always stay in the {11r} harbor for a month, because there are many storms during this season.

Now I would also like to relate how Tunis was conquered by the Turks through treachery and how His Imperial Majesty retook the city and returned it to its deposed king.

When we had landed at Djerba with our ships, Barbarossa,[54] the Turkish emperor's admiral, wrote from the sea to our commander, who had thirty galleys.

---

48. *twenty-three of our men [. . .] seventeen corpses*: this passage is not entirely clear in the manuscript. Perhaps twenty-three of their men were thrown overboard, seventeen of whom were already dead, and six who were still alive but severely wounded.

49. *aquam*: water.

50. *Djerba*: an island off the coast of Tunisia. "Hierbis" in the 1558 German manuscript. For this identification, see Ritter, "Ein deutscher Sklave als Augenzeuge bei der Eroberung von Tunis," 201n68.

51. *Tripoli*: the modern-day capital of Libya. "Trÿpoll" in the 1558 German manuscript. In 1530, Tripoli was ceded to the Knights Hospitallers by Charles V until it was taken by the Ottoman Empire in 1551. See Whitworth Porter, *Malta and Its Knights* (London: Pardon and Son, 1871), 57, 74–75.

52. *pull the long feather*: probably a quip about the weight of the wooden oar.

53. *rye*: the German reads "Korn" (literally: "grain"), but in Sturmer's time, this umbrella term would have been used to refer to the most common grain of a region. Judging from Sturmer's background, this was most likely rye.

54. *Barbarossa*: Hayreddin Barbarossa (ca. 1478–1546), the corsair and later grand admiral of the Ottoman Empire.

[He informed him] that, as early in spring as possible, he was to go to Capo Cartago[55]—which is three miles from Tunis—with his armada to help seize the city of Tunis. This was carried out. Through certain circumstances and self-interest, the good city of Tunis was conquered by the Turks as follows.

There were two brothers in Tunis. The eldest was in command and kept the youngest under his thumb. In addition to that, the older king wielded his power in a tyrannical manner,[56] {11v} wherefore his subjects favored the younger lord and sent him to the Turkish emperor along with letters of recommendation from the authorities of the city of Tunis. For the reasons mentioned above, they desired to have the younger lord as their king. The young lord subsequently pledged to pay tribute to the Turk if he would help him become king.

The Turk promised [the younger brother] the following: He would give him an armada and help him win the kingdom. However, treachery betrayed its own master.[57] Barbarossa had eighty galleys, so the good young hero boarded a galley, believing he would become king of Tunis. But what did Barbarossa do? He marooned him on a desert island and left him there to starve.

Meanwhile, when the Tunisians learned that the young lord was to arrive with a large armada, they drove the elder brother into the mountains. We had already traveled from Djerba to Capo Cartago with our armada {12r} and awaited Barbarossa, who arrived with his armada shortly thereafter. All cannons were fired, and the day after, we sailed to a harbor by the name of Cap Bon,[58] which lies seven miles from Tunis. When we arrived in Cap Bon, the young lord's banners were raised, as though he were there himself. People soon came from the land to bring many victuals on board. [We] pretended to the Moors that their king was feeling a little unwell and could not come to them.

---

55. *Capo Cartago*: probably Cape Carthage, modern-day Sidi Bou Saïd.

56. *The eldest [. . .] tyrannical manner*: the "tyrannical ruler" mentioned by Sturmer is Moulay Hassan, who ascended the throne in large part thanks to his mother's intrigues and proceeded to have two of his older brothers assassinated. However, a third brother, Rashid, managed to escape and sought Barbarossa's aid in reclaiming the throne, which ultimately backfired. See Gonçalo De Illescas, *Segvnda parte dela historia pontifical y catholica* (Barcelona: Emprenta de Jaime Cendrat, 1606), 256–58.

57. *However, treachery [. . .] own master*: Sturmer quotes the German proverb, "Untreue schlug seinen eigenen Herren." Literally: "Disloyalty struck its own master."

58. *Cape Bon*: situated in northeastern Tunisia. "Bona" in the 1558 German manuscript. For this identification, see Ritter, "Ein deutscher Sklave als Augenzeuge bei der Eroberung von Tunis," 203n75.

From there we sailed to La Goulette, the port of Tunis, which lies only three or four Italian miles from the city, which is itself about three miles away from the place where Carthage once stood. When we arrived at the port, the Moors had already received tidings from the aforementioned city of Cap Bon that the supposed king and his armada were there, so the masses prepared themselves to receive him, believing him to be on the ship.

There are two paths that lead {12v} into Tunis, and they are divided by a stretch of water two miles wide. Barbarossa had been informed which route the nobles would take to receive the king. So, as they approached La Goulette from one side, Barbarossa went along the other side of the water. By the time Barbarossa had almost reached the city, the treachery was discovered. The Moors turned [against the Turks], for they were great in number, but Barbarossa dominated the field. [After the battle] there were probably about two thousand men left on each side. Thus was Tunis conquered through treachery.

I stayed with the Turks for about two months. After that, we went on another voyage and we acquired rich booty, for a captured Christian who rows receives the same part of the booty as his master. However, in the end, when it comes to dividing up the loot, the master is allowed to take the captive's share as well, which means that the slave has worked for nothing.

{13r} Now, I would like to speak further of the ousted king.[59] When the Moors saw that their treachery had backfired, a number of them returned to the deposed king, prostrated themselves before him, and swore renewed allegiance. For his part, the king of Tunis [decided to go] to war against Barbarossa, but he was too weak [to overpower Barbarossa], so he tried to win over the nobility for himself through gifts and presents, as is now customary. May God rectify this; if one has money, one can easily influence circumstances in one's favor.

When the displaced king realized that he stood no chance against Barbarossa, he sent his son—who would afterward gouge his father's eyes out[60]—to [Charles V] and begged to become his tributary. His Imperial Majesty promised to assist him in regaining his lands and people.

---

59. *ousted king*: Moulay Hassan.

60. *gouge his father's eyes out*: after being reinstated as the ruler of Tunis by Charles V, Moulay Hassan was blinded and deposed by his son Hamid. See Kenneth Meyer Setton, *The Papacy and the Levant, 1204–1571* (Philadelphia: American Philosophical Society, 1976), 397.

His Imperial Majesty was nevertheless more concerned with his [own] lands than with helping the king for the following reasons: {13v} The position of [Tunis] in the Mediterranean, not more than thirty miles from Sicily, was ideal. In the year following the city's conquest [by Barbarossa], [Charles V] would come in person with a massive armada.[61] When His Imperial Majesty came to Tunis and lay in Sardinia with his entire armada, one of his small ships, which was bound for Holtze,[62] was captured by Turks and brought to Tunis. The captives were then taken ashore and brought before the commander, a man by the name of Casso Diaboli.[63] [The captives] were asked by an interpreter how strong His Imperial Majesty was with his armada and how soon he would arrive. I entered and listened; it was good news for me. Whereupon the skipper answered that [the armada] was about forty thousand men strong and that it would arrive as soon as the winds changed.

Then an old Turk spoke in his language, "Wollacheÿ {14r} billacheÿ Spanien gavor kolckmas, Italian gavor kolckmas, Ilman gavor kolckmas iauis kopecke,"[64] which means in our language: "We should not fear the Spaniards, and the same goes for the Italians. The Germans, however, are tough dogs; we learned that the hard way in Hungary."[65] Having heard this, I hurried to see a friend of mine and tell him the good news that His Imperial Majesty would soon come to relieve us.

Soon after, my master came onto the galley, ordered me to his presence, and said, "You should know that your father and all his kin are coming here, but we will face them and capture them, so you will have more company." I answered, "Everything lies in God's hands." He retorted, "Your gods will not help you." No more than eight days after this episode, however,

---

61. *[Charles V] would come [. . .] massive armada*: one year after Barbarossa conquered Tunis in 1534, Charles V successfully seized it from him. Large parts of the subsequent narrative are devoted to the Habsburg conquest of the city.

62. *Holtze*: this reference is unclear.

63. *Casso Diaboli*: Aydin Reis, a prominent captain who served under Barbarossa and whom the Spanish had nicknamed "Cacha-Diablo."

64. *Wollacheÿ [. . .] kopecke*: what Sturmer writes differs from the translation he gives. What he most likely meant was (in Ottoman Turkish): *Vallahi billahi İspanyol gavur[dan] kork[u]lma[z], İtalyan gavur[dan] kork[u]lma[z], [ama] Alman gavur[dan] kork[u]l[ur] yavuz köpek*. Literally: "Forsooth, forsooth, the Spanish heathens are not to be feared and neither are the Italian heathens. But the German heathens are to be feared; they are wild hounds." The comment about Hungary is entirely absent from the Turkish Sturmer attempts to write.

65. *we learned [. . .] in Hungary*: this phrase of Sturmer's translation is not actually contained in the Turkish quote Sturmer gives. He is referring to the Battle of Mohács (1526), in which Suleiman the Magnificent defeated Ludwig II, king of Hungary and Bohemia.

His Imperial Majesty arrived with one thousand galleys and five hundred ships; they were the armadas of Spain, {14v} Italy, and Rhodes, or Malta.

Less than half an hour before, I had gone to fetch water about a quarter of the way from La Goulette. Had I but stayed a little longer, I would have seen the galleys arrive. I would have hidden there and gone to His Imperial Majesty in the evening and pointed out all the opportunities [for attack] and His Imperial Majesty would have been able to conquer La Goulette the next day, since [the Turks] were poorly prepared. They did not believe that they would be overrun so soon, although they had already been warned by the aforementioned skipper, who had been captured from [Charles V's] armada.

I had hardly taken the water barrel off my shoulder when I saw twenty galleys rowing toward us—it was the day on which the Turks celebrate their Easter;[66] were robbed [?] now and then.[67] Immediately, we, the captured Christians, were led to Tunis, and once there, {15r} we were regrouped now and then and put in chains. We were about fifteen thousand men of all nations. His Imperial Majesty besieged La Goulette for about three months before it was finally conquered.

It happened about three days before the Feast of St. James,[68] when approximately fifty of us captured Christians were released from our quarters to fetch water and quench our thirst. We had not gone far when we heard dreadful shooting. In the morning, around the time the bell struck three, His Imperial Majesty attacked La Goulette. The Turks drove us back and chained us more firmly than before.

---

66. *their Easter*: since there is no Easter in Islam, it is likely that Sturmer is referring to the other great feast celebrated by Muslims, Eid al-Adha, or the "Feast of the Sacrifice," which commemorates Ibrahim's willingness to submit to God's will by sacrificing his son. See Ian Richard Netton, *Encyclopedia of Islamic Civilization and Religion* (Abingdon, UK: Routledge, 2008), 170–71. In Spanish, a language that Sturmer declares himself proficient in, the feast is also known as "Pascua del Cordero," which translates as the "Easter of the Lamb." This could explain why Sturmer mistook it for the similarly named Christian holiday.

67. *were robbed [?] now and then*: "wahren hin vndtt wieder spolieret" in the 1558 German manuscript. It is unclear who was robbed. The correct translation for "spolieret" in this context is also not certain.

68. *the Feast of St. James*: Sturmer may be referring to Saint James the Great, the patron saint of Spain, whose feast is celebrated in Western Christianity on 25 July. Saint James was commonly depicted as "the Moor slayer" due to a Spanish legend from the ninth century, according to which he miraculously led an outnumbered Christian army to victory against the Moors. It is possible that Sturmer was trying to make a symbolic comparison with the saint at the expense of historical accuracy, as Charles V's siege of La Goulette began on 14 June and ended a month later. It is also possible that Sturmer's memory simply failed him or that he lost track of time during his captivity. See Francisco Márquez Villanueva, *Santiago: Trayectoria De Un Mito* (Barcelona: Ediciones Bellaterra, 2004), 188–93.

Not more than three hours later, La Goulette had been taken by force. My master then returned to his house in Tunis and had me fetched from prison. I often argued with my master's Turkish servants, who frequently said, "When the Christians come, we will beat them all to death and take them as captives." I objected, however, that His Imperial Majesty would {15v} hit so hard and cannonade La Goulette so violently that no one would be able to tell where the wall had stood—which was exactly what happened.

When the sun started to set, some Turks told my master, "Wollacheÿ billacheÿ bihem Oliman, gavor ahabedÿ,"[69] "Verily, the German infidel had spoken the truth." And they proceeded to inform him of our previous debate, whereupon my master asked me, "What do you think we should do now? Will we be able to keep Tunis?" I told my master that it would be wise to make preparations for his escape, for Tunis is not a fortified city wherein one would want to be caught unprepared. My master answered that he himself doubted this. It was then that my master vowed that after two more years of service, he would set me free. However, I did not believe him. But by God, I should not have doubted him.

A few days later, His Imperial Majesty came within about half a mile of Tunis with his cavalry and infantry. {16r} There, Barbarossa confronted him with a number of field guns, which His Imperial Majesty soon took, after forcing him to flee.

The previous evening, [the Turks] had held counsel together about how to deal with this predicament and came up with the following plan: The fortress of Tunis was garrisoned by six hundred Turks. Their orders were to set the fortress on fire, along with all the captured Christians, as soon as they saw Barbarossa losing ground. The following morning, [Barbarossa] would try to establish whether he could put a stop to His Imperial Majesty's advance.

When the assault began, about one hundred *Mamluks*,[70] who are renounced Christians, remained among the six hundred Turks. These [Mamluks] went to the captives and told them, "If Barbarossa loses the battle, [we will carry out] his sentence. However, if you vow to intercede for us with His Imperial Majesty so that we may be released along with our belongings, {16v} then we will unshackle you and free you today and slay all the Turks."

---

69. *Wollacheÿ [. . .] ahabedÿ*: in Ottoman Turkish: *Vallahi billahi bizim Alman gavur hak dedi*. Literally: "Forsooth! Forsooth! Our German heathen has spoken the truth."

70. *Mamluks*: the word "Mamluk" is derived from an Arabic word that means "slave." However, the status of Mamluks was above that of ordinary slaves, as they were primarily soldiers. The use of Mamluks as a major component of Muslim armies was a distinctive feature of Islamic civilization.

They were deemed trustworthy because they had vowed by their faith and their honor to side with His Imperial Majesty. But I was on the battlefield with my master. After this had been decided, Barbarossa marched into the field in the early morning with several thousand men.

Meanwhile, the captured Christians had taken control of the fortress. The Turks had taken two pennants[71] from the Spaniards on watch, which were fixed to the gates by the tail end, as is customary during war. These were taken down. When Barbarossa realized that he could not do the emperor much harm, he wanted to return to the fortress and put into action that which he had ordered his villains to do. But when it became obvious that he was hurrying toward the fortress, the gates were opened and good cannons were set up and fired bravely at them. The two Christian pennants were flown as well. {17r} It was then that [Barbarossa] realized the severity of his plight.

Against my will, I found myself among the troops out on the field. I would have preferred to stay in the fortress, where at the time I would have become rich as well, given that most of the Turks' treasure had been left behind. As His Imperial Majesty was about to enter the fortress, the [Christians] refused to allow him inside until he promised to uphold everything they had promised the Mamluks. Therefore, His Imperial Majesty declared before everyone there that, on pain of death or losing one's possessions, no *Mamluk* was to be harmed. For this purpose, they all had to wear a white piece of cloth around their left arm so that they could be identified. Many captured Christians became rich that day because most of the Turks' treasure was kept there. Had I been there, I would have made not only myself but many others rich also, for I knew very well where to look.

I nearly forgot to relate how the deposed {17v} king came to His Imperial Majesty at La Goulette. His Imperial Majesty had been stationed on the field in front of La Goulette for about eight days when the dethroned king came to him. Upon receiving tidings of his arrival, the emperor arranged his troops into neat lines and allowed [the deposed king] to pass through. When he was halfway through the camp, all cannons, both on land and water, were fired, which amazed him greatly.

To return to my subject, those of us who were out on the field with Barbarossa did not know which way to retreat. At last, they decided to go to Bizerte[72]—the town I helped conquer after I had been delivered—where

---

71. *pennants*: it is unclear what the exact function of the pennants was in this particular situation.
72. *Bizerte*: a Tunisian city. "Beserte" in the 1558 German manuscript.

Barbarossa still had nine galleys. Had the emperor's men not been too tired to follow us, they would have slain us all; this was truly an "every man for himself" situation. However, the men of the king of Tunis came after us with one thousand horses and took everything the Turks {18r} had wanted to keep, except their guns. We were all in dire need of water. Indeed, many actually died from thirst during the march, for we did not take the direct path but went straight into the mountains, since the Moors were after us.

After walking with them for about three days, I thought to myself, "You could hide in a bush along the way, if you make an effort." I thought about it briefly and begged our Lord God to help me divine just how I could get away from my master's encampment. I had a right to this, for he had promised to free me after serving two more years, as mentioned before. While the march went on, I stepped aside, pretending that I wanted to relieve myself. I wandered farther and farther into the mountains and crept into a bush.

When my master noticed my absence, he asked his servants, who had not left the path, where I was. One of them said, "He went into the forest and is probably {18v} answering the call of nature." However, as time passed and I failed to come back, my master called me, "Olyman Gavor!"[73] which means in our tongue: "Unrighteous German!" for they believe that their creed makes them righteous and [ours makes] us unrighteous. For his part, this "Olyman Gavor" lay still and prayed to God. Several Turks turned back, called my name, and searched for me. I sometimes saw them, but they never saw me. They came close to the bush [where I was], which made me break out in cold sweat.[74] Had they found me, it is unlikely that they would have let me live, but since they did not, they continued with their journey. Nevertheless, I lay still. I had not eaten that day, but I was not hungry. However, I was very thirsty. I still had half of what would amount to a shilling of bread now, and several dates. I ate a little, thinking of the days ahead, and not long after, our dear God sent merciful rain. I searched for water in puddles and drank it although it was warm, and I thanked God that I {19r} had it.

As night fell, I still did not know what to do or where to go and I could still hear people coming and going. Finally, toward morning, I climbed a high mountain and crept into a crag there. At daybreak, I would try to figure out where I was so that I could continue my journey at night. Nevertheless, once morning broke, I looked around and realized I was still lost.

---

73. *Olyman Gavor!*: in Ottoman Turkish: *Alman gavur*. Literally: "German heathen!"

74. *break out in cold sweat*: "ich schwitzete Judas Schweis" in the 1558 German manuscript. Literally: "I sweated Judas's sweat."

At around ten hours past midday, I looked around once again and begged my dear God continually to deliver me from the heathens. It was then that I heard a disturbance coming from the mountains and imagined several squadrons of horsemen coming toward me. Instead, I saw a herd of deer dashing forward followed by two lions, which gave me a fright. As they came down the mountain, a lion up ahead lay in wait for them under the crags, leaped from the side, and caught a deer. {19v} The other two joined him shortly after and they all ate their meal.

I made my escape and begged God for mercy. During the day, I lay still in the mountains, for I could not move by day, but only at night. This continued for almost four days and I had not eaten anything substantial. I started feeling feeble, but I remained rational and cautious. I thought to myself, "It does not serve your purpose to keep wandering about in the wilderness. Next, a pride of lions will come and devour you and then nobody will know what became of you, which will grieve your dear parents deeply." I considered that I could no longer fight my hunger and thirst and I thought to myself, "You will want to be on your way by the morrow. If you come across the men of the king of Tunis, you will be safe, for they are your friends. However, if it is Barbarossa's men you come across, then you will say, 'I am a righteous one.' If they ask where you are headed, you will {20r} say that you could not keep up with your comrades because you fell ill on the way." And this was true: The foul water I had drunk on the way had made me ill. Having considered all of this, I therefore climbed down the mountain by day and made my way to Tunis.

I had not been on my way for long when I saw about sixty horsemen coming my way. They were Moorish subjects of Barbarossa. I braced myself and cried to God for help, and He showed me mercy in that our encounter went well. I was dressed in the Turkish manner as they came toward me. Once they had reached me, they asked me who I was. I answered them in Turkish that I was a Mussulman, which in German means "a righteous one." They asked me whither I was bound [and told me that] this was the way to Tunis. I replied that I was completely lost and did not know myself where I was headed. They said, "Do you want {20v} to come with us? We want to reach the encampment!" I would have preferred to continue on my way, however, had I taken my leave of them then, they would have realized that I was a Christian right away, since they had found me on the way to Tunis. Well, what was I to do? I had to choose the lesser of two evils!

As we were traveling, one of them asked me how long ago I had converted and adopted their creed, for my manner of speaking made it obvious to them that I was no real Turk. I answered that I had become righteous long ago; that was required at this time. As they say: *Necessitas frangit legem*.[75] However, in saying I was a righteous one, I did not renounce my faith in God, for we are righteous through our belief in our Lord Christ, who is the maker of righteousness.

Not far from a town called Raf Raf,[76] we set up camp and ate. My martyrdom was only beginning, but God sustained me.

{21r} After we had eaten and the horses had been fed, [my traveling companions] got together to confer among themselves. When I saw this, I suspected they were discussing me, which was indeed the case. As they broke up, a priest[77] among them called me to him and said, "My brothers suspect that you are not a righteous one, since we found you on the way to Tunis. So, come with me to the side, and I will verify that you are circumcised. You cannot refuse that!" I was very shocked when I heard this, but I managed not to show it, for every cloud has a silver lining. It so happened that many years prior, while in Spain, an evil two-legged worm had bitten my foreskin off,[78] which is something the Turks generally have removed. When the priest looked at me and beheld the *signum*,[79] he bellowed in his language, "Wollachey billachey muselmander kesly,"[80] which means in German: {21v} "Forsooth! Forsooth! He is a righteous one and has been circumcised."

Thus did God blind him. The story is uncouth, but I must be truthful in my confession if I am to be granted absolution, and I may as well be given credit for [my candor]. [The Moors] had been treating me well, especially

---

75. *Necessitas frangit legem*: literally: "Necessity breaks the law." Figuratively: "Necessity justifies breaking the law."

76. *Raf Raf*: a commune in Tunisia. "Raffat" in the 1558 German manuscript. For this identification, see Ritter, "Ein deutscher Sklave als Augenzeuge bei der Eroberung von Tunis," 210n109.

77. *priest*: Sturmer writes "Priester" in the 1558 German manuscript. Islam, however, does not have a homologous role to the one played by priests in Christianity. Either Sturmer was not aware of this, or he simply could not find a German word to describe the rank of the religious leader who examined him.

78. *two-legged worm had bitten my foreskin off*: Sturmer seems to be referring to a woman, possibly a prostitute. It is not entirely clear what happened to his foreskin. He could have actually been bitten, or perhaps he suffered from a sexually transmitted disease.

79. *signum*: Sturmer euphemistically refers to his foreskin as his "signum," a word he likely borrowed from the Vulgate, which states in Genesis 17:11: "et circumcidetis carnem praeputii vestri, ut sit in *signum* foederis inter me et vos," a command from God that translates as: "and ye shall circumcise the flesh of your foreskin, and it shall be a *token* of the covenant between me and you."

80. "*Wollachey billachey muselmander kesly*": in Ottoman Turkish: "*Vallahi billahi müslümandır kesili.*" Literally: "Forsooth! Forsooth! He is a Muslim and has been circumcised."

the priest, but I still did not trust him because of what he said to me. He had told me he had friends in Blackamoor Land[81] and wanted to move there, and, should I want to come with him, promised not to enslave me and that it would not cost me a penny. I was inclined to accept his offer but decided against it. I thought to myself, "Perhaps he saw that you are not circumcised and will sell you when you reach your destination." I was wrong, however, as I would learn later on.

That day we decided to stay put, but the next day {22r} we arrived in a city called Constantine. The dethroned king of Tunis had remained there, waiting for His Imperial Majesty to arrive and restore his lands to him. He then became His Imperial Majesty's tributary and gave him twenty thousand ducats annually and twelve Moorish horses. His Imperial Majesty retained La Goulette.

After we entered the city, I saw several Turks sitting in a house and I approached them to see if I knew any of them, but I did not. I thought to myself, "It is better to die with the Turks than with the Moors; [the priest] might lead you into Blackamoor Land and sell you there." However, I did not intend to stay with the Turks for long. As soon as an opportunity presented itself, I would run away. I returned to [the Moors], thanked them for their charity and told them I had found my former companions. The priest then told me, "My son, may God guide you and {22v} keep you." His words made me regret our farewell right then and there, for they convinced me that he had meant well all along. I had regarded him with suspicion, but now I wished I had gone with him instead, for I would have seen more things under the pretense of being a righteous one, although I did not fully trust him. The priest and two others accompanied me; they wanted to see which companions I was joining.

We approached the Turks, greeted them, and said, "Salamalekim affendelar,"[82] which means: "Greetings, gentlemen!" To this they answered, "Malick salam sonen geldÿ,"[83] or: "Thank you. You are all welcome." Not long after, they asked where we had come from. The priest replied, "We came from

---

81. *Blackamoor Land*: this term appears in the 1558 German manuscript as "Schwartz-Mohrenlandtt" and seems to refer to sub-Saharan Africa, given that the word "blackamoor" was sometimes used in early modern Europe to distinguish North Africans from those who lived south of the Sahara.

82. *Salamalekim affendelar*: in Ottoman Turkish: *Selamun aleyküm efendiler*. Literally: "Peace be upon you, gentlemen."

83. *Malick salam sonen geldÿ*: in Ottoman Turkish: *Ve aleyküm selam, [hoş] geldi[niz]*. Sturmer writes "sonen," an incomprehensible typographical error; the correct phrase is *hoş geldiniz*. The expression translates as: "And upon you, peace. Welcome!"

Tunis and found this young fellow lost on the way, and he has accompanied us this far. We did not want to believe his claim that he is a Mussulman. So, I examined him and found that he is circumcised. You should give us {23r} credit for this." This worked greatly in my favor, as I was taken for a righteous one. In this manner, I had to make my way precariously through life by the grace of God. Shortly after, the Moors took their leave of the Turks and I stayed in the company [of the Turks].

This city of Constantine is a large city, able to summon [an army of] up to forty thousand men on foot and on horseback. From there, we traveled to a city called Bresie,[84] where we stayed several days. I was the youngest among them, so I had to fetch everything they needed, and until my time [to escape] eventually came, I did this gladly.

[However], it was then that my martyrdom began once more. While on my way to fetch a jug of water from the well, I encountered a Moor from Tunis who knew me and my master well. He said to me, "Where have you come from? You must have run away from your master!" I would have liked to answer, "My master is here," but I was concerned {23v} that he might want to visit him, and then I would have been shamed. So instead I replied, "Sir, do not expose me! I will do anything you ask. Help me get to Tunis, and I will honestly requite it!" His response was, "Your countrymen hold my father captive in La Goulette. If you can free him, I will bring you to Tunis." I gave him my word; I intended to do it. I would probably have promised him even more and later kept as much of my word as I could. He showed me his home, where his two sisters lived. When it suited me, I was to come to [his] house and he would shelter me. In the evening, when I was fetching water again, I dropped the jug and went to my companion. The Turks noticed my absence the following day and not knowing where I was, they made my disappearance public and asked if anybody had taken in a fellow matching my description. But the Moors {24r} are not very well disposed toward the Turks whom Barbarossa had brought into the country.[85] It so happened that the people of the town wanted to go to Tunis within ten days to pay homage to the king once again, so in time my Turkish companions departed. When the time came that we were due to travel to Tunis, who could be

---

84. *Bresie*: Ritter, "Ein deutscher Sklave als Augenzeuge bei der Eroberung von Tunis," believes this to be Béja, a Tunisian city between Constantine and Tunis (212n117).

85. *the Turks [. . .] brought into the country*: "the Turks" in question are either janissaries or the administrators sent to North Africa by the Ottoman Empire after Barbarossa sought support from the Ottoman sultan.

happier than I? But the contrary happened. My companion had equipped me, given me a goat's skin that contained his food, and put a small dagger in my hand, and thus we began our journey.

When we were a quarter of a mile away from the city, two Moors appeared, attacked me, and said, "Where are you going? You must have run away from your master!" I retorted, "I have no master; I am my own master!" My companion did nothing to defend me. He would later tell me in Tunis that he had been afraid that they would discover I was a Christian, which would have put him in great danger {24v} because the townsfolk had become the Christians' great enemies after over one hundred of them had been slain at La Goulette. So I was forcibly led back to the town.

The two Moors then told me, "If you have any money, give it to us. You may then go on your way." I had no money, so I offered to give them the gown I was wearing instead. I was told to take it off, and, as I did, my loincloth slipped from my body. When they saw this, they attacked me, saying, "We have to verify if the rumors are true, and you are indeed a righteous one." Once they had taken a look, they shouted, "He is an unrighteous one!" For they had doubted me because the *signum* was too large. The children came and promptly threw stones at me. Then, a tall, large man came and said, "My two brothers were killed by your people; you shall die at our hands today!" Now I was really in trouble. As he spoke, he picked up a {25r} large stone and threw it at me but missed. He then said, "Lead the dog out onto the field and kill him."

However, I begged our Lord God to grant me mercy and to aid me, which soon came about. As I was being led to my death, two of the Moors who had encountered me on the way [to Tunis] noticed me. They were respectable men and did not understand why I was being treated thus, so they approached me and asked what they were about to do to me. [The other Moors] answered that I was an unrighteous one and since my people had killed many of the townsfolk, they were determined to lead me out [of the town] and have me strangled.

Then the two men, who were my angels, said, "You should not say that he is an unrighteous one, for our priest examined him and found him rightly circumcised, so you are about to do this man great harm." Then they added, "And even if he were a Christian, which he is not, you should consider that our lord is now an ally of {25v} his lord. Indeed, [Charles V] has bestowed land and people on our lord. Think of the repercussions if you insist on carrying out your plans. So set him free!" This was done and they let me go.

At that moment, I felt newborn once again, but my trials were not yet over. Now I was on my own and free, but I could not continue my journey alone.

In this little town there was a Moor from Granada[86] with whom I had often conversed while the Turks had been around. I now kept company with him and revealed to him that I desired to go into the service of the king of Tunis, if only I had a good companion; I could not make the journey alone. He replied, "I think it ill-advised as well. Let me see if I can find someone to go along with you." But he turned out to be a traitor.

The next day I came to him again and he said, "Today, a nobleman—an {26r} Alarb[87]—will arrive, who is heading for Tunis. He is a good friend. For my sake, he will take you with him and also help you reach the king." The next day, the Alarb arrived with two horses and pretended to be friendly to me, as if he really intended [to help me]. Later, I would learn what agreement they had made between them. We continued together and became acquainted. When it was past noon, I was given a horse. I mounted [this horse] and he mounted another and we continued onward, and I assumed I would get to Tunis. In this manner, he led me to his living quarters, which were tents, for Alarbs have no houses. They live out on the fields due to the great quantities of livestock they own—camels in particular. Indeed, they trek to new locations every two months to pasture their livestock.

As I entered his lodgings, a band of Moors surrounded me as sparrows do the owl. It was as if they had never seen such a man before. {26v} I was then given food, but they did not reveal what they intended to do with me until the rest of the people were gone again. Then my companion's father, a priest who spoke Turkish quite well, came and told me, "You, Gavor"—which means in our language: "You, unrighteous one"—"So you really thought you would make it to Tunis, as you had been led to believe!" It was then that I realized I had been betrayed. "If you want to regain your freedom, you will have to give us one hundred ducats, for you are a Christian!" I argued that I was a righteous one, but it was all to no avail; I had to dance to their tune. They offered to take me within one mile of Tunis. From there, they wanted me to write to my people so that they would bring me one hundred ducats.

---

86. *Granada*: the last Muslim outpost in Spain, which surrendered to the Catholic monarchs in 1492. As a result, many Morisco Spaniards left Spain to avoid Ferdinand and Isabella's policy of forceful conversion. "Granaten" in the 1558 German manuscript.

87. *Alarb*: possibly someone from a nomadic North African tribe (Ritter, "Ein deutscher Sklave als Augenzeuge bei der Eroberung von Tunis," 214n120). However, as the word "Alarb" literally translates as "the Arab," it could possibly mean someone who speaks Arabic or comes from the Arabian Peninsula.

[I was also to inform them] that I was being held in a place that was not under the rule of the king of Tunis, but under [that of] the *Scheryffen*.[88] I was left with no choice. I was made to promise that {27r} I would not write anything else besides what I had been told. I wrote my letters—one in Spanish, the other in German—and was assigned a Moor who would deliver them in La Goulette.

By then, His Imperial Majesty had left La Goulette with his armada, [but had left behind] two thousand Spaniards occupying the port, along with several German gunsmiths. The messenger was dispatched and delivered the letters. But what did the commander do? He took the Moor captive and said, "When you deliver the captured Christian here, you will be set free." But this was not what I had ordered.

When the Alarbs received the news, they thought that I had given instructions [in my letter] for the Moor to be taken prisoner. They had brought me to within approximately half a mile of Tunis, but when [it became evident that] the messenger would remain there, they took me back again. Who was more unfortunate than I? They left the Moorish messenger behind {27v} and tied me to a mule, which took me back into the mountains. After we had arrived, my legs were bound together and tied to a stick, so that I was suspended upside-down, and two churls, who were carrying the stick on their shoulders, flogged the soles of my feet with a rod. I thought my eyes would bulge out of my head, but I endured it, although I was innocent.

After I was with them for almost two months, they started treating me a little better, since I now had to eat out of one bowl with the dog.[89] Once they had eaten, they would put my helping on one side of the bowl and the dog's on the other. The dog would finish his share promptly and immediately start biting my hands, for he wanted to eat mine as well. [The Alarbs] found this amusing.

My daily chore was to grind as much flour as they required with the mill, for they did not bake more than they ate in one day. They had no {28r} baking ovens either but used an earthen griddle; they laid one cake into it, and when it was done on one side, they turned it over. And when they

---

88. *Scheryffen*: probably a nomadic North African tribe (Ritter, "Ein deutscher Sklave als Augenzeuge bei der Eroberung von Tunis," 215n121). Alternatively, the adjective *Sharifian* is used to designate descendants of the Prophet Muhammad himself.

89. *eat [. . .] with the dog*: this episode highlights just how bad his treatment must have been before if eating with a dog was an improvement.

traveled—which, as I mentioned before, occurred frequently—I had to load the provisions onto the camels. I was allowed to wander freely by day but was secured with a chain and lock when night fell.

They wanted to find me a wife there, wherefore I was expected to adopt their faith, for my master's father was a priest with two daughters. But I retorted, "How am I supposed to adopt your faith if I do not yet understand your language properly?" Because I played along like this, they believed that they would eventually succeed and started treating me better. My master, the Alarb, had two wives: one was dark-skinned and the other was white. In my opinion, the conduct of the dark-skinned wife seemed more devout and God-fearing, for she prayed regularly {28v} in the early morning, at noon, and in the evening. And whenever I passed her unwarily during her prayers, she would look at me and say, "O, afa wole,"[90] which means: "Oh, poor you." Whatever else was on her mind was between her and God, but in my opinion, it seemed as if she wanted to be rid of me.

Our merciful God did not wish me to remain with the heathens any longer. One evening, as the black woman was about to secure my chains, my master called her and she left the key behind. Whether she did this on purpose or not, only she knows. When night fell, I took a few handfuls of wheat from a sack by my head and put it in a bundle. My comrade the dog always lay beside me, for he was both my dining and my sleeping companion. After I had made certain that everyone was asleep, I crawled out of the tent, which had been pitched next to {29r} a mountainside due to the wind, and was followed by my comrade, the dog. I then fell to my knees and heartily begged our Lord God to help me out of my prison. [I made] many promises in that moment but kept very few later.

After completing my prayer, I began my journey. When I walked farther away than the dog was accustomed to, he barked and began to howl. The dog ran to the tents, baying incessantly, causing everyone in the tents to wake up and start chasing me, as I would later learn from the Alarb. Nevertheless, my faithful God protected me through His dear angels. As soon as I heard the noise the dog was making, I slipped even farther away, but avoided the road. A little way farther on, I came to a path between two mountains that I had to take. When I had passed through it, I soon saw a village of tents. The dogs became aware of me, so I made a detour and

---

90. *O, afa wole*: the meaning of this is unclear. "Afa" could possibly stand for "anta," meaning "you." "Wole" could stand for "welī," an expression of dismay.

intended to return to my path once I had passed the village. {29v} Before I could take a good look around, I found myself again near the tents I had tried to avoid. This would turn out to be a great stroke of luck, but I did not know it at the time, and [I thought] my God had not heard me. I therefore fell to my knees once again and begged our faithful God to send His dear angels to guide and lead me, so that I would finally regain my freedom unharmed. Necessity teaches one to pray.

I therefore marched straight into the mountains, which were a good way from the path. However, whenever I perceived the slightest movement, I kept still. I was so light-footed that I did not know whether I was walking or flying. When morning broke, I came to a level field not far from a ruined castle where we had camped once during our retreat from Tunis. In the twilight, I thought I glimpsed four riders approaching, and since the field [provided no cover], it was not possible to flee. I therefore thought {30r} to myself, "If these riders are the ones chasing you, you will not be able to escape them, but if they are other travelers, you will greet them and let them pass." As I approached them, [I saw that] it was four oxen, each with a bag of wheat on its back, and two men driving them. I greeted them: "Salamalekim."[91] They thanked me and replied, "Malick salam,"[92] and passed.

I made for the castle, for there was a small stream nearby. Once there, I pulled out my wheat, soaked it, and ate my meal. Then I went deeper into the mountains, lay down under a tree, and slept. I had walked seven miles that night.

Later, when night fell, I resumed my journey and had to travel through some high mountains, which abounded with monkeys and guenons,[93] of which I saw many. They came close and hissed and screamed at me, making my hair stand on end, {30v} but they did not harm me.

As the third hour past midnight drew near, I arrived at the city of Tunis, whose gates were still closed. When they opened, I crossed the city's threshold wearing my *bornis*, a coat with many drapes. Also, the soles of my shoes had worn out almost completely, so I had swathed my feet in cloths. When the Moors saw me enter in such a "stately" manner, they said to each

---

91. *Salamalekim*: in Arabic: *s-salām ʃalēkum*. Literally: "Peace be upon you."
92. *Malick salam*: in Arabic: *wa ʿalaykumu s-salām*. Literally: "And upon you, peace." The "m" in *Malick* is probably an error. The actual word would be pronounced with a sound similar to "w."
93. *guenons*: small, long-tailed monkeys.

other, "Hodde mausy muselman, hodde ansara,"[94] which in the Moorish tongue means: "He is not a righteous one but an unrighteous one." When I arrived at the city center, however, I found two Spanish soldiers who had been on watch at the fortress during the night. They still carried their halberds[95] with them, for the king of Tunis did not much trust his Moors, given their past treacherous behavior, of which I have spoken previously.

When the Spaniards saw me, they said, "Qui nos vienne allia," which means: "Who goes there?" I {31r} walked up to them quickly, greeted them, and said, "Dios vos de bonos dies Signoros." That means: "Gentlemen, I wish you a blessed day!" They thanked me profusely: "Ben venuto."[96] "We extend our welcome to you!" They asked me if I wanted to drink brandy with them, and in that moment, the Moor who was pouring it recognized me and asked where I had come from. I told him I had started my journey not far from Bresie the day before yesterday, and I told him where my master was. He said, "You must have had a good angel, otherwise you would have been torn apart by the lions."

The Spaniards, who were listening to my conversation with the Moor, asked me about my country of origin, and I said I was German. Upon this, they answered, "By God, may you be the one who sent us the Moor with the letters!" I answered, "One and the same." They said, "The messenger is still incarcerated. You may make him your servant. Our commander, Captain Sperea, will {31v} be happy to hear that you are here because you have served under him before."

We did not waste any words. We stepped into a boat and sailed for La Goulette, where I was reunited with my captain, who was very happy to see me and gave me three doubloons[97] as a present. Then, several German gunsmiths who knew me arrived and gave me this and that. The captain then asked what I wanted to do with the Moor I had sent to him with the letters, since he could become my slave unless I decided to release him.

---

94. *Hodde mausy muselman, hodde ansara*: in Arabic: *hādha māhū-shi misilmīn, hādha anṣāra*. Literally: "This one is no Muslim; this one is a Christian."

95. *halberd*: a combined spear and battle-ax.

96. *"Qui nos vienne allia"* [. . .] *"Ben venuto"*: it must be noted that, although intelligible, Sturmer's Spanish is not consistently idiomatic.

"Qui nos vienne allia?": in Spanish: "¿Quién viene por allá?" Literally: "Who goes there?"

"Dios vos de bonos dies Signoros": in Spanish: "¡Que Dios os dé buenos días, señores!" Literally: "May God grant you a good day, gentlemen."

"Ben venuto": in Spanish: "Bienvenido." Literally: "Welcome."

97. *doubloons*: Spanish gold coins.

However, I set him free and demanded no ransom. I instructed him to tell my master good things and that he had seen me. But, should I encounter him again some time, I would pay him back dearly for having held me captive for so long in contradiction with His Imperial Majesty's orders. I also gave him money for provisions.

This is almost all my captivity and {32r} release, recounted word for word. Now I would also like to make it known how I have fared from then until today.

While I was earning well again and acquired a good pay of four salaries of sixteen ducats per month, the city of Bizerte remained occupied by the Turks. The king of Tunis had sent his son with ten thousand men on foot, and Andreas Doria with his armada of thirty galleys. We sailed to Bizerte. At the time, I was in the Spanish regiment on one of the galleys. There I found my friend who had helped me sell my wheat in Lisbon and who had been my journeyman[98] at first, but now I was his. Such is the way of the world.

When we neared the city of Bizerte, we foot soldiers[99] were put on land, not far from the Moorish cohorts. Several high-ranking Moorish officers came to have a look at our unit and among them was my [former] master, the Alarb, from whom I had recently escaped. I said to my companions, "Now you shall see some wondrous things, {32v} if you will excuse me." I approached him then, but he failed to recognize me right away in my new outfit.[100] I took hold of his horse's bridle and said to him in the Moorish tongue, "So we meet again, sir." The Moor dismounted, fell to his knees before me, and begged for mercy, for he realized that he had done me wrong. He vowed to give me half his share, should we, with God's blessing, seize the city by force. However, I was not to complain about him. What was I to do? This was not the time to make accusations. Less than an hour later, the galleys opened fire and captured the city by force.

When the Turks realized that [the city] was lost, they fled through the gates, only to fall into the hands of the Alarbs. Thus, my [former] master

---

98. *journeyman*: a worker skilled in a particular trade who works for someone else.

99. *foot soldiers*: "Knechte" in the 1558 German manuscript, which refers to the "Landsknechte," the widespread mercenary foot troops that evolved in the late fifteenth century and dominated warfare throughout the early modern period.

100. *new outfit*: "in den Federn" in the 1558 German manuscript, which literally means "in the feathers."

acquired plenty of booty and, when it was all over, he came to me with countless Turkish garments, weapons, and suchlike and said, "Take whatever suits you, for you deserve everything, and {33r} your virtue suggests that you must be of aristocratic descent. Not only did you not report my misconduct—although you had the opportunity and every right to do so—but you also released the messenger, who could have been yours, without demanding any ransom, and you even gave him provisions for the road."

"Come with us to our quarters; we would like to honor you formally," declared all the Moorish gentlemen. I thanked them but I did not deem it opportune, and I took what suited me from the Alarb's booty and left the rest to him. Thus we parted ways.

From Bizerte we sailed off to Naples, where we were paid and put on leave. So, I had a few hundred ducats for myself, but as they say, "Male quæsit male perdit"[101]—"Thus one gains, and thus one loses." By then, I had already forgotten all my tribulations. I was living at the whim of my earthly appetites and did not remember how my loyal God had delivered me. However, the Lord observed me closely and kept score, {33v} and when my ledger was full, He came in His time to call me to balance accounts and punished me rigorously.

From Naples, I sailed again to Sicily, where we loaded a ship with grain. On the way, we battled some Turkish galleys but managed to escape unscathed. Finally, we arrived safely with our ships in Andalusia at a city called Seville, where we handed over the grain and received our payment. Meanwhile, war with France had broken out.[102] Therefore, three ships of Orleÿ[103] were prepared to occupy the island Aÿs in the Canaries[104] Then, God granted us the good fortune to capture a French ship that had taken seven Spanish merchant vessels—booty that was now ours. When winter approached, we sailed to Spain again, reached Seville with our booty, and received our pay there.

---

101. *male quæsit male perdit*: literally: "wrongly gained, wrongly lost."
102. *war with France had broken out*: most likely a reference to the Italian War of 1536–1538, a conflict between Francis I of France and Charles V for control over territories in northern Italy.
103. *Orleÿ*: this reference is unclear.
104. *Aÿs in the Canaries*: probably one of the Canary Islands (Ritter, "Ein deutscher Sklave als Augenzeuge bei der Eroberung von Tunis," 221n142).

{34r} In the meantime, Orleÿ had prepared six ships, which were meant to sail to Peru to fetch the emperor's gold. I was made master gunner of these ships and received a good salary. We were meant to return with twelve ships that had sailed before us, because the French usually preyed on such vessels. We sailed from Sanlúcar[105] in the name of God and arrived in the Canary Islands on the eighth day. There, we refilled our water supply and sailed to an island called Santo Domingo,[106] where we collected as much gold as was available.

We then sailed to Nombre de Dios,[107] which is also a port. Most of the gold comes from there. When we came within one hundred miles of the Indies,[108] we lost sight of the North Star but saw the South Star[109] rise and set instead. Thus our beloved, beautiful world floats across the skies. Just what are we so smug about? We are but poor little worms.

Here we loaded our freight and saw that {34v} there were lindworms,[110] which they call *lagarti*,[111] as well as tiger-like beasts[112] and fish in the water called sharks.[113] All of them devour humans, something I occasionally saw myself. The lagarti normally remain in the water, and the tiger-beasts on land. The latter is very similar to a lion, but it is not as strong and hairy.

On our way back, we could not use the same route we had taken on the way over, so we took a different one. The wind and the current were against us. Therefore, we rowed three hundred miles out to sea until we managed to see the North Star again, which was very near the horizon.

Steersmen are to a large degree astronomers. Among their instruments there is the quadrant, which resembles a half moon with digits. The steersman will sit with it in the sun at noon and make a mark where the sun,

---

105. *Sanlúcar*: Sanlúcar de Barrameda, a city in Andalusia, Spain. "Sankt Lucas" in the 1558 German manuscript.

106. *Santo Domingo*: Sturmer could be referring to the island of Hispaniola, where the city of Santo Domingo is located; "Santo Donigos" in the 1558 German manuscript.

107. *Nombre de Dios*: located in the Colón Province in Panama, it was a major port of call for the Spanish treasure fleet.

108. *the Indies*: Sturmer is most likely referring to Central and South America.

109. *South Star*: the true south star (Sigma Octantis) is too faint to navigate by. It is possible that Sturmer is referring to the Southern Cross, but this is composed of four stars, not one.

110. *lindworms*: in Germanic lore, lindworms are mythical, dragon-like creatures.

111. *lagarti*: in Central America, the word "lagarto" can refer to either crocodiles or caimans.

112. *tiger-like beasts*: based on the subsequent description, Sturmer probably means cougars.

113. *sharks*: "Tÿbron" in the 1558 German manuscript, a transliteration of the Spanish word "tiburón," which means shark.

shining through the hole, hits the digits. And in {35r} the evening, he uses an instrument which he aims at the North Star, so that he can mark at what degree it stands in relation to the sun. He then consults his book and calculations, which enable him to determine where we are, what land lies before us, and how far away it is.

No steersman is allowed to sail from Seville before having been examined. If he has already worked there as a steersman, his name will soon be found in a book. If not, he will be tested, and if he answers well, he will be allowed to proceed; if not, he must stay home or travel as a boatswain.

On the way back, we reached an island called Pannamar,[114] where we found the remainder of our armada with the [aforementioned] twelve ships. Then we sailed in the name of God from there through the Canary Islands. After we made it through them, a devastating storm arose {35v} that drove us close to Brazil. I suspect devils, rather than humans, must live on that island. They danced with lights every night.

Of the twelve ships, [the one carrying] the fleet admiral leaked so much that it almost sank during the storm. It carried most of the gold. God showed us His mercy and the storm subsided, so we managed to salvage the people and the gold. After that, we let the ship sink with her cannons. There was nothing else we could do. Our Almighty God helped us, so we made it safely back to Seville, where we received our payment and were put on leave.

From Seville, I wrote to my dear, blessed father about how I had fared during all this time. However, he found it impossible to believe that anyone could endure so much. Thus, he kept my letter but did not show it to anybody. In Seville, I enlisted as a gunsmith and sailed back through the Mediterranean to Sicily. Our ship was {36r} loaded for Candia, called Cretam in Latin.[115] There, we loaded Malmsey and Muscat wine for London in England. Candia lies not much more than forty miles[116] from Constantinople. Our dear God favored us by granting us a safe round trip and we arrived in London in England, where we received our payment.

---

114. *Pannamar*: Sturmer is probably referring to an island off the coast of Panama.

115. *Candia, called Cretam in Latin*: Candia, known as Heraklion today, was a term used interchangeably to refer both to the island of Crete as a whole and its capital.

116. *forty miles*: this is probably a typographical error. The linear distance between Crete and Istanbul (formerly Constantinople) is around seven hundred kilometers, which would be over four hundred miles.

In the name of God, I sailed from there to Gdańsk on an English ship, and after that, I went back to Malbork[117] to my father, who did not recognize me until I revealed myself. Soon, four days later, he had a feast prepared to celebrate the prodigal son's homecoming and to rejoice in his future.

While sitting at table, after we had eaten almost everything, my father said, "My dear son, strangers have told me that you were held captive by the Turks. While our friends are gathered here, {36v} you must tell us all about it!" He did not let on that he had received my message. So I started and told them almost exactly the same story I have written here. Only afterward did he admit that he had received my letter.

I was home not more than fourteen days before I loaded several shipments of wheat onto a ship, which Hans Balser took to Lisbon. My father pestered me to stay home and join his business, for he was nearing seventy, but I did not want to obey him. I thought I knew better. So we sailed to Lisbon in the name of God, and [then to] England, [where] we stayed with the ship and its goods. Thus, four hundred florins[118] vanished again.

I crossed back home and again loaded several shipments of wheat onto another vessel; the skipper was called Cale Caspar. My father insisted that I should stay in the country, [since] I had already had my fair share of adventures. He wanted to find a wife for me, but I could not spare a {37r} thought for that. We sailed to Lisbon, had a good voyage, and arrived safely. I stayed there for almost four years and made good money over time, for I had found someone with whom I could do business.

Then, not God, but rather the troublesome devil guided a citizen of Gdańsk to me. He sold me approximately forty loads of wheat at thirty-two ducats per load. He kept the wheat in the ship and gave the crew several thalers[119] to spend on drinks in exchange for them drenching the wheat. Once the wheat had swollen, its weight increased so that it seemed as if there were five shipments more than he had loaded in Amsterdam. When it was delivered on land, [I saw that] it was damp in several places and said, "Hans Wÿdau, why is the wheat so wet?" He answered, "On our way over, the wind was somewhat against us and provoked high waves,

---

117. *Malbork*: a city in Poland that belonged to Prussia in Sturmer's time. "Marienburg" in the 1558 German manuscript.

118. *florin*: a Florentine gold coin.

119. *thaler*: a currency widely used in Europe from the late fifteenth century.

of which several got into the ship." His words convinced me and I gave that immoral man my trust {37v} and my money. He received about 130 *portugaleser*[120] from me. Then, I myself sewed it into a canvas doublet for him. After the wheat had lain for several days, it heated up and became infested with worms. There was nothing I could do; I had to give it away, almost for free. I kept not even two hundred ducats from all that wheat.

In the meantime, my father had died, and from time to time I found myself reflecting on the pious life[121] I had led since escaping my imprisonment. I felt a sense of trepidation come over me and thought to myself, "Why do you persist in pursuing this unholy life, bereft of the word of God? Were God to meet you right here, He would judge you as the person you are right now. You should return to your fatherland, do penance, become pious, and enter the holy state of matrimony."

I therefore made up my mind and returned home. Soon after, I traveled to Königsberg,[122] where I found an honest person to be my {38r} wife: Peter Brandes's blessed widow. At first, everything seemed to be going well. I was rich, well thought of by everyone, had a great many friends, and only mingled with important people. Thus, I made my way in the world and truly believed myself to be the cream of the crop. I got myself into many fights all around me.[123] I was harmful to my neighbor.

In the blink of an eye, God reversed my fortune by wondrous means and I lost almost everything. I had not one friend left. One person might interpret this one way, somebody else another. In the end, even my dear wife, from whom I was supposed to receive comfort, turned against me—not

---

120. *portugaleser*: since Sturmer was living in Lisbon at that time, it is likely that he means "portugueses," a kind of coin minted in Portugal and a quintessential monetary symbol of the age of discovery. However, it should also be noted that several European nations, including Germany and Poland, minted their own coins called "portugalöser," which were inspired by the Portuguese gold coins. See António Miguel Trigeiros, "Portuguese Coins in the Age of Discovery," *The Numismatist* 104, no. 11 (1991): 1728–35.

121. *pious life*: either Sturmer is being sarcastic here or there is a mistake in the 1558 German manuscript. The manuscript reads "gottseliges Leben" (pious life), when it is clear from the context that Sturmer has led an "ungottseliges Leben" (impious life).

122. *Königsberg*: formerly part of the Kingdom of Prussia, it is now known as Kaliningrad, a Russian exclave.

123. *all around me*: the meaning of this sentence is not entirely clear in the 1558 German manuscript: "Feder Hansen vndt ich verwahrre mich auch in so viell Händell, ich wolte es nur allenthalben habenn."

unlike Job's wife.[124] Indeed, even my dear godfather, Doctor Morlinus,[125] had plenty of contact with her. However, even in my weakest moments, when the devil was rejoicing, I remembered that the God who had delivered me from Barbary in such a wondrous manner was still present. {38v} I always comforted myself with this.

However, a punishment deferred is not a punishment forgotten. Our Lord God had been watching me for a long time, and He had likewise reminded me to change my ways. But avarice had even taken hold of me when I resolved to do a good deed, or when God let His word be heard, etc. I heard it clearly but my thoughts were with the potash works,[126] the finance office, the storehouse, the beer jug, my coffers. When I woke up early in the morning, I always had a long list of things to do during the day. This often contained more than thirty tasks, but no task from our Father,[127] which ought to have been at the very top.

Our dear God gave me the insight that all of this happened on account of my sins and to gain the knowledge of His true word; to bring me thus to the understanding of His true word and that everything happened for my own good. For eight years, my faithful God mercifully preserved me through His holy word. {39r} After taking all my possessions, He also took my dear, pious spouse. Soon after her [death], I also took to my bed and nearly followed her, but my hour had not yet come.

But now that I have almost nothing left, I can only pray to God and sigh, "Abba,[128] dear Father, it is time to be merciful again." My faithful God will come, for He does not wish to see me in distress any longer. Instead, He will once again offer me His gracious, bountiful hand, and He will give me more than He has taken from me, just as he did with poor Job. Given your

---

124. *not unlike Job's wife*: Sturmer is referring to Job 2:9–10: the prophet Job, even after losing his possessions and children and being cursed with boils that covered him from head to toe, refused to curse God. His wife, however, cursed God and Job for their misfortunes.

125. *Doctor Morlinus*: it is not clear to whom Sturmer is referring. It could be the Wittenberg theologian and reformer Dr. Joachim Mörlin (1514–1571), whose Latin name is "Doctor Ioachimus Mörlinus."

126. *potash works*: "Aschhoffe" in the 1558 German manuscript. The reference is not clear. It could refer to a storehouse for wood ash.

127. *thirty tasks, but no task from our Father*: the 1558 German manuscript reads "30 Perselen, aber kein Persell vom Vatter Vnser." Although the exact meaning of the terms "Perselen/Persell" is not clear, the context makes Sturmer's intended meaning fairly obvious.

128. *Abba*: from the Aramaic word for "Father." In the New Testament, God is addressed in this manner on three different occasions.

request, I could not withhold all of this from Your Honor. With this, I ask that Your Honor remember me in your diligent prayers. May [God] keep us: here, temporarily, and over there, for all eternity, in the name of Jesus Christ, his dear Son. Amen.

Completed on 20 October 1558

Balthasar Sturmer

Figure 2.1 Title page of Antonio de Sosa's *Topography of Algiers*
Source: *Topographia e historia general de Argel* (Valladolid, 1612); Res/2 H.afr. 266, urn:nbn: de:bvb:12-bsb10867104-8; Bayerische Staatsbibliothek München

CHAPTER II

ANTONIO DE SOSA, *TOPOGRAPHY OF ALGIERS*: ATTEMPTED ESCAPE OF MIGUEL DE CERVANTES

1612 Spanish print edition; selection

Captivity in Algiers 1577

The following short excerpt provides a detailed description of one of Miguel de Cervantes's multiple attempts to escape from Algiers before he was ransomed in 1580, after five years of captivity. The section is part of the Spanish *Topography and General History of Algiers* (1612), which was most likely written by Miguel de Cervantes's fellow captive Antonio de Sosa in the late 1570s. The *Topography* was published decades later under the name Diego de Haedo. Recent research by María Antonia Garcés and Diana de Armas Wilson makes a convincing case for Antonio de Sosa as the true author of this multivolume work on Algiers.[1] Antonio de Sosa's (or Diego de Haedo's) *Topographia e historia general de Argel* (1612) together with Luis del Mármol Carvajal's *Descripción general de África* (1573) and Diego de Torres's *Relación del origen y suceso de los xarifes y del estado de los reinos de Marruecos* (1586) are typical of the Spanish discourses about North Africa in the second half of the sixteenth century.[2] One could go

---

1. María Antonia Garcés, ed., *An Early Modern Dialogue with Islam: Antonio De Sosa's* Topography of Algiers *(1612)*, trans. Diana de Armas Wilson (Notre Dame, IN: University of Notre Dame Press, 2011).

2. For a good survey of sixteenth-century Spanish accounts of North Africa, see Mercedes García-Arenal, "Spanish Literature on North Africa in the XVI Century: Diego Torres," *Maghreb Review* 1–2 (1983): 53–59.

[91]

so far as to claim that a large portion of these texts of Iberian origin are "encyclopedic compilations."³

All three authors, Mármol, Torres, and de Sosa, were captives in North Africa at some point in their lives. Unlike most northern European returnees, who put their own captivity experiences at the center of autobiographical first-person narratives, Antonio de Sosa and his fellow countrymen typically composed encyclopedic compilations of general knowledge about North Africa. De Sosa deals with the different facets of North Africa, including the demographic features of different ethnic and religious groups, Algiers's political and military organization, and other aspects of life among Spain's and Portugal's southern adversaries. The main thrust of these texts on North Africa was to provide as much useful information as possible about the "enemy," always envisioning a potential military or colonizing intervention in which this intelligence might come in handy. At the beginning of the seventeenth century, with the Spanish crown shifting its attention to the New World colonies and to northern Europe with its dangers of Protestantism, the interest in these encyclopedic texts about northern Africa declined dramatically. Therefore, the publication of these texts is more or less restricted to the later parts of the sixteenth and to the very early seventeenth century.

It seems likely that the geographic proximity of the Iberian Peninsula to North Africa resulted in omnipresent firsthand oral testimonies of captivity by returnees from Barbary. This information overload meant that there was most likely little incentive for former captives to put their personal experiences down in autobiographical writing. The general lack of an

---

3. António Saldanha's *Crónica de Almançor* is a Portuguese example of this type of encyclopedic compilation of knowledge about North Africa in the sixteenth century. On Saldanha, see Peter Mark, "'Free, Unfree, Captive, Slave': António de Saldanha, a Late Sixteenth-Century Captive in Marrakesh," in *Mediterranean Slavery and World Literature: Captivity Genres from Cervantes to Rousseau*, ed. Mario Klarer (London, New York: Routledge, 2020), 99–110. For a modern edition, see António Saldanha, António D. Farinha, and Léon Bourdon, *Crónica de Almançor, Sultão de Marrocos (1578–1603)* (Lisbon: Instituto de Investigação Científica Tropical, 1997). There are also hybrid texts that include more traditional slave experiences of Iberian origin while still containing encyclopedic sections. For one such example, see João Carvalho Mascarenhas, *Memoravel relaçam da perda da nao Conceiçam que os turcos queymàraõ à vista da barra de Lisboa; varios successos das pessoas, que nella catìvàraõ. E descripçaõ nova da cidade de Argel, & de seu governo; & cousas muy notaveis acontecidas nestes ultimos annos de 1621. atè 1626* (Lisbon: Na Officina de Antonio Alvares, 1627).

audience for *personal* Barbary narratives in Portugal and Spain could have encouraged Iberian authors to resort to this highly idiosyncratic encyclopedic set of discourses instead. Texts such as de Sosa's illustrate a culture-specific way of coping with Barbary captivity in the southern European regions near North Africa. The encyclopedic textual coverage of Barbary served a highly political and utilitarian purpose, as it provided valuable and directly applicable information in the case of military confrontations or diplomatic exchanges. This utilitarian agenda did not prevent these authors from inserting at times highly personal episodes, as is the case with the account of the unsuccessful escape of Antonio de Sosa's fellow captive Miguel de Cervantes.

Notes on the Present Translation of Antonio de Sosa's *Topography of Algiers*: Attempted Escape of Miguel de Cervantes

This translation is based on the first print edition: Antonio de Sosa [Diego de Haedo], "Dialogo segvndo, de los martyres de Argel," *Topographia e historia general de Argel, repartida en cinco tratados, do se veran casos estraños, muertes espantosas y tormentos exquisitos, que conviene se entiendan en la Christiandad: con mucha doctrina, y elegancia curiosa* (Valladolid: Diego Fernandez de Cordova y Oviedo, 1612). Digitized collection: http://bdh-rd.bne.es/viewer.vm?id=0000079195 .144r-191v.

The numbers in brackets { } in the text always indicate the beginning of a page and refer to the original page numbers of the 1612 edition. The translation introduces additional paragraph breaks to enhance the readability of the narrative. Because this historical print edition only gives a page number for individual leaves, the letter "r" (recto) indicates the front of the leaf and "v" (verso) indicates the back of the leaf. Special thanks go to Diana de Armas Wilson, Alfonso Merello Astigarraga, and Camila Torres Carrillo for their invaluable assistance with clarifying numerous cases of doubt.

Antonio de Sosa [Diego de Haedo], "Second Dialogue, of the Martyrs," *Topography and General History of Algiers, Divided among Five Books, Which Will Exhibit Strange Cases, Horrific Deaths, and Extraordinary Tortures that Christianity Needs to Understand: With Copious Doctrine and Curious Elegance* (Valladolid: Diego Fernández de Córdova y Oviedo, 1612), 184r–185r

Translated by María Antonia Garcés

{184r} [. . .] In that same year, in 1577, during the first days of September, some Christian captives in Algiers, all prominent men, among them many Spanish and three Mallorcan gentlemen—all in all there were fifteen of them—plotted to have a brigantine or a frigate[4] from Mallorca come and pick them up. It was supposed to take them on board one night and bring them to Mallorca or Spain. The arrangement was made with a Mallorcan Christian who had been liberated from Algiers. Viana was his name; a man with much nautical experience and of the Barbary Coast. He departed from Algiers with the intention and purpose of returning in a few days.

During this time, all fifteen {184v} Christians had hidden in a secret cave in the country house of *Alcaide* Hassan,[5] a Greek renegade. The country house was located in the east, about three miles from Algiers and not too far from the ocean. The cave was comfortable and very appropriate for this purpose, namely, to provide the best and safest place for the Christians to hide and wait for the ship.

Only two Christians knew about this. One was the country house's gardener, who had made the cave long before and was always on the watch in case somebody came. The other was a man who had been invited to come along in the brigantine, and who had been born and raised in the village of Melilla.[6] [This is] a town on the Barbary Coast under the rule of the king of Spain, in the Kingdom of Tlemcen,[7] two hundred miles from Orán[8] in

---

4. *brigantine or a frigate*: in the early modern period, warships with square-rigged sails.

5. *alcaide*: from the Arabic *al-qā'id*, meaning "leader" or "captain." De Sosa uses it to refer to a warden or keeper.

6. *Melilla*: an autonomous city belonging to Spain, situated on the northwestern coast of Africa. It shares a border with Morocco.

7. *Kingdom of Tlemcen*: originally a Berber kingdom located in northwestern Algeria. In 1554, it became part of the Ottoman Empire. It appears in the Spanish text as "Tremecén."

8. *Orán*: a city in Algiers that was controlled by Spain at the time.

the west, and one hundred miles from Vélez and the rock.[9] As a Moor, he was an unbeliever, but he later became a Christian and was then captured a second time. He called himself El Dorador,[10] and his main responsibility was to buy (with the money he was given) everything the men in the cave needed and to bring it discreetly and secretly to the country house.

Diligent and true to his word, Viana the Mallorcan began to assemble a group of experienced sailors as soon as he arrived in Mallorca (I heard this from three Christians who traveled with him). He did this quickly, for he was supported by the viceroy of Mallorca (to whom he had delivered letters from the aforementioned Christians and gentlemen). A few days later, the brigantine was ready, and so he left Mallorca for Algiers on the last days of September 1577, exactly as he had intended.

He arrived on 28 September. According to their plan, he approached the coast at midnight, close to where the cave and the Christians were (he had observed the cave carefully before he left). He intended to land and alert the Christians to his arrival so that they could embark with him. Unfortunately, the moment the brigantine or frigate's prow touched land, some Moors who were passing by spotted the Christians and their ship despite the darkness and started to yell at the top of their lungs: "Christians! Christians! Ship! Ship!" Those on the vessel heard this and were forced to sail away to avoid detection and left without achieving their goal this time.

Therefore, some days passed and the Christians in the cave believed that the brigantine was late. They did not know that it had arrived and left, nor whether it would return. Nevertheless, they were extremely confident that the Lord God would redeem them and that Viana, as a man of honor, would keep his word. In this way, there in the cave (which was damp and dark, and which they did not leave all day long, so some of them were already sick), they found consolation while hoping for their escape.

Precisely at that moment, the Devil, enemy of all men, blinded El Dorador (who, as we have mentioned, provided them with food) and persuaded him to become a Moor once again, repudiating the faith of Our Lord Jesus Christ a second time around. He then decided that there was much to be gained from the king, the Turks, and especially from the masters and owners

---

9. *Vélez and the rock*: Peñón de Vélez de la Gomera, a Spanish enclave on a rocky peninsula off the Moroccan coast.

10. *El Dorador*: literally: "dorador" means "gilder" (a craftsperson who performs gilding). However, it could also mean someone who hides evil deeds or words behind a pleasant mask.

of the captives who were hiding in the cave. Therefore, on the feast of Saint Jerome, on 30 September, he went to King Hassan,[11] a Venetian renegade, and asked for his consent to become a Moor. He added that he intended to do him a favor by disclosing the whereabouts of a certain cave that hid various Christians who were awaiting a ship from Mallorca.

The overjoyed king thanked El Dorador for the tidings and, tyrant that he was, planned to keep all the captives for himself, against all reason and convention. Without wasting any time, he summoned his *basha*[12] (the person in charge of guarding his Christian slaves) and asked him to send for other Moors and Turks. They were to follow the Christian who wished to become a Moor and go to the country house of Alcaide Hassan. There, hiding in a cave, they would find fifteen Christians, {185r} who were to be captured along with the gardener.

The basha followed the king's command at once and took with him eight or ten Turks on horseback and another twenty-four on foot. Some were carrying guns and cutlasses; others were carrying spears. Their guide (leading the way, as Judas once did) took them to the country house, where the gardener was apprehended. They then headed for the cave revealed by this new Judas and forced the Christians to come out. All were captured by order of the king and taken to his presence. In particular, they bound the hands of one Miguel Cervantes,[13] a leading gentleman from Alcalá de Henares,[14] who had masterminded the whole affair and was therefore held responsible for it.

The king was delighted at the sight of them and commanded that they be taken to his *bagnio*,[15] where they were to be heavily guarded (in his mind, they were already his slaves). Only Miguel Cervantes was ordered to remain in his palace. He endured many questions and terrible threats, but the king never managed to discover who had concocted or known about the scheme. He suspected Friar George Olivar, a member of the Order of Our Lady of Mercy[16] and the Commander of Valencia (who had been

---

11. *King Hassan*: Hassan Veneziano, regent of Algiers from 1577 to 1580 and 1582 to 1587.

12. *basha*: a high-ranking official in the Ottoman world. It appears in the Spanish text as "Baxi."

13. *Miguel Cervantes*: Miguel de Cervantes (ca. 1547–1616) was captured by Barbary corsairs in 1575. He was ransomed five years later in 1580. In the 1612 edition, he is sometimes referred to as Miguel Cervantes and sometimes as Miguel de Cervantes.

14. *Alcalá de Henares*: city in central Spain.

15. *bagnio*: the prison or slave quarters where slaves lived.

16. *Order of Our Lady of Mercy*: a Catholic order also known as the Order of Our Lady of Mercy for the Redemption of Captives, or Mercedarians.

sent as a redeemer by the Crown of Aragon),[17] because that Judas Dorador had persuaded the king of the friar's involvement. Being the tyrant that he was, Hassan the Venetian thought this the perfect opportunity to apprehend the friar and extort a fortune from him.

Despite all his threats, however, the king never managed to get anything out of Miguel Cervantes other than his admission to being the plan's sole author (he cast all the blame upon himself, like the honorable man he was). The king ordered him to his *bagnio*, taking him as a slave as well. Nevertheless, he had no choice but to return him, along with another three or four captives, to their original masters.

Afterward, Alcaide Hassan was notified of everything that had occurred in his country house, that is, of the Christians being arrested there along with his gardener. He rushed to the king's house and pleaded insistently with the king to mercilessly effect justice upon all involved, and, especially that he, Hassan, be allowed to punish the gardener as he pleased. He displayed the full extent of his wrath and outrage against the gardener. The king imitated him and severely punished all the other Christians who had hidden in the cave.

It was a wondrous thing how some of them had been confined without being able to see the light—except at night when they left the cave—sometimes for seven months, sometimes five or fewer. They were often succored by Miguel de Cervantes, who by doing so risked his own life. He was on the verge of losing it on four different occasions when he was nearly impaled or hooked or burned alive because he had sought to liberate many others. Indeed, if his determination, industry, and machinations had been met with some good fortune, Algiers would be Christian today, for he aspired to nothing else.

In the end, the gardener was hung by a foot and died by drowning in his own blood. He was a native of Navarre and a very good Christian.

One could tell an extraordinary tale of the feats of Miguel de Cervantes and the things that occurred in that cave during the seven months that the Christians spent in it. Hassan Pasha,[18] king of Algiers, used to say that his Christians, his ships, and indeed the whole city were safe because he kept that wretched Christian under heavy guard. That is how terrified he was of

---

17. *Crown of Aragon*: a composite monarchy that was created after the merging of the County of Barcelona and the Kingdom of Aragon through marriage. It existed from 1162 to 1716.

18. *Hassan Pasha*: de Sosa means Hassan Veneziano (see note 11).

Miguel de Cervantes and his plots. Had he not been discovered or betrayed by those who were supposed to help him, his imprisonment would have been blissful, despite being one of the cruelest captivities in Algiers.

The king assuaged his apprehension by buying [Miguel de Cervantes] from his master for five hundred escudos[19] and then locking him up in a cell for many days. He later doubled the demand and asked one thousand escudos for his ransom, which [Miguel de Cervantes] managed to pay, in great part thanks to Friar Juan Gil, the then redeemer of the Order of the Most Holy Trinity[20] in Algiers.

---

19. *escudos*: the Spanish escudo was a gold coin introduced in the 1530s.
20. *Order of the Most Holy Trinity*: the Trinitarians, a Catholic religious order founded in the twelfth century. It undertook large-scale missions to ransom Christian captives in the early modern period.

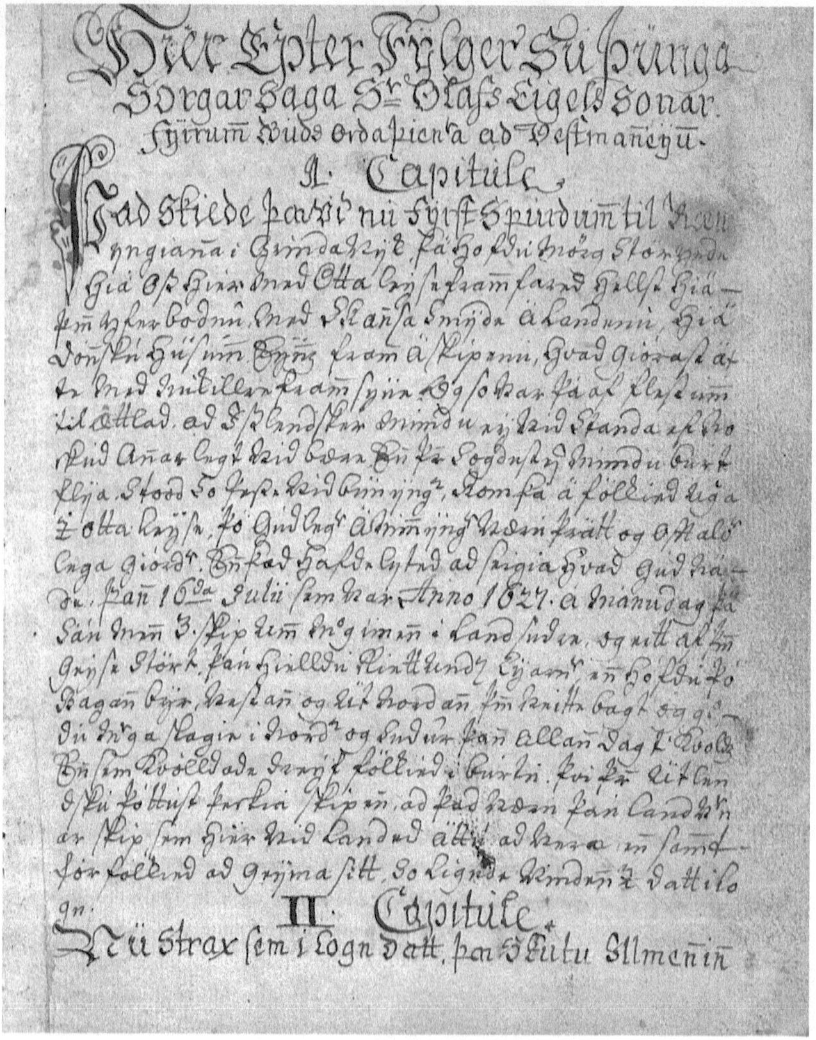

Figure 3.1 First page of a surviving manuscript version of Ólafur Egilsson's narrative
Source: *Sorgarsaga Sr [Séra] Olafs Eigelssonar* [ca. 1770]; shelf number: Lbs 769 4to skr.
C. 1770, National Library Manuscripts, National Library of Iceland, University Library.
Digital image courtesy of Landsbókasafn Íslands (National Library of Iceland).

CHAPTER III

ÓLAFUR EGILSSON, *THE TRAVELS OF REVEREND ÓLAFUR EGILSSON*

Undated Icelandic manuscripts; selection

Icelandic raid and captivity in Algiers 1627–1628

The Travels of Reverend Ólafur Egilsson is one of many writings documenting the *Tyrkjaránið*, the infamous raid on the Icelandic coast by Barbary corsairs in 1627.[1] However, only one narrative account by one of the captives themselves has survived—a pious Lutheran minister who was captured together with his pregnant wife and their two children. It recounts the surprise attack by the corsairs, the grueling passage to North Africa, the treatment and selling of the captives in Algiers, and Reverend Ólafur's laborious journey across Europe to Denmark in an unsuccessful attempt to raise ransom money. It also features typical descriptions of people and customs, North African flora and fauna, and the city of Algiers. It stands out as the only Barbary captivity narrative that provides a detailed account of a large-scale corsair land raid for human booty.

When two cooperating groups of corsairs—one from Salé[2] and one from Algiers—set sail for Iceland in the summer of 1627, they were about to

---

1. The following information on Ólafur Egilsson is based on Karl Smári Hreinsson and Adam Nichols, eds. and trans., *The Travels of Reverend Ólafur Egilsson: The Story of the Barbary Corsair Raid on Iceland in 1627* (Washington, DC: Catholic University of America Press, 2016); and Þorsteinn Helgason, "Historical Narrative as Collective Therapy: The Case of the Turkish Raid in Iceland," *Scandinavian Journal of History* 22, no. 4 (1997): 275–89.

2. Salé broke away from Morocco briefly in 1627 to form an independent corsair republic.

strike in a region that Barbary pirates had never touched before.[3] The party from Salé, consisting of a single ship, arrived on 20 June. They pillaged the southwest coast of Iceland for a little over a week, taking fifty or more captives (an exact count is hard to come by), and then returned to Salé. The Algerian party, consisting of three ships, arrived on 5 July. They first raided Iceland's southeast coast, where they took more than one hundred captives. Thereupon they sailed westward, reaching the island of Heimaey, one of the Westman Islands located off Iceland's south coast, on 16 July. Over the course of three days, they captured 242 men, women, and children, and then set sail for Algiers on 19 July. It is estimated that the two parties together took well over four hundred captives. As Reverend Ólafur vividly depicts in his first few chapters, the desperate attempts by the surprised islanders to escape or defend themselves were hardly successful. They had become victims of a well-organized military attack by professionals for which they were not at all prepared.

Reverend Ólafur Egilsson, born in 1564 and in his sixties when the raid took place in 1627, was among those helpless civilians who were unable to resist or evade the corsairs. Men, women, and children were taken on board the corsair ships that reached Algiers a month later, where the captives were sold on the slave market. Reverend Ólafur was separated from his family and then ordered to travel to Denmark to seek ransom money from King Christian IV of Denmark (1577–1648), sovereign over Iceland at the time. Reverend Ólafur traveled to Copenhagen via Livorno, Genoa, Marseilles, and Enkhuizen (Holland). However, his request for ransom money was declined by the king, who was in the midst of the Thirty Years' War (1618–1648). Fortunately, Reverend Ólafur's wife was ransomed in the 1635–1636 Danish ransom venture to Algiers, and they were reunited in 1637.[4] However, he never saw his children again.

---

3. It is commonly accepted that the Barbary corsair raid on Iceland in 1627 was a single coordinated attack led by the Dutch renegade Jan Janszoon van Haarlem, also known as Murat Reis. The Icelandic documents make it clear, however, that there were two separate sets of corsairs who descended upon Iceland in two separate raids, led by two separate commanders. Murat Reis ("Amóráð Reis" in the Icelandic documents) commanded the corsairs from Salé. Murate Flamenco ("Móráð Flaming" in the Icelandic documents) commanded those from Algiers. At the time of the raid, Murat Reis was admiral of the Salé corsairs; Murate Flamenco was one of the foremost corsair captains of Algiers. For Amóráð Reis, see Björn Jónsson, *Tyrkjaráns-Saga* (Reykjavík: í Prentsmiðju Íslands, 1866), 13, 15–16; for Móráð Flaming, see Jónsson, 32, 67.

4. *his wife was ransomed [. . .] 1637*: for details of the ransom paid for Reverend Ólafur's wife, whose name was Ásta Þorsteinsdóttir, see Jón Þorkelsson, ed., *Tyrkjaránið á Íslandi 1627* (Reykjavík: Prentsmiðjan Gutenberg, 1906–1909), 436. For her return to Iceland, see Þorkelsson, 5, 299.

The observations Reverend Ólafur made during his adventures appear unusually accurate and impartial. His descriptions of people, animals, and cities are those of a keen observer relatively uninterested in sensationalist exaggerations and distortions. Although he collectively vilifies the corsairs and describes how he himself is manhandled and brutally beaten by the "Turks," he follows the convention of depicting the renegades of European origin as the most remorseless adversaries. However, he also frequently mentions humane aspects of his captors, who appeared to be "quiet and well-tempered in their manner," and who "were even kind to the children" and, once in Algiers, provided the captives with ample food.[5]

Reverend Ólafur puts the *Tyrkjaránið*, or Turkish Raid—as the corsair attack came to be known in Iceland—in a clearly religious context, paralleling his fate with that of characters from scripture, particularly Job. All chapters are concluded by a theological formula or complemented by a biblical reference, frequently an incorrect one, most probably because Reverend Ólafur had no Bible at hand when he was writing. The *Tyrkjaránið* was such a severe shock to the Icelandic population that it has become deeply engrained in the Icelandic collective memory, where it has remained prominent to the present day.

The specific passages from the *Reisubók* in this anthology were selected because of their unique depictions of a land raid by Barbary corsairs. Reverend Ólafur's account is a rare testimony of this highly lucrative corsair practice, not uncommon in the early seventeenth century, which included similar incidents in Madeira in 1617 and Ireland in 1631,[6] during which hundreds of men, women, and children were abducted. Whereas anyone going to sea in the early modern period had to take into consideration the possibility of a corsair attack, the island population of a place as remote as Iceland was hardly prepared for such a confrontation.

---

5. Other narratives written by European captives in Algiers at this time display a similar combination of negative and (often grudgingly) positive assessments of North African corsairs. For an instructive comparison and contrast between Reverend Ólafur's observations and those of Emmanuel d'Aranda, see Toby Wikström, "Was There a Pan-European Orientalism? Icelandic and Flemish Perspectives on Captivity in Muslim North Africa (1628–1656)," in *The Dialectics of Orientalism in Early Modern Europe*, ed. Marcus Keller and Javier Irigoyen-García (London: Palgrave Macmillan, 2018), 155–70.

6. See Henry Barnby, "The Sack of Baltimore," *Journal of the Cork Historical and Archaeological Society* 74, no. 220 (1969): 101–29; Robert Pentland Mahaffy, ed., *Calendar of State Papers, Ireland, 1625–1632* (London: Eyre and Spottiswoode, 1900), 617.

Many letters, historical narratives, and other writings documenting the *Tyrkjaránið* have been preserved, indicating the Icelandic population's great need to process this event, both at the time and in later centuries. Also, Reverend Ólafur's narrative, which he wrote upon his return to Iceland in 1628, was copied numerous times during subsequent centuries and was widely distributed. The original manuscript, along with any early copies, are lost, and thus no manuscripts predating 1728 have survived. None of the extant manuscript copies or the printed Danish versions of the *Reisubók* reflect the original shape of Reverend Ólafur's manuscript accurately. This is why Karl Smári Hreinsson and Adam Nichols carefully constructed their translation using the most reliable sources from the late eighteenth and the early nineteenth century, including the Thott 514 manuscript and the recently discovered Skógar 1981 manuscript.[7]

Notes on the Present Translation of Ólafur Egilsson's *The Travels of Reverend Ólafur Egilsson*

The extracts from the *Reisubók* in this anthology are taken from: Karl S. Hreinsson and Adam Nichols, eds. and trans., *The Travels of Reverend Ólafur Egilsson: The Story of the Barbary Corsair Raid on Iceland in 1627* (Washington, DC: Catholic University of America Press, 2016).

Of Reverend Ólafur's original twenty-seven chapters, eight are included here: chapters 3, 4, 6 through 8, 10, 11, and 14 (all telling of the reverend's fate from the raid up to the point where he leaves Algiers for the European continent). His secondhand accounts of the fates of other captives as well as his description of the manners and customs of Algiers have been omitted. Omissions are marked with ellipses [. . .]. I wish to thank Karl S. Hreinsson, Adam Nichols, and Trevor Lipscombe for generously giving permission to reprint these sections here, as well as for Adam Nichols's input for the footnotes.

---

7. Manuscripts: Sighvatur Einarsson, *Reisubók séra Ólafs Egilssonar* (Skógar MS. Skógar Museum, Iceland); Hannes Pétursson, *Reisubók séra Ólafs Egilssonar* (MS Thott 514, Thott Collection, Copenhagen); *Reisubók séra Ólafs Egilssonar* (MS Landsbókasafn 153, National Archive of Iceland, Reykjavík); *Reisubók séra Ólafs Egilssonar* (MS Borealis 56, Bodleian Library, Oxford). Editions: Sverrir Krinstjánsson, *Reisubók séra Ólafs Egilssonar* (Reykjavík: Almenna Bókafélagið, 1969); Jón Þorkelsson, *Tyrkjaránið á Íslandi 1627* (Reykjavík: Prentsmiðjan Gutenberg, 1906–1909).

Ólafur Egilsson, *The Travels of Reverend Ólafur Egilsson: A Book by the Reverend Ólafur Egilsson, Who, with Others, Was Captured on the Westman Islands by Turkish Corsairs in the Year of our Lord 1627 but Returned to Iceland in 1628* (Four undated manuscripts)[8]

Translated by Karl Smári Hreinsson and Adam Nichols

Chapter 3: About the Preparations That Were Put into Effect when Word of the Pirates Was First Heard

When news of the pirates' approach first reached Grindavík[9] and southern Iceland, there were many grandiose words and much fearless boasting, not least by the Danish authorities.[10] A defensive rampart was built around the Danish merchant houses on the Westman Islands, and ships were prepared for defense. The Danes boasted that the Icelanders would all flee at the first sign of trouble.

Preparations stood like this until people heard that the pirates had gone away,[11] and that they no longer posed any threat to the Westman Islands. After that, people became careless, despite some warnings that had been given, and this went on until 16 July,[12] which was a Monday. Then people saw three ships early in the morning, off the south coast, one of which was very large. The ships headed toward Heimaey[13] but had a bad wind from the northwest and therefore were slow and had to make many a tack north and south all day long.

---

8. See note 7.
9. *Grindavík*: fishing town in southern Iceland.
10. *the Danish authorities*: Iceland was under Danish rule at the time.
11. *the pirates had gone away*: Reverend Ólafur is referring to the contingent of Salé corsairs who first made landfall at Grindavík on 20 June and who, after successfully raiding Grindavík and unsuccessfully assailing Bessastaðir, set sail again for Salé a little over a week later. They had therefore been gone for more than two weeks by the time the Algerian corsairs appeared at Heimaey.
12. *16 July* [1627]: Europe used the Julian calendar (introduced by Julius Caesar in 45 BCE) until the end of the sixteenth century, when the Gregorian calendar was officially adopted. Catholic countries switched to this new calendar fairly quickly. Protestant countries did not. Denmark only adopted the Gregorian calendar in 1700. Iceland was a Danish possession in Reverend Ólafur's day, so all the dates provided by him are Julian dates.
13. *Heimaey*: the largest of the Westman Islands off Iceland's south coast.

When the three ships were first seen that morning, all the people were called to the Danish merchant houses for defense and strongly prohibited from leaving. They stayed there all day until evening.

When night had come, however, the people went away, because the Danes began to say that they thought the three ships must be part of the defensive force that had been sent to protect Iceland.[14] Then all the people went back to their homes and laid aside their preparedness.

And so these servants of Satan, the father of all ungodliness, got their will.

As the Lord says, everything is mine that is under the sky. We are the Lord's. Job 41:11.[15]

Chapter 4: About the Evil Attacks and the Methods Used to Capture Some of the People

The next day, when the wind had dropped, the evil pirates[16] lowered three boats overboard—which they call *slúffur* and which are quite large—and very quickly put three hundred men into them and then rushed ashore. There were English fishermen[17] in these boats who guided the pirates to an unusual landing place[18] [at the south end of the island] where nobody in living memory had ever before managed to come ashore.

The pirates landed so suddenly that the people found it hard to escape. They rushed with violent speed across the island, like hunting hounds, howling like wolves, and the weak women and children could not escape, especially on the farms above the volcanic lava fields, because the pirates had a shorter way there. Only a few of the people who were strongest, or had nothing to carry, or did not pay attention to anybody else, managed to avoid capture. I, with my weak group, was quickly taken.

Some of my neighbors managed to escape quickly into the caves or down the cliffs, but many were seized and bound. Some were able to gain

---

14. *the defensive force [. . .] protect Iceland*: Reverend Ólafur is referring to the warships that the Danish Crown sent out each summer to patrol Icelandic waters. In the summer of 1627, the Danish fleet was late.

15. *Job 41:11*: "Who hath prevented me, that I should repay him? whatsoever is under the whole heaven is mine" (King James Version [hereafter KJV]).

16. *the evil pirates*: these were corsairs from Algiers.

17. *English fishermen*: after attacking the East Fjords, the Algerian corsairs sailed westward along Iceland's southern coast toward Heimaey. On the way, they captured an English fishing boat and forced some of the crew to serve as guides.

18. *unusual landing place*: a spot named Brimurð, near the southeast tip of the island of Heimaey.

their freedom again, but who, exactly, I cannot tell, for I and my poor wife were among the first to be captured.

We struggled for a long time, along with others, until we were beaten and struck with the butts of their spears and had to give in. I have since wondered that they did not kill us all with their beatings. I think most of those attacking us were English.[19]

We were then herded to the Danish merchant houses [at the harbor at the island's north end] and there put into the new house, where many other Icelanders were already imprisoned.

Of this, there is an example in Holy Scripture: Genesis 14.[20] And the women of Media with children: Numbers 21.[21]

Whatever happens, we are the Lord's.

[. . .]

Chapter 6: About How the People Were Treated by the Evil Men and Put into the Danish Fieldstone House, and Then Taken Forth and Placed on Board a Ship

On Tuesday, as those of us already captured sat in the Danish house where we had been driven, the evil pirates gathered together everyone else whom they had taken, and in that crowd I saw my children. It was by now midday. The three houses where we were kept could no longer contain all the people, so the pirates ordered us to stand on the pavement in front of the houses, where we were surrounded by those evil men.

When I came out of the house and saw their commander,[22] I went up to him with my poor wife, and we fell on our knees in despair in front of him and his under-captain and begged for mercy, but our begging did no good. When I saw their headgear, I knew that these pirates were Turkish.

---

19. *English*: these Englishmen would have been renegades (European Christians who had converted to Islam). There were many European renegades among the ranks of the Barbary corsairs at this time.

20. *Genesis 14*: in Genesis 14, Abraham's nephew Lot is taken captive.

21. *Numbers 21*: Reverend Ólafur was thinking of Numbers 31:9: "And the children of Israel took all the women of Midian captives, and their little ones, and took the spoil of all their cattle, and all their flocks, and all their goods" (KJV). Reverend Ólafur sometimes gets his biblical references wrong, probably because he did not have a Bible at hand when he was writing.

22. *their commander*: although Reverend Ólafur does not name him, this was Mórað Flaming.

Then all those taken prisoner who were considered to be in acceptable condition were transferred to the pirates' ship in two ten-oared boats. The Icelanders were ordered to row against a sharp easterly wind, and they were beaten and flogged with ropes. Then we were forced onto the pirates' biggest ship, which had lain there at anchor in the deepest part of the harbor and had never come near the shore. When the pirates on that ship saw us climb miserably aboard, they rejoiced. There were men on that ship already, in chains, who had been captured in the east of Iceland.[23] We expected that we too would be put in chains, but this did not happen. Instead, we were given bread to eat and water to drink (though the water was bad), and the other prisoners were released from their chains and also given bread, which they ate ravenously, because they had suffered from hunger until then. Then some of the evil pirates went back to the island to fetch more of those they had captured. Looking toward shore, we saw the Landakirkja church in flames.

A short time thereafter, I was called to the stern of the ship and commanded by the pirate captain to sit down. At once, two of the Turks took my hands and bound them tightly together while others bound my feet. The captain then beat me, striking and kicking me along my back while I screamed helplessly with the pain of it. I do not know how many blows he gave me, but he beat me as hard as he could until I was too hoarse to scream any longer. Then a man was brought forward who spoke German.[24] He asked me if I knew about any money that might be anywhere. I said forcefully that I knew of none and wanted only that they beat me to death quickly and have done. They left me alone then, raised me up, and ordered me back to the bow of the ship. I could hardly stand or walk, so badly had they hurt me. My fellow Icelanders had compassion for my miserable plight, but the evil pirates just laughed.

God tests his people, and as it is written: He wanted to humble you, to know what was in your heart. Deuteronomy 5.[25]

---

23. *captured in the east of Iceland*: before attacking Heimaey, the corsairs from Algiers had spent two weeks raiding southeastern Iceland, where they took more than one hundred captives.

24. *German*: although he never explicitly says so, Reverend Ólafur spoke German. Many educated Icelanders of his time did.

25. *Deuteronomy 5*: Reverend Ólafur is thinking of Deuteronomy 8:2: "And thou shalt remember all the way which the Lord thy God led thee these forty years in the wilderness, to humble thee, and to prove thee, to know what was in thine heart, whether thou wouldest keep his commandments, or no" (KJV).

Chapter 7: About Events in Preparation for Sailing

In the afternoon of that same day, the pirates brought more captives to their ships. They gave one man from the East Fjords his freedom, for he had a crippled hand. In the middle of the evening, we were taken belowdecks, where there were other prisoners, and given some food. That night each lay where he was, as best we could find the space.

On Wednesday morning, the pirates brought in still more people, and we saw smoke from the Danish houses, and they were said to be all afire in one great burning. It was then that I first heard the sorrowful news of the death of that man of God, Reverend Jón, and that his people were all taken.[26]

For the whole of that day, the evil pirates were continually coming and going from the ship, and on each trip they came with more wretched people as prisoners.

But so that you, honest reader, should know the truth, I must say that after the people came aboard the ship at this time, the pirates did not annoy anyone except me, but behaved well toward them all, and were even kind to the children—though this does not make the story any happier.

[. . .]

The most accurate reckoning of the number of Icelandic people killed is thirty-four. There were two hundred and forty-two people captured in all, and by Wednesday evening, all were aboard the Turkish ships.

Remember that suffering is part of this world and do not be discouraged.[27]

Believe that we are the Lord's.

Chapter 8: About Our Journey to Barbary and What Happened During That Voyage

On Thursday morning 19 July, about midmorning, the pirates weighed their anchors. These evil people made sail at the same time as the big ship that

---

26. *Reverend Jón [. . .] his people were all taken*: there were two parishes in Heimaey at this time: Reverend Ólafur ministered to one; Reverend Jón Þorsteinsson ministered to the other. Reverend Jón was murdered in a cave where he and his family had taken shelter. His wife and two children—a son and a daughter—were taken captive. In Icelandic history, Reverend Jón Þorsteinsson is often referred to as Reverend Jón the Martyr.

27. *Remember that suffering [. . .] do not be discouraged*: "And ye have forgotten the exhortation which speaketh unto you as unto children, My son, despise not thou the chastening of the Lord, nor faint when thou art rebuked of him" (Heb. 12:5, KJV).

lay off eastward. Then they saw the *Crab*—the ship they had captured from the Danes—leave the shore. When they had unreefed the sails, they shot off nine cannons and joined their little fleet of ships together. Then they set their course by Elliðaey Island[28] and then southward, and kept that course for three weeks, with the best, most direct fair wind they could wish for.

Now the ungodly shall perish suddenly, as is written.

When the poor Icelandic people saw their homeland disappearing behind them, there was much wailing and lamentation all that first day. When, finally, the wailing diminished, they tried to comfort each other in their plight with God's words, women as well as men, both young and old, because God had given these people true understanding about their salvation.

Praised should be the name of the Lord.

Though some people remained silent, many talked about the fate of others who had been led away into captivity and about how the Lord preserves His people in distress. For Him, nothing is impossible.

On the next Saturday thereafter, 21 July, people were fetched from one of the other Turkish ships and brought aboard the big one where I and my people were, among them the two Margréts and Jón Jónsson.[29] I and my wife and our children were separated from the other people and put in a place by ourselves, and some clothes were given us to lie on. The pirates made a place for us to sleep every night with an old sail and a big tent that they had stolen from the Westman Islands. As it was dark down in the hold where they imprisoned us, lamps burned day and night.

They gave us all food at mealtimes. They had stolen a barrel of beer and one of mead from the Westman Islands. As long as these lasted, they were given us to drink. The pirates had chopped up many of the wine and beer barrels in the Danish merchant houses and burned the rest. Most mornings, we got two bowls of spirit—of aqua vitae.[30] The Turks never drink anything other than water.

On 30 July, my poor wife gave birth, after the proper time, to a boy child who was named after the blessed Reverend Jón Þorsteinsson. God should always be thanked. I myself baptized the child as if we were back on land, but my heart was filled with grief.

---

28. *Elliðaey Island*: one of the Westman Islands off Iceland's south coast.

29. *the two Margréts and Jón Jónsson*: the wife and daughter (both named Margrét) and the son of Reverend Jón Þorsteinsson (who was murdered on Heimaey during the corsair attack).

30. *aqua vitae*: brandy.

When the evil pirates heard that a child had been born, and heard the child crying, they gathered in a crowd. Two of them gave old shirts to wrap the child in.

Have pity upon me, friends, because the hand of God has touched me.[31]

On that voyage, there was one of the pirates on our ship who washed himself normally every day in water. He was also washed by others during the month that we were traveling. The honest woman Margrét said that this pirate had killed her husband. All this washing could not make him clean, even though he might have held to the words of Moses, to wash clothes and bathe in water.[32]

But we believe that we are the Lord's.

[. . .]

Chapter 10: About How It Went (to the Best of My Knowledge) for the Good People Who Had Been Captured and Were Taken to Algiers

When the poor Icelandic people were put on land [in Algiers], such a huge crowd gathered that I think it was impossible to count their number. They did not come for any cruel purpose, but only to look at the poor captives. We Icelanders were separated from each other—friend from friend, children from their parents—and driven through the streets, from one house to another, to the marketplace where we were put up for auction as if we were sheep or cattle.

The people who had been captured in East Iceland were offered for sale first, the men being kept separate in some houses, the women in other houses. This went on until 28 August, by which time most of the East Icelanders were sold.

After that, the people from the Westman Islands were brought to the marketplace, which was a square built up of stones with seats encompassing it all around. The ground was paved with stones that appeared glossy—which I understand is because they were washed every day, as were the main

---

31. *Have pity [. . .] touched me:* "Have pity upon me, have pity upon me, O ye my friends; for the hand of God hath touched me" (Job 19:21, KJV).

32. *the words of Moses [. . .] water:* "And the Lord said unto Moses, Go unto the people, and sanctify them today and tomorrow, and let them wash their clothes" (Exod. 19:10, KJV).

houses, sometimes as much as three times a day. This marketplace was next to where their local king[33] had his seat, so that he would have the shortest way there, because, as I was told by those who had been there a long time (and were and are still Christians), their laws concerning the sharing out of captives were as follows.

First and foremost, the captain got to have whichever two of the captives he wanted. Then their king (if I may call him that) took every eighth man, every eighth woman, every eighth boy, and then every eighth child. When he had taken these, the people who remained were divided into two groups, one for the shipowners and one for the pirates themselves.

We poor Westman Islanders were taken to the marketplace in groups, each of thirty. The Turks guarded each group in front and behind and counted heads at each street corner, because the inhabitants of that place will steal such captive people if they get the chance.

When we came to the marketplace, we were placed in a circle, and everyone's hands and face were inspected. Then the king chose those whom he wanted from this group, every eighth, as I mentioned earlier.[34] His first choice among the boys was my own poor son, eleven years old, whom I will never forget as long as I live because of the depth of his understanding and knowledge. When he was taken from me, I asked him in God's name not to forsake his faith or forget his catechism. He said with great grief, "I will not, my father! They can treat my body as they will, but my soul I shall keep for my good God."[35]

I have to say with Job: What is my strength, that I should hope?[36] Were one to try to weigh my misery and suffering all together on a scale, they would be heavier than all the sand in the sea.[37]

---

33. *local king*: the Ottoman governor of the city, commonly known as the *basha*.

34. *Then the king [. . .] mentioned earlier*: Reverend Ólafur's description of the process of selling captives in Algiers differs from that of other European writers of the time. In the reverend's account, the captives were taken to the slave market, where the basha went to examine them and make his choices. Other writers make it clear that newly arrived captives were first taken to the basha's residence, where he chose those he wanted, and only after that they were taken to the slave market to be auctioned off to the general public. Exactly why Reverend Ólafur should be confused about this is unclear.

35. Reverend Ólafur never saw his son again. This brief exchange between them was the last contact they ever had. According to Björn Jónsson, Reverend Ólafur's son ended up in Tunis. See Björn Jónsson, *Tyrkjaráns-Saga* (Reykjavík: í Prentsmiðju Íslands, 1866), 68.

36. *What is my strength, that I should hope?*: Job 6:11, KJV.

37. *Were one to try and weight [. . .] the sand in the sea*: "Oh that my grief were thoroughly weighed, and my calamity laid in the balances together! For now it would be heavier than the sand of the sea: therefore my words are swallowed up" (Job 6:2–3, KJV).

The other Icelanders were moved from there to another place, and one of the Turks led two groups of ten around a stone column with loud screaming that I did not understand. I and my wife and our two younger children, a one-year-old and a one-month-old, were taken from that place up to the king's hall,[38] and there we sat with the children in our arms for two hours. From there, we were then taken to the king's prison, where we spent that night. From that time on, I do not know what became of the rest of the Icelandic people.

Ah! I would like to comfort and strengthen the people with my words, but I cannot. And whether I speak of such things or not, my suffering does not lessen.

Whatever happens, we are the Lord's.

Chapter 11: About What Happened to Me and My Family Thereafter

The next day, around midday, there came two captains, one German and one Norwegian, who were also captives, who said they were supposed to fetch us. Carrying the young children, my wife and I followed them for a long distance through many streets until we came into the house of one of the Turkish chieftains. At once, the younger child was given clothes and a cradle. Also, my wife was given clothing after their custom, and we were given food, though I was not allowed to eat with her.

To tell the truth, we captives were given ample food. Evenings and mornings, we had bread warm from the oven and good porridge groats with fat[39] put into it, and as much as we could want of apples and grapes. What was left in the evening of the bread was given to the horses in the morning, but the porridge was either thrown over the wall or—if I may say so—down into the privy. Nothing else was given us to drink other than lukewarm, brackish water.

Straight after the meal at this chieftain's house, I was taken away to another house where I had to wander alone all that day until night, when those who lived there came home. They were soldiers of the chieftain in

---

38. *the king's hall*: the basha's (the Ottoman governor's) palace.

39. *porridge groats with fat*: Reverend Ólafur seems to be referring to couscous and butter, a traditional Algerian dish.

whose house my wife and children were kept. I stayed in that place for three or four days. Thereafter I was taken a long way from there to a house where two men from the Westman Islands were already kept, Jesper Christiensson and Jón Þorsteinsson, a blacksmith. We all three were kept there, as if in prison, and watched.

Two or three days later, I was brought in front of some of the Turks of the highest rank, apart from the king, and by them commanded to go and seek money from my gracious sovereign, King Christian of Denmark, to ransom my wife and my children, who were with their mother. The Turks demanded a total of twelve hundred dalers which they call "Stück von achten."[40] Upon this, I had to kiss their hands.

Then I was returned to the same house to which I had originally been brought. I could walk freely there now within the confines of the walls[41]—which I and Jesper did—but I could not visit my wife and children except very seldom, even though I very much wanted to see them.

Oh misery upon misery! I want to say, as did David: The Lord will lift up my head and smite the enemies that surround me.[42]

[. . .]

Chapter 14: About How I Was Driven from Algiers and How Things Went on My Miserable Travels

On 20 September, I was taken from the house where I was imprisoned by four men and brought to the street where the house containing my wife and babies was located. I begged the men who had fetched me with all humbleness and prayer that I might be allowed to say goodbye to my wife and the children who were with her, all of whom were deadly ill.

---

40. *dalers [. . .] "Stück von achten"*: the "daler" mentioned here is the Danish rigsdaler, which was the standard silver coin in use in Denmark at this time. As Reverend Ólafur notes, the rigsdaler was equivalent in value to a Spanish coin known as a "piece of eight" ("Stück von achten").

41. *I could walk [. . .] walls*: houses in Algiers during this period had inner courtyards surrounded by walls that formed the outer structure of the house. Reverend Ólafur likely means here that he was allowed to walk about within the courtyard inside the walls of the house where he was being held.

42. *The Lord [. . .] enemies that surround me*: Reverend Ólafur may be referring to Psalms 27:6: "And now shall mine head be lifted up above mine enemies round about me [. . .]" (KJV) and Psalms 3:7: "[. . .] thou hast smitten all mine enemies upon the cheek bone; thou hast broken the teeth of the ungodly" (KJV).

I was hardly allowed ten words with them, however, and then my captors callously pulled me away. Oh, distress upon distress:

To lose both babies and wife
makes one despair,
but the returns into eternal life
all separations repair.

Now, in the name of Jesus, the Lord says: "I am the one who made thee, and formed thee from the womb, and I will pour my spirit upon thy seed and my blessings on thine offspring. Be not afraid." Isaiah: 44.[43]

After this painful meeting with my family, I was taken to the street where the official who was to issue me a safe-conduct lived. I was to give this safe-conduct, written in many different languages, to any Turkish pirates who might capture a ship on which I was a passenger. The document explained that I should neither be killed nor interfered with because I was acting as a messenger. I still have this document and have shown it to several people, including the archbishop of Copenhagen.

In order to receive this safe-conduct, I had to kiss the pirates' hands again. That same day, I was put aboard an Italian ship.[44]

---

43. *Isaiah: 44:* "Thus saith the Lord that made thee, and formed thee from the womb, which will help thee; Fear not, O Jacob, my servant; and thou, Jesurun, whom I have chosen. For I will pour water upon him that is thirsty, and floods upon the dry ground: I will pour my spirit upon thy seed, and my blessing upon thine offspring" (Isa. 44:2–3, KJV).

44. Reverend Ólafur's request for ransom money was declined by King Christian IV of Denmark (1577–1648), who was occupied with the Thirty Years' War. His wife was ransomed in 1636 as part of a Danish ransom venture to Algiers. However, it appears that he never saw his children again.

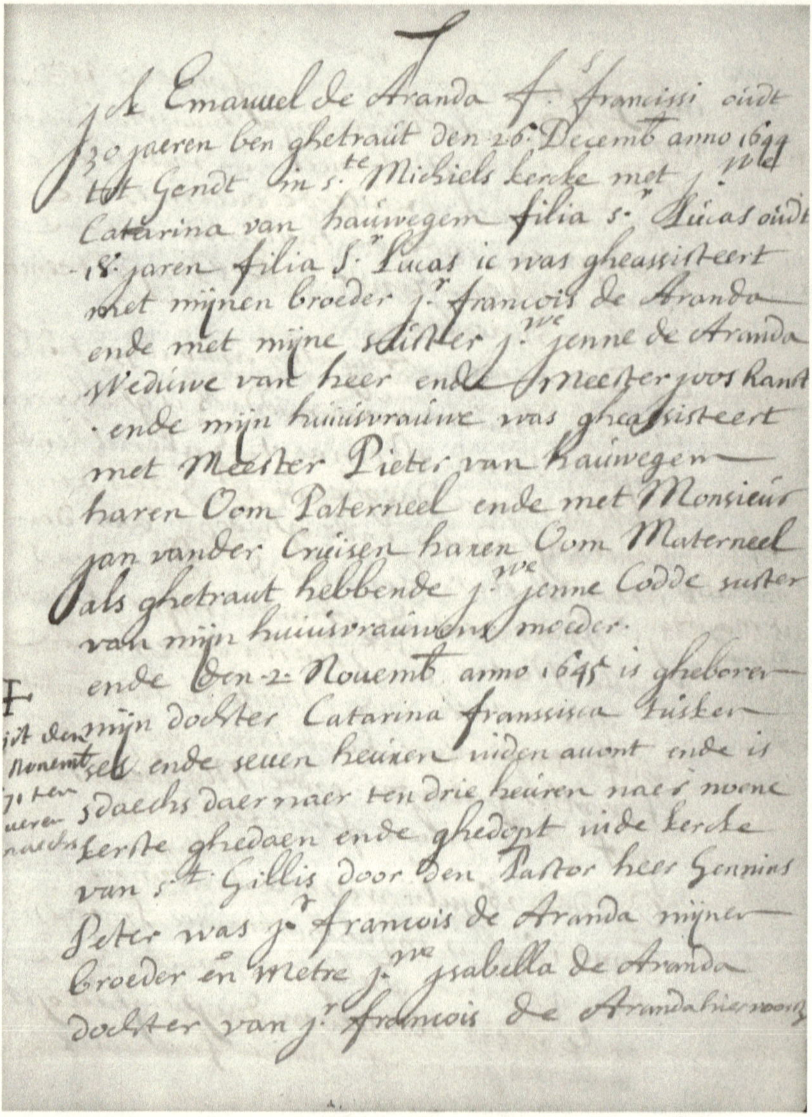

Jck Emanuel de Aranda f. francissi oudt
30 jaeren ben ghetrauwt den 26. Decemb anno 1644
tot Gendt in s.te Michiels kercke met j.ue
Catarina van hauwegem filia s.r Lucas oudt
18 jaren filia S.r Lucas ic was gheassisteert
met mijnen broeder j.r francois de Aranda
ende met mijne suster j.ue jenne de Aranda
weduwe van heer ende Mr Meester joos kant
ende mijn huijsvrauwe was gheassisteert
met Meester Pieter van hauwegen
haren Oom Paterneel ende met Monsieur
jan vander Cruisen haren Oom Materneel
als ghetrauwt hebbende j.ue jenne Codde suster
van mijn huijsvrauwens moeder.
ende den 2 Nouemb anno 1645 is ghebooren
mijn dochter Catarina franssisca tusschen
ses ende seuen heuren inden auont ende is
sdaechs daernaer ten drie heuren naer noene
kerstene ghedaen ende ghedoopt inde kercke
van s.t Gillis door den Pastor heer Gennins
Peter was j.r francois de Aranda mijnen
broeder en Metre j.ue Jsabella de Aranda
dochter van j.r francois de Aranda hiervoorn

Figure 4.1 A page from Emanuel d'Aranda's autograph manuscript
Source: Emanuel d'Aranda, *Relation de la Captivité en Algérie de Emmanuel de Aranda 1640.1642.* (n. d.), fol. 1; Castle Van Loppem Foundation, West Flanders, Belgium.

CHAPTER IV

EMANUEL D'ARANDA, *SHORT STORY OF MY UNFORTUNATE JOURNEY*

Undated Dutch manuscript; complete captivity narrative

Captivity in Algiers 1640–1642

For most printed Barbary captivity narratives, it is close to impossible to gauge the degree to which editors, translators, and publishers influenced or shaped the text. A major exception to this rule is Emanuel d'Aranda's[1] seventeenth-century account, one of the most popular printed specimens of the genre. A surviving autograph manuscript in d'Aranda's own hand, presented here in English translation for the first time, provides readers with a privileged insight into d'Aranda's original authorial intentions, unaltered by editorial interventions.

In 1640, while on a voyage to Spain, the Flemish nobleman Emanuel d'Aranda was taken captive by corsairs, transported to Algiers, and released after one and a half years of captivity in exchange for North African slaves who were in European hands. Emanuel d'Aranda's account became the most popular Barbary captivity narrative of the seventeenth century. Being widely available across Europe in numerous editions and translations, it soon became an almost prototypical slave narrative: It opens with a short prologue about the sea voyage that leads relatively quickly to a grippingly portrayed pirate attack and subsequently describes the sale of the first-person narrator at a slave market in North Africa. Episodes of day-to-day life in North

---

1. *Emanuel d'Aranda*: other variants of d'Aranda's name include Emanuel de Aranda, Emmanuel de Aranda, and Jac Emanuel de Aranda.

African captivity, the diplomatic efforts leading up to the release of the captive in 1641, and his return home in 1642 make up the rest of the narrative.

D'Aranda's text in no way presents an exception to standard Barbary captivity narratives. On the contrary, its content and choice of topics makes it a typical example of the genre. However, d'Aranda's narrative stands out from other European slave accounts set in North Africa through the marketable treatment of its subject matter, which makes the text easily comprehensible for the general reader. This includes clear explanations of nautical concepts and descriptions of Algiers, including its economy based on slavery and piracy. The simplicity of the depictions extends like a guiding principle throughout d'Aranda's account. Further narrative elements with audience appeal also come into play, for example, the manner in which the nobleman Emanuel d'Aranda tries to lead his owner astray by passing himself off as a simple soldier in order to keep the ransom demand as low as possible. The easily comprehensible and gripping narrative style, d'Aranda's own character (which is sometimes reminiscent of figures in picaresque novels), and the background information about North Africa and Algiers made d'Aranda's text probably the most successful and widely distributed North African slave account written by a European. Shortly after its composition, d'Aranda's testimony appeared in French, English, and German print publications.

What makes d'Aranda's text singular is the fact that it was so popular in such a wide array of countries despite political, cultural, and religious barriers. The Catholic d'Aranda managed to fascinate Protestant audiences just as much as his Catholic readership. This is all the more remarkable given that d'Aranda's text appeared in the second half of the seventeenth century, at the tail end of the greatest intra-Christian conflict, that is, the Thirty Years' War (1618–1648). Against this backdrop, a "crossover" voice like d'Aranda's is unexpected and presents a unique testimony to the translation work done in the early modern era that bridged not only linguistic, but also political and religious barriers.

However, what distinguishes d'Aranda's text more than anything else—above and beyond the fact that it was made accessible to a surprisingly diverse European public through numerous translations and editions—is that the original manuscript of the slave account composed in d'Aranda's own hand is still extant. A few years ago, this manuscript surfaced at an auction and is now in the possession of the Caloen family, the descendants of one of Emanuel d'Aranda's companions during his captivity.[2] In this anthology, the best-selling captivity narrative of the Flemish nobleman Emanuel d'Aranda about his experiences in the early 1640s is made accessible for the very first time through a translation of his autograph manuscript. The manuscript in d'Aranda's own hand documents the author's original intentions, before publishers, editors, or translators could alter the narrative for their specific marketing purposes (see fig. 4).

The bound autograph manuscript includes the 138-page captivity account in a clearly legible script, written in the same hand as the short 13-page family chronicle that precedes the captivity narrative proper. With the exception of the title—*Relation de la Captivité en Algérie de Emmanuel de Aranda 1640.1642*—both the narrative and the preliminary sections are entirely rendered in Dutch. The family chronicle records births, baptisms, and marriages from 1644 to 1684 in the same handwriting as the captivity narrative, so it is very likely that this is, in fact, an autograph manuscript by Emanuel d'Aranda himself. This is also corroborated by the fact that the last entry in the manuscript dates from 1686, the year of Emanuel d'Aranda's death.[3]

D'Aranda's autograph is a singular textual witness to the original intention of the author and how this authorial intention differs, in some circumstances, from published versions, that is, those edited by printers and publishers. As a result, it is possible to reconstruct, via the original manuscript, an extremely vivid picture of the appropriation of personal, autobiographical reports during the early modern period through comparison with the different published or translated versions. In contrast to d'Aranda's surviving handwritten autograph, the printed d'Aranda accounts in Dutch, French, German, and English contain, in addition to the slave narrative proper, several dozen "relations." These vignette-like episodes or scenes of a few paragraphs' length on all kinds of topics relating to piracy and slavery differ very starkly in the respective print versions and are missing entirely from the handwritten manuscript. The extant autograph manuscript allows for a rare case study of early modern publishing practices. It brings to light the commercialization of eyewitness reports before the great breakthrough of the novel as a genre.

2. Lisa F. Kattenberg, "The Free Slave: Morality, Neostoicism, and Publishing Strategy in Emanuel d'Aranda's *Algiers and It's Slavery* (1640–82)," in *Mediterranean Slavery and World Literature: Captivity Genres from Cervantes to Rousseau*, ed. Mario Klarer (London: Routledge, 2019), 152–74.

3. Kattenberg, "The Free Slave," 156.

Notes on the present translation of Emanuel d'Aranda's *Short Story of My Unfortunate Journey*

This translation is based on the undated autograph manuscript: Emanuel d'Aranda, *Relation de la Captivité en Algérie de Emmanuel de Aranda 1640.1642* (n.d., MS, Castle Van Loppem Foundation, West Flanders, Belgium).

Instead of the French title given on the front page of the bound manuscript, this translation uses d'Aranda's own title, which he provides directly before the start of his captivity account: *Kort verhael van mijne ongeluckighe reyse, doen ic ghevangen wiert, van de teurcken. en van het geene ic inde slaevernie ghepasseert hebbe. ende op wat maniere dat ic wederomme mijne liberteyt verkregen hebbe (by my jac Emanuel de Aranda)*.

The present edition does not include the thirteen unnumbered pages of genealogy that precede the actual narrative. The Barbary narrative proper is translated in its entirety, that is, from the numbered pages 1 to 138 of the original autograph manuscript. The numbers in brackets {} in the text always indicate the beginning of a page and refer to the original page numbers of the manuscript. Punctuation has been standardized, and paragraph breaks have been added in order to enhance the readability of the narrative.

The Castle Van Loppem Foundation is in possession of the manuscript. The castle is in the vicinity of Bruges and was built in the nineteenth century by Charles van Caloen, a descendent of d'Aranda's travel companion, Jean-Baptiste van Caloen, who is also mentioned in the captivity narrative. I have to thank the Caloen Foundation, in particular its curator, Véronique van Caloen, for providing me with scans of the manuscript, as well as for allowing me to transcribe the Dutch original and to produce an English translation of this unique document. Thanks also go to Frederiek ten Broeke, who did the first transcription of this manuscript and provided input for the translation.

Emanuel d'Aranda, *Short Story of My Unfortunate Journey, during Which I Was Captured by the Turks, of My Experiences during Slavery, and of How I Regained My Freedom (by Me, Jac Emanuel de Aranda)* (Undated manuscript, Castle Van Loppem Foundation, West Flanders, Belgium)

Translated by Almiria Wilhelm

{1} Having lived in Spain for a year, and having satisfied my curiosity to see the country and learn the language, I decided to travel to the Netherlands. Because I had, on the way to Spain, taken the route past Sanlúcar, during which trip I had been in great danger of being captured by the Turks,[4] I decided to return via San Sebastián: first, thus to avoid the dangers of the seas as much as possible, and second, to see Castilla la Vieja and Biscay. Acting upon this decision, I departed from Madrid on 1 August 1640 and arrived in San Sebastián on 14 August. Here, I found two English ships waiting to set sail with the first fair wind. As the wind turned that same night, I embarked {2} on the following day, which was 14 August,[5] and we left with this fair wind.

Our cargo consisted of wool, iron, and patacons.[6] We had barely sailed a mile into the sea when the wind fell. It proved contrary the next day also, so we were forced to laveer,[7] waiting for the wind to turn favorable. After traveling for four days, we found ourselves at the latitude of La Rochelle, where we met with a French pirate frigate, which had set sail from La Rochelle. This frigate observed us from afar. Having seen that we were English ships, it came within firing range, and the captain of the frigate sent out a boat with three or four soldiers to inspect our ship from the inside and to examine our captain's passports, which he showed them. [Our captain] also gave them a tip in the end (which {3} happens at sea, as it does on land; if, despite being in possession of a passport, one nevertheless meets soldiers on the way, one

---

4. *Turks*: D'Aranda uses this term to refer to a broader group of largely Ottoman and Arabic people from North African countries surrounding the Mediterranean Sea. It has been translated literally into English from the term used in the manuscript ("Teurcken").

5. *the following day, which was 14 August*: the manuscript reads "tsanderdaechs," meaning "the following day." D'Aranda's use of dates does not make sense here, since "the following day" should be 15 August. The 1666 English print edition corrects this mistake by making 13 August his arrival date.

6. *patacons*: while this was one of the many names given to the Spanish silver peso, it was also used for a Dutch silver coin that was much in use in the Spanish Netherlands. See Wiert Jan Wieringa, *The Interactions of Amsterdam and Antwerp with the Baltic Region, 1400–1800* (Dordrecht, Netherlands: Springer, 2013), 16.

7. *laveer*: nautical term meaning to sail against the wind.

gives them a tip). After these soldiers had visited our ship, they informed their captain that they had seen our captain's passport and that he was free to leave. Hereupon the frigate departed and her captain cried out to our captain to stay on guard, since Turkish pirates were present at the mouth of the English Channel (but our captain relied on his king's power, because the ships of the English king sometimes sail to the end of the Channel to clear it of the Turks). He considered neither the great danger nor his own vulnerability but sought to continue his voyage, for he thought it impossible {4} that the Turks would dare to venture this far. The wind continued to prove contrary, so we laveered, barely making progress.

It had now been seven days since we left San Sebastián and we were still only at the coast of Brittany in France. On the same day, at two o'clock in the afternoon, we saw two ships. Believing them to be merchant ships, we sailed toward them instantly, and then we saw but one [merchant ship], which was the smaller one. And, as we noticed, it came straight toward us. As soon as our captain became aware of this, he ordered the sails taken in, so that our ship would slow down, for he said that it was not the English custom to flee. Since our sails were being taken in while {5} the ship that followed us was under full sail, it rapidly came so near to us that we could easily see that it was a caravel.[8] It did not fly its flag (which is very suspicious at sea), but as our captain had little experience, he immediately ordered a boat to be put out to sea to ask who they were, believing it to be a French or Dunkirk privateer.[9] The Turks who were in the caravel (as we heard afterward) saw that we expected them and had put a boat out to sea, all of which are normal things to do when a fight is intended. Mistaking the inexperience of our captain for cunning and the desire to fight, {6} the captain of the caravel ordered his men to take in the sails immediately, so that he would not come closer to us. In the meantime, night fell, but despite this, the caravel stayed in sight and installed a lantern at her stern. We saw clearly that the lantern served as a signal to any ships in her company. We pointed this out to our captain, but to no avail. All we could get from him with our fair words was that we should ready our ship in order to be able to defend ourselves somewhat, and with these preparations we spent the night.

8. *caravel*: a light, fast sailing ship much in use in the Mediterranean and beyond from the fifteenth to the seventeenth century.
9. *Dunkirk privateer*: privateers in the service of the Spanish Empire operating from Flemish ports, including Dunkirk, which was under Spanish rule at the time.

Of the four cannon pieces that were aboard, {7} there was only one that we could use properly. All this happened with our sails taken in, so that neither we nor the caravel could do anything but keep each other in sight. Having passed the night in this manner, it was now about five o'clock in the morning (being 22 August) when we discovered two large ships sailing toward us. We begged our captain to use the sails, but he remained obstinate. Each of us gave our opinion, but this was useless. At about ten o'clock in the morning, the two large ships joined the caravel without showing their flags. They came so close to our side that they were within firing range {8} and then they let Turkish flags fly from the sterns of their ships. A Christian slave who was aboard the largest ship cried out in Flemish: "Strike for Algiers"[10] (one can imagine how pleased we were to hear this). We proposed to our captain to offer them the thirty-two thousand patacons[11] we had on board on the condition that they would first set us ashore on the nearest Christian land, for it sometimes happens that when the Turks capture a ship by treaty, they put the Christians ashore on Christian land. But our captain only asked whether they had good accommodation for him, whereupon the Turks immediately answered that they did. Without further ado he jumped on a boat with two {9} or three of his shipmates, rowed to the Turkish ships, and gave himself up to his enemies.

The Turkish soldiers, eager to plunder, immediately came with their boat and boarded our ship. The captain of one of the Turkish ships came aboard first. He was a renegade[12] and an Englishman by birth. He immediately asked me where I was from and whether I was a merchant. I answered that I was a Dunkirker and a soldier by profession.[13] He answered in Flemish, "Have patience, brother. This is the fortune of war; today for you, tomorrow for me." I gave this captain the money I carried with me. Immediately, another Turk came {10} and stuck his hand in my pocket. He took out my case, my handkerchief, my rosary beads,[14] and my church books.

---

10. *"Strike for Algiers"*: d'Aranda is probably referring to one of the two following maritime expressions: "to strike sail," meaning to lower the topsails as a sign of submission or respect; alternatively, "to strike colors," meaning to lower the flag ("colors") as a sign of surrender at sea.

11. *thirty-two thousand patacons*: this is quite an impressive amount of money; later, on p. 19 of the manuscript, we learn that d'Aranda was sold on the slave market in Algiers for 220 patacons.

12. *renegade*: in the manuscript, d'Aranda uses the term "verlogende Christen" ("heretical Christian") to refer to renegades (Christians who had converted to Islam).

13. *Dunkirker [. . .] soldier by profession*: d'Aranda disguises his real identity as a nobleman to avoid astronomical ransom demands. Dunkirk is a historically contested area in modern-day northern France. In 1640, it was part of the Spanish Netherlands.

14. *rosary beads*: this is one of the few references to d'Aranda's Catholicism.

He returned the latter with my handkerchief, but he kept my case, by reason of which he said I was a barber.[15]

Having plundered the deck and the deckhouse of the ship, they took us to one of their ships by boat, leaving a dozen Turks to manage the ship they had captured from us. Since the wind was easterly, they turned immediately toward the Spanish coast. After sailing for two days, we saw the North Cape of Galicia, also called *finis terre*.[16] Until now I had felt like someone deep in a dream, seeing strange apparitions, {11} noticing the different languages, the strange clothing, and the superstitious ways of praying. But since sadness would not find me any food, which my hungry stomach was now demanding, I joined four Christian slaves who had become companions. Although they only got some ship's biscuit from the Turks, they sometimes made pottage[17] from rice or from something else that they had brought with them onto the ship from ashore. Note: these were slaves who had come from Algiers with the Turkish ship, because the Turks use Christian slaves as sailors on their ships.[18]

The wind continued to be {12} favorable. It was now eleven days since we had been captured. We got to a passage that is called the Strait of Gibraltar. In this passage, the Turks typically perform a lot of superstitious ceremonies such as throwing a little can filled with oil into the sea, believing that this can will make its way to a nearby mountain, which the seafaring people call the "monkey mountain."[19] The Turks believe a marabout[20]—a holy man—lives there, who, so they say, is nourished by the oil the people throw into the sea in his honor. Furthermore, in honor of this holy man, they put little wax candles on the guns while they sail through the passage, which is done {13} with much ceremony and prayer.

On the third day after passing through the Strait of Gibraltar, we arrived at the city of Algiers in the morning. The captain of our ship ordered the guns to be fired as a sign of victory, and the shots brought all the curious people in the city to the shore. I had slept chained to the other newly captured slaves that night. The ship had already cast anchor when we were

15. *barber*: d'Aranda uses the term "Barbier" in the manuscript. In the seventeenth century, this term could also be used to refer to a surgeon.

16. *finis terre*: Cape Finisterre on the west coast of Galicia, Spain.

17. *pottage*: a thick soup or stew, typically made from vegetables, pulses, meat, etc.

18. *Note [. . .] ships*: this is a note d'Aranda provides in the manuscript text itself.

19. *"monkey mountain"*: the Rock of Gibraltar is still famous today for its wild population of Barbary macaques.

20. *marabout*: a Muslim holy man.

finally cut loose. As soon as I was set free, I went up to the deck of the ship and I saw that the seaside was full of *Alarbes*, or Saracens[21] as we say in Flemish. I asked the captain what kind of people they were. He answered {14} that they were poor people and farmers, for they wore nothing but two or three ells of white cloth, which covered their limbs like serge.[22]

Here, our tragedy begins. The owners of the ships that had captured us now brought us new slaves ashore. They conducted us to the market where the Christians are sold, to see if anyone there knew us.[23] From there, they led us to the house of the *basha*[24] (that is the governor, although some called him king, because he was the viceroy of the Kingdom of Algiers), so that he would receive his share, which was one out of every eight Christian slaves. This basha sat in a room of his palace with his legs crossed (in the same way that tailors here are seated), on a large seat covered with blue tapestry. {15} He had a fan of feathers in his hand and he was dressed in a long gown made of red silk. He wore a turban on his head. Before we were brought to him, he had been informed that Vlamertinghe was a rich nobleman, and so he chose him as his share. This was a great misfortune for both of them, because the aforementioned Vlamertinghe, though a nobleman, was not wealthy, which the basha would not believe, demanding a large ransom.

After we had been to the basha's palace, we were brought to the house of an honorable Turk who owned the ships that had captured us. As we entered his house, he asked us in Italian whether we had eaten anything that day, whereupon we answered that we had not. {16} He immediately ordered a basket of bread and grapes to be brought to us. We stayed in this house for eight days, until some other Christian slaves, who had been taken before us, were sold. In the meantime, we slept on the stones in the gallery of this house. We were not allowed to leave. Some Dutch slaves sometimes came to bring us stolen goods, though we did not look for them very much, as we had already been informed that one Christian slave often betrays the other in order to receive the goodwill of his masters. Alli Pegelin and another honorable Turk came to visit us in order to find out if anyone of us had the

---

21. *Alarbes, or Saracens*: "Alarbes" refers to Arabs. "Saracens" refers to the Arabic people of the Levant; "Sarasinen" in the manuscript.

22. *serge*: strong woolen fabric.

23. *if anyone there knew us*: d'Aranda is most probably referring to the practice of bribing existing slaves into teasing out information about the newcomers' true identity to gauge their ransom value.

24. *basha*: a term used for high-ranking officials in North Africa as well as for the governor of a city. In August 1640, the ruler of Algiers was Abu Djamal Youssef Pasha (ruled 1640–1642). "Bassa" in the manuscript.

money {17} to pay our ransom. We insisted that we had no hope of getting any ransom, except what good people would grant us through alms.

It was now 12 September. The Christians who had been captured before us (as I mentioned before) had now been sold. Therefore, we were led once more to the market where the Christians are sold. An old crier, who walked with a staff because of his age, took me by the arm. He led me across the market several times and the people who were interested in buying me asked what country I came from, what my name was, and what my profession was. To all of this I answered {18} with deliberate lies. I said that I was born in the land of Dunkirk, that I was called Jacques van Zevere, and that I was a soldier by profession. They looked at my teeth and checked whether I had any sores on my hands caused by hard labor. Then they had us sit on the ground in two rows and the crier took the first in line and led him through the market three or four times, crying, "*Arrache*," which means in Turkish, "Who offers more?" The first one sold was placed on the other side of the market, starting a new row. While one after the other was being sold, I sat on the ground between Jonker Jan Baptiste van Caloen and Reynier Saldens. {19} Notwithstanding the sadness we found ourselves in, Reynier said with great patience, "There is a fair in my village at Coelscamp today. If we were there, we would be eating waffles with our friends." I answered, "We are at a lovely fair here too." I had barely said this when the crier grabbed me by my sleeve and led me as he had done with the men before me, calling, "Arrache, arrache." I heard several Turks bidding, yet could not understand how much they offered, so I asked a Christian slave who understood their language how much they were offering, and he told me, "This one offers one hundred and ninety patacons, that one two hundred." The last one offered two hundred and twenty patacons, whereupon {20} the sale was concluded. The man who bought me was a renegade called Saban Galan.

As the basha has the right to rebid, we were once more led before him and he was told what price each one had been sold for. He took three of us, namely Jonker Jan Baptiste van Caloen, Saldens, and myself, for the same price that we had been sold for. He told us that he was well informed that we were rich noblemen, but notwithstanding our noble backgrounds, he sent us to the stables of his palace. Here we found ourselves in the company of about two hundred and fifty Christian slaves, whom he used as rowers in his galleys. We remained here for twenty-one days without being allowed to go out. We were given two loaves of bread every day.

{21} It was now the end of September, at which time the galleys make their last journey of the year. The slaves each made what provisions they could. By order of the basha, each slave was given five ells of linen cloth. I received my share, which at that time proved useful to make a shirt, for the shirt I had was full of lice. The day the galley had to leave, six or seven young barbers came to the stables we resided in to shave the beards and heads of all the slaves, as is the custom on the galleys. When all this shaving was done, the captain of the galley and the basha's steward came and brought all the slaves out of the stables and into {22} a large courtyard in order to choose the slaves they needed to row the basha's galleys. We, as new slaves, were very anxious. Thank God they passed us, saying that they would still keep us (because we had only been captured very recently). The basha's galley departed, accompanied by three other galleys. In the meantime, we stayed in the stables with the sick slaves who had not boarded the galley. The basha now believed that he had been informed of the truth—that we were neither noblemen nor rich, as he, being greedy for profit, had believed. He had us brought to the hall of his palace once more, where Alli Pegelin was present, who told us in Spanish, "Christians, I bought you {23} from the basha, but at a very high cost" (this Alli Pegelin was a general of the galleys). He sent us immediately to his house, together with a few Jews who were present there. There we found around forty Christian boys of all nations, whom he keeps in his house for his magnificence. There were also twenty Christian female slaves to serve his wives, but these slaves were rarely seen, because they were always kept at home. In addition, there were another ten to twelve Christian slaves to do the housework. But we were immediately sent to the *bagnio*,[25] which is to say a place or prison where the galley slaves live.

This bagnio was a street at his house, accessed by a narrow door. Upon entering, one came immediately, {24} after five or six steps, into a spacious vault that received light through bars from above, but so little that lamps were necessary even in the afternoon. In this vault, there were as many as twenty taverns owned by Christian slaves. Most of the Turks come here to drink. *Faciunt peccat nefandum.*[26] In this bagnio, we were five hundred and fifty Christian slaves all belonging to one master—the abovementioned Alli Pegelin. He did not give sustenance to any of these slaves. The only consolation we had was that we were given three or four hours a day to search for sustenance.

---

25. *bagnio*: the prison or slave quarters where the slaves lived.
26. *Faciunt peccat nefandum*: "They commit an unnamable sin." Islam forbids the consumption of alcohol.

Some of the slaves own taverns, others serve in the taverns, still others steal or team up with four or five men to steal purses. {25} Others earn a living by trading.[27] In the bagnio there is a table for trading, a part of [whose proceeds] are donated to the church to assist the sick Christians. The priests who live as slaves and stay in the bagnio fare very well with everything they receive from charity. One can observe from this that God never leaves those who belong to Him. I can say that in the twenty months that I was there, I never saw any priest in poverty—that is to say, with any lack of food, drink, or clothing. And it rarely occurs in Algiers that priests have to work. Usually, the priests reach an agreement with their owners for two or three patacons a month. Then they start living in the bagnios, where the churches are, for the Roman Catholic religion is {26} publicly practiced in four different churches.

I will move on from the description of the bagnio and turn to my personal experiences. On the first night after arriving in this new lodging, I worried about where to sleep. As I did not know anyone, I took my coverlet (which I had received at the basha's lodgings) and went to the *azotea*,[28] which is the flat roof of the house. All houses in Algiers have a flat roof, like in Italy. This seemed the most convenient place and there I found two French slaves who were crusaders from Malta.[29] They asked me what news there was from Christendom, and as I was telling them, {27} I heard the guard (this is the Turk who supervises the slaves and makes sure they do their work every day) below in the courtyard of the bagnio. He called out that a number of slaves had to go to work at dawn on the following day. The guard had barely left the bagnio when I saw an old man, an Italian by birth, who was also a slave of Alli Pegelin. He carried a large pack of woolen and linen clothes. He started to cry: "Arrache, arrache." I asked the French slaves what this meant. They answered, "Since our master does not offer any subsistence to his slaves, most of them live upon what they steal and every evening, the booty of the preceding day is usually sold."

{28} On the following day, before sunrise, the guard came to the bagnio once more. He cried out: "Get up, you dogs!" (this was his good morning), and he conducted us to a suburb of the city named Babaloet. There we found all the tools necessary to make ropes, and without asking us if we knew this trade, he put us to work. Saldens and I were appointed

---

27. *trading*: "tuisken" in the manuscript, which is most likely related to "tuisen" ("swapping" or "trading").

28. *azotea*: a flat roof that can be walked on; Spanish term, from the Arabic: *as-suṭayḥ*.

29. *crusaders from Malta*: d'Aranda most likely means Knights of Malta.

to turning [the wheel], which we did with all our force, while the guard kept crying out: "Forti." We thought this signified that we should turn as hard as we could, but in the lingua franca[30] (the common language used there to make sure that the slaves of all nations understand the Turks—which is a language reduced from Italian), *forti* means "keep still." Because he could not get us to hold still by shouting, he came to teach us with canes what FORTI {29} means. We carried out this trade for five or six days. Because I was not used to this kind of labor, I lay down from tiredness on the flat roof of the house as soon as we arrived home. The abovementioned French slaves were touched with pity and asked me whether I would like a place to sleep with them. I accepted heartily and took a sleeping place in a small room, or rather, a pen where they slept.

Once the ropes had been made, we had to learn a new trade once again, and this one was much more painful (for people who are not used to it) than the former one. This work consisted of pounding wheat. I carried out this trade with great effort and little progress, as I have barely any strength. {30} So the guard who observed us said to me: "Stand still, you dog, you are still untamed." When the wheat was pounded and put into bags, a small amount accidentally fell on the ground. The guard said to me, "*Pilla esso perro,*" meaning "Pick that up, you dog." But because I did not understand what pilla meant, he hit me three or four times on my back, which became full of blood because I was not wearing a doublet.[31] When the wheat had been put into bags, he gave each of us a bag to carry. I had barely walked twenty steps when the bag began to slide from my head because of my lack of strength. The guard came to help put it up again, but he gave me three or four blows in my face with his fist, making blood run out of my nose and {31} my mouth, which forced me to try to carry the bag (notwithstanding my lack of strength). After a few steps, the string that tied up my trousers broke under all the strain. I fell on the ground again with my bag. I adjusted my trousers and put my bag on my head again until I arrived at my master Alli Pegelin's house. Here I fell down on the ground again out of tiredness. But the hardest work of all had barely started. I had to carry the bag up the stairs, which was totally impossible for me. But as God knows the strength of man, His Godly providence allowed my companion Saldens, who had already unloaded [his bag], to see me lying there when he came down the

---

30. *lingua franca*: for more on lingua franca, see Joanna Nolan, *The Elusive Case of Lingua Franca: Fact and Fiction* (London: Palgrave Macmillan, 2021).

31. *doublet*: a close-fitting, padded jacket in use from the fifteenth to the seventeenth century.

stairs. He was touched {32} with pity, and said to the guard, "Don't you see that this Christian is ill?" He took my bag and carried it upstairs. Everyone will understand how pleasing this deed was for me.

I was very downhearted and Saldens led me to a tavern in our bagnio to console me (since Saldens still had a bit of money that he had hidden when we were captured), where he called for a flask of wine. We did not have to pay for the food; whether one eats or not, one only has to pay for the wine. While we were eating and drinking something, Jonker Jan Baptiste Caloen joined us. He had been employed that day to push a loaded mule, and since the streets in Algiers are very narrow, it is the custom to shout "*Belech*,"[32] meaning "Please wait." But as Caloen {33} did not yet know about this custom, he did not shout anything and ran down a notable Turk, who thereupon wanted to attack him with his knife (because it is customary for the Turks to wear long knives in their waistbands in the cities, instead of a sword). But luckily there were a few Turks on the street who spoke on behalf of Caloen, saying that he was still unmannered and did not know the local customs yet. And so we passed the evening, telling each other about the adventures of the day, and furthermore, seeing that we had to work every day without receiving any food, we asked our master for advice on how we could earn money {34} to live from. We could not perform any trade and we were neither bold nor fast enough to steal. We decided to go to an Italian merchant named Franco Capati to ask him for one hundred patacons, on the condition that we would return the same amount to him at Antwerp, with a profit of 21 percent. We executed this decision the next day, and thank God the merchant was content for each of us to stand surety for the others. We four, namely Saldens, Caloen, Vlamertinghe, and myself, immediately received four patacons each.

The next day, we had to dig up the vineyard, {35} which was hard labor. As we went home to the city, the guard kept me company. I said to him that I was sick and weak, and that if he would employ me for some lighter work, I would give him four reals[33] a month. He agreed to this on the condition that I gave them to him a month in advance, which I gladly did. He said to me, "From now on you will only have to carry four pots of water to the house of the basha's guard every day." This was the chief guard, for as there were five hundred and fifty slaves all belonging to one master, there

---

32. *belech*: from the Arabic *bālak*, meaning "watch out" or "take care."
33. *reals*: the real was an early modern Spanish coin; "realen" in the manuscript.

were also five or six guards. I was very happy with my new {36} employment. The wife of this chief guard was a black woman. She was born in Sevilla in Spain, but she was an apostate. She had a good disposition, sometimes giving me a piece of bread or a plate of pottage. This happened when she bathed and I had brought a lot of water, or when I had carried bread to the oven. I carried out this task for some days with great satisfaction, but as no one can continue in such luxury, it once happened that I brought water in my ordinary can to the *tinaga*[34] (which is a container wherein water is kept), when I found an English woman in the house. I asked if she would like to drink a glass of Spanish {37} wine with me. I do not know if the black woman became aware of this, but on the next day I got my leave, and from that day on I had to work with the other slaves again.

My usual work was to serve the bricklayers. I started to get used to this life. It was now the month of December, when the Turkish ships stay at the coast of Andalusia, knowing that the fruits and wines are sent out at that time. It happened at this time that the Turkish ships conquered a ship that was made in Dunkirk and was called *De Peerle*.[35] It came from Málaga. I did not dare to go down {38} to the sea, as I had once been in Málaga and was afraid of being recognized. On the evening of the arrival of this ship, Mathias Perez came. He was born in Antwerp and had been captured together with us. He said, "A boy has come with the ship from Dunkirk and he asked me if I knew two Christians named Caloen and de Aranda." I hereupon begged him not to ask for these persons again and I said that these men were known under different names among the slaves: Caloen was known as Jan van den Berge and de Aranda as Jacques van Zevere. I immediately went (not without great fear of being recognized) to bring this news to my friends, {39} namely Caloen, Saldens, and Vlamertinghe. We immediately decided to speak to our master, in order to reach an agreement concerning our ransom before we were recognized, for our master still believed that Vlamertinghe was a great nobleman and that we were his servants. But we thought it would be sensible, before we spoke to our master, first to ask the new slave if the duty would be carried out to release us, and also to advise him not to speak of us. We told Mathias Perez to inform the new slave that he would find us on the following day on the terrace of the bagnio at around nine o'clock in the morning.

---

34. *tinaga*: a large cistern used to store water. See James Wilson Stevens, *An Historical and Geographical Account of Algiers: Comprehending a Novel and Interesting Detail of Events Relative to the American Captives* (Philadelphia: Hogan & M'Elroy, 1797), 297.

35. *De Peerle*: The Pearl.

Mathias Perez did this, and {40} on the next day, at the appointed time, the new slave came to the terrace. When he saw me, he said with a sad expression, "Sir, I am sad to see you in this condition." I answered, "Leenaert, don't call me sir. My name is Jacques van Zevere here." Thereupon he told me at length how our friends in Spain knew of our misfortune. Only fourteen days before, Peralta and Woestwinckele, both Dutchmen born in Bruges, had had a drink to the health of their friends who were aboard the galleys, believing that we were still on the galleys. I advised [the new slave] to remain silent about who we were and promised to help him as much as possible. But as he saw that I did not have much to give, {41} he gave me three *camafeas*[36] (which he had kept hidden) and told me to sell them or pawn them in order to help myself. And I pawned them at a maximum worth of 10 patacons. This money came at a very convenient time, for our hundred patacons had been consumed, and the merchant had not received any notice that the exchange at Antwerp had been paid.

Five months had passed now since our arrival in Algiers, during which time a response from Flanders could have been expected. And so, we, being Caloen, Saldens, and myself, went to the house of our master and kissed his hand or his sleeve (as is the custom there). We said to him that we understood that he had reached an agreement with some of his slaves about their {42} departure on a certain ship from Livorno,[37] which lay ready in Algiers to set sail for Livorno. They would continue to stay imprisoned there until their ransom was paid.[38] We asked him if he would agree to the same conditions with us. He asked, "Why do you want to go to the prison of Livorno? If you pay me here in Algiers, I will lower your ransom by a third." We answered him that we could write daily to our country from Livorno and would receive a reply quickly, while in Algiers there was barely the possibility to write once every six months and the letters often arrived in bad condition. We urged him so much {43} that he was persuaded to believe us. He asked, "How much are you willing to pay for your freedom? I will send you to the prison of Livorno." I answered, "If my lord would be so kind as to [name a sum], for [my lord] may value me at a sum I would not have dared to offer."

36. *camafeas*: probably related to the Spanish term "camafeo"; carved gems or cameos.
37. *Livorno*: a port city on the Ligurian sea in western Tuscany, Italy.
38. *imprisoned there until their ransom was paid*: this passage indicates that European slaves could be transferred from North Africa to Livorno in Italy and stay in the bagnios there until the ransom money from a slave's home country arrived. Such a procedure required a high degree of mutual trust between the Muslim and Christian parties involved. To my knowledge, d'Aranda's narrative is the only one that describes this particular practice.

And so he demanded two thousand patacons,[39] whereupon I said that it was impossible for a poor soldier like myself to collect such a sum. I said that I would rather stay in Algiers than make a promise that I could not fulfill and which I would have to die for in the prison of Livorno. I said that the highest amount I could offer in Livorno was five hundred patacons. He answered, "You offer too little. I am leaving town now and when I return, we will speak again." These words {44} gave me much comfort. I estimated that the five hundred patacons I had offered would prove to be sufficient.

The next day was 18 February 1641. Our master was out of town with a few slaves to make them cut wood for the construction of a galley in the coming year. We worked as usual on a certain house that our master had us construct in the most elevated part of the city (the city is built entirely against a mountain). The way up was so difficult that neither a packhorse nor a mule could get there, so all materials had to be carried up by men. In the morning, the guard sent us to work at sunrise. As Vlamertinghe had an injured arm, he did not have to work. When we left, we asked him {45} to prepare some rice for when we returned from work. While we were busy working, two Turks came into the bagnio to ask for three slaves from Dunkirk, named Jan Baptiste van Caloen, Emanuel de Aranda, and Reynier Saldens. Nobody knew these slaves, so they showed a certain certificate in Latin. The Spanish slaves who read it could not understand it and believed it was Flemish or English. The Turks who had brought the certificate said it was a language that was only spoken by the priests and noblemen in the land of Dunkirk. The Christians who stood nearby thereupon thought it had to be Latin. They immediately called a slave who was generally known as "Frans the Student," {46} for he had studied. (He was born in Mol in De Kempen). When he read the certificate, he presumed from the signs that it must concern us. He said to the Turks that he knew us but that we were busy working. In the meantime, Caloen and Saldens, who did not pay as much attention to [the danger of] punishment as I, had skipped work. They were hidden somewhere in a corner of the bagnio playing cards when Frans the Student came to them and said, "There are two Turks downstairs who come from Dunkirk and have brought a letter for you." Caloen and Saldens immediately went to the two Turks, who instantly gave Caloen a letter from his father. He was very happy and the Turks, finding us all {47}

---

39. *two thousand patacons*: the ransom price is extraordinarily high when compared with the "two hundred and twenty patacons" (p. 19 of the manuscript) that his new master paid for him on the slave market.

in Algiers, were also happy, for their contract required them to release us from whatever part of the barbarian land we might be in. They immediately led Caloen and Saldens to the house of Barbeer Assan, the father-in-law of Monstafa Ingles, who had been captured in Bruges.[40] [Monstafa Ingles'] mother was happy that she would see her son again.

Until now, I did not know what had happened, for I preferred working one or two hours extra to the risk of being punished. It was now afternoon and we had started working at sunrise. The guard let us go. I was very hungry and I walked to the bagnio, hoping that Vlamertinghe had cooked something. When I entered the bagnio, I met Frans the Student, who said to me, {48} "Jacques, I have some good news for you. You are a free man. Two Turks from Dunkirk have come for you, and Saldens and Caloen went with them." I was not hungry anymore and went to search for Caloen and Saldens immediately, and eventually found them with the Turks. As soon as Caloen saw me, he said to the Turks, "That's Emanuel." I asked them immediately about my parents. They answered that my mother did not know about my misfortune yet and that my brother was well. They came with us to the bagnio and told the guard not to make us work anymore, for we were free. We were very happy that day and drank to the good news with our friends. But little did we know that joy in the home means sorrow waits at the door.

{49} We meant to spend the following day as happily as the one before, but a Jew came to the bagnio, sent there by the wife of our master Alli Pegelin (who already knew what had happened). He said that the basha wanted to speak to us and he led us to the palace of the basha, who let us in. We were there for two hours without knowing what they wanted to say, when the steward came to us with a stick in his hand. He said, "You dogs, which of you has written to his country to get some Turks?"[41] To which we answered nobody, explaining that our parents had done this without our knowledge. The steward looked very angry to hear this {50} and he beat Caloen and myself a couple of times. He said, "I will come to you tonight still to cut your ears and noses off." Saldens answered, "Have patience." For this answer,

---

40. *who had been captured in Bruges*: as we will learn later, Monstafa Ingles is one of the North Africans in European captivity who will be exchanged for d'Aranda, Caloen, and Saldens. This passage marks the beginning of the long-winded liberation process of d'Aranda and his companions. Unlike other Barbary narratives that relate the "standard" ransoms based on the payment of an agreed sum of money from Europe, d'Aranda's account is one of the very few texts documenting a prisoner exchange across the Mediterranean.

41. *to get some Turks*: d'Aranda and his two companions were eventually ransomed in exchange for seven North Africans in European captivity, referred to here as "Turks."

he got a couple of blows with a stick as well, and the overseer said, "You will not escape as easily as you think, for you are not the slaves of Alli Pegelin, but of the basha, and you have only been lent to Alli Pegelin. And the basha does not have any need for Turks as your ransom; he only wants money." This was brought about by the wife of our master Alli Pegelin during his absence. For there is a law generally accepted by all countries that fall {51} under the influence of the Great Turk[42] stating that every Turkish soldier, however poor his condition may be, may set free any Christian he wants to, on the condition that he pays his master the acquisition price and that he swears he does this in order to free himself, or another soldier, from slavery. But the basha said that this law did not apply to his slaves, since he represented the Great Turk, who was not subject to such laws. In the meantime, we wrote a letter in Spanish to Monstafa's grandmother (for she was born in Spain and was driven out with the Moors) and we informed her of all that had happened to us in this new prison. And [we told her] to be mindful of her grandson,[43] who was still in our control, {52} and that we would take revenge on him for any wrong done to us. She was very moved by this letter and immediately went to speak to the basha's wife. She begged her not to treat us badly, which the basha's wife promised. Monstafa's grandmother immediately informed us of this, first, so that we would not have to fear, and second, to prevent us from writing to Flanders, telling them to treat the Turks who were in their hands badly as well. Our master, Alli Pegelin, had not returned from his journey yet.

In the meantime, we were locked up in the basha's house without anyone from outside being allowed to visit us. Nevertheless, this sometimes happened, {53} but with great secrecy. We each received, as our daily portion, two small loaves of bread, which were not sufficient to fill our bellies. But it was our good fortune that the head chef of the basha was French by birth, but now a renegade. He had been a servant of Mr. Samois (a Knight of Malta, mentioned above).[44] And as this chef knew that we had come to know Mr. Samois very well in the bagnio of Alli Pegelin and that we were good

---

42. *Great Turk*: historical term for the ruler of the Ottoman Empire. At the time when d'Aranda was captive in Algiers, this was Ibrahim (1615–1648), sultan of the Ottoman Empire from 1640 to 1648.

43. *grandson*: the manuscript reads "neefve," meaning "nephew"; however, d'Aranda means "grandson."

44. *mentioned above*: d'Aranda mentions these Knights of Malta on p. 26 of the manuscript, when he first takes refuge on the roof of Alli Pegelin's bagnio: "I found two French slaves who were crusaders from Malta."

friends, he gave us oil, vinegar, figs, and tobacco. Here we suffered the greatest misery of our time as slaves. We slept on the ground in a little room with ten to twelve other boys who were covered with lice. Even when we did nothing but pick off lice all day, we were covered again after lying beside the boys for an hour. {54} The steward patrolled the back of the house all day with a stick in his hands and always found someone to beat. The only diversion we had was that all slaves, of whom the basha took his part (which is one out of eight, as I have stated above), came to sleep together with us on their first night before they were sent to the bagnio of the basha. And as ships were captured every day, we heard daily what was happening in almost all of Christendom.

When we had been in this misery for eighteen days, our master Alli Pegelin returned to the city. The two Turks who had come for us went to greet him right away and explained to him that there were seven Turks who were to be traded for three Christians, and they told him that they would pay as much for us {55} as we had cost him. Alli Pegelin thereupon answered, "I buy my slaves for profit, not to free Turks." They answered, "We are poor soldiers, and you know very well the privilege we have." Whereupon he said, "The poverty the six of you live in touches me and your privilege is also well known to me. But the seventh is rich and should not receive this privilege, for he was born in Algiers and no one born in Algiers can be a soldier, for the Turks keep the inhabitants of the city of Algiers as subjects and keep them under their rule with force. And since the Turks have almost been defeated by the inhabitants of Algiers two or three times, no one who is born in Algiers may be registered as a soldier. {56} Therefore they also cannot enjoy the privileges that the soldiers enjoy. But if you will follow my advice, then I will receive money and you will receive the three Christians without having to offer much." This pleased the Turks, so Alli Pegelin advised that the two of them should reach an agreement with the grandmother of Monstafa Ingles (he was the one who was born in Algiers and could not enjoy the privileges of the Turks), on behalf of the other five who were still in Flanders. [They would do this] in such a way that the rich grandmother of Monstafa would buy Jan Baptiste van Caloen. Because [the others] were poor, they would, between the six of them, buy Emanuel de Aranda and Reynier Saldens. This advice pleased the Turks and they put it into practice by visiting the mother and the grandmother of {57} Monstafa Ingles. They asked whether she would be prepared to buy Jan Baptiste Caloen, while they would buy the other two. The mother and the grandmother happily accepted this condition. When this was done, the two Turks went to Alli

Pegelin and told him that they had reached an agreement. Then the question arose how much they would offer for Emanuel de Aranda and Reynier Saldens. They agreed on five hundred patacons. Monstafa's grandmother and mother also went to speak to Alli Pegelin on the same day, in tears. They said the Christians had captured their son as a slave and that there was no other remedy to free him but by [trading] a certain slave from Dunkirk named Jan Baptiste van Caloen. For that reason, they came to ask him, for the love of God, {58} to sell that slave to them. Alli Pegelin said, "To serve you, I will happily sell him. But you should know that this slave is a friend of the king of Dunkirk, and that he cannot be bought for a lower price than six thousand ducats." These women were very distressed to hear this answer. They called us to tell us that Alli Pegelin wanted six thousand ducats for Jan Baptiste's ransom, but that they did not have so much money and that there was no way to gain our freedom but for us to contribute to this ransom. Hereupon we replied to the one who had brought us this message that we would not pay a dime and that they could let us hang if they would not set us free, which same fate would await her son. And while all this happened, {59} nine weeks and three days had passed, during which we stayed in the basha's house in great misery and sadness. Then Monstafa's mother finally reached an agreement[45] with Alli Pegelin for 1,400 patacons, on the condition that this money would be counted before Jan Baptiste Caloen left Algiers. With this agreement, we could leave the basha's house.

When I was at liberty to move through the streets again, I thought of the fact that I was no longer a slave, for it had saddened me greatly to be locked up for so long. On the first night that we spent outside the basha's house, Caloen went to sleep in the house of Monstafa Ingles's grandmother and Saldens and I went to sleep in the house of one of the two Turks who had come for us. He was named Cataborne Monstafa. He lived in a *funducke*,[46] which was a house where many {60} soldiers live together, like a barracks, as we would say in Flanders. This funducke was a large square house with

---

45. *reached an agreement*: Alli Pegelin, the owner of the three captives, had no interest in simply exchanging them for North African slaves in European hands, since this would jeopardize his original "investment" at the slave market. In order to not lose out on his "return on investment," he sells two of the slaves, Saldens and d'Aranda, to the Turkish negotiators, and one, Caloen, to the wealthy mother of a Muslim captive still held in European hands. Only after all North African "stakeholders" had reached a financial agreement could the actual trans-Mediterranean exchange of captives take place. This transaction shows the underlying economic complexity of what, at least at first sight, seems like nothing more than an exchange of slaves across the Christian–Muslim religious divide.

46. *funducke*: related to the Arabic *funduq*, meaning "inn" or "hotel."

galleries, and it had two stories. Every soldier had his own separate room, which was usually kept very neat by boys, for every soldier had common Christians or renegade boys as slaves. Our new master, Cataborne Monstafa, served us very well that evening, as far as his means allowed. He said that he could not be blamed for the fact that we had to stay such a long time in the basha's house during the preceding days.

Saldens went to live in the house of a Turkish nobleman named Mahomet Celebi Oiga, whose nephew was one of the five Turks who were still in Flanders. The grandmother and the mother of Monstafa Ingles, who complained about the money they had had to pay for Jan Baptiste Caloen, were a continual annoyance to him, {61} because they wanted half of the 1,400 patacons. We hurried as much as possible and asked for our freedom in consequence of the contents of Caloen's father's letter. Thereupon the two Turks said (and not without reason), that this would put them in danger of losing their money and their companions (for the contract that had been made in Flanders required that they send us to Christian land immediately upon finding us). Therefore, we were obliged to form a new contract with them, agreeing that they would set one of us free, who would go to Flanders to pick up the five remaining Turks and return with them to Ceuta or Oran.[47] These are two cities that are in the possession of the king of Spain, {62} although they are situated in Africa. It was decided that I should be dropped off with the pirate galleys on Spanish land. But my misfortune was that a barbarian king named Benali, who was a subject of the Kingdom of Algiers, rebelled. This caused a civil war, and the basha now needed the galleys for himself and would not allow them to be used for piracy along the Spanish coast, as was usual in this season. In the meantime, a ship from Livorno lay ready in Algiers to return to Livorno. Our comrade Saldens, who also wished to regain his liberty quickly, urged the Turks and Caloen so strongly that they finally let him go to Livorno with the ship. I was very sad when I saw him leaving while I had to remain behind. Our only consolation was his firm promise {63} to come to Ceuta in time with the five Turks, which he later did.

In the meantime, I remained with my new master, Cataborne Monstafa. Although he was poor, I enjoyed good days with him, for he often said to me, "Emanuel, do not be sad and just imagine that you are the master and I am your slave." I ate from one plate with him, sitting beside him with my

---

47. *Ceuta or Oran*: Spanish enclaves on the coast of North Africa.

legs crossed, as is the Turkish custom. He wanted to make good cheer and he often said to me, "Emanuel, is it not wise of me to make good cheer, for I have no wife or children and when I die, the basha will inherit my possessions, according to the Turkish custom." All these conversations did not please a certain renegade slave who served him. He washed the linen clothes and guarded the money {64} and also performed some other tasks for his master that a woman would normally do. He constantly mumbled, "You eat too much. There are many days left before you will receive your wages and you are not ashamed of being drunk every day. This is not the life of a noble Turk." But notwithstanding all these exhortations, [the master] was drunk every day. One day, while he was drunk, he quarreled with a *bulcebas*[48] (meaning a captain of the infantry), responding to a scornful remark by calling him a Christian. The bulcebas put in a complaint at the first meeting of the council for this injury. Thereupon, my master was condemned to receive fifty strokes on his buttocks with sticks, and furthermore, he was banned, having to serve in the army against Benali for six months. I was very sad about my master's misfortune. {65} He said to me, "Emanuel, from now on you will live at the house of Mahomet Celebi Oiga. I hope that, with God's help, you will have gained your liberty before I return. If I had money, I would have shared it with you." Whereupon I answered, "Master, I know about your poverty and I thank you for your good treatment." He said, "When you are in Flanders, send my greetings to all your friends, and especially to Jan de Melgaer, for he offered me good beer to drink."

I went immediately to the house of Mahomet Celebi Oiga. After I had greeted him, I said, "Cataborne Monstafa has left to join the army and he asks you to offer me a place to stay." Thereupon he answered that he would gladly have done so, but that he did not {66} have any place for me to stay. He said this because Saldens had spoken too familiarly to his wife, which had made him jealous. Finally, after much pleading, he was pacified and he gave me a room above the stables to live in, which was completely separated from the house. During the first days, I was astonished that the mistress did not speak to me, for she spoke Spanish and the lingua franca very well, and the women generally looked for any chance to speak to the Christians. I tended my master's horse and I went to the well every day to bring water for the family without being commanded to do so. And little by little I came

---

48. *bulcebas*: from the Turkish *bölük başı*, meaning "the commander of the *bölük*." A bölük is a small military unit.

into the good grace of my mistress. Daily I bought meat, fruit, and all that was consumed by the family. Gradually my mistress's tongue loosened and she started to talk to me, saying, "Emanuel—may God give you {67} your liberty—are you a poor man in your country?" I answered, "I am a poor soldier." She said, "You may say whatever you please, yet you are not like Gregorio." He was another Christian slave who also lived there with me. This Gregorio served as a gardener in a country house outside the city that my master owned. This slave was a native of Galicia and he was a fisherman by trade. She asked me questions every day with great curiosity, for she spoke Spanish very well. Physically she was pleasing to behold; the beauty of the women of the barbarian land lies in their opulence and devoutness. I went to the market every day and did all she asked of me. I went to mass every day (for which she gave me time).

Mahomet Celebi Oiga was a well-mannered man, temperate in his eating and drinking habits. He was very devoted {68} to his religion and he was curious as well. He asked me about the way of life in Flanders and whether we Christians were Papists, by which he meant Roman Catholics. In the meantime, Caloen was at the house of Monstafa Ingles's grandmother, where he had much to suffer. When he was in the city, he had to stay in a room with heavy chains weighing one hundred pounds attached to his leg. Sometimes he was in a country house, situated three miles from Algiers, where he was often left hungry. In the meantime, Monstafa Ingles's friends, who had paid so much money for Caloen, began to long for some news from Monstafa. As this news did not arrive, they started saying that the king of France had captured the land of Dunkirk {69} and they began to threaten [Caloen], saying, "If we don't receive any news within four months, we will make you pay the ransom." And while sea journeys are subject to many accidents and misfortunes, and while I also knew that my companion had to be on his way with the five Turks, I was often overpowered by anguish and fear. But as God not only allows diseases, but by His grace also provides medicine to cure the sick, I found comfort with my mistress, who often consoled me when I was sad.

I had been living in this last house for six months when I got my first letter, which had been written in Ceuta, from my companion Saldens. In this letter, he informed me that he was there with the five Turks and that we should come to {70} Tétouan[49] immediately, where the exchange should

---

49. *Tétouan*: a city in northern Morocco.

take place according to the agreement we had made. Concerning the seven hundred patacons that Monstafa's mother expected from Caloen's father, he said that [Caloen's father] would rather let his son die. But in the margin of the letter was written in Latin: *haec propter bene stare*,⁵⁰ which words we immediately scribbled over. We gave the letter to Monstafa's mother to read, which she did, and since the letter only mentioned five Turks, without any particular mention of their names, Monstafa's mother said that her son was not among them and that Caloen should either deliver her son or she would have him burnt, unless he paid a ransom of six thousand patacons. {71} But on the same day, she received a letter from her son, which made her very happy and us as well, who trusted that she would be reassured by this. But happiness and sadness succeed each other, and she had barely read the letter when she ordered Caloen to be put in chains. She said that [Caloen] was the reason that his father would not pay the seven hundred patacons. But notwithstanding this new trouble, we kept our courage up, and at last we saw a ship, heavily laden and awaiting only a fair wind to leave for Tétouan, where we had to be for the exchange with the Turks who were at Ceuta. What worried us most was that, if we missed this opportunity, we might not get such a chance again for four or five months.

{72} We agreed among ourselves to get the advice of a certain renegade. He was a reformed colonel who was known among the Turks as Saban Galan. He was a man who, except for his religion, was known as an honorable gentleman. I went to speak to him and said, "The good reputation of your lordship brings me here to ask for your counsel in my misery." He asked who I was, and I said that I was Emanuel de Aranda, born in Flanders, and that I was one of three Christians who were to be exchanged for five Turks who had been captured by people of Dunkirk on the caravel of Barbeer Assan. "According to a certain contract we made seven months ago here in Algiers, my companion left for Flanders and has come back to Ceuta with the five Turks. {73} And according to the contract, they should now send us to Tétouan, so that the exchange can be concluded there, but they do the contrary, and after we have incurred heavy costs in order to bring the Turks from Flanders to Ceuta, instead of sending us to Tétouan, they have put my companion Jean Baptiste Caloen in chains. They demand seven hundred patacons and they want the Turks to come to Algiers."

50. *haec propter bene stare*: the Latin is not clear. It could possibly mean "this because of his good standing."

After hearing this story, he said, "I will investigate this case and you can come for an answer tomorrow." On the next day, I went to find him, as he had asked me. His answer was, "I have now been fully informed of your affair. Monstafa's mother does all this in order to see if she can get any more money from Caloen. {74} [This is] what you should do now: Do not make any promises and remain at ease, and you will leave with the ship that is ready to depart. Although Monstafa's mother is threatening you, she would not dare to keep Caloen or you here." I thanked him heartily for his advice and I offered him payment, which obliged me to pay twenty-five patacons when I arrived in Tétouan (which I indeed paid when we were in Tétouan).

I immediately brought this answer to Caloen, who was in a little cellar with chains attached to his leg. He was greatly comforted when I told him that we would, without any doubt, leave with the first ship and that we would not have to pay a dime. While I spoke to him, Monstafa's grandmother came to confront Caloen, {75} [demanding] that he pay the seven hundred patacons, but Caloen mocked her, from which she gathered that I had given some advice to Caloen. She was angry about this and came to speak with my mistress, Mahomet Celebi Oiga's wife. She said, "Why don't you put Emanuel in chains? For he comes to my place every day to give bad advice to his companion." My mistress answered, "Emanuel serves me very well and I have no reason to put him in chains." And when I, as usual, brought oats for the horse in the evening, (my master was not at home), my mistress told me all that had happened. The next day, I went to Caloen and I was telling him what Monstafa's grandmother had said to my mistress {76} when she came to us and said to me, "Yesterday I was at the house of your master. Had it not been for me, your mistress would have put you in chains as well." Whereupon I answered that I was very thankful to her and that I already knew what good references she had given me. She became very angry about this answer and she sent a Turk to my master to complain about me: about my coming to advise Caloen every day, and [saying] that I was the reason that Caloen did not promise the seven hundred patacons. She requested that he put me in chains immediately or that he would at least send me to her house to be put in chains together with Caloen.

This was accordingly done, without the knowledge of my mistress, because I was taken from the streets to the house {77} of Monstafa's grandmother, where I was immediately fastened to Caloen's chains, which only measured three feet but were incredibly heavy. She put us in a little cellar. Here we discussed what end our situation would lead us to, for I feared constantly that she would force us into something by beating us. When we had been there for three or four hours, a Christian slave named Gregorio (mentioned above), came to us, sent by my mistress. He told me that she was very sad and had not known of this and that she would send me food if I had need of it. And [she said] that I should keep up my courage and that nothing bad would happen to us, for this was all planned by Monstafa's grandmother. We were {78} happy about this message and we immediately sent this Gregorio to the bagnio of Alli Pegelin to a certain tavern keeper in order to ask him to send us a flask of wine and a plate of food. This was immediately done. As Gregorio had been sent by my mistress, Monstafa's grandmother did not dare to forbid him to come to us.

When night had fallen, the grandmother came to us with the keys to close the pen we were in. She said to us, "Be careful what you do! This is the last night and the ship will be gone tomorrow. If you want to regain your freedom, you must either promise the seven hundred patacons or you will have to die here." Caloen immediately answered, "My father refuses to give you this and I do not have anything. Hang me, if you want, but know that Monstafa will be treated in {79} the same way." After more such discourse, she closed the pen we were in and left. The following day, at daybreak (it being St. Andrew's Day[51]), she came to tell us, "The wind is fair and the ship will leave this night." Whereupon we bravely answered, "Send us there if you want to have Monstafa back, otherwise we will stay slaves and he as well." Although we spoke so bravely, we were not without fear.

Around noon, two or three slaves came to visit us. They had to leave with the same ship. They had been put up to this by us and they came to say goodbye. They asked Monstafa's grandmother if she longed for her grandson and they said that they would soon board the ship {80} that left for Tétouan and from there to Ceuta. There they hoped to find Saldens with the five Turks to tell him of the misery we were in. They said goodbye to us, showing great hurry. These exchanges immediately altered the attitude of the old woman, for now that the ship was to leave soon, she began to cry out, almost like a lunatic, "Oh Christians, for the love of God, take off these chains and board the ship so that my Monstafa may return, in the name of God." She called her female slaves and made them bring us hammers and instruments to remove our chains. To provoke her even more, we said, "Because of your greed, you let us lie here in chains, and in the meantime the ship will leave

---

51. *St. Andrew's Day*: the feast of Andrew the Apostle takes place on 30 November.

and your grandson will stay a slave with the other four Turks, and their friends will say that it is your fault {81} that they [have to] spend such a long time in slavery." While making these suggestions, we managed to take off our chains. She said to me, "Go and look for your master, so that he can speak to the captain of the ship."

It was the time of the day when my master was in the mosque (this is a church), so I first went to his house to thank my mistress for the care she had taken of me. She was very happy, first, because I had been freed from my chains, and second, because I was surely close to freedom now. It was now the time at which the *salah*[52] (which is the prayer) had ended, so I went to the door of the mosque to await my master. We went together to the captain of the ship to speak to him. He told us that there was as yet no opportunity for departure, but that he would set sail with the first fair wind. {82} I returned home with my master, preparing myself as much as possible to bring some provisions onto the ship with me. My mistress gave me cheese from Mallorca to carry with me onto the ship and twelve to fifteen pounds of white ship's biscuit as well. Caloen also got some provisions from Monstafa's parents. We thought all was ready for us to leave when another misfortune arose: a Turk had to go with us to Tétouan and he wanted fifty patacons for his effort. [Monstafa's parents] wanted us to pay, but we agreed that we would pay one half and they would pay the other.

It was now 8 December 1641, Our Lady's Day, when the wind turned to the east (this was the direction we needed). I said farewell {83} to my master and my mistress, who wished me well. I went aboard with Caloen. On the ship we met some other Christian slaves who were also going to Tétouan to negotiate about their liberty. There were also some Moorish and Jewish traders. When we had boarded the ship, a gun was fired as a sign that the toll collectors should come to visit the ship to see if there were any Christians on board who were not free. For after the Christians have paid their ransom to their masters, they still have to pay large sums before they are allowed to continue. After they had inspected our ship, they returned to the city with their boat. They asked us to tell our captain to leave immediately, for the toll collectors are not allowed to return to the city before they see that the ship they have inspected has set sail. {84} This is done so that [the ship] cannot take away any [slave] after they have been inspected. We started our journey with a fair wind until we arrived at an unfortunate place named Cabo de

---

52. *salah*: a canonical prayer performed five times daily.

Tenes.[53] (I call this place unfortunate because the emperor Charles V lost the largest part of his galleys in this place on 27 October 1541 as a result of bad weather. This occurred when he meant to conquer Algiers.) Here, the wind began to turn contrary again, so we were forced to return to Algiers.

We arrived there once more on the morning of the next day, and we were very sad that the wind had not served us well. I returned to my master's house. He and his wife welcomed me. I stayed there again for fourteen days until the wind turned to the east. I boarded the ship for the second time. We fared well and we saw (during the short time {85} that we sailed by), Formentera,[54] the islands of Ibiza, yes, and even the coast of Valencia in Spain. But this was all to no avail, for at the end of eight days, we were happy to return to Algiers (because of the bad weather we had constantly had), where we arrived on 29 December. The people of the city who saw our ship return thought it had already made its journey to Tétouan. I was very tired, for during the entire eight days that had passed, I had been in the lower part of the ship, in a little place seven feet long and nine feet wide. We were there with nineteen persons and some of them were constantly sick and had to spit and vomit the whole day. This caused such a stench that I was surprised that we did not all get sick.

{86} I jumped ashore as fast as I could and I immediately went to the house of my master, who was very surprised to see me yet again. I told him about the misery we had suffered in those eight days. I was very sad that we had not finished our journey, but I was happy to be able to refresh myself ashore. I was also happy to be able to see the celebrations of the Turks during their Easter, which they call the Easter of Ramadan, for they have different Easters.[55] During my previous year in Algiers I had not seen these celebrations, for they took place during the time we were in the basha's house, which we could not leave, as I said above. This feast lasts eight days and is celebrated with {87} the greatest solemnity. Outside the city, the Turks held horse duels every day, called *juego de cañas*[56] in Spanish, and the children are pulled along by Christian slaves in little carriages, which are especially made by the slaves, who receive tips in return. There are Christian slaves who

---

53. *Cabo de Tenes*: Cap Ténès, Algeria.
54. *Formentera*: the smallest of Spain's Balearic islands in the Mediterranean.
55. *Easter [. . .] for they have different Easters*: Islam does not celebrate Easter; d'Aranda means periods of religious fasting.
56. *juego de cañas*: literally: "game of reeds." This was a tournament in which participants threw reeds at each other (instead of real weapons).

know how to make a profit during these celebrations by selling children's items to the children. Every day during these eight days there are wrestling games between the Moors. Some of them are very experienced in this art. Most of the Turks (although it is against their law) celebrate Easter by drinking, which they do with great appetite, for they have been fasting for a month before this Easter, though they only have to fast during the daytime. This fast, which they call Ramadan, is so rigorously enforced {88} that if someone is caught eating during daytime during the fast, molten lead is poured in his mouth, in accordance with their laws. But at night they are allowed to eat, and since no one should neglect to eat at night during the fast, drums are beaten up and down the streets at night to remind everyone of the fast and to eat something. This Easter is also pleasant for the Christian slaves, for just as we give tips to our servants on New Year's Day, the Turks give tips to their slaves during Easter. Moreover, they do not put their slaves to work on the first three Easter days.

These celebrations ended and the wind continued to prove contrary until 14 January 1642, when we boarded {89} the ship for the third time. We were barely in the steady seas when the wind turned contrary again. But as we had returned twice, some had mocked our captain, saying that he did not understand navigation. This had provoked him, and he said that he would not return to Algiers until he had finished his journey, even if he had to sail the seas for another year. And as the wind continued to prove contrary, we laveered with the contrary wind, and on the eighth day we were only at the latitude of Oran, which is about forty miles from Algiers. That night, the Turks who kept guard on our ship discovered two ships that followed our ship continuously. They were very anxious, fearing that these were Christian ships, {90} and at sunrise they saw that it was the admiral of Algiers, named Amet Arrais. He was born in Dunkirk. He was accompanied by another pirate ship. Our captain spoke with them and asked if they had seen any Christian ships. When he heard that they had not, we sailed on and arrived at Tremesen[57] within four days. Here, we lowered the anchor and unloaded some quintals[58] of tobacco and other wares. Several Jewish and Moorish merchants remained there as well. Tremesen had been a renowned kingdom in the past, and the king of Algiers had to pay tribute to the king of

---

57. *Tremesen*: probably Tlemcen, which lies northwest of Algiers and was the capital of the Kingdom of Tlemcen from the mid-thirteenth to the mid-sixteenth century.

58. *quintal*: a unit of weight formerly equal to one hundred pounds (although the exact weight could vary by region).

Tremesen at that time. But at the present time, Tremesen pays tribute to Algiers, and the basha who resides in Algiers appoints his *caya*[59]—that is, his lieutenant—as an overseer in Tremesen. {91} This kingdom lies at the furthermost edge of the territories that are under the command of the Great Turk, for the neighboring country is the Kingdom of Fez,[60] whose king is at peace with the Great Turk. But notwithstanding this peace, the king of Fez and Morocco is sometimes at war with the king of Algiers, claiming that he does not violate his peace [treaty] with the Great Turk. Likewise, those from Algiers are often at war with those from Tunis, though both are subject to the Great Turk.

After we had been anchored here for three days, the wind seemed to turn to the east, and so we continued our journey again. As I have said, some Jewish and Moorish merchants remained ashore in Tremesen, so there were now {92} as many Christians as Turks on the ship (though there were also twenty-three Jews). In Algiers, we Christians had agreed to leave the ship if the right occasion presented itself, for as we had been on board twice before, we had observed all opportunities. And as we now saw a good opportunity, we decided to put this plan into action, for we had some tools for this eventuality. The one who was largely responsible for this was a Spanish slave who slept on the deck of the ship with eight other Christian slaves. We slept with fifteen Christian slaves in the locked lower part of the ship, but with the help of the Christians who were upstairs, we could have opened the hatch without any of the Turks noticing, {93} if this had happened the way we had planned it (but God did not wish this). One night, when we were all ready and only awaiting the signal to open the hatch to get to the deck and take over the ship by force, the Spanish slave who was to give the signal became frightened or neglected to give it. After that, we never had such a good opportunity again, for as we came closer to the Spanish coast every day, they kept guard more vigilantly because they approached the land of their enemies so closely. It was now 9 February 1642. We were at the latitude of Málaga and early in the morning we saw two large ships, which caused our captain and the other Turks {94} on our ship more than a little fear, because our ship could not avoid passing them. Our mast was cleft, so our ship could not get under full sail to sail away from them. When they came near us, we could see

---

59. *caya*: *kethüda* or *kahya* in Ottoman Turkish, meaning "steward" or "lieutenant."

60. *Kingdom of Fez*: a region in northern Morocco that was known by this name from the time of the Idrisid dynasty in the late eighth century.

that they sailed under the Dutch flag. The captain of our ship immediately ordered all Christians to go below and had us locked up there, making a boat ready to flee to the barbarian coast with the most important Turks (as I was afterward told by the Turk who supervised Caloen and myself). But these ships, as they were trading ships (as we learned two days later), did not mean to start a fight unless they were forced to. Our captain, seeing that these ships passed by {95} without approaching us, was very happy to have escaped such peril.

On the next day at seven o'clock, we had a fair wind and we saw a pirate from Salé.[61] He came to us to ask if we had seen any Christian ships. He told us that the ships we had seen were Dutch ships that traded along the barbarian coast. This occurred within sight of Gibraltar, and as the wind was favorable to us, we continued our journey. We arrived at the bay of Tétouan on 12 February 1642, where we lowered our anchor. This bay is situated one and a half miles from the city of Tétouan. The mouth of the river, which was previously supposed to serve as a harbor for Tétouan, is situated {96} just one mile from the city, but the father of the present marques de Santa Cruz, who is a general of the Spanish galleys, has made this river completely unusable by letting some ships sink in it. He did this to obstruct the pirate ships that set sail at that place every day to plunder the Spanish coast. We had lowered our anchor in this bay and were all glad that our journey was completed, for we hoped to be able to sleep ashore that evening. However, the sea was very rough because of the east wind for, with the east wind, the Mediterranean Sea forces her water into the *Oceano*—which we call the Spanish Sea.[62] For this reason, the captain did not want the boat to be put out that evening. He feared some accident because of the sea level, for this place lies almost {97} directly between the two seas, causing great turbulence in the water and forcing us to cast two more anchors into the sea. Our misfortune was that we could not get to the calmer sea anymore because of the strong wind. During the entire night the storm increased, and on the next day it was completely impossible to get to the shore. The captain and the other Turks on the ship, seeing that the bad weather did not improve, became very anxious. They knew no remedy and feared that

---

61. *Salé*: the base of the feared Sallee pirates; Salé broke away from Morocco briefly in 1627 to form an independent corsair republic.

62. *Oceano—which we call the Spanish Sea*: the Atlantic; European sailors referred to the Atlantic as the "Mare d'Espagna." See Pınar Emiralioğlu, *Geographical Knowledge and Imperial Culture in the Early Modern Ottoman Empire* (New York: Routledge, 2016), 134.

any moment the cables might break and that the ship would crash against a rock and break into a thousand pieces, without a hope of anyone on the ship staying alive.

Now the captain, who was desperate, had {98} a certain Christian slave (who only expected to be struck on the neck), called from the place where we were locked up. He was called Hans Maurus and was a man with great experience in navigation. He was asked if he could give any advice to prevent the forthcoming peril, whereupon he answered, "If it pleases you to follow my advice, I see a way (with God's help) to save the lives of all men here. But the ship will be lost." The captain asked, "In what way?" He said, "The foresail must be made ready in such a manner that it can be pulled up gently. Thus, we will turn the ship and let it run onto the sandbank. Otherwise the ship will be driven toward the rocks by the strong wind and it will break into a thousand pieces." {99} This advice met with approval and the foresail was prepared as directed. This was done around noon.

The wind continued to grow stronger and stronger and as the Turks are very superstitious, they all went to read their *assala*[63] together, which is their common prayer. They promised to offer alms if they were delivered from this peril, and seeing no miracle, they turned to sacrifice, which is the last remedy they use to become reconciled with God when they are in peril. This is done in the following manner: they take a live sheep (and for this reason there are always live sheep on the Turkish ships) and, with the greatest solemnity, cut it in four parts and throw these parts over the four corners of the ship into the sea. In the meantime, {100} we Christians commended ourselves to the mercy of God. Night began to fall and the wind increased constantly. The Turk who had the task of locking us up in the evening came to lock us up as usual. We asked him to free us if the ship should run aground, so that everyone could try to save his own life. He made that promise.

It was around midnight on the night between 12 and 13 February 1642 and it was just full moon when our strongest anchor cable broke. And as the other two anchors had short cables, the ship, because of the force of the wind, dragged the two remaining anchors with it. We thought we would drown helplessly, but the hatch that locked us in was opened by the Turks who were {101} on the deck. They called to us, "Come up here, Christians, for we have to perish together." We leaped up so eagerly that we obstructed one another, for only one could pass through at a time. When we were upon

---

63. *assala*: from the Arabic *al-ṣalāh*, meaning "daily prayer."

the deck, we found a scene much like Judgment Day, for at the back of the ship the Turks were crying out loud to their prophet Mahomet. At the mast, there were about twenty-three Jews, loudly calling for Moses, Abraham, Isaac, etc., and their other patriarchs and prophets. And we Christians called out to Jesus and Mary. Among us Christians, there were some heretics from different sects who prayed in their own way. And in this confusion, the two dragging anchors were cut off {102} so that the ship would not be unattended.[64] The sail, which had been readied, was hoisted, whereupon the front of the ship swung toward the shore with astounding swiftness. The Christian slave Hans Maurus, of whom I spoke above, said to us in Flemish, "You should all expect to be hit on your heads," fearing that parts of the rigging—yes, even the mast itself—would fall, but, thank God, in less time than it took to say a Miserere[65] and without anything falling down, the ship hit the ground and burst apart. It fell slightly to one side, from which side most of the people who were aboard jumped out. When I saw this, I also decided to jump out, but from the front side, from the bowsprit. I went there, and when I arrived, {103} I found another Christian slave who stood on the bowsprit and was ready to jump. Some who followed me said, "Hurry, jump." I did not do this until I saw that the ones who had jumped before me had found ground beneath their feet. When I saw this, I commended myself to God and jumped in the water, which reached up to my girdle. I was very glad and I approached the shore, but a wave then covered my head with water, so that I was forced to swim three or four strokes. Another [wave] hit me and I was thrown on land. I praised God and I immediately called out to Caloen, for though I had seen him jump, I did not know if he had come ashore. He had the same fears for me. We found {104} each other right away, and we congratulated one another on having reached the shore. I went to look for the Turk who had come with us as our supervisor. I found him among some Christians, Turks, and Jews who all stood together, or better said, huddled together like a herd of sheep. [They did this] to avoid dying from cold, for they were completely wet from head to foot. Gradually we all gathered together except for a Jewish boy called Abramico, of whom no one aboard had heard a word or seen a sign.

Here on the shore we were (thank God) safe from the perils of the sea, but not from the barbarians who live there on the fields. If they found out

---

64. *not be unattended*: the manuscript is unclear; it reads "nieuers aperen."
65. *Miserere*: a reference to Psalm 51, which is a prayer for mercy.

{105} that a ship had been stranded, they would come to plunder it and kill us. For that reason, the captain immediately sent two Turks (who had been there before) to the governor in Tétouan, which was one and a half miles away, to inform him of our accident and also to ask him for protection against the barbarians. All this happened during the night while we stood there and almost died of cold. Our good fortune was that one of the Turks had a tinderbox (for they often carry a tinderbox in their bag to light tobacco) and we made a fire. First, we set fire to some dry bushes that grew there on the land. Then, when we had fire, we constantly threw {106} sticks, barrels, and all else that the sea cast ashore from the wreck of our ship onto it. We spent the whole night by this fire.

At daybreak, the barbarians came to see if there was anything to steal, but the people from Tétouan came immediately with many horses to transport to the city the goods that we had saved. The governor of Tétouan came in person with twenty horsemen, who were armed with lances in the African way. The Turk who supervised us hired a horse to transport his luggage and himself, for as the storm had decreased slightly, all the luggage of the passengers and most of the cargo had been saved, but was wet. Caloen and I also hired a horse, {107} and we rode together, as wet as we were. At about noon, we arrived in Tétouan. A Jew who had come with us showed us a tavern in the Jewry (this is the place where the Jews live). We agreed to pay one patacon a month for lodging. After we had been in Tétouan for two days, a *cafila*[66] (that is, a group of people traveling together) left for Ceuta. Two men who were civilians from Tétouan went along with them. They went to Ceuta as hostages, and the Redeeming Fathers of the Order of the Most Holy Trinity[67] (who were in Ceuta) would then come to negotiate bravely with the governor of Tétouan for the release {108} of the Christian slaves. We were glad to have such an opportunity, for sometimes the people of Ceuta and those of Tétouan do not have any communication with each other for three or four months. We sent a letter to Ceuta with this cafila (having confidence that our companion Saldens was still there, for he had written to us from that place).

---

66. *cafila*: from the Arabic *qāfilah*, meaning "company of travelers."
67. *the Order of the Most Holy Trinity*: the Trinitarian Order is a Catholic religious order also known as the Order of the Most Holy Trinity for the Redemption of Captives. It was founded in France in 1198 by St. John of Matha. It undertook large-scale missions to ransom Christian captives in the early modern period.

Two days later, the cafila returned with two Redeeming Fathers of the Order of the Blessed Trinity. Their arrival occasioned great joy, both among the Christian slaves and among the pagans, for the former hoped to receive their freedom and the latter hoped to gain money. We went to greet the Fathers and we received a letter from a Spanish nobleman called Don Martin de Penalosa, who was in Ceuta. He sent us the following message: {109} "Your companion Reynier Saldens was tired of staying here in Ceuta and has gone to Gibraltar to entertain himself. But he has given me the task of supplying you with anything you might find necessary. As I understand from your letter that you are in need of two hundred patacons, I will order a Moorish merchant called Alli Tagarino to put two hundred patacons at your disposal. This same Alli Tagarino will stand bail for you, so that you are free to live in the city without having to go to the *masmorra*"[68] (this is the prison). "In the meantime, I will write to Gibraltar immediately so that Reynier Saldens may return here and that the exchange with the {110} five Turks (who, praise God, are all well) may take place soon." We were very happy with this news, but as I said above, happiness at home means sorrow waits at the door.

The five Turks who were in Ceuta were bailed out by two rich Turkish merchants who often resided in Ceuta. They walked freely about the streets without being put in prison. As our companion Saldens was not in Ceuta, Monstafa Ingles wrote to Tétouan that Saldens had promised seven hundred patacons to contribute to Caloen's ransom and that they would therefore put us in the masmorra until we also agreed to keep this promise. The instigator {111} of this business was the Turkish captain Hibraim Arrais. He had said in Ceuta that we had promised the seven hundred patacons before we left Algiers. The Turk who guarded us went to bring this letter to the people who had been recommended to him by Monstafa's grandmother. They thought it good to put us in the masmorra, first, to see if they could get anything from us, and second, to satisfy their correspondents from Algiers. The Turk who supervised us told us what they had arranged and that he had no part in the matter, and without further ado he conducted us to the masmorra. This is a dungeon that lies {112} about thirty feet underground and is divided into three parts, of which the greatest part is twenty-eight feet long and twenty-four feet wide. One hundred and seventy Christian slaves usually occupied this place. This prison receives no light but what comes

---

68. *masmorra*: a prison or dungeon. From the Spanish *mazmorra*.

from three barred windows, which are situated at street level, and each of these barred windows has a rope and a hook attached to it. When Christians pass by during the daytime, they charitably bring bread, meat, water, or anything else [the prisoners] want—provided that they pay for it—and pass it through the bars with the hook. This is because the guard of this masmorra will not let anyone enter unless they bribe him. There are no toilets in this prison, so pots are hung on the walls. These pots are emptied every evening, at which time the guard opens one of the gratings. {113} All the pots are then lifted up with a hook. For every pot, the guard receives a coin (which is a great cruelty), and all who stay in the prison must sleep on the floor and are not allowed to hang beds against the walls. As there are so many people and there is so little space, as I said, the people all sleep crowded together. This causes so much heat in the summer and so many lice and fleas that it is considered worse than rowing in a galley.

We were there during the winter, but what troubled us most was that the whole floor was covered with people at night. Then, at the most unexpected moment, a few Moorish boys came and threw water and filth through the barred windows. {114} This sometimes happened three or four times in one night and caused such alarm that everyone had to get up to avoid being trampled by someone else. Caloen and I had our sleeping place in a small corner, as a favor from a Knight of St. Jacob[69] who was called Don Hieronimo de Penaroa. He was born in Cordoba and was also a slave, and he formed a great friendship with us. He told us that there, in the masmorra we were in, he bought his dinner together with four other slaves for ten shillings a month. Caloen and I joined this Don Hieronimo and his companions in paying ten shillings a month. We were served at noon and in the evening; that is to say, we filled our stomachs. While we were in all this misery, {115} our companion Saldens had returned to Ceuta. He received the letter in which I informed him of all that happened; [of] how we were in the masmorra, and how the five Turks were the cause of this, for they had written that we should be put in the masmorra until we consented to [pay] the seven hundred patacons which, they said, they had been promised when they were still in Dunkirk. To show that neither Caloen nor I had made any promise, I also sent him a letter, written in Turkish, from the Turk who supervised us. In this letter, he said that we were not guilty and that

69. *Knight of St. Jacob*: d'Aranda most likely means the Order of Santiago, also known as the Order of Saint James of the Sword. This Spanish Christian military order was founded in the twelfth century.

we had made no promise but to pay the twenty-five patacons for him and our fare of passage on the ship on which we had come. But though this Turk said {116} that he had written these things, I wrote to Saldens to let someone read the letter [first] and only pass it on if he thought it was right. And [I wrote] that he should immediately put the five Turks in chains and also put them in the masmorra of Ceuta, which is much worse than the one in Tétouan, for that one has no light from outside and is situated under an oven, which constantly gives off heat.

At this time the Redeeming Fathers, of whom I spoke above, returned to Ceuta without having freed any Christians, because they could not reach an agreement with the governor of Tétouan. Before the Redeeming Fathers free a Christian, {117} they make an agreement with the governor in this or a similar manner: that they shall pay a third in coupons,[70] up to about a dozen [coupons], another third in pearls, up to about as many, and another third in money. The misunderstanding was that the governor wanted neither the pearls nor the coupons for the price the Fathers had estimated. Also, he wanted the Fathers to buy thirteen Christian slaves who were in his possession. The Fathers did not want to do this, for these slaves were Portuguese or Frenchmen and the Fathers said (and not without reason) that as long as there were Spanish slaves, they could not redeem slaves of other nations, for the alms they brought had been given in Spain. Hence {118} the Spaniards were preferred above others. Because of these differences, the Fathers returned to Ceuta with the cafila.

I gave my letter to a young Dutchman who also went to Ceuta with the cafila. He gave my letter to Saldens personally and told him that he had seen us the day before in the masmorra. Saldens was very disturbed by this. He immediately went to look for the five Turks and put them in the masmorra. He said to the captain [of the Turks]: "*Pilla baso.*" This is what the Turks say when they want to beat Christians and it means "lie down on the ground." Four people then have to hold [the prisoner] by the hands and feet and take his clothes off. The person who beats him hits him on {119} the back or on the buttocks, whatever he prefers, and to make them more fearful, he holds a rope in his hand. While the captain made himself ready to lie down, the four remaining Turks trembled with fear. Just at that moment, two Turkish merchants passed and said to Saldens, "What are you doing with

---

70. *coupons*: the manuscript refers to "bonnetten." It is not clear what the exact nature of these coupons was; it could refer to a type of bill of exchange.

these unhappy slaves?" Whereupon he answered, "I want to finish off two or three of those ungrateful dogs [by beating them] with a club. I released them on bail and let them walk freely through the streets and they have caused my companions to be put in the masmorra (notwithstanding that they had a pledge), where they are now still {120} suffering a thousand miseries. And these dogs walk through the streets here and write a thousand lies to gain money unjustly." Then the merchants spoke with the Turks and said to Saldens, "Don't hit these slaves; we will stand bail that your companions will arrive with the first cafila." Saldens said, "But in the meantime, my companions will die of misery in the masmorra." Whereupon the merchants said, "We will write to Tétouan tomorrow saying that your companions should be released immediately from the masmorra." Saldens and the two Turkish merchants went to speak to the governor of Ceuta immediately, who at that time was the marquess of Miranda.[71] {121} He gave [them] a letter to send to the governor of Tétouan, which contained the following: "Send me two Christians named Jan Baptiste van Caloen and Emanuel de Aranda. I promise on my Christian faith and on my nobility, that as soon as said Christians stand here at the gates of Ceuta, I will release the five Turks named Monstafa Ingles, Hibraim Arrais, Alli Tagarino, Rodes Monstafa, and Monstafa Oiga."

As I said above, the Redeeming Fathers had returned from Tétouan to Ceuta because they could not reach an agreement with the governor. While they had been {122} in Tétouan, a prestigious Jew from Ceuta had gone to Tétouan specially to mediate between the Redeeming Fathers and the governor. The letter [from the governor of Ceuta] was given to this Jew so that he would personally hand it over to the governor of Tétouan. He did this, and we were freed from the masmorra immediately and were given the liberty to walk wherever we wanted in the streets. We immediately went to the Jewry where we had our lodging, which had been kept for us by the Turk who [had] supervised us while we were in the masmorra. While we were in the masmorra, some {123} strange things happened. Two Spanish soldiers of the garrison of Penon de Velez[72] (which is a fort belonging to the king of Spain, although it is situated in Africa), due to their great poverty, came to give themselves up in order to become renegades and slaves.

71. *marquess of Miranda*: Juan Fernández de Córdoba y Coalla, marqués de Miranda de Auta (1595–1664), governor of Ceuta from 1641–1644. The marqués de Miranda was also a Knight of the Order of Santiago.
72. *Penon de Velez*: Peñón de Vélez de la Gomera, a Spanish enclave on the northern coast of Morocco. A *peñón* is a type of fort, typically situated on a rocky offshore island, built by the Spanish Empire.

They were not allowed to convert [to Islam]. They were put in the masmorra by those who had found them, in order to be sold to the galleys from Algiers in the summer, which usually pass by at that time.

We walked freely every day, both inside and outside the city, while waiting for the cafila to [be ready to] leave. Caloen and I each bought a white coat and a red cap. {124} This is the garb of a Christian slave when he receives his freedom. All Christian slaves who wished to do so gave letters to us, so I had as many as three hundred letters from Christian slaves. As there is nothing that does not end, God was willing also to put an end to our slavery. The Jew who had come from Ceuta to mediate with the governor of Tétouan about the disagreements between the governor and the Redeeming Fathers had now resolved these differences. He left on the following day, being 23 March 1642. Every hour felt like a year to us. We hired two horses from a Moor who traveled with the cafila. We prepared two hens, {125} salted and peppered, to take with us on the way, and a large flask of wine. We left Tétouan on foot, accompanied by many Christian slaves we knew, till about a quarter of a mile outside the city, where all who went with the cafila gathered. Here, we happily mounted the horses that had been prepared for us and said goodbye to the Christians who had kept us company up to that point, but who now, unhappily, had to return to the city.

We rode about two miles that evening until we arrived at a field that is the last place inhabited by people on the road between Tétouan and Ceuta. Here, we and all the people in the cafila dismounted {126} and all the loaded mules were unloaded. Two or three Turkish men immediately cut some branches and other wood with their sabers and at once they began to make a fire. Because some rain falls at night in the month of March, we all sat together by the fire. Everyone offered whatever they had brought with them to eat. We offered our hens. I asked the Turks and Moors who sat around us if they did not want to eat with us, but they answered that they were not allowed to eat our food because the hens had been killed by the hands of a Christian. I said, "I swear to God that a Turk has killed them." {127} (Which was true). They believed me and we ate together. After we had eaten, each of us took a place by the fire to sleep. We left one hour before dawn. On the whole route from the place where we had slept to Ceuta, which was five miles, we found not only no people, but also no sign that any people had ever lived there, except for one place with some walls that had fallen over. A Turk who was with us shot a wild boar with his gun. Because they were going to cut the boar in four pieces and take it with them to Ceuta,

Caloen gave them two patacons.[73] Before the cafila arrives at Ceuta, it has {128} to take a route along the coast so that the sentinels of Ceuta can see the cafila. Taking that route indicates that we come in peace. When we had come within musket-shot of Ceuta, a Moor told Caloen and myself that we had to stay there until the five Turks who were to be exchanged with us had arrived. I gave my church book to a Jew I knew, who would enter the city with the cafila, so that he could give it to Saldens as a sign that I was there. He would then do what was needed for us to enter the city. This happened around nine o'clock in the morning. We stood there till about three o'clock in the afternoon before we saw anyone other than the Moor who was with us {129} and who kept us there until the five Turks arrived.

We could not imagine what the reason could be that we had to wait so long. At three o'clock in the afternoon, we saw about thirty horses coming through the gates of the city, all lightly armed in the Moorish way. One of them, who had a light horse, found the fields, and then the others followed and stationed themselves along the roads. The captain of these horsemen said to us, "Your companion speaks with the governor concerning your entrance to the city." In the meantime, a company on foot came from the city and stationed itself between the horsemen {130} and the city. Behind them followed many Turkish and Moorish slaves[74] with heavy chains attached to their legs and large pots of water on their necks. They came to fetch water from a well, which was situated between the city gates and the infantry. This takes place every day with the same care, first, out of fear of being ambushed by the Moors, and second, so that the slaves do not escape. We saw all this without anyone looking for us.

We wondered what took our companion Saldens so long to come and speak to us. The reason was that, in his letter to the governor of Tétouan, the governor of Ceuta had promised to release the five Turks as soon as we {131} arrived at the gates of Ceuta. But he did not dare to do this, because a small ship from Tangier was expected in Ceuta, and if the five Turks had been permitted to go to Tétouan, they would have informed the people of Tétouan of this. The pirate frigates of Tétouan would then wait somewhere for this ship to pass. We were in the great danger either of having to return

---

73. *Because they were [. . .] two patacons*: presumably Caloen wanted part of or the whole boar, but this is not clear in d'Aranda's text. On p. 134, d'Aranda mentions that they gave the head of the boar to the governor.

74. *Turkish and Moorish slaves*: this passage is quite remarkable, since it shows, side by side, the two Mediterranean slave economies: the European captives in Muslim hands (such as d'Aranda), and the North African captives in European bondage (i.e., the Moorish and Turkish slaves from the Spanish enclave of Ceuta).

to Tétouan or to stay where we were for two or three days, outside the gates. But our companion Saldens, assisted by Don Martin de Penalosa, was able to influence the governor so much that he called the five Turks to him. He told them, {132} "It is true that I gave my word to the governor of Tétouan that I would set you free as soon as the two Christians arrived here. The two Christians are now at the gates, waiting to come in. But I cannot let you go until the expected ship has arrived. If you are content that the two Christians enter, I promise that I will let you go as soon as the ship has arrived. In the meantime, you are free to roam the streets here, by day and night, like all other free people. If you do not accept this, I will not let the Christians enter." They answered that they were content with the two {133} Christians entering [the city], that they trusted the governor not to wrong them, and that they would wait until the ship arrived.

Saldens had all the above news sent to us by the man with whom he lodged, so that we would not have to wait longer for it. He informed us that he would come and get us (but he had to speak to the governor first). He did this half an hour later, accompanied by Don Martin de Penalosa, who assisted him in everything. We were both very happy when we saw our companion whom we had longed for so much. We embraced each other, he wished us much happiness, and we went into the city together. Here we went to kiss {134} the hands of the governor. We gave him the head of the wild boar we had brought with us, as I said above, as a present. On our way from the palace of the governor to our lodgings with Saldens, we met the five Turks, who welcomed us and embraced us. They came with us to the tavern, where we gave them something to drink. They asked about their friends in Algiers and we told each other about our adventures. This happened on 24 March 1642. A certain friend wrote these two inscriptions, the first one concerning the day of my capture and the second one concerning the day of my liberation. {135}

CHRONICUM CAPTIVITATIS.

MENSIS AUGUSTI DIE XXII, CAPTUS FUIT.

CHRONICUM REDEMPTIONIS.

MARTII XXIIII, REDUCTUS FUIT.[75]

---

75. *Chronicum . . . fuit*: Chronicle of [his] captivity.
　On the twenty-second day of the month of August, I was captured.
　Chronicle of [his] redemption.
　On March 24, I was freed.

We were here in Ceuta for eight days, waiting for the departure of a brigantine,[76] on which we wanted to leave. It was a brigantine with fifteen benches[77] on each side. We passed from Africa to Europe in five hours. We were afraid of being captured again until we reached Gibraltar, which is the first city in Spain. We were there for three days, and we went to visit Our Lady's Chapel of Europe,[78] situated {136} a quarter of a mile outside the city, which lies close to Africa. All those who have friends that are slaves frequently visit this chapel. We still wore our white coats and red caps. And so we traveled to Cádiz, and on the way, in the taverns where we dismounted, all the people from the villages or cities we passed who had friends in slavery came to see if we had any letters or messages from their friends. This is why people who are freed from slavery wear white coats and red caps—so that everyone knows that they are freed from slavery. When we were in Cádiz, we got ourselves some Christian clothing and traveled from there to Madrid. The three of us stayed there for two months. {137} After that, Saldens went away to the army with his old master, the marquess of Solero. Caloen and I went to San Sebastián, and from there we passed through France without passports, trusting the certificates we had, which proved that we were freed from slavery. We boarded a ship in Rouen and arrived in Dover in England. Two days later, we arrived in Bruges, which I had yearned for so long. My late mother, who had not known about my imprisonment, was still alive [at the time]. She and all my friends were overjoyed about my arrival (this happened on 22 August 1642, just two years after I had been captured). But after a short time, God wished {138} this happiness to be mixed with sorrow, for shortly after my arrival, my brother-in-law and my mother died. From this we learn that in this life, joy and sorrow succeed each other constantly. God, give me and all people eternal peace in the Lord. (*Finis*). Jac Emanuel de Aranda.

---

76. *brigantine*: a two-masted sailing ship equipped both for sailing and rowing. The brigantines' speed and maneuverability made them popular pirate ships.

77. *benches*: rowing benches for the galley slaves who manned the oars.

78. *Our Lady's Chapel of Europe*: the Shrine of Our Lady of Europe, located at Europa Point, the southernmost point of Gibraltar.

L'ESCLAVE
RELIGIEUX,
ET
SES AVANTURES.

A PARIS,
Chez DANIEL HORTEMELS,
ruë S. Jacques, au Mécénas.
M. DC. XC.

Avec Privilege du Roy.

Figure 5.1 Title page of Antoine Quartier's narrative
Source: Antoine Quartier, *L'esclave religieux, et ses avantures* (Paris, 1690); Bibliothèque Nationale de France.

CHAPTER V

ANTOINE QUARTIER, *THE RELIGIOUS SLAVE AND HIS ADVENTURES*

1690 French print edition; selection

Captivity in Tripoli 1660–1668

The testimony of the French Catholic Antoine Quartier is one of the rare instances of a Barbary captivity narrative set in Tripoli.[1] Quartier composed a first draft of *L'esclave religieux* a few years after his enslavement in Tripoli (1660 to 1668). Upon his return to France, Quartier became a Mercedarian,[2] answering a religious calling that had already developed during his captivity. The text was published in 1690, more than twenty years after Quartier's return home from slavery in Tripoli. *L'esclave religieux* complements the *Histoire chronologique du royaume de Tripoly*, an unpublished, 1200-page narrative about Tripolitan captivity. The *Histoire* has been attributed to the French physician Girard, who was also a slave in Tripoli shortly after Quartier's return home.[3] Both texts are rare testimonies of captivity in North African regions beyond the cities of Tunis and Algiers or the regency of Morocco. In addition to their value for the study of corsairing

---

1. *The Religious Slave* was attributed to Antoine Quartier as late as the 1970s and had hardly any impact on scholarship until that time. See Guy Turbet-Delof, "Le père mercedaire Antoine Quartier et sa chronique tripoline des années 1660–1668," *Les Cahiers de Tunisie* 8, nos. 77–78 (1972): 51–58. On Quartier, see Gillian L. Weiss, *Captives and Corsairs: France and Slavery in the Early Modern Mediterranean* (Stanford, CA: Stanford University Press, 2011), 54–56, 69.

2. *Mercedarian*: the Mercedarian Order is a Catholic order that undertook large-scale missions to ransom Christian captives in the early modern period. It was founded in Spain in 1218 by St. Peter Nolasco.

3. See Gillian L. Weiss, "A Huguenot Captive in 'Uthman Dey's Court: *Histoire chronologique du royaume de Tripoly* (1685) and Its Author," in *Piracy and Captivity in the Mediterranean: 1550–1810*, ed. Mario Klarer (London: Routledge, 2019), 234–57.

and captivity, the two texts are also indispensable sources for the history of Tripoli in the seventeenth century in general.

Despite being one of the very few surviving Tripolitan captivity accounts, Quartier's text features some prototypical Barbary narrative sections. These include dramatic capture scenes, the complexities of ransom activities, and Quartier's insistent exhortations to readers to assist with the ransom of those still in slavery. After his capture, Quartier was moved from one master to the next, until he finally became the property of the *basha*.[4] Quartier's narrative contains some unique experiences, most importantly the section in which he describes the time he spent in the countryside, where he was forced into agricultural labor. He reports that, as a slave of the basha, he was obliged to do particularly arduous tasks under miserable conditions, for example, farming for months in the desert in extreme heat.

The experience of excruciating work on the desert fields that Quartier depicts is not unusual for Barbary captives.[5] However, only very few Barbary captivity narratives actually describe this type of rural work. He writes, "The next morning, we started ploughing the soil with fifty camels, while the other captives were employed to cut the bushes, dig the ditches, and sow the seeds, all of which was done in twenty days" (157–58).[6] The conditions were so bad that Quartier claims: "Since our departure, we had only eaten grass snakes, lizards, and crocodiles" (158).

On top of the harsh labor that Quartier claims he had to perform during his captivity, the plague ravaged Tripoli for one and a half years from 1662 to 1664. He reports that about six thousand inhabitants of the city and the surrounding rural areas died. The death toll among the European slaves was five hundred—a comparatively small number considering the disadvantageous and unhygienic conditions in which they lived. Quartier asserts that he contracted the disease while working as a nurse but managed to recover from it.

Perhaps because of his own profound faith, Quartier demonstrates curiosity about and interest in the manifestations of the religious practices of the Muslim and Hebrew communities in Tripoli. However, Quartier dwells most

---

4. *basha*: the term "basha" was frequently used to refer to the governor of a city.

5. See Robert C. Davis, "Rural Slavery in the Early Modern Mediterranean: The Significance of Algiers," in *Human Bondage in the Cultural Contact Zone. Transdisciplinary Perspectives on Slavery and Its Discourses*, ed. Raphael Hörmann and Gesa Mackenthun (Münster: Waxmann Verlag, 2010), 81–94.

6. Page numbers correspond to those in the original historical edition used for the translation in this anthology.

on those who converted from Christianity to Islam because, as he puts it, "The door to freedom is open to all who renounce their faith" (foreword). In other words, conversion to Islam provided great opportunities for renegades. He deliberately emphasizes the fact that "the renegades live without religion" (19) and represents those who "turned Turk" in the worst light possible. Quartier himself reports being faced with generous conversion offers. His testimony follows the traditional pattern of most Barbary accounts: He asserts that he rejected this temptation and that his Muslim master generously and benevolently accepted Quartier's display of religious steadfastness.

The theme of remaining faithful to Christianity takes up large parts of the foreword and is an undercurrent that runs through Quartier's entire narrative. For him, those captives who resist apostasy are "no less martyrs than those of the early church" (foreword). Quartier's position on ransoming slaves is quite extraordinary: Of course, he wanted to help free captives in order to ease their lot. However, for Quartier, the ultimate driving force behind ransom efforts was to reduce the number of converts. The more likely prospects were for ransom, the more likely it was that a slave would adhere to his or her faith, even during a long and arduous captivity. The ultimate proof of Quartier's own religious determination and his belief in this very concept is that, after his return to France, he became a member of the Mercedarian Order, which was dedicated to the ransom of Christian slaves from Muslim captivity.

Notes on the present Translation of Antoine Quartier's *The Religious Slave and His Adventures*

This translation is based on the first edition: Antoine Quartier, *L'esclave religieux, et ses avantures* (Paris: Daniel Hortemels, 1690; digitized edition: https://gallica.bnf.fr/ark:/12148/bpt6k104958t).

Omissions in the text have been marked with an ellipsis [. . .]. The lengthy chapter titles have been omitted without comment. Paragraph breaks have been added to enhance the readability of the narrative. The numbers in brackets {} always indicate the beginning of a page and refer to the original page numbers of the 1690 edition. The foreword, however, is unpaginated in the 1690 edition, and page breaks have therefore been indicated with a forward slash (/). Special thanks go to Mark Cruse for his invaluable assistance with clarifying numerous cases of doubt.

Antoine Quartier, *The Religious Slave and His Adventures*
(Paris: Chez Daniel Hortemels, ruë S. Jacques, au
Mécénas, 1690)

Translated by Clara Messiant

Foreword

It is neither the desire to write nor the aspiration to become famous that induces me to publish this work, which I entitled "The Religious Slave," for while I was in chains, I resolved to renounce the world. I have no other wish than to rouse Christians to attend to the redemption of captives by exposing them to a faithful representation of their miseries. I can truly say that, though I suffered in slavery for eight years, my deepest sorrow was to see so many others more miserable than myself, either because they did not have the same strength to bear their pains, or because Heaven did not give them the succor with which it favored me from time to time, / for it is not among the Christians held in Barbary that the proverb occurs: "The consolation of an unfortunate [Christian] is to see people more miserable than himself." Since the door to freedom is open to all who renounce their faith, only those who are animated by the spirit of Jesus Christ remain in chains, continuing united and firm in the face of the cruelest forms of persecution. Therefore, the weight of their chains becomes unremarkable, for they regard themselves as children who are suffering for having the same father,[7] and they help the weakest ones, to prevent them from falling into apostasy.

    I admire the charity of the Christians in France; it makes them descend into the darkest dungeons to help those who are, more often than not, strangers to them. They are comforted, their suffering is relieved, their interests are taken care of, their trial is requested, they are released from jail through the payment of their debts, and / sometimes payments are made to secure their release from the banishment to which the law had condemned them. One cannot praise these acts of charity toward one's fellow man enough, but [how] can one not complain that compatriots, friends,

---

7. *the same father.* Quartier means the Christian God.

parents, brothers, young children, frail girls, clergy, priests, and people of extraordinary merit are forgotten? No one considers that they are in danger of losing faith at any moment and succumbing to the harshness of the torments they bear. These torments are no less cruel than those of the first martyrs. It is true that the slaves can end their suffering once they have the means to redeem themselves, but they are no less martyrs than those of the early church, for they suffer for the name and the faith of Jesus Christ when they could break their bonds by abandoning Christianity. Their martyrdom lasts even longer [than that of the early martyrs], for the / former did not stay long in jail and were often killed as soon as they were arrested, whereas the captives suffer all their lives. Their only bed is the ground; hunger, thirst, and nakedness follow them like shadows; the food given to them barely suffices to keep death away and to preserve a life that becomes more wretched by the day. Nevertheless, they are forced to work without respite. The stick and the whip are their only forms of instruction. These infidels do not take illness, weakness, and helplessness into account. They strike without distinction when what was commanded has not been done, and, ordinarily, they ask for more than can possibly be done in order to use this as a reason to mistreat the captives and oblige them to take the turban.[8]

/ The most dangerous persecutions are the temptations they use to seduce the slaves who could not be weakened through suffering. There is no sweetness or apparent tenderness that they do not use to deceive them. They take pains to discover their biggest weakness and try to surprise them with it. If the captive likes [sensual] pleasures, they use good food and all that is hedonistic. If he is moved by kindness and has lost the hope of being redeemed, they promise him greatness, they pretend to sympathize with his disgrace, they show him respect and affection, and they offer him freedom. The renegades,[9] above all, glory in perverting the Christians. They convince themselves that the fetters of the slaves reproach them incessantly for their own apostasy and that their crime diminishes when they / share it with other guilty parties. This is why they spare no violence, cruelty, and mercy, no feasts, gifts, time, or sorrow to force [the Christians] to follow the teachings of the Quran. These infidels are both the judges and the persecutors of captives who resist them and they never tire of making them suffer.

8. *take the turban*: convert to Islam.
9. *renegades*: Christians who converted to Islam.

Those, on the other hand, who declare with awful blasphemy that they want to adopt the law of Mahomet are instantly free. Their masters give them their daughters in marriage and obtain important positions for them and, seeing themselves thus replete with wealth, honor, and reputation in a short time, [these apostates] forget their faith and homeland easily and become the biggest persecutors of Christians. What was most deplorable for me was / to see young boys and girls being brutalized just like the other slaves. The fragility of their age, the delicateness of their sex, and everything that nature could inspire in their favor could not touch the hearts of these tigers. But what gives comfort is that one always finds young children so fortified by [God's] grace that they praise the virtues of God in the midst of the harshest torments. I saw a fifteen-year-old boy who, while he was being beaten in order to force him to renounce [Christianity], shouted how sweet it is to die for Jesus Christ.

All of Christian Europe knows what is happening in Turkey, in the kingdoms of Tripoli, Tunis, Algiers, Morocco, and Fez, and along the Mediterranean coast. Particularly in France, the Reverend Fathers of Mercy, / who made several celebrated redemptions a few years ago, are famous, so that it can be said that they hear the cries and groans of these unfortunate people. Woe, then, to Christians who are indifferent to the cries and disgraces of their brothers.

I would be happy if the story of my captivity were to make an impression on my readers' minds and encourage their charity toward the slaves. I describe the city of Tripoli, the state of the kingdom, and the customs of the inhabitants, and say something about Tunis, Algiers, and great Cairo. I recount the adventures of a few Christians, because they are similar to [my experience] and they are part of it. The reader should not be surprised if he finds this similar to a novel;[10] the country of the corsairs is the scene of all kinds of events and novelties. The smallest / capture they make of Christians often provides extraordinary material capable of filling volumes. I added nothing to my story and I deliberately omitted many things that could have embellished my work. I do not expect my work to be successful; we live in a century in which, of the many books that are published, few deserve success. [. . .]

---

10. *similar to a novel*: It is quite remarkable that as early as 1690, Quartier compares his narrative to the genre of the "novel" ("Roman" in the 1690 French text) and its setting to "scenes" ("theatre" in the 1690 French text). Like authors of early novels, Quartier also stresses the authenticity of his narrative, claiming that he "added nothing" to his "story" (introduction).

{5} [. . .] The Dutch vessel on which I embarked[11] to go to Constantinople was called *Le Fleur de Lys*. It was {6} half armed for battle and half filled with goods and carried passengers from various countries. A Greek woman was on board, as well as her two little girls aged between eight and ten years, whom she had had with a Venetian nobleman. He had captured her for her beauty and had brought her to Venice. After his death, she left to return to her country. As soon as the vessel was in suitable condition to sail, we left the harbor with a favorable wind that allowed us to arrive at Zante[12] in a short time. We did not stay because of the earthquakes that are frequent on the island. The inhabitants pointed out the neighboring lands to us, which were in ruins, and some houses that were recently knocked down. One day, as we were enjoying ourselves after dinner, the room that we were in shook so much that the stones of the door cracked, which forced us to leave the room immediately, and we had scarcely boarded when the house collapsed. We thanked Heaven for protecting us from this peril and continued our trip along Candia,[13] where all the Ottoman forces {7} were besieging the capital.

There is, of course, a difference between travels overland and those made on the sea. During the former, the diversity of the manners and customs of the people and the singular beauty of the countries makes the traveler forget, partly, about his fatigue. At sea, on the other hand, one is in a state of continual repose, having no other occupation than to pass the time and to share one's adventures with one's companions on the vessel. [Traveling] from Venice to the archipelago, we discovered, on the right, the lands of the Republic,[14] the March of Ancona,[15] Loreto, and the provinces of Abruzzo, Pozzuoli, and Calabria in the Kingdom of Naples; on the left, Dalmatia,[16] the Republic of Ragusa,[17] Albania, Epirus,[18] Bossine, Morea,[19] and Candia. We were on our guard as we approached Candia; the noise of

---

11. *embarked*: Quartier does not provide a date for his departure from Venice, but it was probably in the year 1660.
12. *Zante*: Zykanthos, a Greek island in the Ionian Sea.
13. *Candia*: now Crete. Formerly a colony of the Republic of Venice, it fell to the Ottoman Empire during the Cretan War (1645–1669).
14. *lands of the Republic*: the Republic of Venice.
15. *March of Ancona*: a semi-independent republic under papal control. It became part of the Kingdom of Italy in 1860.
16. *Dalmatia*: a historical region of Croatia. It was under Venetian rule at the time.
17. *Republic of Ragusa*: a maritime republic centered in Dalmatia, in what is now southern Croatia.
18. *Epirus*: a historical region on the Ionian Sea, now shared by Greece and Albania.
19. *Morea*: the Peloponnese peninsula in southern Greece.

the cannons of the Turks came down to us, and we were right to dread their navy. We were close to the islands of the archipelago when, one night, our captain told us that he had been lucky enough to have come from Holland to Venice without any danger, notwithstanding the number {8} of pirates roaming the Mediterranean Sea. We congratulated him on his good fortune and he brought us food and two bottles of malvasia[20] to express his gratitude. It was a happy feast, for there were people from different nations who created a bizarre concert of languages, which was very pleasant. After plenty of drinks, a Flemish priest confessed that he was going to Greece or Armenia to live there, because that is where priests can get married, and he had the intention of entering this sacrament before dying. As we were about to withdraw, the sentinel, who was descending from the mast, told the captain that he had seen a few sails in the distance. We retired, hoping the night would put distance between us, but at daybreak we saw four vessels no more than ten miles away from our ship, rushing toward us. Their rapidity made us think they were corsairs, which obliged the captain to give his orders. He made a public prayer, urged {9} each one of us to hold his position and defend his life and liberty against the enemies of the Christians, and arranged things so well that we were ready to fight.

An Italian bark that we had met in the Gulf of Venice, two days after our departure, had been taken by these pirates who, having been informed of our passage [by the Italian bark], put all sails to the wind to reach us before we could anchor off the isles of the archipelago and by this retreat avoid battle. But all the speed we could muster was useless because of the weight of our vessel, which was loaded with goods. The boldest of the four corsairs, named Beyram Rais, a Provençal renegade, saluted us with twenty-four cannon shots, but the shots fired from the stern caused more damage than all the rest. Hally Rais, a Greek renegade, attacked us on the same side. Morat, a Dutch renegade who commanded a French-style vessel equipped with forty-eight cannons, damaged us badly and, in short, we were subjected to the enemy's cannon shots followed by musket shots, arrows, and grenades.

{10} One holds some truces (on such occasions) in order to bring the wounded down into the hold and to throw the dead bodies into the sea, which the fish profit from; they never fail to go near the ships at the sound of a cannon. Meanwhile, our captain, who was a very brave man, crossed

---

20. *malvasia*: also known as malmsey, this is a wine made from one of the ancient Mediterranean Malvasia grape varieties.

the vessel and, seeing that the flank of the starboard was damaged and some of the cannons inoperative, he, with no reinforcements, made the enemies believe we had an equal force by arming the other side, although there were four pirate [ships] against one merchant ship. While one of the corsairs passed back and forth, Beyram Rais prepared to board us after the grappling hooks were thrown. We retreated to the stern to surprise these infidels, thirty of whom boarded our ship with sabers in hand. The fire from our muskets and from two short cannons loaded with scattershot were so effective that only six survived. One of them received a ponton shot[21] in his body while he was leaving and a saber blow to his head, but these wounds did not stop him from running after the one who had wounded him, and he fell down dead after six steps.

The {11} opium the Turks eat before fighting makes them furious, and they go heedlessly into battle without fearing any danger, screaming like ferocious beasts to terrify the Christians. Our captain thought the barbarians would not attempt to attack again, but ashamed of such a shameful retreat, they tried to attack us a second time. Our weapons fired so much and so precisely that they were forced to withdraw once again with a considerable loss. I was wounded during this battle by the shot of an arrow in the stomach and a splinter of wood in the kidneys. I would have been killed if the baldric[22] had not parried the blow. One of my closest friends was killed by a musket he received in the lower abdomen, and on my left, a gentleman named Grimonville, born in Rennes in Brittany,[23] was badly wounded in the face. The Order of Our Lady of Mercy for the Redemption of Captives redeemed him after I left Tripoli in Barbary. Although I was wounded, the captain ordered me to guard the bow, and while the enemies were going a little farther away to {12} hold council, he asked me to see why the cannons would not shoot. I went down to the bottom of the vessel, where I found only dead bodies and dying people. The carriages of the cannons[24] were broken and had fallen over dying persons. I heard nothing but moans, shouts, and groans, and I saw horrific scenes everywhere.

I arrived just in time to prevent a Dutchman from setting fire to the gunpowder. This desperate man would rather make us perish than allow

---

21. *a ponton shot*: "coup de ponton" in the 1690 French text. The reference is unclear.

22. *baldric*: a belt worn over one shoulder, typically used to carry a weapon or other piece of equipment.

23. *Rennes in Brittany*: a city in northwestern France.

24. *carriages of the cannons*: a structure on which cannons were mounted, allowing them to be maneuvered and fired.

[us to fall into] slavery. Having gone back upstairs, I heard the lieutenant suggesting to the captain that they escape in the rowboat because the bow was on fire, the stern smashed, and our defeat unavoidable. As I was explaining to them that we were going to fall into the hands of the Greeks of the archipelago, who have no religion and no pity, a cannon shot halved the captain's body, whose head and shoulders were swept into the sea, and the rest fell down at my feet. How alarmed I was by this fatal blow, which removed all the hope we had! The lieutenant entered the captain's room, where I followed him. A cannon shot had {13} broken his safe into pieces and scattered a large quantity of gold sequins.[25] The ones that I took on the lieutenant's advice nearly cost me my life. Leaving the room was not as easy as entering it. The poor lieutenant lost his right thigh because of a cannon shot and, as I was comforting him, we raised a white flag at the stern, which was the signal that we were surrendering.

When the Turks boarded our ship, the lieutenant embraced me and told me that he would rather throw himself into the sea than spend the rest of his life in Barbary in the deplorable state he was reduced to. I begged him not to give himself up to despair, but as soon as I left him to think about myself, he threw himself into the sea. I was first arrested by two Turks who searched me superficially and took two crowns that I had in my pockets. Two renegades searched me more thoroughly and found what they were looking for. The two Turks who had arrested me earlier were present. One of them, furious at having taken so little advantage of me, struck at me with a saber, which I avoided by fleeing. The Christians {14} were once again inspected and the officers and merchants were dispossessed of their beautiful clothes. Seventy of us survived the battle, among which were thirty wounded, and we had lost more than fifty men. As I was one of the first to go down into the main rowboat of the enemies, the Greek lady with her two daughters by her side saw me. She begged me to help her and her eldest child down and gave the youngest daughter to a new captive who, on his descent, tripped on the edge of the boat and fell down, which caused him to let go of the girl, who fell into the sea, where she could not be saved. The mother, overwhelmed with grief by the loss of her daughter, her goods, and her liberty, uttered pitiful cries to Heaven, and her misfortune moved the most insensitive corsairs. This desolate woman died of sadness in the seraglio of the basha of Tripoli after three years of captivity, and, as a final misfortune,

---

25. *sequins*: Venetian gold coins minted from the thirteenth century onward.

she saw her daughter, whom she had raised in Venice in the true religion, converting to Islam.

We twenty captives were conducted to the vessel of Morat Rais, the squadron chief. As soon as we arrived, we were searched a third time, {15} this last time more rigorously than the two other times. The sailors even took off my drawers and they left me only my shirt. I stood there in the guise of a criminal who is going to make a public confession, and without the help of an Italian renegade, who covered me with old rags, I would have suffered even greater misery during the rest of the journey.

The corsairs, while returning to Tripoli, again attacked a Christian ship, one that was carrying supplies and munitions to Candia. Before attacking this ship, which defended itself with much vigor, they locked us in the bottom of the hold. We were subjected to all imaginable miseries in this place of darkness: hunger, thirst, the uninterrupted groans of the injured people, and the excessive heat almost killed us. During the battle, which lasted more than eight hours, we made futile good wishes for our brothers, for they could not resist the infidels' attacks, and seeing their ship almost sinking, they were forced to surrender. As soon as [the ship] was in the hands of the Turks, we were allowed to go upstairs between the two decks to breathe fresh air. {16} During our sea trip, I was obliged to sleep on the riggings. It was during the heat wave, so that in the mornings, when I got up, the pitch and the tar removed some pieces of my flesh, which increased my wounds.

We arrived in Tripoli at the end of July 1660, when Osman, the Greek renegade,[26] was basha. The barbarians were very pleased about the two large hauls. They found more than forty thousand crowns in the ships without [taking into account] the goods, which were estimated [to be worth] more, as well as one hundred and fifty Christians, who embody the principal wealth of the country. All the new captives were taken to the castle to be introduced to the basha, before whom a Christian scribe asked the name, age, country, religion, art, and skill of every captive. The richness of the loot consoled the basha for the death of the officers who had been killed in the battle. Among them were two lieutenants, eight gunners, thirty Turks, and nearly forty renegades, without counting the wounded persons, whose number equaled that of the dead. After the basha had reserved the youngest

---

26. *Osman, the Greek renegade*: 'Othman Pasha (ruled 1649–1669) from Chios, Greece, who had renounced Christianity, was basha of Tripoli at the time.

and {17} most beautiful Christians for his palace and to serve his wives, he gave us each a garment, a pair of shoes, and a hood.

At night, we were taken away to the prisons, where we found several captives who exhorted us to be patient. In the morning, the prison guards drove us to the bazaar, a public square where [captives] are sold. Here the captives are half naked and are inspected by many Turks, Arabs, and Jews, who are pleased to walk around and examine the ones they want to buy. They are good at distinguishing the slaves of quality from the common ones by the feet, the hands, and the physiognomy. The basha took the rest of the slaves, taking into account those for the Levantines,[27] who make up the naval force and receive a portion of all booty. An Arab called Salem Chastel purchased me for one hundred and fifty crowns. On the way home, he stopped at a café to show me to his friends, who were smoking and drinking coffee. They congratulated him on buying me and prayed to their prophet that I would convert to their religion.

{18} Before speaking of the miseries and the adventures of my captivity, it is appropriate to give the reader a description of the city of Tripoli,[28] which we called Tripoli of Barbary to distinguish it from those of Syria and of Romania, which bear the same name. The city is located on the African sea, between Tunis and Alexandria in Egypt. It is quite well built, and the houses are very low and look like convents, so that women cannot be seen. The castle, which controls the port and where the basha {19} and his wives reside, is located to the east, by the seaside. On the left side there is the city gate, which has been the only [entrance] for more than forty years, the Turks having closed one on the landward side, which the Arabs from the countryside attacked several times, [wishing] to become the masters of Tripoli. On the left side, there is the arsenal, close to a square called La Fosse,[29] where ships are built. On the west side, there is an old fortress with walls made of earth that dominates the city. The Jews are not far from it and live alone at this end of the city as infamous and despicable people. The harbor is spacious and the ships are safe there, surrounded by rocks and protected by the castle and by another fortress called Mandrix, which dominates the big harbor. There are eighteen mosques in Tripoli, without

27. *Levantines*: Ottomans sent to North Africa (as opposed to the North African natives), who served as soldiers by land (janissaries) and sea.

28. *description of the city of Tripoli*: Quartier's description of the city matches visual representations of the time, e.g., Merian's engraving of Tripoli (see fig. 5.2).

29. *La Fosse*: literally: "the Pit."

[counting] those in the countryside, which are more beautiful and whose towers are higher, and they are more frequented by the Muhammadans because the Great Marabout[30] resides there, whereas in the city, the renegades live without religion. The climate is very hot and it rarely rains, but the evening dew is so plentiful during the night that it fertilizes {20} the earth and makes it produce [a harvest] three times a year. Every garden in the countryside and in the land near the city has its wells with their basins to water [the gardens] if needed. One does not see any snow or ice during the winter, and the inhabitants are pleased when it rains two or three times a year. The fruits are such ones as hot countries produce; they are abundant and so excellent that a person can eat ten pounds a day without feeling sick. Among others, there are many dates, which are palm fruits. They last all year, and without them the slaves would be in danger of starving. For each tree, the basha earns five French shillings per year, and for each well, two crowns, which makes a considerable income because of the quantity of both in the countryside around Tripoli. Seven or eight leagues away from the city, the country is deserted, and the Arabs live only in tents, as in Egypt and other abandoned African countries.

Tripoli is inhabited by [people of] all nations. All the civic, naval, and garden work is done by the {21} captives, because the real Turks live in an idle and effeminate way; the barbarians are lazy, without art and without industry, and are satisfied with little, and do not work except in case of necessity. The doctrine of these infidels consists entirely of keeping the Prophet's laws, of having as many women as they can feed, and of hiding their treasures in the hope of enjoying them in the next world, as Muhammad promised them in the Quran, if they follow his law exactly.

Regarding the renegades, they are debauched and dedicate themselves to stealing to provide for their needs; these criminals are constantly at war with the Christians after they have apostatized. They flee the Turks' company in order to live freely. They mock the teachings of the Quran and despise the Arabs. The Jews conduct most of the trade and manage all of the import taxes due to the basha, who knows exactly where to find them when he needs money. Besides the wool and leather of Barbary, which are valuable in France, the biggest trade of Tripoli is the flow of goods that the corsairs take from the Christian merchants at sea, {22} as well as the ones the pilgrims from all over Africa bring to Mecca when they return from the pilgrimage

---

30. *Great Marabout*: a marabout is a Muslim religious leader.

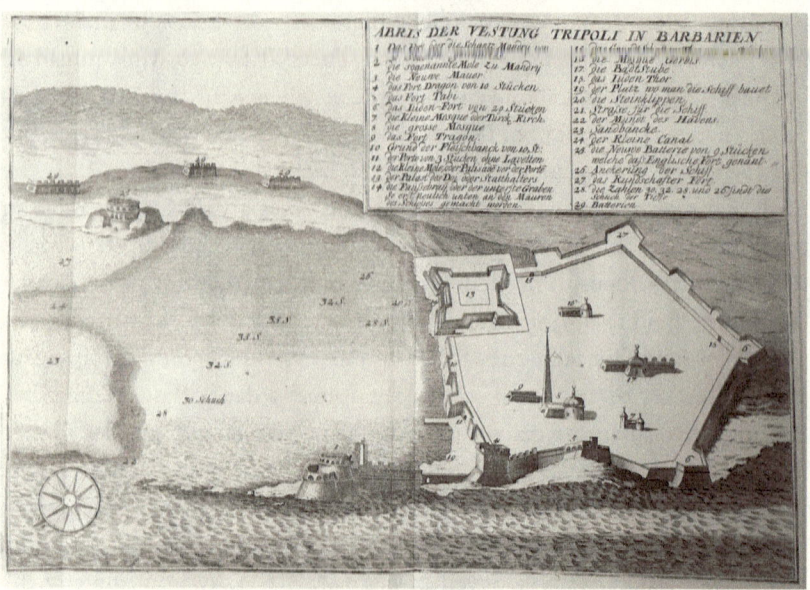

Figure 5.2 "Outline of the Tripoli Fortress in Barbary"
Source: Matthäus Merian, "Abris der Vestung Tripoli in Barbarien" (Frankfurt, 1646); Mario Klarer, private collection.

they do every year to see the tomb of their prophet. The captives are the principal wealth of the country, and most of them are owned by the basha. It is true that the captains and officers may have some to serve them, but the merchants of the country and the Jews purchase slaves only to traffic them. Those unfortunates sleep in three different prisons; there is one more in the castle where those intended for the service of the basha and his wives are obliged to retire at night, and another one outside the city, which is called La Galère de Terre[31] of Tripoli, where those Christians sleep who work in the countryside. All of the administrative positions are occupied by renegades, who command all the naval, arsenal, and production work. All the administrative positions are held by renegades, who direct all the work of the navy, arsenal, and manufacturers. The Turks and the Arabs carry out the policing and judicial duties; judgments are rendered by the basha three times a week in the presence of his *cadis*.[32] There are only four governors in the whole

---

31. *La Galère de Terre:* literally: "land galley," i.e., a prison.
32. *cadis*: a *cadi* (also *qadi* or *kadi*) was a judge in the Ottoman Empire.

kingdom of Tripoli: in the naval cities {23} of Benghazi and Derna close to Alexandria, and Zoara,[33] and Djerba off the coast of Tunis. [This is because] the ground, except in the province of Gibel—which is quite fertile—is a desert, and the Arabs live only in tents. They are rebellious toward the basha and taxes are collected [from them] with weapon in hand there.

At the time of my captivity, Tripoli was ruled by the Greek renegades, Tunis by the Italian and Islander renegades, and Algiers by the Andalusians and Granadians who had left Spain. Although the state of Tripoli is called a kingdom, its government is more like a republic than a monarchy, and the Great Lord is more a protector than a sovereign. The renegades and the militia have all the authority. They choose their basha and have no other master than the one they give themselves. This basha rules absolutely, obeys the Great Lord only for show and out of self-interest, and defers to the orders of the Sublime Porte[34] only when he wants to. But often the persons responsible for his good fortune destroy their own handiwork and sacrifice him for their interests and their fury, so that greed, {24} rebellion, and cruelty can be said to be the true rulers of Tripoli.

The French and Dutch renegades build the best war vessels, as they are the most courageous and experienced on the Mediterranean Sea. The Provençals are wicked; they kidnap their families and friends to revenge themselves for not having been redeemed, without considering that these people were perhaps helpless to do so. That is why we call them the curse of the cities of Marseille, La Ciotat, and Toulon, where most of the sailors held captive in Tripoli come from. [. . .]

{155} [. . .] Every year in late autumn, the basha sends one hundred captives to the distant countryside of Tripoli, near Alexandria, close to the small river of Mesrata, to plough the plains, which are more fertile than the ones {156} around the city, where there is only quicksand. After the captives have sown, during the winter and until the harvest, they are occupied with pulling out bulrushes with the strength of their arms to make the rigging that is used by the ships while they remain at the harbor. Once harvest time has come, they collect the seeds, which are transported to Tripoli. I was usually one of the unfortunates intended for this painful work, which lasts eight months. Before our departure, we were allowed to go to the city to say goodbye to our friends, the Christian merchants, who are aware of

---

33. *Zoara*: Quartier is probably referring to what is now Zuwara, Libya, a coastal city situated approximately one hundred kilometers west of Tunis.

34. *Sublime Porte*: the central government of the Ottoman Empire.

the miseries the captives suffer during the journey and who do not fail to feed them with biscuits and some other food. A surgeon I knew gave me some ointments and also had the kindness to teach me how to use them. He assured me that the Arabs would come to me when in need and that I would make some profit from them. He was a prophet, for I practiced surgery without paying for the privilege, and in a short time I passed for a skillful man.

We left Tripoli at the end of December with two hundred camels, which {157} were carrying the seeds we had to sow and our supplies made of biscuits, oil, onions, and salt. There was a huge crowd at the exit of the city, curious to see us set off for the countryside like a caravan going to Mecca. After eight days of walking, we arrived at the place. We found only one well on the way to water our animals and to provide us with water for the rest of the journey. We were needlessly frightened by the Arabs, who go looking for pasture for their livestock. They are obliged to change their quarters three or four times a year and choose fertile lands where there are wells, which are rare in the desert. They live only in tents, and when they decamp, a camel carries the women, children, a hand mill, and all their equipment.

On the first day of our arrival, we were occupied with setting up our tents and building an earthen rampart with big ditches to shield us not only from the Arabs, but also from the lions that caused us much alarm during our stay. The next morning, we {158} started ploughing the soil with fifty camels, while the other captives were employed to cut the bushes, dig the ditches, and sow the seeds, all of which was done in twenty days. It is a surprising thing to see that a deserted land, cultivated only negligently, produces so abundantly. Nevertheless, we must not be astonished. God blesses the work of the captives who have watered it with their sweat, mixed with the tears that these barbarians make them shed by demanding of them things beyond their strength. At the end of the seeding, we enjoyed the meat of a camel that had broken its leg by accident in the basin where the animals were watering. It was a delight for us; since our departure, we had only eaten grass snakes, lizards, and crocodiles. We found the camel's meat delicious because we were starving, for the food that was distributed was incapable of giving us enough vigor to withstand the harshness of the work. Every morning before going [to work], each captive was given a pound of biscuits. At midday, on the way back, we had a soup made of grain, seasoned with a bit {159} of oil and Spanish pepper, or dough made with barley flour. In the evening, we only had roots or filthy animals that we found.

The Arabs of the neighborhood camped under tents like us and came three times a week to get their water provisions. They brought milk, dates, pieces of ostrich, and small barley breads that we acquired for pins, scissors, ribbons, and trifles we had brought along and sold for a hundredfold [their worth], because these things are rare in the country. The Turks who guarded us were not angry about this small trade; they sometimes obliged the Arabs to leave their food when the captives could not buy it, as a reward for the trouble [the captives] had in filling the basins of water, and even for their contribution to the maintenance of the tents. The animals go two or three days without drinking, and I have seen horses nourished only by milk during their journey; there is little water in Barbary. [. . .]

{170} [. . .] In March, when the heat {171} becomes excessive where we stayed, I fell ill and so did twenty other captives. We all felt a violent pain in the side and had a malignant fever that killed eight of us in a few days. Some were cured by the treatment of the Arabs, who apply buttons of fire[35] to the painful areas. The others recuperated by sleeping and I was one of those. My recovery came during Ramadan when the Muhammadans eat only at night. The marabout sent me dishes from his table every night.

One day, an Arab whose wound I had healed visited me. He brought me a quarter of an ostrich with grasshoppers, which are rare. These small animals multiply and look for fertile lands at the beginning of spring. There are so many that the air is full of them, and sometimes it prevents one from seeing the sun. They devastate entire provinces, and the countryside where they alight is in a sad state. It is often necessary to put armed guards on the plains to {172} shoot them, so that they do not land, or at least to infect the air with poisonous smoke. The Arabs from the countryside trade [grasshoppers] so much in the maritime cities of Barbary that they make a large profit from these insects, which are now considered a novelty in Paris, like the new peas.[36] The barbarians eat them more than four months a year in the countryside and are as pleased to eat them as the French are to eat quails or

---

35. *buttons of fire*: "boutons de feu" in the 1690 French text. Local doctors applied a painful treatment in which iron rods with heated iron "buttons" on the end were applied to the patient's body. See Giles Milton, *White Gold: The Extraordinary Story of Thomas Pellow and North Africa's One Million European Slaves* (London: Hodder and Stoughton, 2004), 96.

36. *the new peas*: green peas, as opposed to matured, white peas, were a novelty at the time. See Jim Chevallier, *A History of the Food of Paris: From Roast Mammoth to Steak Frites* (Lanham, MD: Rowman and Littlefield, 2018), 77.

ortolan birds. The income made by selling grasshoppers in Tripoli is higher than that of the inhabitants from the Capraia Island in the Kingdom of Naples, who sell quails. These birds, which make a stop on the island every year, are the bishop's main source of income, and that is why the bishop is called the "Bishop of the Quail."

As soon as the work with the bulrushes was done, they had to be loaded onto the camels, which carried them to the seaside, where barks from Tripoli brought them to the city. This task kept us busy for twenty days on uncultivated lands, where our only companions were the fierce beasts {173} that often attacked us, but God preserved us. We ate little bits of biscuit with roots and ostrich eggs that the birds left in the sand. The eggs hatched without any help from the birds because of the sun. As soon as this work was done, we started the harvest. It was pitiful to see the captives, enfeebled by long and perpetual exhaustion, at work reaping in the oppressive heat. What thirst we suffered! Several Arabs died because they did not want to break Mahomet's law, which forbids them to eat and drink during their Lent. We comforted and motivated each other in the hope of leaving the desert soon and returning to Tripoli, where the weight of our shackles would be less troublesome. While we cut the wheat, the animals trod it in the middle of the land in order to bring it to the city with the straw, which is used as food for the animals, as there is no hay and pasture around Tripoli. [. . .]

{188} After my return from the countryside, I stayed in a new prison, of which I had refused to be the notary. To avenge themselves for my refusal, the guards put me to work in the navy, which is one of the hardest [tasks] for the captives, after that of the harvest in the desert. I would probably have perished without the help of Baba Manoly, who allowed me to leave. He had learned that I had taken care of lighting a lamp in the chapel of the new dungeon and that I had been praying every night after the retreat of the Christians [to the dungeon], in order to excite them to some devotion, because we did not have priests and were consequently deprived of the consolation of the sacraments. This good man became fond of me and gave me four crowns so that I could do some trade and be exempted from working by paying the prison guards two piastres[37] a month. More than one hundred captives trade in the city in this way. Some work for Christian merchants,

---

37. *piastre*: originally a Spanish silver coin; a monetary unit common in the Ottoman Empire.

others are shoemakers, tailors, or barbers, and the majority work in taverns. It is true that we were all obliged to work when the {189} boats had to be freighted to go privateering.

My first occupation was to whiten the clothes of the Christian merchants, from whom I received four crowns in two months. This small profit and some other events made me undertake to prepare food, not only for the Christians, but also for the Levantines and the renegades. I cooked French dishes, which attracted most of the renegades, who stopped eating their bad food to eat my stew. It is true that I added pork, which is forbidden by the Quran. The loot continuously won by the pirates meant that I made ten crowns in three months. But I had to leave the inn because a eunuch of the sultana, having noticed that he had often eaten this forbidden meat, wanted to stab me, and without the help of two renegades, who were not as scrupulous as the eunuch, I would have been killed. I had to leave the inn because of this misfortune, for fear of being mistreated by these odious seraglio guards, whom I could only appease with presents. Then I worked as a butcher without the Turks knowing it, for they are not allowed to eat the {190} meat of animals that have been killed by Christians. The merchants and consuls preferred to buy the meat I was selling rather than that of the barbarians. As the barbarians no longer controlled the distribution of the meat that they intended for the Christians, they suspected that some captives were butchers. The Jews, who leased the right to manage the city's salt tax, were warned to be careful with the animals arriving, which the Jews did so thoroughly that they caught me in the act. One Friday, I could not arrive on time to let a steer, six sheep, and four goats in through a secret door guarded by a renegade who assisted me while the city gate was closed and the Turks were praying. The Jews, who were on the watch, saw my cattle close to the seaside while I was away and confiscated them. I did not dare claim them because I was afraid of getting a fine or a punishment, as it is forbidden to let the cattle enter through this secret door. Thereby I lost in one day what I had earned dearly in six months. [. . .]

{214} [. . .] At the beginning of the eighth year of my slavery, I was burdened with all conceivable miseries, and I admit, to my confusion, that at the time, {215} when I had lost almost all the hope I had always had in [regaining] my liberty, Heaven provided the means of obtaining it. Father Phillipe from Pontoise, a Franciscan monk, having arrived in France, solicited my parents so much that they spared no effort to redeem me at the earliest opportunity. [. . .]

{217} [. . .] The hope I had always had of being redeemed was not in vain, for I {218} received news from a bark from Marseille, whose captain, Sir Mirangal, gave me a letter on 8 January, which informed me that he had orders to redeem me. I read the letter in the company of the Sirs de la Barre and Gonneau, Knights of Malta; Grimonville of Rennes; Guibaudet of Dijon; and Chaillou, a Parisian living on the Rue Saint-Denis near the Church of the Holy Sepulchre of Paris. They were surprised to have news from Paris within seventeen days.

Monsieur Giraud, a banker from Marseilles, reading a letter in which the gentleman from Saint Amand, quite well known in Paris, advised him not to lose any opportunity of freeing me from Barbary as soon as possible, found Captain Mirangal. He was awaiting the delivery of his passport to the town hall and [Giraud] asked him to postpone [the departure] for some time in order that the money necessary for my ransom could be counted. The captain replied that he could not wait because his bark was sailing. The banker made use of the authority of the consuls, and upon his explaining to them that I was far from Provence and therefore could not be {219} redeemed for a long time if such an opportunity were lost, they did not issue the passport until [the captain] had received four hundred crowns from the banker, who ordered him to spare nothing for my liberty. Then the captain embarked in his rowboat and joined his bark, which had already passed the fortresses around the city. The wind was so favorable that he arrived at the harbor of Tripoli eight days after his departure from Marseilles.

At night, in the prison, I told the good tidings to my friends, who received this news with great joy and, as soon as prayers were over, the slaves of my acquaintance came to congratulate me. Since the arrival of the captain, I had been exempted from working by paying two crowns a month to the prison guards, not to mention the gift they received from the captain once he had redeemed the slaves, who withdrew to his place until the departure. Mirangal postponed my meeting with the basha for more than a month in order to agree on the price of my ransom. During this time, I visited the gardens in the countryside, which embody all the beauty of the country. The slaves who took care of the cultivation let me in. I found unfortunates {220} who barely remember the mysteries of Christianity, deprived as they were of the sacraments by more than thirty years of servitude. I comforted them as best I could, exhorting them to be patient in their misery and pious in their religion, and wished [for them] that they would be released just as I was. [. . .]

{232} [. . .] Osman, who dearly loved his son, told me that he would surrender to his son's wishes,[38] and that at his son's request, he would release me for four hundred piastres, not including [the fee for] the exit through the gates and several other costs. I withdrew to the castle, unable to suppress my happiness, to share [the news] with my friends. It is impossible for me to explain the joy I felt at that moment, for all pleasures of this world are nothing compared to it. As soon as I arrived at the prison, I entered the chapel to thank God for my release. In the evening, one of the basha's officers came to assure the guard that I was free and he brought me to the house of {233} Captain Mirangal, where I stayed until the departure from Tripoli.

The manner in which slaves in Barbary are redeemed differs. It varies depending on their place of birth and age and the qualities of the captives. Youth, skill, strength, quality, and country are all obstacles to the liberty of a Christian, who cannot break his chains unless he pays twice what his condition or merit are worth, unless he is careful to hide them. This is what happened to Sir Bordier from Geneva, a clockmaker who was presented to the basha by Mirangal on the same day that I was redeemed. Osman, who was well informed that [the captain] had six hundred crowns, did not want to reduce the sum of money he was asking [for Bordier]. After a long disagreement, the captain, who offered five hundred crowns, left the castle without obtaining mercy for his Genevan, who could not help reproaching Savy[39] for his betrayal. The next day, we continued pleading with the basha on behalf of poor Bordier, who was in despair. And to make matters worse, he was recognized by Mimy, a renegade from his country, who informed the {234} basha that the clockmaker had two wealthy brothers living in Geneva who could lend two thousand piastres for his ransom. Bordier told Osman that as he had been made a slave by the corsairs while going to Constantinople, he had lost four thousand piastres, which was all he had. The captain assured the basha that his refusal to release Bordier was making him desperate and that he would not fail to kill himself like Gonneau, a Parisian

---

38. *surrender to his son's wishes*: on a previous occasion, Quartier had begged for mercy to Osman's son, who interceded on his behalf.

39. *reproaching Savy*: Savy, the ship's secretary, revealed the sums the captain had been given for the captives' release.

slave, which had deprived [the basha] of a slave he had loved because of his skill. The basha replied that all these remonstrances were useless and that, in his eyes, the death of a Christian was less regrettable than the death of an ostrich he kept in his palace for his entertainment. Mirangal, seeing how miserly and harsh the basha was, had no doubt that his scribe had revealed to his brother renegade the sums of money intended for the ransom of the slaves. That is why he gave the six hundred crowns he had received in France, as well as the other expenses the captains incur when the money is not sufficient to cover the expenses of the captives for whom they are {235} responsible. After so many sorrows, Bordier left the castle happier than when he had arrived. Bordier would certainly have stayed in Barbary for a long time without the recommendation of the English consul, who was the protector of the Protestants. [. . .]

{275} [. . .] Captain Mirangal was obliged to stay in Tripoli longer than he wished because of two inconveniences. The first one was the injury of his secretary, who was injured at night by a recently redeemed Christian because the secretary had revealed the price of his ransom to his renegade brother.[40] The other was that the basha was waiting for two corsairs who were at sea and were returning with the booty of a ship from Sicily, loaded with rich goods. As soon as they arrived, Osmand Rais, who commanded the navy, ordered our captain to prepare to set sail. This agreeable news made me bid farewell to my captive brothers, whom I could not leave without shedding tears. Many of them gave me letters that greatly advanced their deliverance, thanks to the solicitations I brought to their parents, namely: Sir André de Saint Maximin, Jean Gaumont from Cavaillon, de Lorme from Pont-Saint-Esprit, Potier from Vienne in Dauphiné, Barras from Lyon, Gibeaudet of Dijon, Chaillou from the Rue {276} Saint-Denis, and Grimonville from Rennes. The letters that Blauchon, who was born in Grenoble, gave me did not have the same effect. He had been the gardener of Salem Chastel, my first master, and he had abandoned Calvinism to become a Catholic during the plague that carried off the family of our master. I stayed some days in Grenoble to plead with [Blauchon's] mother in favor of her son, but I could not get anything from this stubborn Huguenot. She told me that she had abandoned him the day she heard that he was not part of her religion anymore.

---

40. *renegade brother*: Savy had a brother named Regep who was a renegade and was valet to the basha.

There is no joy equal to that felt by a redeemed Christian when he is ready to leave Barbary to go and enjoy the comfort of his country. However, I know from my own experience that this joy is disturbed when one thinks of the large number of Christians and friends whom one leaves still in the chains of which one knows the weight.

On a Thursday at the beginning of March 1668, the navy commander told our captain to leave the next day, and the night was passed with celebrations. At daybreak, the sailors started to weigh {277} anchor and prepare all the necessary things to set sail while the captain was at the castle with the newly freed slaves to take leave of the basha, who gave us a passport in Turkish. I remember that he told me, while I was kissing his hand, to refrain from coming to Tripoli again. He did not know that God had destined me to redeem captives, not only in his capital, but also in all of Barbary. Then he ordered two Turks to take us to the bark, which they visited to check that no slave was hidden among the crew. Mirangal gave them a present to discharge them, and as soon as they were in the rowboat, three short cannons and three long guns were fired to salute the castle. It took us more than an hour to get out, because the rocks that surround the harbor make the exit difficult and because we had to pass through all the ships of Tripoli. In the meantime, we prayed to God to grant us a good journey. The wind was so favorable at first that we neared {278} Malta within a few days, where we were pursued by a corsair, who left because he was afraid of falling into the hands of the knights.[41] [. . .]

{287} [. . .] After having been very well treated by the Order of the Grand Master[42] for several days, [the others] left and all arrived in their [respective] countries. Although I intended to reach my dear homeland as soon as possible, I could not help but see the Sainte-Baume desert. I stayed in several towns in order to hand over some captives' letters and to beg their parents to redeem them. Finally, I arrived in my hometown, where my parents were waiting for me. After having thanked them and acknowledged my debt to them for securing my liberty, I went to Paris to give thanks to one of my uncles to whom I was even more indebted and to fulfill what I had promised to God, who was the principal cause

---

41. *knights*: Quartier is referring to the Knights of Malta, who patrolled the Mediterranean, protected Christian merchant ships from falling into Ottoman hands, and freed Christian slaves.
42. *Order of the Grand Master*: the Knights of Malta.

[of my liberty]. I became a clergyman in the congregation of the Reverend Fathers of Mercy so that, in this order, which had since its formation been characterized by its charity toward captives, I could be useful to Christian slaves who suffered the same fate that I had {288} borne for almost eight years of captivity.

I cannot end my work without warning you, Christians, that the charity which is the credit of the clergymen of my order will one day be your downfall if you are not moved by the miseries of the captives. You have the same faith and hope as these children of Saint Peter Nolasco.[43] Why do you not have the same charity? You know that the slaves are incessantly exposed to the danger of becoming infidels and that they suffer from every imaginable misery. Their cries cross the seas to implore the help of your alms. They show you their chains to excite you to compassion. However, you remain indifferent to their moans, your unnecessary expenses prevail over their tears, and it seems that you are contemptuous of their miseries. Can one be more insensitive at the same time that God showers you with prosperity and blessings? But you will not always triumph, and your indifference will not remain unpunished. The cries of the captives, tired of praying to you in vain, will change course; {289} they will ascend to the throne of God and will solicit his revenge against so many indifferent [Christians] who allow so many men, redeemed by the precious blood of Jesus Christ, to perish.

Above all, do not be hopeful for the future: for it is written that on the terrible Day of Judgment, God will hold brother accountable for the life of any brother who died because of him. What will you say to this severe judge when he holds you accountable for a captive who renounced Him in slavery and who would have glorified Him in freedom if you had broken his chains with your alms? But while the indifferent Christians are blameworthy, how much praise do those deserve who generously contribute to the freedom of slaves! Thanks to their help, the Reverend Fathers of Mercy have just redeemed one hundred and fifty [captives] in Algiers who suffered much because of the revolution that took place in the city in recent years. These charitable people are implored to continue [donating] their alms for the benefit of others who remain in the same misery and implore their

---

43. *Saint Peter Nolasco*: a Catholic saint who freed Christians from Muslim slavery and founded the Mercedarian Order.

help. While finishing this work, we learned with great regret that {290} the Reverend Father Charles Piquet, the oldest religious man of the congregation of Paris, died in Pont-sur-Yonne near Sens. He died of fatigues he suffered on the trip to Algiers, where he was sent by Her Majesty to redeem captives.

THE END

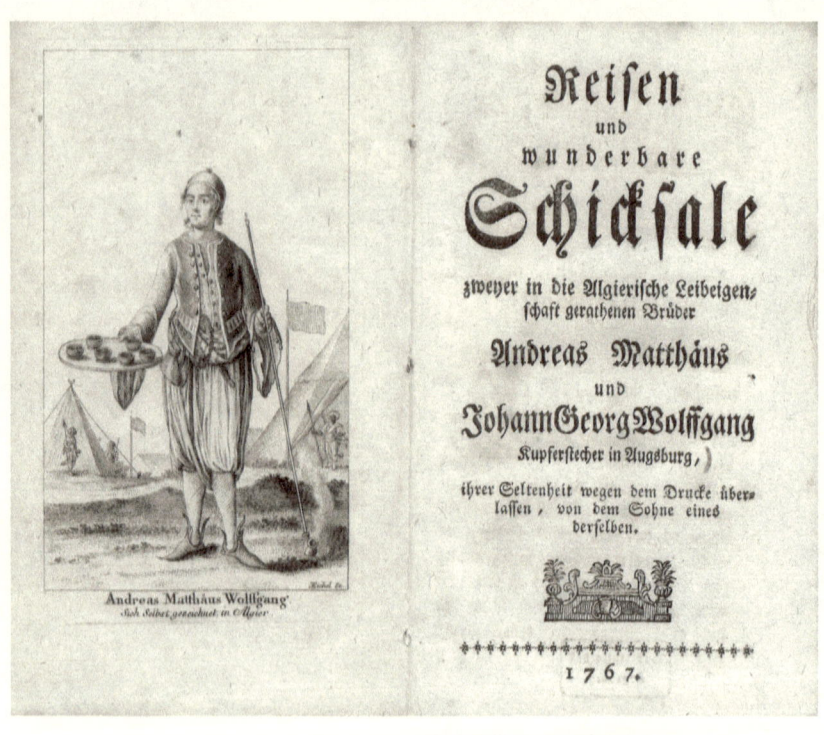

Figure 6.1 Frontispiece of the 1767 edition of the Wolffgang brothers' narrative
Source: Wolffgang, *Reisen und wunderbare Schicksale zweyer in die Algierische Leibeigenschaft gerathenen Brüder* [. . .] ([Augsburg], 1767); S1824, State and City Library Augsburg.

CHAPTER VI

ANDREAS MATTHÄUS AND JOHANN GEORG WOLFFGANG, *TRAVELS AND WONDERFUL FORTUNES OF TWO BROTHERS IN ALGERIAN BONDAGE*

1767 German print edition; complete text

Captivity in Algiers 1684–1688

The account of Andreas Matthäus Wolffgang and Johann Georg Wolffgang, two German engravers from Augsburg, is unlike any other slave narrative because it is accompanied by visual representations that were executed by one of them. The brothers were sent to Holland by their father as part of their training as engravers to hone their craftsmanship. They traveled to England without their father's knowledge and were taken captive in the English Channel by Algerian pirates in 1684 on the return trip. In Algiers, they served as house slaves in the dey's palace until they were ransomed with their parents' money.

The captivity of the two brothers constitutes a unique case study: in addition to the written account (from the brothers' oral testimony), pictorial representations in the form of copper engravings made by one of the brothers have been preserved. It is unclear which brother's son recorded their tale and arranged for the printing of his father's story. The book's title mentions only that the narrative "of the two brothers, Andreas Matthäus and Johann Georg Wolffgang, engravers from Augsburg, who fell into Algerian bondage, [was] submitted for printing by one of their sons on account of its rareness."

The first of the two printed editions of their slave narrative (1767) contained an image of Andreas Wolffgang as an Algerian house slave (see fig. 6.1). In addition to the frontispiece of the printed account of the brothers' captivity, over a dozen additional engravings of male and female representatives of North African groups, made by Andreas Wolffgang himself, have survived.

[187]

These include depictions of the dey (see fig. I.4), Algerian Jews, Muslim women, corsairs (see fig. 6.2), captains, and other members of groups that characterized the multicultural setting of Algiers. These images are the only known pictorial self-testimonies by Europeans in North African captivity.[1] In addition to the artistic dimension, the Wolffgang brothers' captivity distinguishes itself through the fact that both were house slaves to the ruler of Algiers and thus had a privileged perspective of North African captivity in the immediate surroundings of the dey.

However, before we learn about their work in the dey's palace, the narrative affords glimpses of the legal conditions that came into effect after the takeover of their ship by the corsairs: "all the Englishmen and the goods belonging to the English found on the ship were separated [from the rest] and, due to a treaty established between these two nations, delivered to the English consul. The remaining people, however, were all made slaves" (11).[2] The Wolffgang brothers' testimony makes clear that North African corsairing did not occur in a lawless space but was variously regulated through bilateral agreements with Barbary states, in this example, between Algiers and England.[3] To put it another way, the English passengers and seamen as well as the ship's English cargo were restituted after capture on the basis of contractual agreements.

The ruler—in this case, the dey of Algiers—was entitled to a fixed portion of the booty, which included the younger of the two Wolffgang brothers, Johann Georg. This part of the loot was contractually set between the corsairs

---

1. Ernstpeter Ruhe, "Zwei Augsburger Künstler in 'Algierischer Leibeigenschaft': Die 'Wunderbaren Schicksale' der Brüder Wolfgang," *Oriente Moderno* 91 (2011): 1–17; Ernstpeter Ruhe, *Porträt des Künstlers als Sklave: Zwei Augsburger Kupferstecher als Gefangene in Algier (1684–1688)* (Würzburg: Königshausen & Neumann, 2017); Ernstpeter Ruhe, "Images from the Dey's Court: The Artist as Slave in Algiers (1684–88)," in *Mediterranean Slavery and World Literature: Captivity Genres from Cervantes to Rousseau*, ed. Mario Klarer (London: Routledge, 2019), 212–40.

2. Page numbers correspond to those in the original historical edition used for the translation in this anthology.

3. On the distinction between formal and informal norms regulating slave liberation in the early modern Mediterranean, see Daniel Hershenzon, *The Captive Sea: Slavery, Communication, and Commerce in Early Modern Spain and the Mediterranean* (Philadelphia: University of Pennsylvania Press, 2018); Daniel Hershenzon, "The Political Economy of Ransom in the Early Modern Mediterranean," *Past & Present* 231, no. 1 (2016): 61–95. For the role of Jews as intermediaries in this process, as well as for the Jewish community in Livorno, see Karl Klaar, "Georg Kleubenschedl von Stams, Sklave in Tunis und seine Befreiung 1612–1636," *Tiroler Heimat* 1 (1928): 182–85; Renzo Toaff, *La nazione ebrea a Livorno e a Pisa: 1591–1700* (Florence: Olshki, 1990); Frattarelli Fischer, *Lucia. Vivere fuori dal ghetto: Ebrei a Pisa e Livorno (secoli XVI–XVIII)* (Torino: Zamorani, 2008); Eliezer Bashan, "Rachat des captifs dans la société juive méditéranéenne du XIVe au XIXe siècle," in *La société juive à travers l'histoire*, ed. Shmuel Trigano (Paris: Fayard, 1993), 4: 463–72; Haim Zeev Hirschberg, Eliezer Bashan, and Robert Attal, *A History of the Jews in North Africa. From the Ottoman Conquests to the Present Time* (Leiden: Brill, 1981).

Figure 6.2 Engraving by Andreas Matthäus Wolffgang: "An Algerian corsair captain"
Source: Jeremias Wolf, *Trachtenbuch, Sammlung von 142 teilw. kolorierten Trachtenbildern* [Augsburg etc., ca. 1700–1750], Chalc. 116, fol. 44; Bayerische Staatsbibliothek München.

and the respective protecting power under whose flag they operated and was an integral element of privateering in the Mediterranean. Eventually, the Wolffgang brothers' ransom was transacted with the help of a Jew in Algiers who organized the exchange of money with the brothers' parents through an acquaintance in Livorno. Toward the end of the narrative, we learn that both brothers, upon their return, had to work off the ransom money advanced by their father by creating copper engravings in their father's atelier.

The Wolffgang brothers' account marks a shift in the genre of European captivity narratives set in North Africa. After the publication of Daniel Defoe's *Robinson Crusoe* (1719), many returnees tried to integrate elements of this successful novel into their authentic autobiographical accounts. This mechanism is apparent and conspicuous in the Wolffgang brothers' narrative. Merely the fact that the brothers went to sea in defiance of their father's wishes parallels Defoe's successful novel. Authentic captivity accounts oriented themselves narratologically and content-wise to *Robinson Crusoe* and the Robinsonade genre that rode on the coattails of Defoe's novel. Thus, the Robinsonade and authentic, real-world eyewitness reports of North African captivity intersected as late as the early nineteenth century.

Notes on the Present Translation of the Wolffgang Brothers' *Travels and Wonderful Fortunes of Two Brothers in Algerian Bondage*

This translation is based on the first edition: [Andreas Matthäus Wolffgang and Johann Georg Wolffgang], *Reisen und wunderbare Schicksale zweyer in die Algierische Leibeigenschaft gerathenen Brüder Andreas Matthaeus und Johann Georg Wolffgang, Kupferstecher in Augsburg* ([Augsburg]: [Conrad Heinrich Stage], 1767).

The text consists of two parts: the captivity narrative itself, which is part of this anthology, and a patrilineal family tree, which has been omitted here. The authorship of the first part remains a matter of debate, but the information in the biographical section strongly suggests that Gustav Andreas, the eldest son of Andreas Matthäus and the only son of the brothers still alive at the time of publication, was the one who wrote it down or who at least provided the story to an anonymous writer.[4]

---

4. See Ruhe, "Zwei Augsburger Künstler in 'algierischer Leibeigenschaft,'" 1–17.

The narrative went through two text editions: one published in 1767, preserved in eight copies, and another published in 1769, preserved in four copies. The second edition (1769) underwent a harsh editing process at the hands of the publisher, Conrad Heinrich Stage, which is why the original 1767 text has been reproduced in this anthology. The numbers in brackets { } in the text always indicate the beginning of a page and refer to the original page numbers of the first edition.

Andreas Matthäus and Johann Georg Wolffgang, *The Travels and Wondrous Fortunes of Two Brothers in Algerian Bondage, Andreas Matthäus and Johann Georg Wolffgang, Engravers from Augsburg, Submitted for Printing by One of Their Sons on Account of Its Rareness* ([Augsburg]: [Conrad Heinrich Stage], 1767)

Translated by Robert Spindler

{3} Dear Sir!

You had the courtesy to ask me for news of the fortunes of my father and his brother in Algiers and the circumstances that drove them to and from that place. [These circumstances] are indeed wondrous, and it is my pleasure to tell you as much {4} as I am able to remember of my late father's manifold narrations; not so much because I believe that I am telling you wholly unheard-of things, but rather to preserve within our friendship the memory of a rare case [such as this one] among people of our position and way of life. Here you have the authentic narrative of an occurrence that cannot be indifferent to you, if not for its rarity, then at least for the persons whom it concerns.

It was in the eighty-fourth year of the bygone century[5] that the two brothers, Andreas Matthäus and Johann Georg Wolffgang, by means of incessant pleading and requests, finally induced their father, Georg Andreas Wolffgang, to allow them to travel to Amsterdam in order to establish themselves in the art of copper engraving. {5} Their father had good reasons for sending Andreas, the older one, ahead, but keeping the younger one with him a while longer. Thus, the older one departed and immediately found the opportunity to work and practice his art for half a year in Cologne by the Rhine.

---

5. *eighty-fourth year [. . .] bygone century*: in other words, it was the year 1684.

However, the fraternal love that these two brothers had always had for each other made this separation very difficult for them. They wished nothing more than to be together, and both badgered their father—one with persistent letters, the other with continuous verbal requests—until he finally let himself be persuaded to allow the younger one to follow [his brother] and to give them both permission to travel to Amsterdam together. Nevertheless, certain forebodings, which his fatherly heart felt, caused {6} him to send his sons with well-considered orders, explicitly forbidding them from undertaking any further travels and, in particular, not to go to sea for any reason whatsoever.

At that time, Wilhelm Bauer, a native of Augsburg and a close relative of [the Wolffgangs], resided in London. He had settled there and lived in favorable circumstances. Therefore, after they had worked in Amsterdam for several weeks, [the brothers] believed they owed this relation and compatriot a polite letter to pay their respects. This they did, and not only did they receive a similar letter in return, but also a polite invitation to take a jaunt and visit him in London. This proposal was good, and welcome as such, but [it was] {7} dangerous on account of the turmoil in England at the time,[6] and definitely forbidden due to their father's command not to venture out to sea. However, their lively and reckless youth found [the invitation] too agreeable to decline. Since they doubted that their father would consent to this, they therefore decided to deceive him in an innocent, albeit condemnable manner. After they had settled on a departure date, they wrote home, in the hope that a month would pass before they received an answer from Augsburg. This period of time should have sufficed to sail to England and come back to Holland without their parents noticing the slightest irregularity. The plan had been perfectly thought out and wanted for nothing—except success, over which they had no control, as they ought to have known. {8} They thus arrived safe and sound in London and were kindly received. For fourteen days, [they] were regaled with much goodwill and the best [food and drink]. But with this, the happy part of their journey was already at an end.

For the crossing to Holland, they found two Dutch ships ready to sail. One of them was a light vessel, and [Andreas] secured it right away, ignorant,

---

6. *turmoil in England at the time*: this is most likely a reference to the Rye House Plot, a conspiracy by a cabal of dissidents who intended to assassinate King Charles II and his brother, the future James II. The plot became public knowledge in June 1683. See Melinda S. Zook, *Radical Whigs and Conspiratorial Politics in Late Stuart England* (University Park: Pennsylvania State Press, 2010), 102–13.

however, of the fact that [his] younger brother had already booked another one. Unfortunately, due to the good company his younger brother had found on board, and in order that they could travel together, [Andreas] let himself be persuaded to transfer his luggage from one boat to the other, which was a heavily loaded merchant ship. This was the first step toward their imminent mutual misfortune.

{9} They sailed out of the Thames with favorable winds, [but as they were crossing] the middle of the Channel, secure in the hope of arriving in Amsterdam soon, they suddenly found themselves pursued by three Turkish corsairs. This was indeed an extraordinary stroke of bad luck, inasmuch as no pirate ship had ventured that far into the Channel for a hundred years. The light Hollander[7] soon hoisted all her sails and, due to her agility, evaded them without problems. The heavy merchant ship, however, could not follow it. [The corsairs] thus caught up with [the merchant ship], and they had no choice but to surrender to the terrible words, "Strike [your colors] before Algiers"[8] without lifting a sword. For [the ship] was neither supplied with cannons nor manned with soldiers. It is easy to believe that the confusion in the hearts of the two brothers was even greater than [that of the others aboard] the conquered ship. Suddenly, they thought about {10} London, whence they had come; then of Amsterdam, where they had intended to go; and then of Algiers, whither they would be taken. They did not dare to consider how their parents would take the news, now that the punishment for defying their father's instructions had caught up with them. They stood at the threshold of a life full of woe and could hardly hope that their friends would hear anything of their misfortune, let alone assist with their release.

While having these self-blaming and self-exonerating thoughts, they were bound with heavy irons and fastened to the beams below deck. Distasteful rusks and rice soaked only in water was all the nourishment they were given to [keep them] from starving. In this sad condition {11} they circumnavigated France—which they had not wished to see under these circumstances—Spain, and Portugal. They went through the Strait of Gibraltar and finally arrived happily, if one can say so, at their unhappy destination in Algiers. There, all the Englishmen and the goods belonging to the English found on the ship were separated [from the rest] and, due to a treaty established between these two

---

7. *light Hollander*: the light vessel that the older brother had wanted to take.

8. *strike [your colors] before Algiers*: "to strike colors" means to lower the flag ("colors") as a sign of surrender.

nations, delivered to the English consul. The remaining people, however, were all made slaves, and the ship was declared [to be] a good prize.

As is well known, the dey of Algiers[9] receives the finest part of the captured goods and the best slaves, purportedly as a "gift." The good looks and lively nature of the younger brother, Johann Georg, gave him the advantage over the {12} other one, [and he was] chosen as a gift for the dey. Considering his misfortune, this was a great stroke of luck and was the [first] step that God's providence had taken toward their release. They were thus separated without any hope of ever seeing each other again in this life. Their tears—the only thing that was left to them in their enslavement—were all they had to bestow upon each other when they parted.

As a royal slave, the younger one did not fare so badly. His garments were clean and [elegant] in accordance with his master's standing, and [he] lived in abundance as regards food and drink. The head chef, to whom he was subordinate, was not only a mild and merciful master, but also a benefactor and sincere supporter of his release. He was a justice-loving {13} and equitable man, who, despite having been born a Turk, had so little pleasure in barbaric behavior that he, instead, took true delight in bestowing good on those slaves who performed their services assiduously and faithfully and in demonstrating his mercy and favor at all times.

In the meantime, unlike the younger brother, [who] endured his status as a slave with relative ease, the elder felt the hardship of his thralldom doubly. He was brought to the public market after their separation and sold together with other [slaves]. He had the misfortune that one of the renegades—commonly known to be the severest masters—glanced at him and finally bought him. Immediately after the purchase was finalized, [his new master] ordered him to follow him home barefoot and in very miserable garments, all of which he had to do without hesitation. {14} At a corner, still about a hundred steps away from his master's home, [his master] ordered him to wait until [he came back to] fetch him once more. It was here that the little Latin he had learned and the French they had studied, due to their determination to visit France, came in handy, for soon a few Turks gathered around him and engaged him in conversation using the lingua franca[10] spoken throughout

9. *Dey of Algiers*: Mezzomorto Husayn Pasha, a notorious Ottoman corsair who reigned as dey (1683–1688) and eventually became Kapudan Pasha. One of Andreas Matthäus's engravings depicts him in full regalia (see fig. I.4). "Kapudan" is the title of the grand admiral of the Ottoman navy. "Kapudan Pasha" means "Lord Grand Admiral."

10. *lingua franca*: see note 30 in chapter 4, this volume.

the Barbary Coast and the Levant, which is pieced together from the languages mentioned above, and in which he could express himself passably due to his knowledge of these languages. It is quite possible that they had been sent by his master to interrogate him, for their questions revolved around his country of origin and his {15} profession. In his confusion, he attempted to help himself by saying that he was from a small village in Swabia, Germany,[11] [where he] was a poor farmhand who had learned nothing but husbandry. Upon hearing this, they laid a map before him in order to trap him and ordered him to show them his place of birth. But since he used his ignorance of geography as an excuse [to sidestep the question], they examined his hands and his bare chest, and they concluded that he could not possibly be what he was posing as, for it did not at all look as though he had ever done any hard labor.

In the middle of these pleasant conversations, his master appeared and was displeased that the spies he had dispatched had not examined him better. Furious, he therefore ordered [Andreas] to follow him home. {16} Upon entering, he was promptly welcomed with blows to the soles of his feet and afterward locked in a dungeon with the other slaves. His first task, which he had to attend to for a few days, was to bring water and wood into the kitchen and to take the waste out of it. Shortly thereafter, it pleased his master to make him a trumpeter. As a result, he was put on a ship to learn how to play the trumpet, but as he was not fond of this profession, he feigned a weak chest and shortness of breath. With this excuse, which was luckily accepted, he was freed from [this task] after a few days and was apprenticed to a cap-knitter instead.

He thus learned the art of making the caps that are produced and sold throughout Barbary in great quantities, since the Turks {17} use them as the base around which they tie their turban. In addition to his main duty of learning cap-knitting, he also had the particular responsibility of bringing meat, bread, and other victuals to the house, given that the seclusion of Turkish women prevents them from [doing] these public tasks. [Consequently,] he often made use of the little leeway [this permitted him] to roam around the city and become acquainted with all its curiosities. On one occasion, his path—or rather a very exceptional act of divine providence—led him to the castle where the dey commonly held court. Nothing could compare to the astonishment he felt when, down from a castle gallery, he

---

11. *Swabia, Germany*: home of the Swabians or "Schwaben," a cultural and linguistic group in southwestern Germany.

heard himself being called and addressed as "Brother Andreas!" He looked up and immediately recognized his {18} brother, who kept beckoning to him to come up. They hugged and spent much time telling each other their stories. The wretched Andreas told his brother of his hardships: the severity of his master and the miserable way of life in which he had to manage with water, bad bread, and a little rice. Therefore, while [still wearing] the same dingy clothes, he was introduced by his brother to his benefactor, the honest head chef, who enquired with great kindness about his circumstances and his master. The younger brother took this opportunity to put in a good word for poor Andreas and beseeched the head chef to include his brother in the dey's retinue, if possible, so that the severity of his servitude would be eased. The Turk gave him as much hope as he could in this matter and instructed him on how {19} he would have to act. He told him that because the dey was not there presently but in his gardens outside the city for the next two or three days, he should look out for the firing of the cannons, which would signal the dey's return. Then he should endeavor to get away from the cap-maker and make his way to the castle as fast as possible. Three days later, he managed this successfully and came to court without hindrance, where he soon had the opportunity to witness the way in which the dey was received. Those who were Turks by birth and had the privilege to kiss the dey's right hand stood to the right; the renegades stood to the left. Behind them were the slaves. Finally, following them, there was [Andreas], the new bondsman. {20} [He] had been instructed to grab the dey's gown and kiss it humbly when he walked past him. [But] as the dey passed and [Andreas] reached for the gown to kiss it, the dey pulled it back and asked what he was doing there. The head chef stepped forward at once and said that this was the brother of his German slave, who performed his services honestly and wanted nothing more than that his brother might be offered the possibility to display the same diligence in serving him. "But," the dey answered, "I have too many of these poor creatures already!" Nevertheless, the head chef continued to persuade him to allow this poor person, who had an exceedingly evil master, to serve at his brother's side. The dey finally agreed and allowed him to remain. The happy {21} slave thus kissed the dey's gown and stayed. However, it was not long before his master came running and demanded to take him home again by force immediately. The dey asked him how much he had paid for his slave, but the renegade demanded his slave back and said he was not for sale. The dey, once again, requested that he reveal how much the slave had cost him, or lose [the dey's] favor, but the renegade insisted on keeping the slave. It was then that the dey let him know his final verdict: he could either tell him the price of the slave, or he could, instead, endure as many blows as said slave had cost in *asper*.[12] Only then did the renegade's dogged determination give way. He capitulated and said that [the slave] had cost three hundred asper. This sum was paid out to him, and {22} the day after, he was allowed to sit at the marshal's table to salve his wounded pride somewhat. In the end, the good Andreas had to attend to him once more at the table, and, as would be expected, [Andreas] was not greeted with the friendliest of faces.

After this, [Andreas] was immediately dressed like the others in the common, clean slave garb. [He] was given good food and drink and [suffered] no deprivation except that of total freedom. The duties that the two brothers had to see to consisted of attending the dey at table, packing the tobacco pipes in the mornings and afternoons, and, in case he had company, serving them coffee.

In this mild thralldom they now had enough time and leisure {23} to deliberate about how to inform their parents of their misfortunes and effect their release. Since this seemed most likely to happen through the Jews, they soon found one who traded with Livorno,[13] and [he] wrote to a friend of his there on their behalf. He also forwarded a letter to their parents, in which they disclosed what had become of them and pleaded for speedy deliverance from their captivity. As distressed as their parents must have been at this message, it was still comforting in that they at least knew that their sons were alive and could be helped. For until then, they had not had any news other than that they had been captured on a Dutch ship in the Channel, but [they did] not [know] whither they had been taken or what else had been done to them. Thus, the good news that they would be ransomed arrived soon enough, {24} and a deal was closed with the Livornese, who transferred money for them to the Jew in Algiers.

During this time, they had the opportunity to visit the inner regions of Africa, although in what they considered to be an uncomfortable fashion. Accompanied by a large escort of soldiers, the dey, with the whole royal household, went more than fifty or sixty miles into the hinterland to collect the usual tribute from the subjugated Moors. The slaves suffered the most,

---

12. *asper*: an Ottoman silver coin used from the fifteenth to the nineteenth century, also known as *akçe*.

13. *Livorno*: a port city on the Ligurian sea in western Tuscany, Italy.

as they were the ones who had to take the tents off the camels and pitch them on the chosen campsite after they had traveled in the scorching heat, sometimes through deep sand. On this journey, just after they had rested for one day, it happened that a heavy gale hit the side of a tent with such force {25} that it knocked over a table with many books on it, among them the Quran. Moved by an exceptional sense of duty, one of the slaves jumped up immediately to pick up the books, since there was no one in the tent except for the dey and themselves. But [the dey] pushed him back before he could touch a single book, with the reproof that were he to merely touch the Quran, [the dey] himself could not keep him from becoming a Turk on the spot. This is certainly evidence that the Turks are very honest, as they do not desire to win adherents from other faiths over to their religion either by trickery or by force.

After they had spent five or six months on this journey and returned to Algiers, they found the letters announcing their redemption {26} already awaiting them. The Jew who had attended to this business was ready to pay out the money, which had been consigned to him in Algiers by Börklin, a native of Augsburg, and his correspondent in Livorno. The honest head chef carried out the negotiations with the dey, who finally released them for eight or nine hundred guilders.[14] Thus the transaction was completed and, all in all, including the exchange of letters and the Jew's fee, their ransom amounted to a thousand guilders. For his part, the Livornese had arranged an advantageous insurance, for he was paid two thousand guilders, of which he would take a thousand for himself in case the two brothers reached Livorno safely, but if they were once again caught by other pirates, he would ransom them using the money he already had in his hands.

{27} Their release had thus come about, and they owed this, for the most part, to the head chef, who, as mentioned before, was an extremely honest and fair man, well disposed toward the Christian slaves. Nothing seemed to anger him except seeing them disagree and start quarreling among themselves, as is not uncommon with slaves. "You dogs!" he often said when he saw them tormenting each other with such spite, "God has let you fall into the misery of slavery. Instead of alleviating your condition through demonstrations of all kinds of friendship, you embitter each other's miserable lives much more through these malicious disagreements."

---

14. *guilder*: a gold or silver coin formerly used in the Netherlands, Germany, and Austria.

After the money for their release had been advanced to the dey, they had their meager luggage—including their slave garments, which {28} they had been allowed to take with them—brought to a ship ready to sail for Livorno. The dey allowed them to remain in the castle until their departure, which they accepted with much gratitude. Only the steady flow of distinguished Turks, who usually came to pay their respects to the dey and to whom they had to serve coffee and tobacco, troubled them and spurred them into departing earlier than they would have had their circumstances been different. "I have released these two slaves, despite [the fact] that they are my best!" the dey once said in their company. The head chef heard these words and feared that [the dey] might regret having granted them their freedom. He therefore advised the two brothers to board their ship as soon as possible. They did this as quickly as they could after {29} expressing their sincerest thanks for his graciousness and care. They embarked and did not allow themselves to be seen on land or in the city anymore. Shortly after this, they sailed away and arrived without incident in Livorno, where they had the "honor" to be kept in quarantine for four weeks, through no fault of their own. Thereafter, they eagerly continued their journey and returned happily to their family in Augsburg.

After such immense misfortune, which had affected them as much as it had their parents—who had ransomed them with their own means, without the help of others—they had the solace of seeing themselves being cared for, in a no less peculiar manner, by divine providence. Indeed, at that time, their father had secured a profitable commission {30} consisting of eight large copper sheets: life-size portraits of the famous Emperor Leopold.[15] After their arrival, [the brothers] helped him engrave them and thus had the opportunity to work off part of their ransom in a laudable manner.

Here you have the notable adventures of our fathers, two skilled artists from Augsburg. [It is a story] which few of their fellow countrymen know, and which even fewer will take pleasure in hearing about.

---

15. *Emperor Leopold*: Leopold I (1640–1705) was a Holy Roman emperor who led Austria through a series of conflicts with the Ottoman Empire. It is interesting that the first commission the brothers were given after their return, which would allow them to pay back some of their ransom money, was precisely the production of portraits of a Christian emperor known for his victories against the Ottomans. See Ruhe, "Zwei Augsburger Künstler in 'algierischer Leibeigenschaft,'" 7.

Figure 7.1 "Captain Lambert was sent from Holland to Algiers with 6 ships, where he hung 125 captured pirates from the yards in full view of this city, and threw them into the sea, bound back-to-back [. . .]"
Source: Pierre Dan, *Historie van Barbaryen, En des Zelfs Zee-Roovers* (Amsterdam, 1684), fol. 80; Mario Klarer, private collection.

CHAPTER VII

ISAAC BRASSARD, *TALE OF MR. BRASSARD'S CAPTIVITY IN ALGIERS*

1878 French print edition; complete captivity narrative

Captivity in Algiers 1687–1688

The very nature of Barbary captivity narratives, seems, at least on the surface, to hinge on the friction between Christianity and Islam as the two driving forces fueling this genre. However, the French account of Isaac Brassard about his captivity in Algiers from 1687 to 1688 is a remarkable departure from this pattern, foregrounding intra-Christian tensions instead. Brassard's text negotiates the denominational antagonisms between Catholicism and Protestantism that dominated extensive periods of the political history of Europe in general and France in particular during the early modern period. The Edict of Nantes (1598) had guaranteed religious freedom for Calvinist Protestants (also known as Huguenots) in France for almost one hundred years. The revocation of the edict in 1685 forced many French Protestants to leave their country for fear of their lives. Brassard and his family were among those forced to emigrate to the Netherlands to escape persecution in France.

After falling into North African slavery, Brassard had to confront pressure from two opposing sides. On the one hand, the French representatives in Algiers urged Brassard to convert to Catholicism to be eligible for official French ransom actions, since liberation efforts by French official agencies did not extend to Huguenots. On the other hand, his Muslim slave masters pressured him to "take the turban," that is, to become a renegade through conversion to Islam, and thereby considerably improve his situation as a captive in North Africa. Brassard resisted both offers because of his unwavering devotion to the Huguenot cause.

Brassard's text is not the only Barbary captivity narrative to "triangulate" intra-Christian denominational tensions between Catholicism and Protestantism before the background of Islam. As early as 1595, Richard Hasleton, a British Protestant captive, quite openly compares the cruelty of the Catholic Inquisition in Mallorca to the Muslim abuse he experienced as a slave in North Africa.[1] During his escape from Algiers in a rowing boat, Hasleton fell into the hands of the Spanish Inquisition in Mallorca. Because of the torture to which he was subjected by the Spaniards, who considered him a representative of the archenemy during the wars between Protestant England and Catholic Spain, Hasleton chose to "escape" by rowing back to Algiers. Being a slave in Muslim captivity seemed less threatening to him than being at the mercy of Catholics.

In a similar vein, Brassard's fellow Huguenots in Catholic France were condemned to the French royal galleys if they did not abjure. Therefore, French Huguenot captives often preferred their unfree status in Algiers to returning to an even worse kind of slavery in France.[2] Bondage in North Africa still offered a slight hope of redemption or, if that was not possible, at least the license to practice their religious convictions under Muslim masters, something their French counterparts did not tolerate at all. Gillian Weiss, an expert on French captives, rightly points out that the "composition of the French slave population in North Africa had always reflected domestic and foreign developments" (79). Like the Catholic Hasleton one

---

1. Richard Hasleton, *A discovrse of the miserable captiuitie of an Englishman, named Richard Hasleton: borne in Braintree in Essex, declaring also his cruell moments during ten years of space, and his vvonderfull deliuerance: being a very strange thing to such as shall reade the same, he being now by Gods prouidence safelie arriued in his ovvne countrie, no doubt to his great comfort. Penned as he delivered it from his owne mouth* (London: Abell Ieffes, 1595). For a modern edition, see Daniel Vitkus, *Piracy, Slavery, and Redemption: Barbary Captivity Narratives from Early Modern England* (New York: Columbia University Press, 2001), 71–95. On Hasleton, see Daniel Vitkus, "Unkind Dealings: English Captivity Narratives, Commercial Transformation, and the Economy of Unfree Labor in the Early Modern Period," in *Piracy and Captivity in the Mediterranean: 1550–1800*, ed. Mario Klarer (London: Routledge, 2019), 56–75; Marcus Hartner, "Pirates, Captives, and Conversions: Rereading British Stories of White Slavery in the Early Modern Mediterranean," *Anglia—Zeitschrift für englische Philologie* 135, no. 3: 417–39; Marcus Hartner, "Toward a New Literary History of Captivity: Adventure and Generic Hybridity in the Late Sixteenth Century," in *Mediterranean Slavery and World Literature: Captivity Genres from Cervantes to Rousseau*, ed. Mario Klarer (London: Routledge, 2020), 47–68.

2. Gillian L. Weiss, *Captives and Corsairs: France and Slavery in the Early Modern Mediterranean* (Stanford, CA: Stanford University Press, 2011), 80. All subsequent references to Weiss follow this edition.

hundred years earlier, the Huguenot Brassard finds himself "enmeshed in a three-way power struggle among Catholic, Protestant, and Muslim leaders" (Weiss 79–80).

Rather than representing the North Africans as the ultimate threat to Christendom, Brassard depicted the bey of Algiers as reasonably well disposed toward the Protestants, whereas the ruler turned against the Catholic captives during a siege of the city by the French, that is, Catholic forces. In the end, only the intervention of Protestant nations such as England eventually guaranteed Brassard's ransom and return to Europe. However, after finally having arrived safely in the Italian city of Livorno, Brassard found himself in danger from Catholic authorities once again due to his religious conviction and Protestant preaching.

Notes on the Present Translation of Isaac Brassard's *Tale of Mr. Brassard's Captivity in Algiers*

Isaac Brassard's narrative has survived as a printed version in a nineteenth-century scholarly journal, upon which this translation is based: Isaac Brassard, "Relation de la captivité de M. Brassard à Alger," ed. H. de France, *Bulletin de la Société de Histoire du Protestantisme Français* 27 (1878): 349–55.

According to the nineteenth-century editor, Henri de France, the original handwritten narrative covered three pages and was written in a very regular hand. The document may have been penned by Brassard himself or may have been dictated to one of his sons. One of his descendants submitted Brassard's account to the editor Henri de France as a testimony to the religious steadfastness of his ancestor.[3] Brassard's captivity narrative proper has been translated in its entirety in this volume. Special thanks go to Renaud Tschirner for his assistance with clarifying cases of doubt with regard to the antiquated French.

---

3. I am indebted to Gillian Weiss for bringing this text to my attention and for the succinct information she provides on Brassard in her book (Weiss, *Captives and Corsairs*, 80–81).

Isaac Brassard, *The Tale of Mr. Brassard's Captivity in Algiers* (Nineteenth-century print version of a handwritten, undated manuscript)[4]

Translated by Camille Jeaneau

On 6 June 1687, I embarked with a great number of refugees on the vessel of Mr. Willanson of Rotterdam to travel from England to Holland. As we neared Brielle[5] and were in sight of Zeeland's coast, privateers from Algiers who were under the command of "le Bouffon,"[6] a renegade from Amsterdam, suddenly appeared with three vessels and captured us.

I was put on the vessel of the Turkish captain Carlg along with several others and was robbed of all my belongings, down to my manuscripts, whose loss pained me most.

Forty days later we arrived in Algiers. During the whole trip I had been very poorly fed and lodged. I felt very ill treated, especially when we had a headwind and it looked like a tempest was coming, for the barbarians blamed these incidents on me and would have thrown me into the sea had I not hidden myself.

Upon our arrival in Algiers, we were all led to the *basha*'s[7] house. The basha kept all the slaves he wanted for himself, myself being one of them, and had us brought to a public house. We spent a whole day there without working. However, on this day, the vicar of the French mission's congregation who lived in Algiers asked me to come to his place. There, he urged me to convert and to have all those who were captured with me convert as well, telling me that, since they were all following my lead regarding their faith, I would thus save my soul and theirs, and above all, I would do the king a great favor, for which he would reward me well.

I answered right away that I was greatly surprised by his suggestion; that I had been made such offers before, and under better circumstances, in France; that I had despised them by the grace of God; and that it was

---

4. Isaac Brassard, "Relation de la captivité de M. Brassard à Alger," ed. H. de France, *Bulletin de la Société de Histoire du Protestantisme Français* 27 (1878): 349–55.

5. *Brielle*: a historic seaport in the Netherlands. "Brille" in the French original.

6. *le Bouffon*: probably Ali Boffoun, a European convert to Islam. See *Revue Africaine: Journal des travaux de la Société Historique Algérienne*, quinzième année, 85 (Janvier 1871): 78.

7. *basha*: a high-ranking official in North Africa and the Ottoman world. The term is also used to refer to the governor of a city.

not likely that I would have more consideration for his. I told him that the more afflicted I found myself, the more I needed my religion to find comfort, and the more it comforted me, the more I felt obliged to persist in my belief. I have always abhorred the Roman religion, even more so since the new persecution in France. I would not do the work of those who undertake to dominate other people's faith and conscience. Far from bringing my fellows in misfortune to embrace such a cruel religion, I would turn them away from it if I found out they were thinking of doing so. Finally, my duty and my own best interest was to bring salvation to myself and my fellow men, and to work first and foremost for God's glory, the King of kings.

On the next day we were given blankets for the night and shoes, with which we were sent to work at the governor's house, half a league away from the city. No consideration was given to my position[8] or my age to exempt me from work. They beat me with a stick to wake me so that I got up from the hard ground where I had been sleeping with no more than my blanket. After that, they had me carry bricks and mortar, forever mistreating me with their words and even more so with the beatings.

It is true that I was forced to do this hard work for a few days only. Since the weakness of my body clearly made it impossible for me, I was given another responsibility for which I knew I was even less qualified. I was made a cook. Though I only had to cook for slaves, it seemed extremely difficult to me, so I asked to be given some other responsibility. I was immediately threatened with a beating. Thus, I had to accept this work, which I performed so badly that I let the rice to feed the slaves burn as well as the cauldron I had put it in. Two Spanish slaves came to me. One of them was so furious that he wanted to kill me, but the other held him back. They even quarreled with each other over this. However, the commander came running, got them to agree, and did not hurt me at all.

On the following day, a young Turk came to take me back to the city. He gave me a heavy load, which I had to carry along with my blanket. As soon as I arrived, I was employed as a mason to build a chapel where mass was held on our prison's grounds. There, I was insulted several times by slaves and got several beatings from the Turk who was in charge at the worksite. After a few days of this work, I was sent to another [workplace] far from the

---

8. *position*: his function as a Protestant minister.

last. Another young Turk, crueler than his predecessor, took me there and beat me with his stick and struck me down because I was not going as fast as he was. When I finally got there, I complained about this bad treatment to the commander. He reprimanded this barbarian strongly, and seeing me so exhausted, he did not make me work.

The vicar [looked like] a Jesuit.[9] At least, he employed the Jesuits' manners and style, always attempting to make me convert to his religion. Pleased that I should be so ill-treated, he let me know that this would no longer be the case if only I became a Catholic, thanks to the money he would give the Turks. I am sure he told the other clerics and priests, as well as the French consul and the vessels' captains, and other people from Provence who were slaves to do everything they could in this attempt [to convert me]. They did all they could to make me look bad in the eyes of the basha's [prison] guard so that he would keep sending me [to work]. He was the commander in the prison where I was locked away and from there he sent the slaves to work. But [the guard] did not always act upon their solicitations against me. At last, he exempted me from work and allowed me to walk around the city, and even outside the city.

However, after that, the vicar I have spoken of and his people acted against me in another way. By giving me the name of "Ducaine" and having me called thus in all places by their emissaries, they made me even more hated and exposed me to the wrath of the people who, on hearing that name and recalling what Mr. Ducaine had done here with the bombings, became very aggressive toward all French people and to me in particular. For this reason, I did not go out much. When I did, I would receive many insults and often harsh beatings.

When in the following year—in 1688—the marshal Mr. Destrée[10] came with a big fleet to bomb these Algerians, I found myself in great and terrifying peril. Every day on which there was a bombing, Turks killed French people by putting them at the mouths of the cannons in the following manner: heads down and feet up, their arms tied to the cannon that was fired against the middle of their body, the fire of the [gun]powder alone ripping and blowing limbs off and scattering them far away.

On the morning of 4 July of this same year, the scribe of the basha's [prison] guard came to find me in a large farmyard where I had been taken

---

9. *Jesuit*: a Roman Catholic order.
10. *Mr. Destrée*: Jean, Comte d'Estrées, a naval commander of Louis XIV and a marshal of France.

with other slaves to keep us away and safe from the bombs. He told me that there were orders to take me away from this place and bring me to some other place together with six refugees in order to subject us to the cannon's torture. I and my fellows followed him and gave each other the courage to face death. I prayed for myself and for them, expressly asking God to grant us the grace to keep faith, to fight the right battle, to finish our path, and finally, to give us the crown of glory and immortality in His paradise. As soon as the prayer was over, the vicar appeared to incite us to give up our religion, assuring us that we would thus find our salvation in the next world and insinuating that we might at the same time still be saved in this one. I answered forthwith that he should leave us to die in peace, that we were all disgusted by this world and were longing for Heaven's peace. I added that his actions made me think that he had something to do with my death, which I would suffer gladly, while praying to God for all my persecutors, for whom I wished [that they would also enter] the paradise I was going to by the grace of my Savior. My fellows in torture showed the same resolution and charity.

This missionary being gone, my companion in ministry and slavery Mr. Jordan came to tell us that a certain Francisco, an Italian, had put him in charge on the basha's [prison] guard's orders and that he would return us to the place from which [the prison guard's] scribe had taken us. The basha wanted neither us nor any other refugee to die; this is what the king declared publicly as he was visiting the slaves' construction work. Having asked whether there were any French present, he was told that there were Lutheran ones. Having asked if there were any Catholics, he was told that there was only one. The basha called the Catholic prisoner and told him that he would be tied to a cannon the next day. As they were about to take him there, he offered [to convert and] become a Jew if they did not tie him to that cannon. This was reported to the basha, who let him live and become a Jew. I heard for sure that when there were no French Catholics left, they would put the Spanish and Italians to death. He had the French slaves put to death—among them the vicar, whose ears and nose were cut [off], and whom the people stabbed several times. His servant the French friar, the French consul, and several merchants and captains of vessels wished to become Turks as long as their lives were spared. The basha refused, saying they were not worthy of taking the Mahometan faith, which did not customarily spare the lives of those who only embraced the religion under threat.

I had been a slave for eighteen months in Algiers and suffered many pains when, at last, I was set free from the bonds of this cruel slavery thanks to the charitable care of our English and Dutch brothers, most particularly the marquis of Ruvigny—father and son—and the knight Sir Chardin. This became apparent in a letter they sent from Greenwich to me and three of my brothers, who were freed with me. Lord Salomon, a Jew living in Algiers, contributed greatly to our freedom. Acting on orders from England, he always kept the basha, who liked him very much, well informed. After [Lord Salomon] paid [the basha] our ransom without delay, he obtained our leave, so that we were set free soon after that.

I left Algiers in good company on an English vessel and we arrived in Livorno[11] on Christmas Day. On the following day, we left the vessel for the lazaret, where they forced all those who come from the east to stay a few days to protect themselves from the contagious [diseases] we might bring with us.[12] We stayed there for five days. After that, Mr. Xalxberner, the Dutch consul, had the goodness to invite me to stay at his home, where he treated me honorably and generously until 5 March 1689.

He had wanted to keep me there longer, but since the grand duke of Tuscany had previously ordered me to leave Livorno and his states, having probably heard the stories that were spread about me performing my ministry, I did not consider it suitable to stay any longer. Hence, having found good company, I made my way to Florence, crossed Italy and its mountains covered in snow, and arrived on the 31st of this month in Venice, where I stayed for six days. During this time, I preached for the French pastor in a citizen's private lodging in complete safety. From there, I then went to the Tyrol and traveled through Germany and its terrible mountains, going through Erlangen, the town of the prince of Bayreuth. There, I found a colony of French refugees where some of my scattered sheep dwelled, whom I comforted with preaching. They comforted me too through their positive response and the joy they all told me they had felt at listening to me after [I had] been saved from such evil.

At last, after a long overland journey, I was taken to Groningen. From there, I was brought to Holland on a ship. On 4 June of this year, I arrived

11. *Livorno*: a port city on the Ligurian Sea in western Tuscany, Italy.
12. *lazaret [. . .] bring with us*: this refers to a quarantine.

in Amsterdam at the abode of my colleague Mr. Ysarn, who expected me and where he had me registered in advance among the guest ministers. After so many strange incidents, it seemed clear that the great God had been my true savior. Therefore, I will always admire and celebrate the marvels of His providence and the greatness of His mercy, which He lets me feel so sweetly and powerfully.

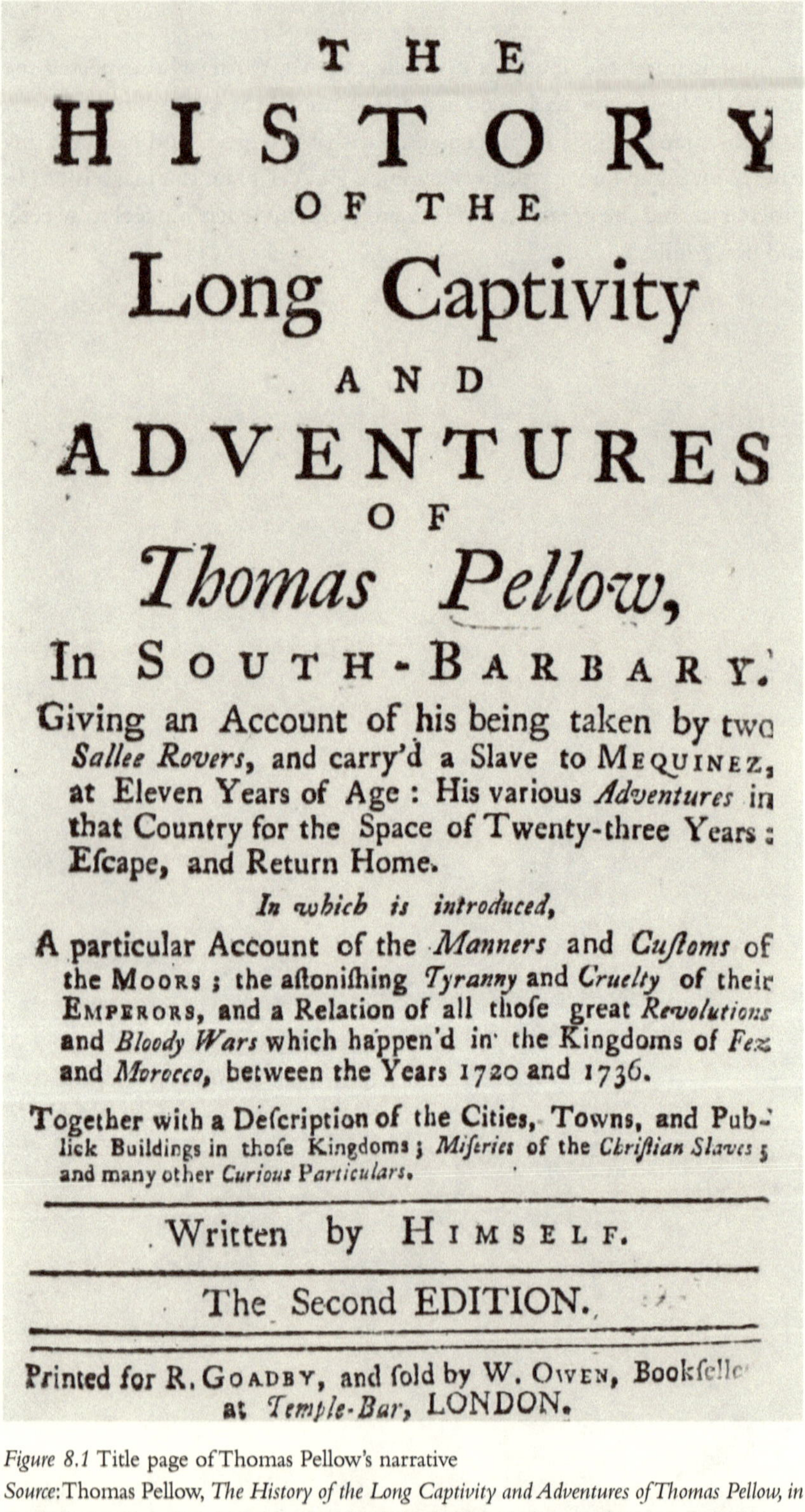

THE HISTORY OF THE Long Captivity AND ADVENTURES OF *Thomas Pellow,* In SOUTH-BARBARY.

Giving an Account of his being taken by two *Sallee Rovers,* and carry'd a Slave to MEQUINEZ, at Eleven Years of Age: His various *Adventures* in that Country for the Space of Twenty-three Years: Escape, and Return Home.

In which is introduced,

A particular Account of the *Manners* and *Customs* of the MOORS; the astonishing *Tyranny* and *Cruelty* of their EMPERORS, and a Relation of all those great *Revolutions* and *Bloody Wars* which happen'd in the Kingdoms of *Fez* and *Morocco,* between the Years 1720 and 1736.

Together with a Description of the Cities, Towns, and Publick Buildings in those Kingdoms; *Miseries* of the *Christian Slaves;* and many other *Curious Particulars.*

Written by HIMSELF.

The Second EDITION.

Printed for R. GOADBY, and sold by W. OWEN, Bookseller at *Temple-Bar,* LONDON.

Figure 8.1 Title page of Thomas Pellow's narrative
Source: Thomas Pellow, *The History of the Long Captivity and Adventures of Thomas Pellow, in South Barbary* [. . .], 2nd ed. (London, [1740?]); Shelfmark: General Reference Collection DRT Digital Store 1418.c.26; UIN: BLL01017699912; British Library.

CHAPTER VIII

THOMAS PELLOW, *THE HISTORY OF THE LONG CAPTIVITY AND ADVENTURES OF THOMAS PELLOW*

[1740?] British print edition; selection

Captivity in Morocco 1715–1738

In 1715, the eleven-year-old English boy Thomas Pellow was captured by corsairs and taken to Morocco, only escaping twenty-three years later in 1738.[1] His fate as a very young slave shows striking similarities with that of the English captive Joseph Pitts and the Danish captive Hark Olufs, also included in this anthology.[2] Like Olufs, Pellow adapted well to the new culture, spent time in close proximity to the ruler, held high military positions in North Africa, and experienced some difficulties reintegrating into his home society after his return. However, unlike Olufs, Pellow leaves no doubt about embracing Islam, which makes his testimony stand out as one of the few Barbary narratives that address the issue of conversion quite openly.

1. On Pellow, see Adam Beach, "African Slaves, English Slave Narratives, and Early Modern Morocco," *Eighteenth-Century Studies* 46, no. 4 (2013): 333–48; Linda Colley, "Going Native, Telling Tales: Captivity, Collaborations and Empire," *Past & Present* 168 (2000): 170–93; Linda Colley, *Captives: Britain, Empire and the World 1600–1850* (London: Vintage Digital, 2010); Magali Morsy, *La Relation de Thomas Pellow: Une lecture du Maroc au 18e siècle* (Paris: Ed. Recherche sur les civilisations, 1983); Robert Spindler, "Benevolent Masters, Despicable *Renegados*: Relativizing Portrayals of Muslims in British Barbary Captivity Narratives, 1595–1739," *Anglistik: International Journal of English Studies* 30, no. 3 (2019): 141–56, in particular, pp. 143–44, 150–52; Robert Spindler, "Identity Crises of Homecomers from the Barbary Coast," in *Piracy and Captivity in the Mediterranean: 1550–1810*, ed. Mario Klarer (London: Routledge, 2019), 128–43, in particular, pp. 131, 134–40. On racial thinking and the enslavement of West Africans in Morocco, see Chouki el Hamel, *Black Morocco: A History of Slavery, Race, and Islam* (Cambridge: Cambridge University Press, 2014).

2. Joseph Pitts, *A True and Faithful Account of the Religion and Manners of the Mohammetans in Which is a Particular Relation of Their Pilgrimage to Mecca* [. . .] (Exon [Exeter]: S. Farley, 1704), reprinted in Daniel Vitkus, ed., *Piracy, Slavery, and Redemption: Barbary Captivity Narratives from Early Modern England* (New York: Columbia University Press, 2001).

[211]

In a European culture that stigmatized returnees from slavery and accused them of having converted to Islam, even when there was no evidence of them having done so, Pellow's tale is a rare example of a captive who actually admits to conversion. However, Pellow takes care to underline the fact that his apostasy was forced through torture and that, unlike a real renegade, in his heart, he never truly converted. Of course, it remains doubtful whether the events leading to Pellow's conversion took place as described. In any case, Pellow's fate improved dramatically as a result of his conversion. He was able to advance quickly on the career path that was open to converted Christians in North Africa, especially in the military. As an adult, he rose to be an officer and participated in a number of military ventures, including slave-gathering expeditions in sub-Saharan Africa.

Despite the career opportunities in Morocco that conversion opened up for Pellow, it also thwarted his one chance of being ransomed. It was during Pellow's stay in Morocco that Charles Stewart was able to ransom close to three hundred English captives—one of the greatest successes in the history of British ransom activities. Pellow, however, could only lament his status as a renegade and point out that "those under my unhappy circumstances" (37) were not among those freed.[3]

As a renegade, Pellow's integration into Moroccan society and culture also included being "allowed" to get married. The narrative renders this occasion as a mass marriage in which the ruler joined "eight hundred young men" with "as many young women" (70). Pellow marries a Muslim woman from an influential family. However, Pellow is conspicuously brief about details concerning his married life and only mentions his wife and children in passing later in the narrative. Both his wife and daughter died while he was on one of his military ventures, before his escape from Morocco became feasible.

Pellow's narrative at times touches upon other themes that must have resonated with his eighteenth-century readers, including long-winded, picaro-like exchanges with the ruler. For example, after his conversion, Pellow was employed as a gatekeeper in Moulay Ismaïl's harem. In this function, Pellow once denied the ruler access to the seraglio. Without having received prior notification, Pellow was unable to tell if it was really the ruler himself who demanded to be let in (18–20). Also, his description of the queen, as "extremely amorous, and the emperor no less jealous of her, which really

---

3. Page numbers correspond to those in the original historical edition used for this anthology.

made my condition very dangerous" (24), must have met readers' expectations of an oriental harem full of erotic temptations.

One final point of interest in Pellow's narrative is his difficulty re-adapting to English society. In a telling scene, Pellow visits the Moroccan ambassador in London, where he dines on his "favourite dish, cuscassoe" (386). The reader gets the feeling that, for the first time since his return to England, Pellow feels at home. After having spent more than two-thirds of his life in Morocco, Pellow's re-acculturation process was not without its difficulties and in many ways resembled that of the Danish returnee, Hark Olufs.

Notes on the Present Edition of Thomas Pellow's *History of the Long Captivity and Adventures of Thomas Pellow*

The present edition is based on: Thomas Pellow, *The History of the Long Captivity and Adventures of Thomas Pellow, in South Barbary: Giving an Account of His Being Taken by Two Sallee Rovers, and Carry'd a Slave to Mequinez, at Eleven Years of Age: His Various Adventures in that Country for the Space of Twenty-three Years: Escape, and Return Home. In Which is Introduced, a Particular Account of the Manners and Customs of the Moors; the Astonishing Tyranny and Cruelty of Their Emperors, and a Relation of All Those Great Revolutions and Bloody Wars which Happen'd in the Kingdoms of Fez and Morocco, Between the Years 1720 and 1736. Together with a Description of the Cities, Towns, and Publick Buildings in Those Kingdoms; Miseries of the Christian Slaves; and Many Other Curious Particulars*, 2nd ed. (London: Printed for R. Goadby, and sold by W. Owen, [1740?]).

Since its publication in 1739 or 1740 (the exact date is uncertain), Thomas Pellow's three hundred page narrative has been edited, republished, and renarrated several times.[4] Due to space constraints, the current selection focuses on Pellow's capture and early career in Morocco, as well as his return to England. Omissions are marked with an ellipsis [. . .]. In case of longer omissions, short summaries in square brackets have been provided to bridge the gaps between different sections. The chapter titles as well as the often

4. See, for example, Thomas Pellow, *The Adventures of Thomas Pellow, of Penryn, Mariner: Three and Twenty Years in Captivity Among the Moors, Written by Himself, and Edited with an Introduction and Notes by Dr. Robert Brown*, ed. Robert Brown (London: T. F. Unwin, 1890). A more recent edition is Thomas Pellow, *The History of the Long Captivity and Adventures of Thomas Pellow, in South Barbary*, ed. Josephine Grieder (New York: Garland, 1973). In 2004, bestselling author Giles Milton renarrated Thomas Pellow's life story in novel-like fashion in *White Gold: The Extraordinary Story of Thomas Pellow and North Africa's One Million European Slaves* (London: Hodder & Stoughton, 2004).

lengthy and outdated explanatory notes of the second edition have been omitted without comment. The numbers in brackets {} in the text always indicate the beginning of a page and refer to the original page numbers in the second edition. Pellow's spelling, punctuation, and capitalization have been standardized to enhance the readability of the narrative.

> Thomas Pellow, *The History of the Long Captivity and Adventures of Thomas Pellow, in South Barbary: Giving an Account of His Being Taken by Two Sallee Rovers, and Carry'd a Slave to Mequinez, at Eleven Years of Age: His Various Adventures in that Country for the Space of Twenty-three Years: Escape, and Return Home. In Which is Introduced, a Particular Account of the Manners and Customs of the Moors; the Astonishing Tyranny and Cruelty of Their Emperors, and a Relation of All Those Great Revolutions and Bloody Wars which Happen'd in the Kingdoms of Fez and Morocco, Between the Years 1720 and 1736. Together with a Description of the Cities, Towns, and Publick Buildings in Those Kingdoms; Miseries of the Christian Slaves; and Many Other Curious Particulars*, 2nd ed. (London: Printed for R. Goadby, and sold by W. Owen, [1740?])

{5} [. . .] In the eleventh year of my age, the second of the reign of our late sovereign lord, King George the First, and of our Lord Christ 1715, I being at the Latin school in Penryn, in the county of Cornwall, and John Pellow, my uncle,[5] being about to proceed on a voyage from Falmouth to Fowey, and thence for Genoa with pilchards, in the good ship *Francis*, Valentine Enes (then of Penryn), merchant, the owner; and I by no means liking my so early rising, and (as I then thought) most severe discipline of the school, so far insinuated myself into my uncle's favour as to get his promise to obtain the consent of my parents for me to go along with him; and which indeed he did, though not without much difficulty, they urging the hardships which probably I might, in my so tender years, undergo thereby, and their ominous fears of our falling into the hands of the Moors, who were

---

5. *John Pellow, my uncle*: John Pellow was the captain of the *Francis*, a merchant ship carrying a cargo of pilchards to Genoa.

then at open war with us, and had, as they saw by the newspapers, very lately taken some of our ships; so that it was with the greatest reluctance and regret that I obtained their consent, which at last I did, and was soon rigged in my sailor's dress; and {6} after taking (as it proved) my so long, long farewell of my friends, our ship sailed from Falmouth to Fowey, where in a few days we completed our cargo; and as soon as all other our necessary business was dispatched, we set sail for our desired port. Of which our voyage it cannot be expected I should give any particular account, as I had never been at sea before, and was entirely unacquainted with the method of keeping a journal; but I well remember that I soon began to repent of my rash undertaking, and heartily wished myself back again, though even to be again sent to the Latin school, my uncle keeping me so close to my book that I had very little or no time allowed me for play; and which, if I at any time presumed to borrow, I failed not of a most sure payment by the cat of nine tails;[6] so that by the time we got to Genoa I thought I had enough of the sea, being every day, during our voyage out, obliged (over and above my book learning) to go up to the maintop masthead, even in all weather.

All which (though very irksome to me then) I now most gratefully acknowledge and plainly see was only intended for my good; and had not our sad misfortune of falling into the hands of the infidels and our long, unhappy slavery prevented it, my uncle would have certainly made me a complete sailor, as he himself was, by those who knew him, allowed to be; but what God thinks proper should be, no human power can prevent.

And now, indeed, the unhappy part of my life draws near; for having made our voyage, our cargoes out and in, and by God's providence bound {7} home, we were off Cape Finisterre very unhappily surprised by two Sallee rovers,[7] and, together with Captain Foster of Topsham (after such small resistance as we could both make), taken and carried prisoners on board of the infidels, as was also the next day Captain Ferris of London, in a ship of much greater strength, having twenty men, eight swivel and eight carriage guns, though they behaved in the bravest manner, fighting ten hours, and with a noble resolution, putting the Moors off, after boarding them three times, and killing many of them; but being overpowered by a superior force, they were also obliged to submit and to become our comrades.

---

6. *cat of nine tails*: a whip used for physical punishment.
7. *Sallee rovers*: pirate ships from Sallee (now Salé).

It is impossible for me to describe the agony I was then in, being separated from my uncle; he being, together with Briant Clarke, John Crimes, and John Dunnal (three of our unhappy men) confined on board one of the Salleeteens,[8] commanded by Ala Hacam;[9] and myself, with Lewis Davies, George Barnicoat, and Thomas Goodman, the other three (our whole number consisting but of eight persons) on board of the other, commanded by Elhash Abdrahaman Medune, the admiral of Sallee,[10] where we were closely confined, and treated after a barbarous manner during the space of one whole month, which the infidels passed in looking sharp out after other prey and in examining into the value of our cargoes, according to our several invoices and bills of lading, the prizes being sent to Sallee for better security and to leave them at more liberty to encounter others during the time of their cruise; but seeing no likelihood of any more prizes, and their provision growing short, they followed {8} the prizes and found them safe at anchor on the outside of the bar of Sallee;[11] when, on a signal from the shore of there being water enough on the bar to carry them over, the prizes were ordered to weigh and got all well in, the Salleeteens casting anchor without till the next day; when, about noon, the infidels being in their jollity, were all on the sudden in an extreme hurry on their discovery of a sail standing right in from sea upon them, they crying out, in great confusion, "Garnoe! Garnoe!" meaning thereby Captain Delgardenoor,[12] who they knew then commanded a British man-of-war of twenty guns on that station; and as they feared so it proved, for it was Garnoe indeed; but alas! too late for our assistance. Medune weighing his anchor, and Ala Hacam slipping his cable, they ran both aground on the bar, Delgardenoor following so near them as in safety he might, some of his shot flying about them, and some of them far beyond them, insomuch that they were both, through means thereof, and a great sea, soon beat to pieces; and almost every one that could swim, swimming for his life; but, for my part, I could swim but very little

---

8. *Salleeteens*: Pellow uses this word to refer to pirate ships and pirates from Salé.
9. *Ala Hacam*: Captain Ali Hakem, a pirate from Salé.
10. *Elhash Abdrahaman Medune, the admiral of Sallee*: Admiral Abderrahman el-Mediouni of Salé.
11. *bar of Sallee*: a hazardous sandbar in front of the Salé harbor.
12. *Captain Delgardenoor*: Captain Arthur Delgarno, who with "his twenty-gun frigate exercised so wholesome a terror over the Sallee men that they never ventured over the bar when he was known to be in the vicinity. Moorish mothers used to frighten naughty children by threatening to 'give them to Garnoe.'" See Robert Brown, ed., *The Adventures of Thomas Pellow, of Penryn, Mariner: Three and Twenty Years in Captivity Among the Moors, Written by Himself, and Edited with an Introduction and Notes by Dr. Robert Brown*, by Thomas Pellow (London: T. F. Unwin, 1890), 335n1.

and which, had I attempted, the merciless sea must soon have overwhelmed me; so I cried to Lewis Davies (who I knew could swim very well) for assistance, though from him I could get none, he saying (and very truly) "That all his strength was highly necessary towards his own preservation; and that should he take me on his back, it would in all likelihood loose both our lives; whereas by his throwing himself into the sea disentangled, and I getting on the mast (which was cut down), it might be a means of preserving both of us;" and which, through the wonderful and ready help of Almighty God assisting (He having ordained us {9} for larger and more grievous trials and sufferings), accordingly happened: Davies committing himself to the waves, and I myself to the mast, from which I was taken by some people in a boat from the shore. As for the Moors, they were under no apprehension of danger from the sea, leaping into it and swimming to shore like so many dogs.

It may easily be imagined what sad terror and apprehension I was under in so dangerous a situation; for though I could see nothing else by being delivered from death than the more grievous torments in my becoming a slave, etc., yet did I endeavour all in my power to avoid it and save myself.

Being now all safely landed, we are in a very low and feeble condition conducted to two separate prisons; myself, Lewis Davies, M. Goodman, and Briant Clark,[13] with divers others of Foster's and Ferris's men, in all twenty-six, to New Sallee,[14] and my uncle, John Dunnal, Thomas Cremer, and George Barnicoat, with seventeen Frenchmen taken in other ships, and the rest of Foster's and Ferris's men, twenty-six more, to Old Sallee, and for three days closely shut {10} up there, and our allowance by the Moors nothing but bread and water, though I must thankfully own that we met with some better refreshment through the goodness of some French and Irish merchants residing there, which was to us in our so weak and disconsolate condition of very great service.

{11} On the fourth day we were all, in number fifty-two, taken out thence and sent prisoners to Mequinez;[15] some being put on mules, some on asses, and some on horses; on one of which my uncle and I were mounted together. [. . .]

---

13. *Briant Clark*: Pellow is inconsistent with the spelling of this name. Previously, he refers to him as "Briant Clarke."

14. *New Sallee*: in Pellow's day, Rabat was frequently referred to as New Sallee. However, according to Brown (ed.), *The Adventures of Thomas Pellow*, in this instance it refers to "the newer castle of two in Sallee" (335n1).

15. *Mequinez*: Meknès, a former imperial city of Morocco.

{13}[. . .] About eight o'clock we all got to the emperor's palace, [. . .] where Muly Smine, or Ishmael, the old emperor,[16] was, who received us from the hands of the Salleeteens, giving Ala Hacam, in exchange for every one of us, fifty ducats; but out of this was paid back again one-third, and a tenth as a customary tribute; and Medune, the admiral, for not fighting Delgardenoor, had the very extraordinary favour bestowed upon him of losing his head.

And now are we ordered to be separated as follows, viz. myself, Richard Ferris, James Waller, {14} Thomas Newgent, and three other boys taken in a French ship, sent to the Kubbahhiatin, or place where the tailors work and the armoury is kept, and where we were directly employed in cleaning the arms. All the foremast men, save two who were wounded, were put to hard labour; and the captains, with the two wounded men, to the Spanish convent; whence, after some short exemption, they were put to hard labour also; and, after some little time, again exempted, and sent to the house of one Mr. Ben Hattar, a Jew, in a place called the Judaiary,[17] he having procured this of the emperor; and, as everything relating to our affairs passed through the hands of him and his agents, it was, no doubt, very much to his advantage.

After some time, I was taken out of the armoury, and given by the emperor to Muley Spha, one of his favourite sons (a sad villain), born of his wife Alloabenabiz, by whom he had in all ten children, viz., seven sons and three daughters. My business now, for some time, was to run from morning to night after his horse's heels; during which he often prompted me to turn Moor, and told me, if I would, I should have a very fine horse to ride on, and I should live like one of his best esteemed friends. To which I used to reply, "That as that was the only command wherein I could not readily gratify him, I humbly hoped that he would be pleased, of his great goodness, to suspend all future thoughts that way, for that I was thoroughly resolved not to renounce my Christian faith, be the consequence what it would." Then said he, in a most furious and haughty manner, "Prepare yourself for such torture as shall be inflicted on you, and the nature of your {15} obstinacy deserves." When I humbly entreating him, on my knees, "Not to let loose his rage on a poor, helpless, innocent creature," he, without making any further reply, committed me prisoner to one of his own rooms, keeping

16. *Muly Smine [. . .] the old emperor*: Moulay Ismaïl Ibn Sharif (1645/46[?]–1727), sultan of Morocco from 1672 to 1727.
17. *Judaiary*: the Jewish district. In Morocco, they were typically walled quarters and were known as *mellahs*.

me there several months in irons, and every day most severely bastinading me,[18] and furiously screaming in the Moorish language, "Shehed, Shehed! Cunmoora, Cunmoora!," in English, "Turn Moor! Turn Moor!,"[19] by holding up your finger. Of which cruelty my uncle hearing, he came one day, and with him one John Phillips, to see if it might be in their power to give me any relief; and which indeed was not, although they very heartily endeavoured it, gaining nothing by their so very kind and Christian-like intention but many severe blows on themselves and, on me, a more frequent repetition of them than before.

And now is my accursed master still more and more enraged, and my tortures daily increasing; insomuch, that had not my uncle, and some other good Christians, through his means, notwithstanding his so late ill usage and repulse (even to the extreme hazard of their lives), privately conveyed me some few refreshments, I must have inevitably perished, my prison allowance being nothing but bread and water; so that I was, through my severe scourging, and such hard fare, every day in expectation of its being my last; and happy, no doubt, had I been, had it so happened; I should certainly then have died a martyr, and probably thereby gained a glorious crown in the Kingdom of Heaven; but the Almighty did not then see it fit. My tortures were now exceedingly increased, {16} burning my flesh off my bones by fire; which the tyrant did, by frequent repetitions, after a most cruel manner; insomuch, that through my so very acute pains, I was at last constrained to submit, calling upon God to forgive me, who knows that I never gave the consent of the heart though I seemingly yielded, by holding up my finger; and that I always abominated them and their accursed principle of Mahometism, my only trust and confidence being firmly fixed on Him, and in the all-sufficient merits of His only son Jesus Christ, my Saviour.

I was kept forty days longer in prison on my refusing to put on the Moorish habit; but I at length reflected that to refuse this any longer was a very foolish obstinacy, since it was a thing indifferent in its own nature, seeing I had already been compelled to give my assent to Mahometism. Therefore, rather than undergo fresh torments, I also complied with it, appearing like a Mahometan; and I make no doubt but some ill-natured people think me so even to this day. I pray God to forgive them and that it may never

18. *bastinading*: a beating administered to the soles of the feet.
19. *Shehed, Shehed! [. . .] turn Moor!*: "Shehed" refers to the Arabic cognate imperative verb *shahhid* or *itshahhid*: "utter the profession of faith!" "Cunmoora" most likely derives from the Arabic *kūn*, meaning "become." "Moora" is not an Arabic word but probably refers to "Moor."

be their mishap to undergo the like trials; and which, if it should, that they may maintain their Christian faith no worse than I did mine.

I was now delivered once more from my prison and chains; and, at the command of the emperor, put to school, to learn the Moorish language, and to write Arabic;[20] and in the latter I should have certainly been a tolerable proficient, had not my master's insolence and violent death by the emperor's orders prevented it; for after being with him about three months, during which he had often called me Christian dog and most severely beat me, it coming to the emperor's ears, he {17} was by his order instantly dispatched by tossing him up and so breaking his neck.

After this, I was put no more to school to learn the language, but immediately into the hands of Emhamenet Sageer, whose business was to train up and instruct youth how they should speak and behave before the emperor and in the war; he having for such purposes under his care about six hundred boys; and with whom I had not been above a fortnight before I had the charge of eighty of them committed to me, I being made their *alcaide*,[21] or captain, to see they kept clean the walks (during all intervals from exercise) in the emperor's garden, where {57} he and his favourite, Queen Hellema Hazzezas[22] (in English "the beloved") were used to walk. In this station I had not been but a very little time when the queen, coming one day into the walks before I had the power to hide myself in a little house set there for that purpose (and which, at her approach, we were commanded always to do), happened to see me, and the next day begged me of the emperor, which he readily granting, ordered us immediately out one by one till she should see the same person; and after the first, second, and third were presented, and turned back again, he ordered their captain to appear, when I instantly appeared, and the queen saying I was the same she would have, I was forthwith given her, and by her again to her favourite son Muly Zidan, a youth of about eight years of age and then resident with his mother in the palace of Sherrers, where she, with thirty-eight of the emperor's {18} concubines and several eunuchs, were closely shut up, and to which I was made chief porter of the innermost door, that is to say, of the door next without

---

20. On captives and foreign languages, see John Gallagher, "Language-Learning, Orality, and Multilingualism in Early Modern Anglophone Narratives of Mediterranean Captivity," in *Renaissance and Early Modern Travel: Practice and Experience, 1500–1700*, ed. Eva Johanna Holmberg, special issue, *Journal of the Society for Renaissance Studies* 33, no. 4 (2019): 639–61.

21. *alcaide*: from the Arabic *al-qā'id*, meaning "leader" or "captain." Pellow was fifteen years old at the time.

22. *Queen Hellema Hazzezas*: Halima el-Aziza, one of the four main wives of the sultan.

that of the entrance into the galleries leading to the several apartments, and where none could gain admittance but through me; as indeed none were to be admitted, the emperor only excepted, nor him neither, in case he should offer to come without giving notice, at an unseasonable hour; as once indeed he did, and though he had gained admittance in at the several outer doors, yet was he by me denied; for how could I tell it was him when he was on the one side and I on the other of a thick door close shut; and allowing, as by his being let in at the several outer doors and his usual way of knocking, I might have very little reason to doubt it, and which might likewise have induced me to open it, yet, what did that signify to me, when I had positive orders before (as no doubt had all the rest) to admit none after such an hour, without being before advised of it, and of some certain signs to be given accordingly on the outside of the door; and further, my orders were, that in case anyone should attempt to enter at such an unseasonable hour and not immediately depart after his first and second knocking and denials of entrance, but should presume to knock a third time without giving the signs as aforesaid, I should then fire through the door—as indeed I had now an occasion to do.

The emperor being admitted, as aforementioned, in at the several outer doors, and knocking at mine, I demanded aloud, "Who was there?," to which I was answered, "Muly Smine," and which, indeed, by his voice and usual way of knocking, I was pretty well assured it was. However, I told him that I {19} very much doubted it; for that I had never known His Excellency to come at such an unseasonable hour, without my being preadvised thereof; and which, as I then was not, he should at his peril be gone, or I would present him with half a dozen bullets through the door, which he prayed me not to do, for that it was actually himself, and that if I would not let him in, he would certainly chop off my head the next day, knocking again louder than before; but, on the contrary, if I would admit him, he would give me such a fine horse (calling him by his name), with all the rich furniture belonging to him, and would make me a great man. I told him I would not do it if he would give me all the horses and furniture in the empire; for that as I was entrusted and commanded by the renowned Muly Smine or Ishmael, the most glorious emperor in the world, to keep that post inviolable against all impostors and intruders whomsoever, and as I had but too much reason to believe him such, I would not on any terms open the door, be the consequence what it would, being thoroughly resolved not to betray my trust; therefore it was in vain for him any longer to persist.

When he changing his note from rewards to threats and knocking again, I fired all the bullets which I had ready by me in a blunderbuss,[23] quite through the door, which indeed (he keeping himself close on one side, as I before imagined) could in nowise hurt him; and on his seeing my so resolute resistance, and no likelihood of his admittance, he returned as he came, highly threatening me for keeping him out, and as much commending those at the several outer doors for their so readily letting him in, assuring us that we should on neither side lose our reward; and indeed we did not, being very early {20} in the morning all ordered out, and all those who gave him admittance had some their heads cut off, others cruelly used; and myself, after being highly commended for my fidelity, rewarded with a much finer horse than that he offered to give me in case I would betray my trust. [. . .]

{24} [. . .] Now am I, after my hard keeping, again become in pretty good plight, being allowed very good eatables, as beef, mutton, and cuscassoo[24] (of the nature of which I shall speak by and by), I having in a manner now nothing else to do than to eat my meat, and be careful of my young master's and the queen's motions, and especially those of the latter, who I found was about to cut me out some new work; so that I was obliged to walk like one walking on the brink of a dangerous precipice, whence, should he happen to make but the least wry step, he is sure to tumble down and break his neck. The queen, in short, being extremely amorous, and the emperor no less jealous of her, which really made my condition very dangerous and might through some unforeseen accident (let my behaviour be never so innocent) happen to prove of very bad consequence to me, therefore I thought it highly prudent to keep a very strict guard upon all my actions. [. . .]

{26} [. . .] Now it is my chief business and greatest concern to study how to oblige the emperor, his dear Hellema, and my young master;[25] but the latter I confess I did not mind, though he was by nature cruel enough, and I had seen him, even in the seventeenth year of his age, kill his favourite black with his own hand by stabbing him into the belly with a knife, and only for coming very accidentally where he was feeding a pair of pigeons and their flying away for a few minutes. Yet, I say, I did not much mind him,

---

23. *blunderbuss*: an antiquated, short gun with a flared muzzle.

24. *cuscassoo*: couscous, a dish made by steaming crushed durum wheat (or other grains). Pellow also spells it cuscassoe (386).

25. *young master*: one of the sultan's sons whom Pellow had to serve for a time.

as having much higher objects to observe, the queen being in a particular manner kind, and often recommending me to the emperor's good liking as a careful and diligent servant, as indeed I really was, so far as I thought might be consistent with my advantage and safety. But I thinking this service very precarious, and that I was every moment exposed, and in danger of her poison, or his sword, I humbly intreated her to desire the emperor to find out for me some other employment, wherein I might be less suspected, and not altogether out of the way of obliging her; which she readily complied with, I being directly ordered by the emperor to quit this dangerous office and to wait on him at his palace for such future commands as should be by him enjoined me. A sudden and pleasing alteration indeed; and though my new business might be attended with more masculine exercises, yet was I well satisfied that it could not be with more danger and uneasiness, of which I was very soon confirmed, I being strictly charged to be observant {27} of the emperor's commands only and to wait on him on all occasions; and when he pleased to ride out, I was generally mounted on the fine horse he gave me for my fidelity in maintaining my post at the door, always carrying at my girdle a club of about three feet long, of Brazil wood, with which he used, on any slight occasion, to knock his people on the head, as I had several times the pleasure of beholding. For, in short (although I did not know how soon it might have been my own fate), I did not care how soon they were all dead; and indeed, he was of so fickle, cruel, and sanguine a nature, that none could be even for one hour secure of life. He had many dispatched by having their heads cut off, or by being strangled, others by tossing, for which he had several very dexterous executioners always ready at hand; but scarce would he on those occasions afford a verbal command, he thinking that too mean, and his words of more value than the life of the best of them, generally giving it by signs or motions of his head and hand; as, for instance, when he would have any person's head cut off, by drawing or shrinking his own as close as he could to his shoulders, and then with a very quick or sudden motion extending it; and when he would have any strangled, by the quick turn of his arm-wrist, his eye being fixed on the victims. The punishment of "tossing" is a very particular one, and peculiar to the Moors.

The person whom the emperor orders to be thus punished is seized upon by three or four strong negroes, who, taking hold of his hams,[26] throw him

---

26. *hams*: backs of the knees or thighs.

{28} up with all their strength, and at the same time turning him round, pitch him down head foremost, at which they are so dexterous by long use, that they can either break his neck the first toss, dislocate his shoulder, or let him fall with less hurt.

They continue doing this as often as the emperor has ordered, so that many times they [the victims] are killed upon the spot; sometimes they come off with only being severely bruised; and the person that is tossed must not stir a limb, if he is able, while the emperor is in sight, under penalty of being tossed again, but is forced to lie as if he was dead; which, if he should really be, nobody dares bury the body till the emperor has given orders for it. [. . .]

{34} [. . .] About this time came Commodore Stewart, ambassador to Mequinez,[27] with full powers from his royal master[28] to treat with the emperor for the so long desired redemption of the poor English captives. [. . .]

{37} [. . .] Commodore Stewart was conducted to Mequinez from Tetuan[29] by Hamet Ben Ally, one of the Emperor's bashaws;[30] in which embassy, the commodore being a very able, well-accomplished, courteous, and indefatigable gentleman, notwithstanding his often meeting with very great insults and manifest dangers, managed his point so well that in six weeks or thereabouts he procured the enlargement of all the English slaves (those under my unhappy {38} circumstances only excepted),[31] in number three hundred and one, releasing them from their long servitude and chains, and conducting them to Tetuan, where he found shipping ready to transport them to their so long desired homes, there being then more than six years expired since they were first made prisoners, that is to say, those taken with poor unhappy me, who you may imagine could not be allowed to go with them, though I most humbly intreated it by all the means I could devise, all my solicitations being in vain, so that I was obliged to content myself to effect my deliverance by private escape when opportunity offered; to which

27. *Commodore Stewart, ambassador to Mequinez*: the Honorable Charles Stewart (1681–1741) undertook a diplomatic mission to Morocco in 1721 and negotiated an agreement with Moulay Ismaïl whereby around three hundred English slaves were released from Moroccan captivity.

28. *royal master*: George I (1660–1727), king of Great Britain from 1698–1727.

29. *Tetuan*: Tétouan, a city in northern Morocco.

30. *bashaw*: high-ranking official in North Africa and the Ottoman world. The term was sometimes also used to refer to the governor of a city. In other texts in this anthology the word has been translated as *basha*. However, in the case of the texts originally written in English, "bashaw" has been retained.

31. *those under my unhappy circumstances only excepted*: as a renegade, Pellow was not freed.

end the ambassador gave me very friendly advice, together with many other marks of his favour. [. . .]

{70} [. . .] You may now perhaps imagine that, as I was altogether at the emperor's command, I was quite excluded the sight and favour of the queen; which I was not, often receiving very valuable acknowledgments thereof, even from her own hands, and certainly through her means I hitherto fared the better with the emperor. For, in short, she thought she could not oblige me enough, and therefore was oversolicitous in an affair which I had much rather should have been let alone, and such as I thought she would never have urged or consented with herself to have put upon me, it being quite the reverse of my inclinations; yet did she urge it, and obtain it, and was, no doubt, some time in bringing it about with the emperor.

One day, the emperor being on the merry pin, ordered to be brought before him eight hundred young men, and soon after as many young women, who also instantly appearing (as being, no doubt, before ordered to be ready at hand), he told the {71} men that, as he had on several occasions observed their readiness and dexterity in obeying him, he would therefore, as in some part of recompense, give every one of them a wife; and which, indeed, he soon did, by giving some by his own hand (a very great condescension), and to others by the beckoning of his head and the cast of his eye where they should fix. After they were all coupled and departed, I was also called forth, and bid to look at eight black women standing there, and to take one of them for a wife. At which sudden command I, (being not a little confounded, as not at all liking their colour) immediately bowing twice, falling to the ground and kissing it, and after that the emperor's foot (which is the custom of those who desire to be heard, as well as a very great favour and condescension to be permitted to do), humbly intreated him, if, in case I must have a wife, that he would be graciously pleased to give me one of my own colour. Then, forthwith sending them off, he ordered to be brought forth seven others, who all proved to be mulattoes; at which I again bowed to the ground, still entreating him to give me one of my own colour; and then he ordered them also to depart and sent for a single woman, full dressed, and who in a very little time appeared with two young blacks attending her, she being, no doubt, the same he and the queen had before particularly designed for me. I being forthwith ordered to take her by the hand and lead her off, which she holding out to me, I perceived it to be black also, as soon after I did her feet; at which I started back, like one in a very great surprise, and being asked what was the matter, I answered him as before; when he smiling, ordered me to lift up her veil (it being the custom of {72} the country for women to go veiled) and look at her face; which I readily obeying, found her to be of a very agreeable complexion, the old rascal crying out, in a very pleasing way, in the Spanish language, "Bono! Bono!," which signifies, "Good! Good!," ordering me a second time to take her by the hand, lead her off, and keep her safe.

This artificial blackness of her hands and feet was laid on by a certain grass, first made into powder and mixed with water, alum, and the juice of lemons, and is called *el bhenna*,[32] being brought from the river Draugh, about ten days' journey from Mequinez, and still further from Taffilet, and several other places.

At our coming out of the palace, we found her father, mother, sister, and sister's husband, ready to receive us (the latter being a man of very considerable authority, as having under his command one thousand five hundred young men, who go under the name of "Kiadrossams," being all the emperor's brothers-in-law, and are generally at his call in the palace), and received us very courteously indeed, desiring me, as it was the emperor's pleasure to give me his sister, that I would always behave to her as a loving husband, so far as she deserved, and at the same time exhorting her no less in her duty to me. This we both readily promised to each other, and which was indeed by both of us as faithfully performed. Their next request being our acceptance of an apartment (as having none of our own) in this our brother-in-law's {73} house, till such time as we were provided with one of our own which we as readily came into, and together with the old gentry went with them, though we were for the first night lodged in separate lodgings, as I suppose were the rest, being all first obliged to appear again the next day at the palace, there to receive a certificate from the secretary as a ratification or finishing stroke, and each couple fifteen ducats,[33] each ducat 6s. 8d., making in all just £5 in English money, two-thirds for the man and one for the woman, as the emperor's bounty on such-like occasions, before our marriage could be completed. Which being paid, and our certificates delivered, each man paying for them (as the secretary's fee) sixteen

---

32. *El bhenna*: henna.
33. *ducat*: the ducat, originating in thirteenth-century Venice, was a gold or silver coin widely used in Europe and across the Ottoman Empire in the eighteenth century.

blankeels[34] (pieces of money of about twopence in value each), we were all dismissed to make merry with our friends and celebrate our nuptials. As I and my spouse were well accounted of amongst the better sort, we did not want for plenty of wedding guests, nor they for plenty of good eatables, I having provided, at my own charge (over and above that of my brother-in-law's), a fat bullock, four sheep, two dozen of large fowls, twelve dozen of young pigeons, 150 lb. weight of fine flour, and 50 lb. of butter, with a sufficient store of honey, spices, etc. All which, our wedding holding three days, was clearly dispatched with a great deal of mirth and friendly satisfaction. Yet was it the soberest wedding you ever saw, for we had not, among all this great company, one intoxicated person, though they had all as much liquor as they would drink; but such, indeed, as might sooner break their bellies than operate in their {74} noddles,[35] being only water; wine being by their grand impostor and great prophet Mahomet altogether forbidden. And though it is death by his law for any person discovered in drinking it, yet it is by some privately drunk, even to excess, there being great store and very good in Barbary, besides what they catch from other countries. [. . .]

[*Pellow, as a trusted officer of the sultan, participated in numerous military campaigns over the course of his twenty-three years in Morocco. Pellow records no dates for his first escape attempt, but he most likely made his first break for freedom before Moulay Ismaïl's death. The death of Moulay Ismaïl in March 1727 was followed by a period of political turmoil in which three of the old sultan's sons fought for succession. During this period, Pellow, whose wife and child had died in the meantime, attempted another unsuccessful escape. Finally, in 1737, he was able to flee from Meknès and undertook a perilous journey over the Atlas Mountains. Many months later, he reached a port that he identifies as Willadia. Here, he boarded the ship of the Irish captain Toobin and departed on 10 July 1738. On 21 July 1738, he arrived at the port of Gibraltar, where the harbor guards at first refused to let him disembark, believing him to be a "Moor." For the crossing from Gibraltar to London, Pellow secured passage on the* Euphrates *with Captain Peacock.*]

{383} And now is it come to the twenty-fourth day of our passage, when I heard called out aloud from aloft the very much pleasing and

---

34. *blankeel*: a base Moroccan silver coin whose name is derived from its white ("blanca") appearance. See Albert R. Frey, *A Dictionary of Numismatic Names: Their Official and Popular Designations* (New York: American Numismatic Society, 1917), 27.

35. *noddles*: heads.

long-expected word "Land," and which proved to be the western Land's End of England, or Cape Cornwall; and the wind favouring to carry us up the Channel, we crowded a great sail, passed by Falmouth, and kept on all upon the same tack till we got off of the Bill of Portland; when, on account of one of our people falling overboard, we were obliged to bring to; and on our throwing out some empty kegs and rails of timber, he caught hold on one of them; then we hoisted out our boat and had him well on board again. After this accident (which, I thank God, was the first and the last we met with during our passage from Gibraltar), we kept on with this favourable gale to the Downs, passed through, and cast anchor at the Nore, where Captain Peacock found his wife with her brother on board of a man-of-war (of which he was commander), waiting his coming. The next tide we got to Gravesend, and the next up the river Thames to Deptford, where our ship was to be disburdened of her cargo, it being the thirty-first day after our departure from Gibraltar. [. . .]

{385} [. . .] Passing over London Bridge, I soon got to the house,[36] and luckily found one Captain Francis of Penzance, who was commander of one of them, named the *Truro*. And after I had told him my name, he was extremely civil to me and readily offered me a passage in his vessel with him down to Cornwall; which I most heartily thanked him for and with joy gladly accepted of it, telling him I should depend thereon and that I would be sure to give my attendance accordingly. But as I found he could not sail in ten days, I, through the advice of some of my new acquaintance, went to the Navy Office, praying the commissioners kind introducing me to His Majesty; to which they (after they had discoursed me) seemed to be pretty well inclined, ordering me to come to them again, as indeed I did again and again, though all I could get from them at the last was the very extraordinary favour of a hammock on board of a man-of-war.

I told them that I was very much obliged to them, and if I could not get a livelihood through other means on terra firma, but must be again obliged to go to sea, that a man-of-war should be my choice of all other ships; for as I had never made but a piece of a voyage in a merchantman, and that so very unfortunate, I did not care to encounter with a second, which if I should, and again fall into the hands of the Moors, it would soon be out

---

36. *the house*: The King's Head in Pudding Lane.

of my power to encounter with a third. Then I fully resolved with myself to give these worthy gentlemen no further trouble, but to hasten as fast as I could home to the {386} place of my nativity, there to get proper vouchers and recommendatory letters to some worthy person, and return therewith, in order to his introducing me and my petition.

At my going out of the office, I chanced to meet in the street one of Elhash Abaulcodah Perez,[37] the Morocco ambassador's nephews, and whom (as I had been so well acquainted with him before in Barbary), you may suppose I was very glad to see, even much more than ever I was to see him in Barbary. He very earnestly entreating me to go with him to visit his uncle and the rest of my old acquaintance, I told him I fully intended to do it, if I had not met him there. "However," said I, "it may now be so much the better for me, through means of your introducing me." So I went directly with him and was by the old man very kindly received; and after he had discoursed me so far as he thought fit, as asking me how I got off and the like, he told me that he was very glad I was delivered out of an unhappy country and that he wished himself in no happier condition than I was, charging his people to make me very welcome, and if I was disposed to take up with his house altogether as to my eating and drinking, it would please him very much; though this I did not care much to accept of, neither did I, after a blunt manner, refuse it, answering him with a low bow.

And after I had dined there that day on my favourite dish, cuscassoe, and some English dishes, I returned to my lodgings in Pudding Lane; where I had not been but a very little time before a gentleman came in, congratulating me on my being so near to be introduced to His Majesty, and he was soon seconded by several others. I humbly thanked them (as supposing it only their pleasure to say so by way of merriment), and that I wished it were true, though I very much doubted the contrary, by reason I could get nobody to introduce me. "No!" said {387} they. "Why, it is actually in the newspapers!" "Indeed!" said I. "Yes," said they, "it is." On which the newspaper was directly brought forth, and I read in it the following paragraph, viz., "A man is now in town, lately arrived from Gibraltar, in the *Euphrates*, Captain Peacock, escaping there from Barbary, where he had been a slave twenty-five years, being taken by the Moors in the tenth year of his age, and

---

37. *Elhash Abaulcodah Perez*: Abdelkader Peres, a Moroccan admiral and ambassador to England in 1737.

is to be presented to His Majesty one day this week." This I soon found to be one of Mr. Newswriter's truths; for which I told the printer that I thought him very much to blame, for that I had given him no such license, neither could I, without asserting a very great falsity; and as to His Majesty, I believed he knew nothing of the matter. After this I waited on the Moroccan ambassador several times and was always by him and his people kindly received.

Now is Captain Francis ready to fall down the river. The first tide we got to Gravesend, and the next to the Nore, and the third over the Flats and into the Downs, and thence with a favourable gale kept sailing till we got off the Start, where the wind taking us right ahead, and blowing very hard, we let go our anchor, and rid it out there two days, when we moved thence and got that day off Plymouth, and the next, being Sunday, we got about four o'clock in the afternoon safe into Falmouth Pier; whence being to Penryn, the place of my nativity, no more than two miles, I got to the town in the evening.

And as my father's house was almost quite at the other end of the town—perhaps about half a mile—I was, before I could reach it, more than an hour; for notwithstanding it was almost quite dark, I was so crowded by the inhabitants that I could not pass through them without a great deal of difficulty—though this, I must own, was of a different and far more pleasing nature to me than {388} my first entrance into Mequinez, every one, instead of boxing me and pulling my hair, saluting me and after a most courteous manner bidding me welcome home, being all very inquisitive with me if I knew them. Which, indeed, I did not, for I was so very young at my departure and my captivity and the long interval of time had made so very great an alteration on both sides, that I did not know my own father and mother, nor they me; and had we happened to meet at any other place without being preadvised, whereby there might be an expectation or natural instinct interposing, we should no doubt have passed each other, unless my great beard might have induced them to inquire further after me.

And now is the so long lost sheep again restored to his owners, after his long straying and grievous hardships amongst those monsters and ravenous wolves of infidelity, and safely returned to his parents, in the town of his nativity, being the 15th day of October, 1738, and the twelfth year of the reign of our sovereign lord, King George the Second.

To look back upon and seriously to consider the years of my captivity is so frightful and amazing that all must allow that nothing but the almighty protection of a great, good, all-seeing, most-sufficient, and gracious

God could have carried me through it or delivered me out of it. Therefore to Him be the glory, honour, and praise, and may He so order my heart as always to continue a lively remembrance thereof, and so order my ways to live up to His divine precepts during the remainder of this mortal life, that after all these my sufferings ended here, I may be crowned with a glorious immortality in the kingdom of heaven.

FINIS

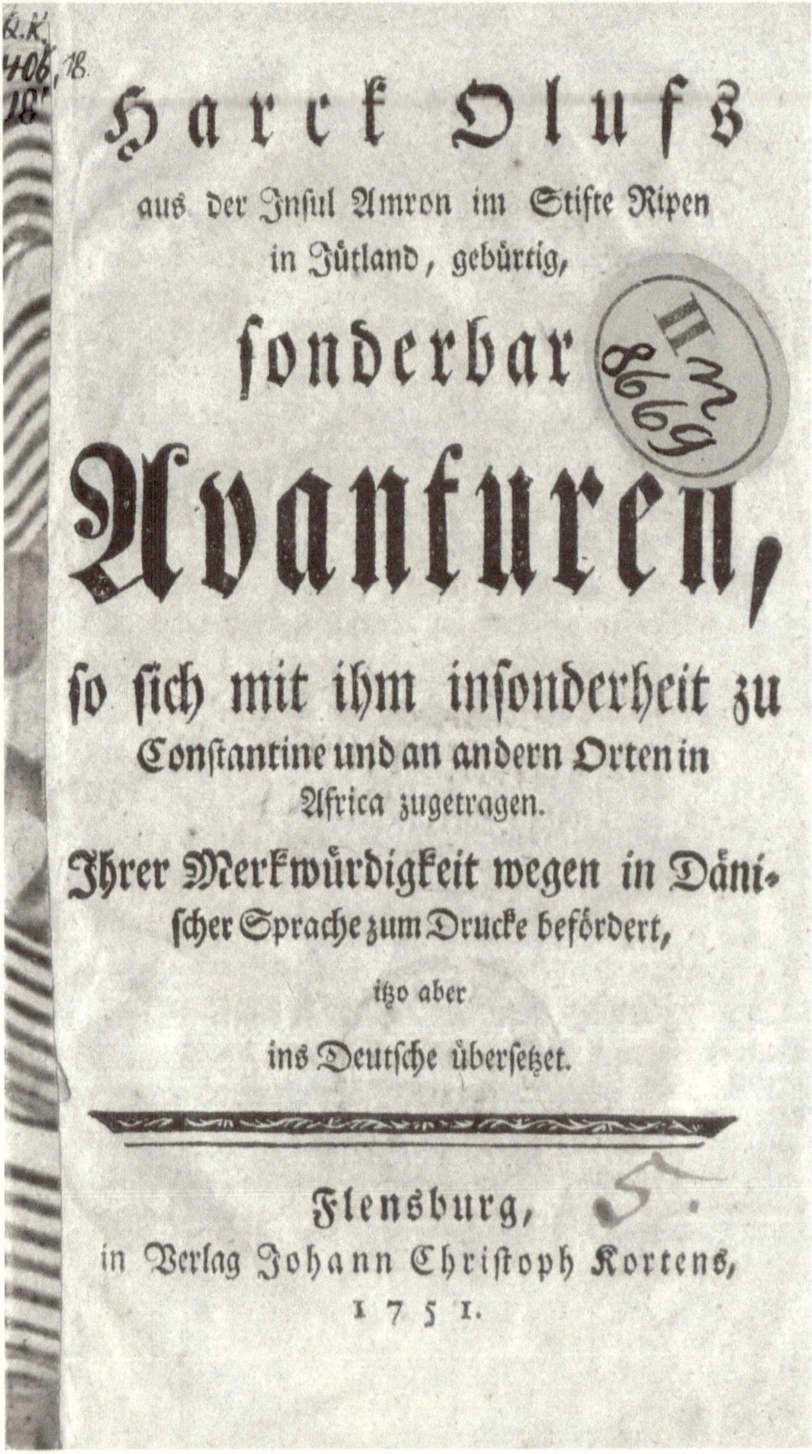

Harck Olufs

aus der Insul Amron im Stifte Ripen
in Jütland, gebürtig,

sonderbar Avanturen,

so sich mit ihm insonderheit zu
Constantine und an andern Orten in
Africa zugetragen.

Ihrer Merkwürdigkeit wegen in Dänischer Sprache zum Drucke befördert,

itzo aber

ins Deutsche übersetzet.

Flensburg,
in Verlag Johann Christoph Kortens,
1751.

Figure 9.1 Title page of Hark Olufs's narrative
Source: *Harck Olufs aus der Insul Amron im Stifte Ripen in Jütland, gebürtig, sonderbare Avanturen* (Flensburg, 1751); PON JIn 8669, QK; Universitäts- und Landesbibliothek Sachsen-Anhalt.

CHAPTER IX

HARK OLUFS, *THE REMARKABLE ADVENTURES OF HARK OLUFS*

1747 Danish print edition; complete text

Captivity in Constantine 1724–1735

The Danish account of Hark Olufs, a native of the island of Amrum in the North Sea during the early eighteenth century, occupies a special place among captivity narratives set in North Africa. Olufs was taken prisoner in 1724 at the age of fifteen while on a sea voyage. What distinguishes his account from numerous other Barbary captivity narratives is the fact that he was able to integrate into North African culture very quickly because of his youth. His social advancement was so great that, at the height of his career in North Africa, Hark Olufs held the position of supreme commander in the bey of Constantine's army. Olufs's account was initially published in Danish in 1747 but appeared in a German translation as early as 1751.

Hark Olufs's testimony corresponds in many ways to the classic captivity narratives from North Africa during the early modern period, describing the author's capture, sale, life in North Africa, and his return from Barbary. As is typical for the genre, Olufs also provides an overview of Constantine and its people, as part of which he also explains the main features of Islam (Olufs 6–12).[1] It is likewise not unusual for the genre that Hark Olufs paints a generally positive image of Islam, respecting Muslims for their religious practice and steadfastness: "They are fervent in their false religion, and one

---

1. Page numbers correspond to those in the original historical edition used for the translation in this anthology.

would be hard pressed to find anyone who acts deliberately against what they consider to be the duties of a Muhammadan" and "one can find as much honesty among the Turks as among us Christians" (8).

Olufs's account stands out from other Barbary narratives because of a number of unique features. For example, it is rather unusual that a returnee chronicles success in North Africa that transcends the fate of an oppressed slave. The "captive's" life presented here differs radically from most slave narratives, because Olufs successfully adjusted to the North African regime, in this case under the bey of Constantine, and was thus able to improve his position dramatically.

Olufs writes that in the first three and a half years of his captivity, he learned the lingua franca spoken in North Africa "as well as Turkish and Arabic" (12). The still-youthful Olufs—all of fifteen years old—was able to adapt to his new cultural environment. Although he does not state this explicitly, it can be assumed that Hark Olufs was only able to make his remarkable career moves in such quick succession because he converted to Islam. We know from many other sources that renegades (Christians who converted to Islam) could become important players in North Africa. These included many pirate captains, military officers, and government leaders. For example, as documented in the narrative by Ólafur Egilsson in this anthology, the foray to Iceland in 1627 by Moroccan and Algerian corsairs was led primarily by European renegades and was only possible because these captains possessed the necessary nautical knowledge to navigate the northern Atlantic.

What differentiates Hark Olufs's testimony from many other early modern narratives is the fact that other surviving documents provide additional information about his life after his stay in North Africa.[2] Thus, we know that Olufs, after his return to his home island Amrum, continued to wear North African clothes and to behave in an outlandish manner, much to the astonishment of the local population. For this reason, Olufs's account provides rare textual evidence of the "successful" acculturation and integration process of a European in North Africa. However, Olufs's experience is also

---

2. See Martin Rheinheimer, *Der fremde Sohn. Hark Olufs' Wiederkehr aus der Sklaverei* (Neumünster: Wachholtz, 2001). All subsequent references to Rheinheimer follow this edition unless otherwise indicated. See also Martin Rheinheimer, "From Amrum to Algiers and Back: The Reintegration of a Renegade in the Eighteenth Century," *Central European History* 36 (2003), 209–33.

a very good example of the problems returnees struggled with after lengthy captivity in North Africa (in Hark Olufs's case, more than a decade).

As already mentioned, Hark Olufs never directly addresses the issue of conversion to Islam. However, it can be assumed—based on the exceptional career he enjoyed in North Africa—that Olufs's account is that of a renegade. Olufs's detailed description of his rapid social and political climb in Constantine includes disturbing events he experienced and gruesome deeds he had to undertake to achieve and maintain his high rank in North Africa. Most startling is Olufs's confession of having twice murdered innocent masons upon the bey's command in order to guarantee the victims' "silence" about the whereabouts of money, which the masons had been ordered to immure in a tower for the bey (30).

Notes on the Present Translation of Hark Olufs's *Remarkable Adventures of Hark Olufs*

This translation is based on the first German edition: Hark Olufs, *Harck Olufs aus der Insul Amron im Stifte Ripen in Jütland gebürtig, sonderbare Avanturen, so sich mit ihm insonderheit zu Constantine und an andern Orten in Africa zugetragen. Ihrer Merkwürdigkeit wegen in Dänischer Sprache zum Drucke befördert, itzo aber ins Deutsche übersetzet* (Flensburg: Johann Christoph Kortens, 1751).

The numbers in brackets { } in the text always indicate the beginning of a page and refer to the original page numbers of the 1747 Danish edition. The translation introduces additional paragraph breaks in order to enhance the readability of the narrative. All transliterations and translations pertaining to languages from the Islamic world have been provided by Stephan Procházka and Devin Stewart.

Hark Olufs, *The Remarkable Adventures of Hark Olufs, Born on the Island of Amrum in the Diocese of Ripen, Jütland; Peculiar Adventures, Which He Experienced Particularly in Constantine and Other Places in Africa. Printed in Danish on Account of Their Remarkable Nature, and Now Translated Into German* (Flensburg: Johann Christoph Kortens, 1751)

Translated by Robert Spindler

{3} Forasmuch as it pleased the Lord to guide me in such a wondrous manner, out of a thousand other men, I was asked to capture and set in print the strange occurrences which befell me, on account of their extraordinariness, so that my story may serve as proof of God's miraculous power, which guides the children of men, and can—if He so wishes—turn the heart of an *unchristian* to lovingness.

On 19 July 1708, I saw the light of day for the first time on a small island called Amrum, located in the North Sea[3] and belonging to the municipality of Ribe in Jutland.[4] Since my fellow countrymen get their sustenance from the sea, {4} I had been very eager to become an able seafarer from my twelfth year onward. After three years of taking part in the occasional voyage, on 10 March 1724, I was captured off the Isles of Scilly[5] in the Channel, and taken to Algiers by a Turkish privateer, along with three of my countrymen, Richard Flor, Jens Nikelsen, and Hark Nikelsen [as well as] Jürgen Oksen of Föhr[6] and three men from the banks of the Elbe. I was sold at the market for one thousand *cartuches*,[7] or one thousand Lübische marks,[8] but the following day, my buyer sold me to another [master], making a profit of one hundred cartuches. I stayed with this master for about fourteen days. My tasks were to grow different things in the garden, to collect mulberry leaves for my master's silkworms, to carry water, and to keep the house clean.

---

3. *North Sea*: "West-See" ("West Sea") in the 1751 German edition. However, Amrum is one of Germany's North Frisian islands, located in the North Sea.

4. *belonging to [. . .] Ribe in Jutland*: today, the island of Amrum is a part of Schleswig-Holstein, Germany.

5. *Isles of Scilly*: a group of more than 140 islands close to the southwestern tip of England.

6. *Föhr*: today, the North Frisian island of Föhr in the North Sea is part of Germany, but in Olufs's time it was under Danish rule.

7. *cartuches*: possibly a corruption of the word "Kuruş," a common unit of currency in the Ottoman Empire.

8. *Lübische marks*: a unit of currency minted in Lübeck from the sixteenth century onward and temporarily adopted by Denmark.

But when the bey of Constantine, by the name of Assin,[9] {5} sent his commissioner to Algiers to purchase slaves, he took a fancy to me, and my master sold me to him for 450 pieces of eight.[10] This Bey Assin can be regarded as a minor king, and he governs the capital city of Constantine, which is a charming fortress city that lies, by my calculations, a twelve days' journey or sixty miles south of Algiers.[11] As far as I know, he was in no way a subject to the Great Sultan.[12] Rather, he was sovereign in his country. By the time I entered into his service, he was already a man of advanced age, hot-tempered, and with a healthy complexion. Stout-hearted and experienced in matters of war, he was often in the field with his army and had disputes with his neighbors, both before and during my time with him. Every year, he would stay at least one month in Constantine. He had two wives, who were served by more than forty male and female servants, including four eunuchs who were commissioned as valets. {6} He himself had thirty to forty footmen to serve him, half of them renegades, who were afterward given the best offices in the country.[13]

Before I go on, I would like to say a few words about the features of the land, about its people, and finally about my own fate. The land is full of peaks, some of them so high that they are permanently covered in snow. However, the areas surrounding the base of the mountains are so hot that if the camels are loaded with snow and start their descent, it will usually melt down to small lumps before they reach the bottom. Additionally, the country is very fertile and yields all kinds of grain, grapes, almonds, dates, figs, pomegranates, watermelons, etc. It is noteworthy that while one province is suited to one activity, another is suited to a different one, so goods have to be shipped regularly {7} from all cities to the camp where the king resides with his queens. Very fine wool as well as wax and honey are exported from the country, not to mention various apothecary ingredients, rare lion and tiger[14] hides, and suchlike. Whether metals other than lead are mined, I do

---

9. *Assin*: Kalyan Hasan Bey was the bey of Constantine from 1713 to 1736.

10. *450 pieces of eight*: Spanish silver coins also known as Spanish dollars or pesos. To put this amount in perspective: later in the narrative (p. 13 of the 1751 German edition), we learn that Hark Olufs's annual salary as the chief-treasurer of the bey was "1,700 pieces of eight."

11. *sixty miles south of Algiers*: the distance is actually about 200 miles (around 320 km) east of Algiers as the crow flies.

12. *Great Sultan*: Ahmed III (1673–1736), Ottoman sultan from 1703 to 1730.

13. *renegades [. . .] best offices in the country*: this is noteworthy, as Hark Olufs's own rise through the ranks while in the service of the bey is congruent with his remark about the renegades.

14. *tigers*: as there were no tigers in North Africa, it is likely that Olufs means leopards or cheetahs.

not know. For those who are born in that land, the air must be very healthy, for it is not uncommon to see people there that reach one hundred, one hundred and twenty years, or more. Now and then, one may experience earthquakes and thunderstorms, especially in summer. On top of dealing with ravenous wild beasts, such as lions, tigers, and suchlike—which often attack humans—the city's inhabitants are also plagued by numerous kinds of venomous snakes and, above all, scorpions, which are found in such abundance in certain areas that one can hardly lift a stone without finding one or two underneath. In addition, irritating flies and mosquitoes {8} frequently disturb the [people's] slumber.

The land is inhabited by Turks and Moors, the latter of which can be either black or white. Their language is different from Turkish, and they call it Arabic. However, both [Turks and Moors], who are under the rule of the aforementioned bey, are known as *Schirck*,[15] which translates as "the people that live in the south." As regards religion, Moors and Turks do not differ from each other much—only slightly with respect to their ceremonies. I must also salute the Turks' uprightness, which is greater than the Moors'. Indeed, as regards their conduct toward each other, one can find as much honesty among the Turks as among us Christians. They are fervent in their false religion, and one would be hard pressed to find anyone who acts deliberately against what they consider to be the duties of a Muhammadan. {9} At daybreak, whoever has been assigned [this task climbs up] a tower or another elevated place and, after sticking one finger in each ear, calls out: "Eschet velej elej lala, Eschet enne Mahammaet arasu lala ella velun Zelleth, ala hoat warth, ala hoat warth."[16] Upon hearing this, everyone rises, and, after washing their hands up to the elbows and their feet up to the ankles, cleaning their mouth and their nose, while at the same time wiping their face and behind their ears with the back of the hand, they hold their usual prayer. This is performed five times a day in this manner, the first time before sunrise. In the Arabic language, the prayer words are as follows: "Al ham dilola Robbi laîro min rachmana rachim mânik jumidin, jâken abeddo, jâken estohiim tokino soratin lâdino en dalohiim al

---

15. *Schirck*: this reference is not clear. Perhaps Olufs means the Arabic word *sharq*, which means "east." Alternatively, the Arabic term *shirk* means "polytheism" or "idol worship."

16. *"Eschet velej [. . .] hoat warth"*: Olufs recalls, in rather broken classical Arabic, the Islamic call to prayer: "Ashhadu an lā ilāha illā llāh, ashhadu anna muḥammadan rasūlu llāh, ḥayya ʿalā ṣ-ṣalāt, ḥayy ʿalā l-falāḥ," which translates as: "I bear witness that there is no God but God. I bear witness that Muhammad is the messenger of God. Hasten to prayer! Hasten to success!"

ham dilolah robbi lâiro min."¹⁷ They believe it is not easy to damn a Turk. They speak with deference of both Christ, whom they call Isa, and of the Virgin Mary, whom they call Lella Maria,¹⁸ {10} but [they refer to] the devil as an evildoer. Their circumcision is not performed before the ages of four, five, or even six. They do not eat pork, and no Muhammadan drinks wine or any other strong drinks, but instead relies on water or sherbet,¹⁹ which is water flavored with raisins but can be prepared in various ways. Their days of fasting, called Ramadan, are held each year for a whole month, and throughout this time, they do not indulge in anything during the day but eat and drink at night. In the last couple of years, my master could not bear to fast, so he ate a little in secret. Their dead are wrapped in linen and thus laid into the earth. The Moors gather together and sing a lament for their dead, while both men and women claw at their chins and foreheads with their nails. When they marry, the bridegroom does not get to see his bride in advance. {11} But after he has eaten and drunk with his guests on the wedding day, during which sometimes a zither is played, he is led into the women's chamber, where the bride is accompanied by other women, who all have their faces veiled. He is then given a sign by which he can recognize the bride. He goes to her and puts the money he has decided to give her as a morning gift in a handkerchief, strikes her with it, and goes into the bedchamber. She follows soon after. He then asks her name twice, but she does not answer until he asks a third time. He then throws

17. *"Al ham [. . .] lâiro min"*: although some parts are missing, this is *al-Fātiḥa*, the first surah of the Quran:

[bi-smi llāhi r-rāḥmāni r-raḥīm] al-ḥamdu li-llāh rabbi l-ʿālamīn, ar-raḥmāni r-raḥīm, māliki yawmi d-dīn, ʾiyyāka naʿbudu wa-ʾiyyāka nastaʿīn, ʾihdinā [ṣ-ṣirāṭa l-mustaqīm] ṣirāṭa lladhīna ʾanʿamta [ʿalayhim ghayri l-maghḍūbi ʿalayhim wa-lā ḍ-ḍāllīn.

Al-ḥamdu li-llāh rabbi l-ʿālamīn.

This translates as:

"[In the name of God, the most Gracious and Merciful]. Praise be to God, the Lord of men the world over, the Merciful and Gracious, who will preside over the Day of Judgment. We serve Thee, and we worship Thee. Show us [the rightful path], the path of those to whom You have shown mercy, [not the path of those who have incurred your wrath] and gone astray.

Praise be to God, the Lord of men the world over."

From his mention of the *muezzin*, the person who calls to prayer, to his depiction of the *wudu*, or "lesser ablution," Olufs's description of the ritual prayer, the second pillar of Islam, is very accurate. See Ian Richard Netton, *Encyclopedia of Islamic Civilization and Religion* (Abingdon, UK: Routledge, 2008), 9, 119–20, 561–62.

18. *Lella Maria*: "Lalla" is a Berber word that means "[esteemed] lady."

19. *sherbet*: from the Ottoman Turkish word *şerbet*. Sherbet is a traditional drink that can be made with raisins or a wide variety of other ingredients. In the 1751 German edition, it appears as "Schorbet."

the handkerchief with the money onto the floorboards and spreads a small carpet on the floor, steps on it, and performs his prayer. In the meantime, the bride takes off her clothes and goes to bed. He follows soon after. Most women are very young when they marry. In my experience, Turks live abstemiously when it comes to food and drink. {12} Not many dishes are served, but many kinds of fruit are supplied at meals. In the morning, they first eat some sort of pastry, and then they drink coffee—tea is not held in high esteem. At ten o'clock, they eat lunch, after which they rest a couple of hours and eat again in the afternoon, at around four o'clock.

Now, regarding my fate in particular, I first served my master as a lackey for three and a half years and, since I had learned the lingua franca[20] during that time—as well as Turkish and Arabic—and, by and by, I had also developed a set of valuable skills, God inspired mercy in my master and he showed me great favor at every turn. He entrusted me with an office of great importance called *hazinedar*,[21] which is what we might call the "chief-treasurer" in our country. I held {13} this office for four years and my yearly salary was 1,700 pieces of eight, in addition to the land, camels, sheep, and such that I acquired. Two scribes, who accompanied me everywhere, were paid by my master, but I personally handed out the wages of twenty servants and sometimes more. Thrice a year I received an outfit richly embroidered with gold and silver. Aside from this responsibility, I was also entrusted with the command of five hundred horsemen, for even as a treasurer I had demonstrated, on various opportunities, while following orders, a kind of bravery that pleased my master. In truth, my courage was more what one might call audacity rather than actual bravery or valor, for [in those days] I was not of a cheerful disposition. Therefore, it was all the same to me whether I lived or died. Even though I was a well-respected man in the region and although many envied my luck, I saw things more clearly. {14} In spite of my wealth, I was a slave, and one slip before my barbaric master, who had the power to do as he pleased, could bring me down as easily as I had been lifted up. Yes, my life constantly hung in the balance. I was permanently surrounded by the five hundred riders mentioned above, who could be considered my master's personal bodyguards.

---

20. *lingua franca*: also known as Sabir, this was used among Italian, French, Spanish, and Portuguese speakers to communicate with each other and with Turkish, Berber, and Arab speakers from the Mediterranean and beyond. It arose around the fourteenth century and remained in use until the end of the nineteenth century. See Viveka Velupillai, *Pidgins, Creoles and Mixed Languages: An Introduction* (Amsterdam: John Benjamins, 2015), 51.

21. *hazinedar*: it appears in the original Danish narrative as "Gassenadahl" or "Gasnadi." The term comes from the Ottoman Turkish *khazīne*, which means "treasure," and *dār*, which means "bearing."

It so happened that a war unfolded between my master and a certain Bu Aziz of Tbessa,[22] who was a kind of minor chieftain and the head of a distinguished family. This Bu Aziz got it into his head that he wanted to seize some land that belonged to my master. I will omit the many daily skirmishes that ensued, in which [the men] continued to fight as long as the other side remained out on the field. Incessant attacks occurred all around. To operate properly under these circumstances, they conducted {15} a different kind of warfare than in our countries. Their strategy relied mainly on a hot-tempered attack. Of these little encounters, the following two were the most important. We were fortunate enough to withstand the first one, but the enemy gained the advantage the second time around. After both sides had seized several thousand camels, horses, sheep, and suchlike, I was ordered to reconnoiter with [my] five hundred horsemen. We noticed on this occasion that the enemy had gone to rest, so we resolved to invade. Our success was such that the enemy took flight, as they probably thought our whole force, which was altogether nine to ten thousand men strong, was there as well. We took fifty-two heads back with us, whereas we lost only five men. We dispatched a courier to bring my master news of our victory.

When we arrived at the tent, the king ordered that {16} everyone who had brought a head with him should come forward and cast it at his feet. He rewarded all of them with money. I received several testimonies of merit, wherefore even the noblest servants were ordered to wait on me, and, from that day on, I was entrusted with the command of the entire cavalry. However, my new position, called *agha ed-deïra*,[23] or colonel of the cavalry, made me the target of much hate and envy. It was not long before I was tasked with attacking the abovementioned enemies. This proved to be ruinous for me and those who were with me, given that while pursuing our fleeing foes, we had to march in single file through a mountain pass garrisoned with [enemy] foot soldiers, who shot part of our men dead. For those who surrendered, the pass was cut off; the rest had to flee to save {17} their lives. I was among the captives. My horse had been shot out from under me.

22. *Bu Aziz of Tbessa*: Bu Aziz ben Nasser was the ruler of the Henanesha, a large Berber clan that enjoyed considerable autonomy under the bey of Constantine and inhabited land in what is modern-day Tbessa in Algeria. See Martin Rheinheimer, "Sklave in Algier: Die Kaperei der Barbaresken in Atlantik und Nordsee," in *Strandungen, Havarien, Kaperungen: Beiträge zur Seefahrtsgeschichte Nordfrieslands*, ed. Robert Bohn and Sebastian Lehmann (Amsterdam: De Bataafsche Leeuw, 2004), 51. He appears in the 1751 German edition as "Boâssâse von Théses."

23. *agha ed-deïra*: this expression is unclear; however, the word *agha* meant "chief" or "master" in Ottoman Turkish and it was usually reserved for servants of the state in military positions.

They had taken my shoulder belt and tied my hands behind my back with it. Forty-five of our captured comrades were massacred. At first, they thought about dealing with us in the same manner, but, since they hoped to receive a good ransom for us, fifteen of us got to keep our lives, and I was among them. However, one of my servants, whom I loved dearly and had brought with me, was stabbed before my eyes.

After we had been taken into custody, Elgia, the consort of Bu Aziz, whom I have mentioned above, came to the prison. She was veiled in the Turkish manner so that not one bit of her could be seen bare, except her eyes and hands, which were painted in different vivid, striking colors in accordance with their customs. She had come to the prison mainly out of curiosity, because she had heard that there was a {18} Christian there. She asked which one of us was [the Christian], and after she repeated the question, I threw myself at her feet, since I clearly stood out among the others anyway. Not only was my complexion very different from that of the other captives, but their gaze was also directed at me. Her questions were manifold. Among other things, she asked whether in our country we believed in a god who rules over heaven and earth. When I answered this question with a "yes," she countered that in Europe they worshiped wooden [figures] and painted pictures. This erroneous view might have stemmed from her having either seen or heard such things about the Catholics. [She further asked] if we had horses, camels, milk, oil, bread, and suchlike. As she was leaving, I shouted [a plea at] her in a moving, yet piercing, tone, so that she would intercede with her master for me, whereupon she answered that I should not shout in this manner. These words I construed as anger, {19} but within a few hours the smith came and unbound me. After that, the sheikh,[24] who is a sort of a prince, showed me favor by summoning me, and much was done to refresh me. This sheikh was a great-grandson of old Bu Aziz, so I was lucky to win his favor. Not only were all manner of good things done for me and given to me for my refreshment, but he also asked his great-grandfather to allow me to go on a hunt with him.

One day, a few hours after noon, they led the horses aside, and the sheikh and the gentlemen who were with him disported themselves by shooting at targets. Meanwhile, I was consumed with thoughts of my fate and absent-mindedly directed my gaze at the horses. The young lord assumed I was contemplating them and asked me whether these horses were as good as those

---

24. *sheikh*: an honorific title in the Arabic language that commonly designates the ruler of a tribe.

I had {20} left behind in Constantine. I did not dare answer this question until I was given the grace to be allowed to tell the truth. "For I have heard," I said, "that it is unbefitting [a gentleman] to say anything but the truth before great lords." Then I told him that the horses I had seen in Constantine, the country of my master, seemed to me just as quick and beautiful. He ordered me to ride on one of them, but, when I failed to praise it emphatically, he let me try his own. I rode him for a little while and sensed an exceptional vigor in him, so it occurred to me that this would be a perfect, if dangerous, opportunity to escape. My heart was beating in my chest. "Oh!" I thought, "If I only could!" I made up my mind quickly, followed my instincts, spurred the horse vigorously, and escaped. I had already put some distance between my captors and myself when they realized my true intentions. {21} They shouted after me, and then twenty to thirty men on horseback started to chase me. They fired several shots at me, but the bullets hit the sand in bursts [instead]. Before three hours had passed, I was completely out of their sight.

I rode at night but grazed the horse in the woods during the day. My food during this time was fruit and a kind of lettuce which grows in that land. Thus, after two nights and a little over a day, I arrived back at the encampment, to my master's great pleasure. After a few disputes, my master and the abovementioned Bu Aziz of Tbessa finally made peace. In my opinion, this truce was very prudent, as my master had perceived some unrest coming from the bey of Tunis.[25] Eventually, a war between the two broke out, whereupon Bu Aziz and my master arranged a carefully considered alliance. {22} In the beginning, luck favored both sides evenly, but in the end, we had the opportunity to occupy the enemy's land with our army. We had been at war with each other for half a year when our provisions finally ran out, for the camels, which supplied us with oil and bread, had been robbed by Murath, a man who was no friend of my master's and lived on the border of the Tunisian land. This shortage compelled us to make a precipitous decision and attack the enemy, come hell or high water. But, as the enemy forces were stronger than ours—although during my time [there], our army, which was forty thousand men strong,[26] had never been

---

25. *bey of Tunis*: this was Al-Ḥusayn ibn ʿAlī (1669–1740), ruler of Tunis from 1705 until he was deposed in 1735.

26. *forty thousand men strong*: it has been speculated that this figure was most likely meant to be four thousand (Rheinheimer, *Der fremde Sohn*, 202n564). Alternatively, in the Abrahamic religions, the number forty is symbolic of perfection, an extended period of time, or a great number. For example, the Israelites wandered the desert for forty years, and Jesus fasted in the desert for forty days.

larger—it was necessary to have good sense and determine the enemy's numbers to some degree. My master and Bu Aziz decided to dispatch someone to investigate these things {23} as thoroughly as possible, and, while taking counsel with each other to decide who might be best suited for this task, Bu Aziz chose me. He said, "The Christian, the hazinedar, is good enough for this [mission]." He knew that I had sneaked away from his great-grandson before, [so he] wanted to do me a bad turn if he could. My master, who loved me and was reluctant to impose such an unfair assignment on me, asked me whether I felt inclined to do it. I answered, "The question here is not whether I feel like it, but rather what does *Afendi*[27]— this means 'my gracious lord'—command." In the end, I consented to his mandate with the additional guarantee that, should it go well, I would be granted permission to return to my fatherland with honor if I so desired.

At night, I approached the camp, which was only a short distance from us on foot, but before I got there, I encountered a few horsemen. I did not know what to do in this quandary, but it occurred to me to cast my saber and my pistols away from myself and pass myself off as a deserter who had something important to discuss with the king of Tunis—if I was given the grace to be granted an audience. When they deduced from my clothes that I must be one of the most distinguished officers, they rejoiced and acceded to my request. The Tunisian bey soon recognized me and asked me why I, the hazinedar and agha ed-deïra, who was held in such high esteem by my master, came to him. I kissed his hand and humbly asked for his protection, which, if denied, would leave my life at his mercy and at that of my former master. For I pretended that [my former master] wanted to kill me due to some missing supplies, whose disappearance from the camp had been blamed on my neglect, even though it was obvious that Murath was the one who had made off with the provisions. My life was dear to me, so should [the bey] {25} spare it, I promised to serve him faithfully if he deemed me worthy. The Tunisian bey was very happy about my arrival and interrogated me closely about whether there really was a shortage of provisions and ammunition in our stock, as he had heard from several deserters. I said "yes," but in truth, there was no shortage of cabbage or munitions. I was further asked whether I was ready to fight against my former master. I answered, "If I had a properly outfitted horse, I would find myself willing to do so, and all

---

27. *Afendi*: the correct spelling in Ottoman Turkish would be *efendi*. This is an honorary title which means "gracious lord." Since Olufs speaks of "my gracious lord," the correct form would be *efendim*.

the more earnestly so because I, a defector, could never expect pardon from him." It came to pass—and I cannot deny it—that, due to the fine manner in which this lord had outfitted me and taken me in, the impulse rose in me to remain with him, contrary to my initial intentions, especially since it was likely that the Tunisian army would keep the field and the Constantinians would be forced {26} to either launch a desperate attack as soon as possible or, on account of the aforementioned shortage, to withdraw hurriedly. [Moreover,] I sensed good faith in this Tunisian bey; I was allowed to move freely among the army and look at the artillery, while simultaneously being closely questioned about the condition of our army and its intentions.

To my annoyance, a few defectors who knew well that I had not fallen out of favor with my master arrived on the third day and deduced that I had been sent to investigate the intentions of the enemy. A renegade who had heard that these rumors had reached the Tunisian bey asked me about the state of my situation. I reacted angrily and demanded to know who had spoken of me in this manner. He answered, "Some of your defectors." I therefore realized that my time had run out and thus speculated about how I might escape. I pretended {27} that I wanted to wage an assault on the enemy. Indeed, this is their way: to invade each other, sometimes with one hundred horses, sometimes with two hundred or more. I was given one hundred men and charged forward with them, but when I came close enough to my people, I made a sign that I wanted to defect to them. They then received me with pleasure and, to my master's great amazement, escorted me into my former camp. Now I was able to furnish exact information on all affairs, [and I] suggested that we attack our enemy that same night and invade [his camp] from a place he could not possibly anticipate, that is, to attack him from behind. The Constantinian soldiers were probably as good as the Tunisians; however, and most importantly, we were spurred on by both our plight and the by hope for booty and abundant provisions. My master even offered to reward those who took certain things that could be seized from our enemy, {28} for example, one thousand thaler[28] for a particular item, and so on.

To make a long story short, it all came down to a deciding battle, which turned out so well for us that our people forced the enemy to retreat in the course of a few hours and captured the enemy camp. In this encounter, however, my master fell off his horse, and since I kept myself close to him most of the time, I offered him mine. I intended to hop back on it once he was firmly

---

28. *thaler*: a monetary unit widely used in Europe in the late fifteenth century.

in the saddle, but we came into such a scrimmage that I could not manage it, yet I succeeded in holding onto its tail in the hope of pushing my way through. However, since I was heavily built and leaden-footed, I had to let go and was left with no choice but to throw myself on the ground among the slain. One of my hands was sprawled out; the other was over my two knives, which the Turks carry on their chest. As I lay in this position for some time, I heard one man telling another, "Here is where I will find {29} some proper equipment. I simply must have this!" He dismounted and began to lift me up and turn me over, but, in that very moment, I grabbed him with one hand and plunged my knife into his chest with the other. He gave out a thunderous howl, and so did I, for [I felt] such a pressure in my chest that, had I not been able to scream, I think I would have died. The horse of the slain man then served me to flee from the battleground, whereupon I found my old master again.

These adventures were the most notable ones that occurred during the war. As regards all the other little incidents, to relate them all would be a long-winded affair. I had massacred many on command and many of my own volition, for I had been entrusted with everything in the last few years, and I had complete power over life and death. My master had aged and thought it preferable that I manage everything. {30} He would sometimes lie down to rest at noon, and [I would have to] carry out the execution of some delinquent or other before he rose again. Among those I killed on command, two master masons are still seared into my mind. Twice during my tenure, my master had the idea to immure a considerable sum of ducats[29] in a tower. Once the master mason had been paid for his efforts, I was commanded to break his neck while he walked down the stairs in front of me, which I had to do if I did not want to risk my own [neck]. For this, my master had two reasons: first, to keep the place where the money was concealed a secret, and second, on account of a superstitious belief held by the Turks, [to ensure] that the soul of the one who had been murdered would hover or watch over the treasure, so that nobody except the owner could lay their hands on it. Thus can Satan take possession of a man's heart once he has been seized by some {31} cardinal vice or other. Now I also want to relate some other curiosities.

It happened that, while I was away from the fatherland, I had the pleasure to see five Europeans who were sent forth by King Augustus of Poland[30] to

---

29. *ducats*: the ducat was a gold or silver trade coin used in Europe from the later medieval centuries until as late as the twentieth century.
30. *King Augustus of Poland*: King Augustus II (1670–1733), also known as "Augustus the Strong." He was king of Poland and elector of Saxony.

gather information about the African continent. The most distinguished one among them was Doctor Johann Hebenstreit.[31] There was also a gardener in that company, a native of the island of Als,[32] who, being a compatriot, was very agreeable to me. As far as I know, a sixth [companion] had died on the journey. My master was very polite to them and ordered me to take care that all their needs were satisfied. It was a joy to present the doctor with a few silver and gold coins, which, as far as I know, were Roman, although they had been found in my master's country. He also received various {32} hides of lions, tigers, and suchlike. I assisted the gardener in collecting different plants, roots, and flowers, the latter of which he kept in a book between gray paper sheets. The doctor had traveled a few miles to inspect an old, crumbling building, the likes of which can be found throughout the land, but whose sumptuousness can still be discerned. Next to this building, a few stones were found, on which Latin letters had been chiseled in former times. When my master made me enquire about the rare things the doctor had discovered there, he found that the doctor appeared as delighted to have found these inscriptions as he would have been had he found several hundred ducats. Upon this, my master laughed heartily and said, "Oh, Christians are such fools!" I know for a fact that the good doctor would have liked to pay me for my services, but I was in no need of money. However, I did ask for an intellectually stimulating book in German because, before I ever set sail, my {33} parents had made sure that I was taught how to read and write. My wish was granted, for as soon as Doctor Hebenstreit arrived in Saxony, he sent Spener's *Reise-Postill*[33] via Livorno and Algiers to Constantine. He had written his name along with wishes for my release on the first page. I still have that book in my possession, for I took it with me to Amrum as a

---

31. *Doctor Johann Hebenstreit*: Johann Ernst Hebenstreit (1703–1757) was a German physician and dean of the medical faculty of the University of Leipzig. Alongside Doctor Christian Gottlieb Ludwig (1709–1773), he led the expedition to North Africa sent forth by Augustus II. See Detlef Döring, "Die sächsische Afrikaexpedition von 1731 bis 1733. Ihre Planung, ihre Teilnehmer, ihre Ergebnisse," in *Eine Afrikareise im Auftrag des Stadtgründers: Das Tagebuch des Karlsruher Hofgärtners Christian Thrann 1731–1733*, ed. Stadtarchiv Karlsruhe, Peter Pretsch, and Volker Steck (Karlsruhe: Info Verlag, 2008), 49–50.

32. *a native from the island of Als*: Christian Thrann (1701–1778) was the horticulturist in charge of the court garden at Karlsruhe, a city located in southwest Germany. He was born on the Danish island of Als, which appears in the 1751 German edition as "Alsen." See Peter Pretsch, "Christian Thrann—Hofgärtner, Entdecker, Unternehmer," in *Eine Afrikareise im Auftrag des Stadtgründers: Das Tagebuch des Karlsruher Hofgärtners Christian Thrann 1731–1733*, ed. Peter Pretsch and Volker Steck (Karlsruhe: Info Verlag, 2008), 29–41.

33. *Spener's Reise-Postill*: Philipp Jacob Spener (1635–1705), a German Lutheran theologian, was the author of *Reise Postille, Aus zweyen Jahrgängen von 1678. und 1679. gehaltenen Predigten zusammen getragen* (1715) (Rheinheimer, *Der fremde Sohn*, 203n580).

token of remembrance. He also carried a book with him in which different friends and benefactors had written their names. He [had] presented it to me so that I would write my name and birthplace in it.

I had been living in Africa eight years when my master decided to assemble a caravan to Mecca, in Arabia, which is a place the Turks consider holy because their prophet, Muhammad, was born there. This caravan or {34} travel company consisted of around six thousand men, of which four thousand traveled at their own expense and two thousand at the expense of my master. The most difficult aspect of this journey was the frequent shortage of water, which [made it necessary to have water] carried on camels in large leather skins. On our way, we came to the place where Hagar and her son had been imperiled by the lack of water,[34] which is westward of Mecca. The well, which is displayed there and regarded as holy, is called *Zamzam*[35] in their language. Thirteen months passed before we completed this journey. Because of the devotion he demonstrated on this journey, my master was honored with the title "Hadji,"[36] which means "the Holy One." Sometime after that, a marriage between one of my master's relatives and the king of Morocco was arranged. I was chosen along with a few others to lead the princess there, but none were granted the honor {35} to see her face, just as with my master's wives, even though I had been in his service for many years. She was carried on a camel with a canopy that resembled a palanquin fixed to its back, and her whole face was covered by a veil. The king of Morocco, whom I was visiting in an official capacity, was at that time Sidim Mahomet, Mula Debbi.[37] The last two words of his title translate to "the Lord of the Gold."[38]

---

34. *the place where Hagar [. . .] lack of water*: Hagar and Ishmael were Abraham's wife and firstborn son, respectively. Acknowledged by all Abrahamic religions, their story is found in the book of Genesis and the Quran, although in the latter Hagar is not mentioned by name. Nevertheless, she is a revered woman in Islam due to the piety and courage she displayed after being banished to the desert. During the hajj, the annual Islamic pilgrimage to Mecca and one of the five pillars of Islam, believers visit the well of Zamzam, the spring that miraculously appeared in response to Hagar's desperate search for water for Ishmael, who is held to be the forefather of all Arabs. It is traditionally believed that this miracle led Abraham to build the Kaaba, the most sacred Muslim site in the world. See Netton, *Encyclopedia of Islamic Civilization and Religion*, 207–09.

35. *Zamzam*: it appears in the 1751 German edition as "Il me Sim." Zamzam is the spring that miraculously appeared to Hagar. See previous note.

36. *Hadji*: from the Arabic ḥājjī, or "pilgrim." It is a title generally used to refer to the men who have completed the pilgrimage to Mecca. Alternatively, it is also a way to address older men, even if they have never been to Mecca. It appears in the 1751 German edition as "Hatje."

37. *Sidim Mahomet, Mula Debbi*: probably Mohammed ben Abdallah, or Mohammed III of Morocco (1710–1790), sultan of Morocco from 1757 to 1790 (Rheinheimer, *Der fremde Sohn*, 203–04n591).

38. *the Lord of the Gold*: his name, as written by Olufs, means "my lord Muhammad, possessor of gold" in Moroccan Arabic: *Sīdi Muḥammad, mūla dahabi*.

In my opinion, some of the most curious things in the country where I was held captive were the following: Between Algiers and Constantine stands a stone of considerable size, which is green both on the outside and on the inside. It is said that those afflicted by fever are cured when a part of this stone is pulverized and consumed, and it is called in their language Hedjar Sidna se Isa,[39] the Stone of the Lord Christ, for {36} it is said that the Lord Christ rested in this place with his disciples. It is also said that some men, whom people call the "Seven Sleepers," are buried in a large country village called M'Gaous.[40] When something is stolen, the suspect is led over their graves, where he has to swear that if he is guilty, he will not be able to walk away without being injured in his head, arm, leg, or any other limb. Culprits then supposedly never fail to be wounded—or so the Turks say.

Still more wondrous are the people who, from time to time, reside in the countryside and can be regarded as the Turks' clerics. They are called marabouts.[41] I myself have witnessed their extraordinary feats, but whether they come to pass through the art of the devil, I do not know. I personally have seen how {37} they ignite fire merely with their breath, thereby lighting up a pipe for example. I was also present when the following happened: One of my master's wives had a swelling above her stomach, as if caused by dropsy, and a marabout was summoned and consulted. He sent for one of his maidservants, and after he had put a copper dish on hot coals and cast some incense on it, he took the maidservant's hand, formed a circle with cotton on her palm and poured some oil in the middle. He then ordered her to hold the circle over the smoke. Then the marabout began to chant with great intensity and it seemed to me that he was mixing many foreign words from all sorts of languages. Indeed, I could not understand anything he produced with his lofty voice. In between

---

39. *Hedjar Sidna se Isa*: from the Arabic *ḥajar sayyidnā ʿīsā*. Literally: "The stone of our Lord Jesus."

40. *"Seven Sleepers" [. . .] M'Gaous*: the Seven Sleepers were seven fabled Christian youths who retired to pray and fell asleep for centuries in a cave in Ephesus to avoid persecution from the Roman emperor Decius (201–251 CE). A similar story appears in the Quran (Al-Kahf 18:9–26), and Olufs seems to refer to a slightly modified version of the legend, in which the Sleepers inhabited the village of M'Gaous (or "Omagus" as it appears in the 1751 German edition). In this story, the Sleepers had been missing for some years before being discovered by a pious man, who upon finding them, decided to build a mosque around them. See Rosemary Guiley, *The Encyclopedia of Saints* (New York: Facts on File, 2001), 304; M. Louis Féraud, "Entre Setif et Biskara," *Revue Africaine: Journal des Travaux de la Société Historique Algerienne*, quatrième année, 22 (1860): 193–94.

41. *marabout*: a saintly or venerated Muslim leader, often believed to have "baraka," or a spiritual quality of blessedness from a divine source that may radiate to others. See Phillip C. Naylor, *Historical Dictionary of Algeria* (Lanham, MD: Scarecrow Press, 2006), 498, 502.

he asked {38} whether she saw something in her hand. She answered, "No." Thereupon, he began anew with the same intensity, until at last she shouted, "I see many people!" He asked, "What people?" She answered, "Distinguished people who want to hold Divan?"[42] He said, "Ask them what ails the woman." She replied, "They say she has been in an evil place where she was harmed." He [then demanded], "Ask what measures are to be taken." She answered, "They say such and such herbs should be collected and cooked. She should drink this infusion and bathe in it." It was done thus, and the woman recovered. But the maidservant fainted. [She] was carried away as if she were dead and did not regain consciousness for twenty-four hours. Sometime later I asked her if she had heard or seen anything. She answered that she remembered nothing, except that she had put her hand over the smoke the marabout had started in his presence, my master's, and mine. {39} These marabouts are capable of many other things. For example, they can thrust their arm into the body of a horse, so that it is colored with blood, and when they pull it out again, they speak a few words, give the horse something to eat and drink right after, and not a single scratch is visible. They also know how to recover stolen goods and many other things. Some of these people walk in beautiful green clothes, which they say is in honor of Christ, who they believe liked this color because of the green stone mentioned above. Others, however, walk around scantily clad. There is also an animal found in the country called a honey badger,[43] which mainly feeds on wild honey and is fairly similar to a pig. The Turks believe that this wondrous animal used to be a marabout or that the soul of a marabout has taken control of it. {40} The reason behind their belief is that when the animal is given a letter or a sheet of paper from a book, it takes the paper between its forefeet and holds it in front of its face. Then it begins to make diverse sounds, as if it could read, and if one attempts to take the paper away from it, it becomes angry and tears it to pieces.

    I must, however, return to my own story, in particular to my deliverance, which occurred shortly after the last war with Tunis. My master had agreed [to my release] and one of the servants of the bey of Algiers had interceded for me by mentioning my faithful services and the success of my various expeditions.

42. *Divan*: the state or imperial council of the Ottoman Empire.
43. *honey badger*: the species is found in many parts of North Africa.

He was the bey's hazinedar, as well as his sister's son. He went by the name of Ali Goje[44] and is said to have become Bey or king of Algiers after my departure. {41} My dismissal was granted in the nick of time, as my master had already turned ninety-five,[45] and every day I [found myself] dreading any event which might change my circumstances, especially as those who enjoy the most favor with the current regent are usually pestered the most by the following one on account of their money. And when their covetousness is insatiable, those from whom they seek to extort greater funds than their lands have to offer are often tormented and tortured to death. Likewise, the lust for money was also one of my master's major vices, although I cannot accuse him of miserliness.

In case [my master] died, I had made plans to flee to one of my wives' gracious brothers, to whom I had promised to return his sister if at all possible. I had also entrusted him with one thousand ducats for safekeeping, {42} but since I did not have to wait long [to leave], it did not grieve me to part with the money. The evening prior to my leaving Constantine, I had various conversations with my master. When tumult broke out in a tent near my master's, he asked me, "What should we do?" I told him it was the Moors, who were mourning one of their bailiffs who had died. "Yes," he said, "that must be it. But what about you? What do you mean to do? Lo! If you travel from here now and go away and die today or tomorrow, I will not take responsibility for your ruin. Be it on your head, for my advice has always been in your best interest. You will be all the more accountable because you, long before your fellow Christians, had the opportunity to become a Muslim." The following day, when I was ready to embark on my travels, I went to my master, kissed his hand, and said, "Afendi! I thank you for the bread and the wages I have {43} received from your hand these twelve years. I ask for your blessing and that you forgive whatever mistakes I may have made." He answered, "I thank you, Captain, for your services, and if I have wronged you, may you likewise forgive me." On hearing his last words, I wept and embraced his knees, but the old master, who also

---

44. *Ali Goje*: taking into account the year of Olufs's release (1735) and the year his captivity narrative was published (1747), the only dey of Algiers that would be consistent with this time period is Ibrahim Kutchuk, who ascended to the regency in 1745 and was the previous dey's nephew as well as his hazinedar. However, given that it appears as if he never went by the name Ali, the veracity of Olufs's claim is hard to ascertain. See H. D. Grammont, *Histoire d'Alger Sous la Domination Turque (1515–1830)* (Paris: E. Leroux, 1887), 302. Olufs uses "bey" instead of "dey."

45. *ninety-five*: this is most likely an exaggeration; he was probably in his eighties (Rheinheimer, *Der fremde Sohn*, 41).

had tears on his cheeks, propped me up, put his hand on my head, and spoke, "Go with God, beware of strong drink, of women, and of the Jews of Algiers, so that they do not take your money." Thereupon he issued me a safe conduct on parchment which I could show in Algiers.

When I arrived there, the bey[46] asked me how long I had been in Constantine. I answered, "Twelve years." He said, "Well, now you can serve me just as long." When I answered that I would consider it an honor to serve such a {44} noble master, he said, "You do not mean it," and he added some scolding words. Nevertheless, he gave me the equivalent of seven *reichsthaler*[47] in gold, as well as a passport, which would have otherwise cost me more than seventy reichsthaler. He added, "For the sake of your master and your loyal service, nothing will be charged." But turning to another lord who was with him, he spoke, "Is it not a shame? We pay for these Christians with our blood, and then we let them leave our country with our wealth." For he knew that my master had allowed me to keep what I had earned, although I could have amassed a much greater fortune, had [the circumstances] not compelled me to gather everything together in such a hurry and sell many things for half their value. It was there that they told me the following story: Four or five slaves of Algiers had secretly planned on building a boat together to escape to Christian lands. {45} One of them had made the others promise that, on the evening when they were set to escape, they would arrive with their boat at a certain garden which belonged to his master and be ready to seize a person whom he would lead to a [nearby] lantern. In the meantime, a silver goblet belonging to [said] master had gone missing, and the slave, understandably, had been held responsible. He, however, denied any knowledge of the matter and instead claimed that he had learned an art in Europe that allowed him to track, or discover, lost items and that he would demonstrate it that evening. To this end, he took his master to a lantern in the garden and vowed that the stolen item would be found there. When they finally came to the spot where the others were, he said, "It should be here." Then the men seized the Turk and took him with them to Christian lands. {46}

My journey [home] was via Marseilles, Lyon, Paris, and Hamburg. In Paris, I saw my former horse, the one I had ridden when I escaped from

---

46. *bey*: the bey or, more commonly, dey of Algiers at the time was known as Ibrahim. He ruled from 1732 to 1745. See Grammont, *Histoire d'Alger Sous la Domination Turque*, 290–302.

47. *reichsthaler*: a silver coin of the Holy Roman Empire used from the sixteenth to the nineteenth century.

Bu Aziz. I had sold it to the French consul in Algiers and it had eventually made its way to the king's stable. When I arrived in Hamburg, my father, Oluf Jensen, came to meet me. He was still alive and had [actually] sent eight hundred marks for my ransom two years earlier. However, when he came to fetch me following a letter from a trader in Hamburg, he found out, to his great sorrow, that they had confused not the names, but rather the persons themselves, because a soldier from Bremen had been released for this sum instead. My father's money was gone, but his son [had remained] in Turkey[48] nonetheless. Shortly after, however, when he received my letters, [in which I spoke] of my prosperity and the hope of my certain redemption, he was somewhat comforted. His hopes were fulfilled when I arrived the following spring and {47} he came to Hamburg again. However, recognizing me proved as difficult for him as recognizing the soldier from Bremen [years] earlier, for he had not seen me since I was a fourteen-year-old boy, but now I was all grown, corpulent, and dressed in elegant clothing.

Thus, I arrived in my fatherland again, healthy and in good spirits, almost at the same time as thirteen years[49] before, when I had been captured. I had brought rare clothes, furnishings, and ready money with me, all of which I had taken from Turkey with my master's knowledge. In Tønder,[50] I had the honor to be introduced to the late King Christian VI,[51] who most graciously listened to some of the things that had befallen me. While I cannot compare myself to Joseph[52] as regards morality, I will dare to do so as regards good fortune. My father had experienced something akin to Jacob's fate with respect to his grief and his {48} joy over [his son's return]. Before [our reunion], it was difficult for him to believe that I was doing so well or that he would ever see me again. The God of Abraham, Isaac, and Jacob, who has protected me to this day despite many dangers, grant me His grace, so that I may remain a God-fearing man and, like Joseph, be mindful of all the evil that displeases Him. May I spend the rest of my days away from the turmoil and agitation of this vain world, in tranquility, faith, and confidence in Him.

48. *Turkey*: Olufs means the Ottoman Empire.
49. *thirteen years*: in actual fact it was twelve years (Rheinheimer, *Der fremde Sohn*, 205n623).
50. *Tønder*: a part of the Duchy of Schleswig in Olufs's time. Nowadays, it is Danish territory. It appears in the 1751 German edition as "Tundern."
51. *King Christian VI*: Christian VI (1699–1746) was king of Denmark–Norway from 1730 to 1746.
52. *Joseph*: a biblical patriarch introduced in the book of Genesis who was sold as a slave by his brothers. After correctly interpreting the pharaoh's dreams, Joseph was promoted to vizier and was eventually reunited with his father, Jacob (Gen. 37–46).

WONDERBAARLYKE
En Merkwaardige Gevallen
Van een Twaalf Jarige
SLAVERNY,
Van een
Vrouspersoon. Genaemt
MARIA TER MEETELEN,
Woonagtig
Tot
MEDENBLIK.

Tot HOORN

Gedrukt, by de Wed: JACOB DUYN, Boek-drukster en Verkoopster op het Oude Noort, by de Nieuwe-steeg. 1748.

Figure 10.1 Title page of Maria ter Meetelen's narrative
Source: Maria ter Meetelen, *Wonderbaarlyke en merkwaardige gevallen van een twaalf jarige slaverny, van een vrouspersoon. Genaemt Maria ter Meetelen, woonagtig tot Medenblik* (Hoorn, 1748); KW 30 B 8, Koninklijke Bibliotheek, NL.

CHAPTER X

MARIA TER MEETELEN, *MIRACULOUS AND REMARKABLE EVENTS OF TWELVE YEARS OF SLAVERY*

1748 Dutch print edition; selection

Captivity in Morocco 1731–1743

At the age of twenty-one, the Dutchwoman Maria ter Meetelen embarked on a journey in men's clothes from the Netherlands through France and Spain, where she enlisted in a regiment of dragoons. Soon, however, her disguise was discovered and she had to leave the unit. Thus commences one of the first known authentic female Barbary captivity narratives. One wonders why Maria ter Meetelen passes over this thrilling episode of cross-dressing and female agency in only a handful of sentences. However, the rest of her otherwise highly detailed narrative, which is devoted to her twelve-year captivity in Morocco from 1731 to1743, makes up for what she omitted in the opening section.

During a four-year stay in Madrid, Maria ter Meetelen married the Dutch captain Claes van der Meer, with whom she left Cádiz for the Netherlands in 1731. Off the coast of Portugal, their ship fell into the hands of Moroccan corsairs. The ship's crew and passengers were abducted to Salé and later moved to Meknès, where they became the property of the sultan. Six weeks after arriving in Morocco, Maria's husband Claes died, leaving her in a precarious situation. To avoid the sultan's harem, the best solution for Maria was to find a new Christian husband. After complex negotiations, Pieter Jansz Iede, a Dutch helmsman who had been a slave in Morocco for twelve years already, agreed to convert to Catholicism in order to be able to marry her. By feigning pregnancy, Maria won some of the sultan's wives over to her side. The sultan ultimately gave his permission for Ter Meetelen to marry Iede. Given that the sultan himself had taken a strong interest in Maria, his approval of the marriage was quite exceptional. Over time, her diplomatic and social dexterity allowed Maria to establish friendly relations with successive rulers and their families, none more so than Moulay Mohammed ben Arbiya, who apparently treated her better than many of his wives.

Maria ter Meetelen's fate as a slave is a perfect example of one of the peculiar forms of slavery found in North Africa in the early modern period. It is tempting to call captives like Maria ter Meetelen "entrepreneurial slaves," since they had to resort to entrepreneurial skills and ideas to make a living in captivity. Like the seventeenth-century British slave William Okeley, who ran a successful import–export business in Algiers,[1] Maria ter Meetelen had to use her business acumen to survive economically. She opened and ran a number of successive taverns to support herself and her family—often without the help of her husband, who was sent away to do heavy slave labor. Eventually, her business allowed her to employ other slaves in selling alcohol. This was possible because the Muslim ban on alcohol did not apply to Christian slaves. Despite her success in the tavern business, her economic situation was extremely precarious, since Morocco was plagued by changes of power. The most extreme example of this was on 1 May 1736, when four kings were proclaimed and removed from power before midday. Nevertheless, Ter Meetelen displayed a remarkable ability to win the favor of successive sultans as well as their mothers and wives. This is particularly surprising since she had to navigate the pitfalls of being associated with the old regime, which could easily have become a death sentence.

In 1743, after a futile, decade-long initiative to free Dutch slaves, the majority of the Dutch captives were finally ransomed. Among them was Maria ter Meetelen with her husband and two children. She published her *Wonderbaarlyke en merkwaardige gevallen van een twaalf jarige slaverny* in 1748. In 1750, by the time Ter Meetelen was forty-six years old, both her remaining two children and her second husband had died. The last trace of Maria

---

1. For more on William Okeley, see G. A. Starr, "Escape from Barbary: A Seventeenth-Century Genre," *Huntington Library Quarterly* 29, no. 1 (1965): 35–52. See also note 40 in the introduction to this anthology.

ter Meetelen is a document that shows her intentions to emigrate to South Africa. Unfortunately, we have no further records about the remainder of her life.

Despite some possibly embellished elements in the narrative, the core of Maria ter Meetelen's account is definitely authentic. In addition to her detailed and succinct narrative that appeared in print in 1748, a substantial number of other documents have survived that corroborate the authenticity of her captivity in Morocco. These include a series of letters that Maria wrote between 1731 and 1743, which were passed on from Morocco to the Dutch consuls in Spain and are now in the National Archive in The Hague.

Notes on the Present Translation of Maria ter Meetelen's *Miraculous and Remarkable Events of Twelve Years of Slavery*

This translation is based on the following edition: Maria ter Meetelen, *Wonderbaarlyke en merkwaardige gevallen van een twaalf jarige slaverny, van een vrouspersoon. Genaemt Maria ter Meetelen, woonagtig tot Medenblik* (Hoorn: Jacob Duyn, 1748).

Omissions have been indicated with an ellipsis [. . .]. In case of longer omissions, short summaries in square brackets have been provided to bridge the gaps between different sections. The numbers in brackets {} in the text always indicate the beginning of a page and refer to the original page numbers of the 1748 edition. Place names have been updated to their modern versions throughout the text and have been annotated with a footnote. Special thanks go to Lisa Kattenberg for her assistance with clarifying cases of doubt with regard to the antiquated Dutch.

Maria ter Meetelen, *Miraculous and Remarkable Events of Twelve Years of Slavery, of a Woman Named Maria ter Meetelen, Resident of Medemblik*
(Hoorn: Jacob Duyn, 1748)

Translated by Almiria Wilhelm

{1} *The faithful record of my amazing travel description, my remarkable and dismal twelve-year slavery, and my happy redemption and joyful return to my beloved fatherland, all described truthfully and from my own experience.*

The course of life is curious, and I will share some of mine with the reader. Since I had been traveling in foreign places from the age of thirteen upward,[2] when I was twenty-one years old, I finally made a decision to undertake a journey through France in men's clothing. Thus I reached Spain, where I was press-ganged into the service of a regiment of Frisian dragoons, in a town named Vitoria.[3] However, I did not remain with them long, as it was discovered that I was not who I had pretended to be.

I dressed myself in women's clothes again and departed for Madrid with the standard-bearer's wife. At last, having been there for some time, I was married on 22 October 1728 to a Dutch captain from Alkmaar named Claas van der Meer. I was then approximately twenty-four years old. As my husband was involved in a lawsuit about his ship at the time, which had been confiscated, {2} we had to wait for our departure. This finally happened on 15 January 1731. On the 27th, we arrived in Carmona, which is less than a day's journey from Seville. We then rented a house again, in Triana across from Seville, and remained there until 27 June, when we applied for a passport to go to Holland. We received this from the ambassador of the States-General[4] and the prime minister of His Royal Majesty. As we saw that there was no end to the matter, we then went to Sanlúcar, two miles from Seville.[5]

---

2. *traveling [. . .] from the age of thirteen upward*: there is evidence that Ter Meetelen worked as a maid in the Dutch provinces of Zeeland and Brabant during some of this time. See Laura van den Broek and Maaike Jacobs, eds., *Christenslaven: De slavernij-ervaringen van Cornelis Stout in Algiers (1678–1680) en Maria ter Meetelen in Marokko (1731–1743)* (Zutphen: Walburg Pers, 2006), 52.

3. *Vitoria*: Vitoria-Gasteiz, Spain. "Sicktoria" in the 1748 Dutch edition.

4. *States-General*: the governing assembly of the Dutch Republic (1588–1795). "Ed: Hoog Mog:" in the 1748 Dutch edition.

5. *Sanlúcar, two miles from Seville*: while it seems indisputable that Ter Meetelen means the port city of Sanlúcar de Barrameda, the distance is closer to fifty miles as the crow flies. "Sint Lucar" in the 1748 Dutch edition.

There, on 7 July 1731, we boarded a Dutch *buys*[6] and set out to sea in it on the 8th. We came in sight of Cape Vincent, where we saw a vessel which we believed to be a Turk.[7] [. . .]

[*On 21 July 1731, they again spied a vessel, purportedly from Algiers. This turned out to be a ruse as it was actually a privateer from Salé, Morocco.*][8]

{4} [. . .] In the meantime, the captain decided to fight off [the privateer] and, to this end, he had the cannons and snaphance muskets[9] readied and great preparations were made to fight. The people seemed little inclined to this. They lowered the sloop and put three muskets in it and some gunpowder in order to flee. So the ship was not equipped against a Turk with twenty pieces [of cannon] and 150 men. We were but eleven people, including ourselves: six men and one boy, and four passengers. [. . .]

[*The ship was looted, but Maria ter Meetelen claims that this did not distress her. The captain gave her preferential treatment and even sent someone to play music with her every evening until they arrived in Salé at the end of July. In August, the captives were transported to Meknès,*[10] *where they were presented to Moulay Abdallah.*][11]

{14} [. . .] Then we came before the king, who examined us and gave my husband and me to the Spaniard and [said] that they should look after us. Therefore, my husband and I were not required to serve the king, but my captain and the passengers had to start work immediately. In the meantime, I was summoned before the *basha*,[12] where I had to disclose what was on the ship. To the captain's relief, I kept quiet about some things. After giving this account, I asked the basha to free the skipper, which I was granted, but this

---

6. *buys*: a type of boat with a small superstructure. These boats could be used both as fishing boats and as merchant ships. See Elisabeth Paling Funk and Martha Dickinson Shattuck, *A Beautiful and Fruitful Place: Selected Rensselaerwijck Papers* (Albany, NY: Excelsior Editions/State University of New York Press, 2011), 2: 104.

7. *a vessel which we believed to be a Turk*: like many early modern authors, Ter Meetelen uses the term "Turk" to refer to a broader group of Muslims from North African countries bordering on the Mediterranean Sea. In this case, she uses the term to refer to a ship from these regions.

8. *privateer from Salé*: a privately owned, armed vessel, in this case from Salé, licensed to attack enemy ships.

9. *snaphance muskets*: guns which were fired using an early flintlock mechanism. "Snaphanen" in the 1748 Dutch edition.

10. *Meknès*: the capital of the Kingdom of Morocco, situated approximately one hundred miles inland from the Atlantic port of Salé as the crow flies.

11. *Moulay Abdallah*: the sultan of Morocco at the time when Ter Meetelen was captured. Moulay Abdallah ruled Morocco several times starting in 1729 (historians disagree on the exact number of times he ruled, but it was certainly at least four times). Ter Meetelen calls him a king and spells his name Muly Abdela in the 1748 Dutch edition.

12. *basha*: a high-ranking official in North Africa and the Ottoman world. In Morocco, the term was also used to refer to the governor of a city.

lasted only for a short period of fourteen days, so the basha did not entirely keep his word.

[*On 8 September 1731, Maria ter Meetelen's husband died and she decided to choose a new husband as quickly as possible in order to avoid either landing in Moulay Abdallah's harem or having to marry a man chosen for her by the sultan.*]

{17} [. . .] I was very afraid of the foreigners[13] for the reason that they had money and would demand to have me through the power of their wealth. Indeed, there were immediately three of them who demanded me of the king. However, I quickly decided to make a choice for myself with the help of the local fathers,[14] whom I would ask for a helping hand in everything.

However, a big difficulty presented itself, as there was not one Roman Catholic among the Dutch. This made it hard to choose one of this nationality, unless one of them was prepared to become Catholic, in which case the fathers would make an even greater effort. I thought, "Now is not the time to wait, but to make a rapid decision before the king gives me to a foreigner." So, in the afternoon on 9 September, I resolved to choose the head of the Dutch community,[15] who seemed to me to be the best of all the Dutchmen. I afterward discovered this to be true. As chance would have it, the fathers paid me a visit that afternoon to comfort me for the loss of my husband and brought me some items which the merchants in Salé {18} had kept for me and had sent to the fathers. This was opportune and saved me, allowing me to go into mourning. I seized the opportunity to beg the fathers to allow me to come to their monastery the following day, since I wished to be guided by their good advice and assistance. This they respectfully granted me and promised to lend me a helping hand wherever they could, which comforted me greatly.

On the morning of the 10th of the same month, I went to the monastery and told the Father Superior my plan, of which he approved. However, the person [I had chosen], though a good man and respected by all the Christians and especially by [the fathers], was of a different religion.[16] This was

---

13. *foreigners*: Ter Meetelen means other Europeans and Jews in Morocco, possibly renegades who had converted to Islam and had managed to accumulate considerable wealth, which gave them leverage with Moulay Abdallah.

14. *local fathers*: members of a Franciscan Catholic order with a presence in Meknès since 1673. See Caroline Stone and Karen Johnson, trans., *The Curious and Amazing Adventures of Maria ter Meetelen: Twelve Years a Slave (1731–43)* (Kilkerran, Scotland: Hardinge Simpole, 2010), 26.

15. *head of the Dutch community*: this was Pieter Jansz Iede, a native of Medemblik, North Holland. He had been taken at sea in 1719 and had been in Morocco for twelve years already by the time Ter Meetelen was captured. He acted as a foreman and spokesperson for the Dutch community of slaves in Meknès (Van den Broek and Jacobs, *Christenslaven*, 55).

16. *a different religion*: Pieter Jansz Iede was Protestant.

an insurmountable obstacle, unless he converted; in this case, [the fathers] would assist me in any way they could. Now, there was another father there who stood up and said, "Oh, Pieter the Fleming[17]—he is a good man and will convert." I thought, "This suits me. Now things will go well." The fathers promised me that they would summon the Dutch leader[18] and see whether they could convince him to become Catholic.

Thereupon, I went home. At the time, I had not yet spoken to the Dutch leader, wherefore I did not know whether he would take this well or badly. So, the same afternoon, he came to me and discussed the matter. He had already been to the fathers and then came to me. He was somewhat against the matter, but was, at the same time, inclined to accept it, but not to convert.[19]{19} By weighing the pros and cons over and over for a long time, he finally resolved to convert and thus to be married to me, since there was no other way to do it. I was very glad about this. We concluded the promises of marriage and, the following day, we went to the fathers. They were as delighted as if they had received a gift of a hundred thousand *rijksdaalders*.[20] They immediately did their utmost in this matter with the basha and the important men close to the king, to try to get the king to agree to the marriage and to conclude it. Christians may only marry there if the king gives them to one another, for we are all his slaves.

Greatly reassured, I returned to my house with the hope that the fathers would arrange this matter, as they were regarded favorably by the king and his grandees. In the meantime, while I was in the house of the woman mentioned previously,[21] I made this matter known. They took it very badly. The man of the house was called Jan Catallana.[22] He went to the king's court daily in order to give out and take back the soldiers' guns every day and to guard the king's storehouses with a few other Christians.

---

17. *Fleming*: a native of Flanders.

18. *Dutch leader*: "hoofmeester" in the 1748 Dutch edition. See notes 15 and 22.

19. *somewhat against the matter [. . .] not to convert*: it was not only a question of religion for Pieter Jansz Iede. By marrying Ter Meetelen, he jeopardized his ransom negotiations, which were underway at the time and which did indeed stall after the marriage (Van den Broek and Jacobs, *Christenslaven*, 55–56).

20. *rijksdaalder*: an early modern coin first issued by the Dutch Republic in the sixteenth century.

21. *the woman mentioned previously*: a Spanish woman and the wife of the Spaniard (Jan Catallana) first mentioned on p. 14 of the 1748 Dutch edition, in whose house Ter Meetelen lived at the time.

22. *Jan Catallana*: the head of all the Christian slaves in Meknès (Van den Broek and Jacobs, *Christenslaven*, 262). In addition to having a spokesperson like Catallana for all the Christian slaves, early modern Muslim cities followed a system whereby the slaves of each nation also had a leader or headman who was responsible for any official exchanges with local institutions/powers (Stone and Johnson, *The Curious and Amazing Adventures of Maria ter Meetelen*, 28). For the Dutch community this was Pieter Jansz Iede.

That evening, he came home and brought me the news that there were three Christians who would demand me of the king and that they had a great deal of money. He thought he was doing me a great service with this, but I answered him immediately that I would rather have a Dutchman in nothing but his shirt than a Spaniard or a Frenchman {20} with a king's ransom. He became extraordinarily angry but did not know exactly how matters stood with me. However, as soon as he was informed of this by his wife and his wife's mother, I was censured in a manner that was distressing to hear; they even spat in my face with rage. I remained silent and let them carry on until they were tired. Then, they tried to change my mind with kind words, offering me the wife's brother. He was a youth of but fourteen years and unbelievably ugly from being overweight. However, I remained steadfast in my intention and [their efforts] were in vain. When they saw that I held to my own nation, they thought of another trick. There was a Jew among the Dutchmen who lived with a basha and had permission to run an inn. He was very rich, and they wanted to marry me to him. They threatened me with the basha, [saying that] if he made a present of but a silken sash and some money, he would then get me. He himself brought this Jew to me, who told me the above, namely that he had money enough, and that if money was an issue, he had friends who would provide him with an *allemoet*, which is as much as a *tak*,[23] and more. I said I preferred to die rather than marry anyone other than the one I had already chosen. They threatened me in all sorts of ways, but I paid no attention to this and remained steadfast. However, every day I had to endure plenty of slander and insults. In the meantime, the Dutch leader had to endure many reproaches and insults and mockery. We {21} could not meet every day, as we wished to, to recount our experiences. We had to bottle things up.

In the meantime, the fathers had advanced the matter so much that it had been brought before the king. On 17 September, he had me summoned early in the morning. Therefore, the woman of the house took off my clothes, right down to my underclothes, and gave me old rags of hers to put on and a tattered nappy for my head. The rags hung around my ears and my hair stuck out at all angles. She did this so that I would look unattractive before the king, for I was young and beautiful, according to the people of that country. I took my zither and my little dog and went to the king's residence.

---

23. *an allemoet [. . .] tak*: "allemoet" and "tak" are archaic Dutch measures for grain (Van den Broek and Jacobs, *Christenslaven*, 263n54).

I had Jan Cornelisz Decker from Zwaag[24] to take me to the king's court. As soon as I got there, I encountered Jan Catallana, who first told me that the king had spoken to him and had said that if I married any Christian other than the Jew, who was his Christian,[25] the king would have me put to death. I answered that the king could do as he pleased and that I wanted no other Christian than the head of the Dutch community. "Well," he said, "do you prefer to die rather than fulfil the king's wishes?" I said, "Yes."

Thereupon, I was fetched by a eunuch and brought before the king. I appeared before the king in a chamber in which he lay with fifty women, each more beautiful than the next, {22} wearing make-up and exquisitely dressed, like goddesses. Each one had an instrument [and was] playing it and singing, thereby creating exquisite music the likes of which I had never heard before. Four of the king's main wives sat opposite the king. They glittered with gold, silver, and fine pearls, which hung around their necks by the pound, and they had precious stones and crowns made of gold, pearls, and precious stones on their heads. Their fingers were covered with gold rings, their arms with gold and silver bracelets, and their legs with gold anklets, each of which weighed a good few pounds. Jewelry hung from their necks to below their bellies. I did not know how they could hold their heads up under all that gold and those pearls and precious stones. Gold rings were braided into their hair and interspersed with gold ducats.

The king lay with his head in the lap of one woman and his feet in the lap of another; one behind him and another before him caressed him. They were also exquisitely dressed, but not to the same extent as the other four. So I presented myself before him in this luxury like a beggar and a crook. The king immediately had the music stopped and had me come closer and sit down. He asked me to play the zither. I could not understand a word the king said, only the gestures he made. I played to the king for a good hour, which pleased him. He spoke to me but I was unable to understand him. {23} However, afterward I found out what he had said. He wanted to know what nationality I was: French or Spanish or Dutch or English, and [he said] that I had to turn Turk,[26] whereupon I would become his wife. I was unable to answer him, as I did not understand what he said. After I had sat with him

24. *Jan Cornelisz Decker from Zwaag*: a native of Zwaag in North Holland, Decker was captured at the age of fourteen and was only freed twenty-eight years later in 1743, along with Ter Meetelen. He also wrote a captivity narrative upon his return home (Van den Broek and Jacobs, *Christenslaven*, 88).

25. *his Christian*: Van den Broek and Jacobs, *Christenslaven*, state that Ter Meetelen means "slave" here (264). It is also possible that Moulay Abdallah did not differentiate between Christians and Jews.

26. *to turn Turk*: to convert to Islam.

for a long hour, a woman came. After she had spoken to the king for a while, she took me away from the king. He had ordered her to make me turn Turk, and once I turned Turk, to dress me exquisitely and bring me to the king like this. This woman had no other role than to dress up young virgins for the king, for he had to have a young virgin every Friday. Furthermore, he summoned all the rest of the women whom he had already enjoyed. He did not approach those who were pregnant, as it is a sin for him to have relations with pregnant women.

This woman took me by the hand and led me along several dark passages to a different part of the palace. Here, I found four more women or young virgins, whom I had to join. One of them was a renegade's[27] daughter who was able to speak a little broken Spanish. She told me that the king had turned me over to her to be converted. I would then be attired as exquisitely as the other four women who sat with the king. I would be dressed and then become the king's bride. Otherwise, the king would have me burned and my {24} flesh would be ripped from my body and I would be put to death with all manner of tortures. I could not understand everything, but they made gestures. However, I said and gestured to them as best I could that I would rather die than turn Turk. Once they understood this, they spat at me and pushed me and scolded me. Then they tried again with pleading and kindness. They dressed me in their beautiful clothes and put a crown on my head and indicated that I would be attired far more beautifully still by the king. They all stood before me with fingers spread and said "Schet,"[28] which means "believe in Mahomet."[29] But when I declined, they tore the things off me again and spat and scolded me again. I was in a difficult situation, but I sought comfort in God and placed myself under his divine protection, although I did not manage to utter a prayer to God. I was hopeful that my God would indeed assist me. In the meantime, food from the king was brought to them, which caused them all to leave me and go to sit in a large hall to eat. They wanted me to come along with them, but I refused to go with them, and so I remained alone in this place. This, then, gave me the opportunity to deliver my prayer to God. I then fell to my knees with my face turned toward heaven. With tears running down my face, [I] begged

---

27. *renegade*: a Christian who has converted to Islam.
28. *Schet*: the *Shahāda*, the Islamic profession of faith, which reads, "There is no God but Allah, and Muhammad is his prophet."
29. *Mahomet*: Mahomet is a common early modern spelling for the Prophet Muhammad (as well as for other instances of the name "Muhammad"). "Magomet" in the 1748 Dutch edition.

God earnestly to fortify me and to uphold me with his Holy Spirit, so that I would be able to suffer the cruelest of deaths rather than to abjure my faith. I {25} did not make my prayer a long one, but kept it short. Under [the influence] of the prayer, I felt relieved, for the fear of death left me. Then I became bold and far preferred to die rather than to forsake my belief, deeming all riches to be as smoke that vanishes. A disgust of them came over me and I experienced a great longing to give myself up as a martyr and to die for my faith in the Lord Jesus Christ. I rejoiced so much in my soul that I cannot describe it; at any rate, the joy was a thousand times greater than the anguish I had felt before.

After the women had eaten, they again tried to get me to become a Moor,[30] but by then I was a lot more self-assured and pushed them away. I indicated that they might as well slit my throat—that I would rather die than turn Turk. They were astounded that I repulsed them so boldly and they scolded me thoroughly and spat at me. Then, I became very faint, for I had not eaten yet. Their stench and the fact that they were crowding me made me want to throw up, but I could not. It was already after midday. They then brought me some milk and bread, but I refused to take it. I tried to make them believe that I was pregnant, but could not explain this to them. I noticed that they became compassionate and from then on, they did not torment me any longer.

I then sought an opportunity to come before the king, who was still sleeping. I went through {26} the long, dark passages again with these women, to the place where the king's hall was. I continued to feign illness. One of the king's eunuchs was there—these are blacks who guard the king's wives in the royal palace. This eunuch spoke a little Spanish. He asked me what ailed me. I replied that I was pregnant and that I wanted to return to my brothers[31] as I was unwell. He then spoke to the women who were with me before answering me. He then said that the king had put me in the hands of the women in order to be converted and that I was not to be brought before him [until I had converted]. I kept on feigning illness, for I noticed that the women were overcome with compassion, and even more so when they heard that I was pregnant, although this was not true.

---

30. *to become a Moor*: to convert to Islam.

31. *brothers*: Ter Meetelen is referring to her fellow Christians; she did not have real brothers in Morocco.

They stopped tormenting me and came to sit by me and comforted me by pointing to heaven as if to say that God would take care of things.

I had not been sitting long before the king came out of his hall and the women took hold of me, one by one arm and the other by the other, and the third took my little dog, and the fourth my zither, and brought me to the king. I was very glad then to make an end of things—[whether I was] to die or go free—but God, who directs everything, allowed me to escape. So, I prostrated myself boldly before the king, expecting only that he would deal me a mortal blow. He pushed me away and I stood up and ran after him and kneeled before {27} his feet a second time and begged to return to my brothers. He pushed me away again. Then, I stood up for the third time and ran after him as far as the door where the king was to exit. I threw myself down in the same manner yet again and said, "Kill me now! I prefer that to turning Turk." Seeing my self-assurance and that I was as unafraid as a lion and blocking his exit from the palace, the king gave me a terrible look, stood still, and finally spoke to the women who were meant to escort him out. [He spoke] particularly with the four who had brought me to him. They then told him that I was pregnant, that I had not eaten the whole day, that I was very ill, and that, from time to time, I was as one dead. They begged the king to let me go. I could not understand this, but after I had learned the language and visited the palace regularly, they told the king's sister this in my presence. I did observe clearly that they were on my side. After hearing what the women had to say, the king turned to me, saying that four men would come for me, who would take me to my brothers. He said this in Spanish so that I could understand him well. I stood up instantly and let the king pass.

The women immediately began rejoicing and displaying great joy. [They] indicated that I should come to visit them. I played along, agreeing to this, thinking to myself that once I was out of here, I would not return so easily. I was very glad that I had {28} escaped so far, but the Christians were in deadly fear and distress, particularly the Christians I lived with, not knowing whether I had already turned Turk. [They] feared that the wife would have to go to the palace daily in order to teach me the language, for she was born in this country and spoke the language as well as the Turks. So there was not a little grief among the Christians and the fathers when they saw the king coming and not me. It took another good half hour after the king's departure before anyone came for me. Then, a eunuch came to fetch me and conducted me to the Christians. [. . .]

[*Maria ter Meetelen was successful in her plan to marry Pieter Jansz Iede. However, her marriage faced difficulties, since the Christians she lodged with tried to sow discord by spreading rumors about Ter Meetelen and her husband.*]

{33} [. . .] My husband got a tavern[32] in a stable among the animals. It looked so dilapidated that the worst horse stables were like palaces in comparison. Hence, my husband did not want to take me there. I pressed my husband so much to see the tavern that he finally decided to take me there. We arrived at this dilapidated tavern and I immediately resolved to stay there. My husband was strongly against this, but it could not be helped. I preferred to stay in that rubbish dump, where I could eat my dry bread, or whatever God saw fit to provide us with, in peace, rather than to stay in the Spanish house with plenty of food and disharmony. I remained firm in this matter and my husband had to fetch all my things from the Spanish house on foot. [. . .]

{34} [. . .] We stayed in that stable until the end of April in the year 1732, when the king's mother[33] returned from her pilgrimage to Mecca, where, according to what she said, Mahomet lies buried.[34] Among others, a French merchant had arrived from Salé as ambassador, who offered to free the French slaves. So, I was chosen to bring the gift and the application letter to the queen with a suitable compliment. I was given an interpreter, who came along and whom I made use of. I had also had a petition written in which I congratulated the queen and begged her for a house. As soon as I had completed my task for the ambassador, I delivered my letter, and the queen granted me the house immediately. She sent people with me who went to the rulers of the city with orders from her to give me the house. [. . .]

[*Moulay Abdallah was deposed in 1734. He was succeeded by Moulay Ali al Aredj, under whose rule Ter Meetelen and her family suffered a great deal. Her tavern was closed and she resorted to selling goods secretly. On 1 May 1736, the political turmoil was so great that four kings were proclaimed and deposed before midday. Moulay Abdallah regained power on 8 May 1736. He sent Ter Meetelen's husband and almost all the other Christian slaves to work on his summer palace. As a result, Ter Meetelen was left alone with her child and fled to the monastery for protection.*]

---

32. *got a tavern*: many slaves in North Africa made a living by selling alcohol, an activity that Islam forbids for Muslims but a "profession" that was open to early modern Christian slaves.

33. *king's mother*: Lalla Khenata, the wife of Moulay Ismail (ruled 1672–1727) and mother of Moulay Abdallah.

34. *where [. . .] Mahomet lies buried*: in fact, the Prophet Muhammad is buried in Medina, not Mecca. See Van den Broek and Jacobs, *Christenslaven*, 271n80.

{64} [. . .] I had been in the monastery for about six days when the basha returned to the city from outside of town. I took my child[35] in my arms and went to the palace immediately without saying anything to anyone, because I knew very well that I would have been stopped. I presented myself before the basha and requested permission to open my tavern in order to be able to earn a living for myself, my husband, and my child. [I also asked] for my rations from the king, which the basha granted me. However, another impediment arose, for the servant of our guard was jealous. He opposed this, with the result that I had to give up either the tavern or the rations. The rations were {65} too much to die on and too little to live off, and I could not share any of them with my husband,[36] therefore, I chose the tavern. I had nothing to begin with, so I had to go and get surety from various Christians—borrowing from one and paying another. In the meantime, my God blessed me so wonderfully that I was able not only to make a living for my husband and children but also to send food and drink to six or eight men daily, which helped the people along. The business grew so large that I had to hire two manservants and a maid, who cost me quite a bit. However, I made money from 24 July to 21 September, when my house collapsed and the king was deposed. In one day, I lost more than 120 ducats worth of wine and brandy in vats and a good further 50 ducats through the collapse of the house. [. . .]

[*Moulay Abdallah was succeeded by his half-brother Moulay Mohammed ben Arbiya in September 1736.*]

The following day, Moulay Mohammed ben Arbiya[37] was proclaimed king. [He] was a {66} good king for us Christians but a child for the country. While this king reigned, we experienced a grievously expensive period, so that from 1737 to June in 1738, forty-eight thousand died of hunger; the living ate the dead, mothers their children. There were no more dogs or cats as they had all been eaten. The bones of the cattle were dug up and crushed between two stones and drunk with water. They ate the plaster from the

---

35. *child*: Ter Meetelen had six children while in Morocco but did not record their births and deaths clearly. Only two of her children survived to make the journey back to the Netherlands with her. Ter Meetelen dwells very little on the deaths of her children. Interestingly, on p. 120 of the 1748 edition, she states that she was so happy to be boarding the ship that was to take them to freedom that she almost forgot her children.

36. *could not share them with my husband*: Ter Meetelen's husband was still working at the summer palace at the time.

37. *Moulay Mohammed ben Arbiya*: in the 1748 Dutch edition he is referred to as Sidi Magomet Ulda Lariba.

walls and straw like animals, for lack of grass. Instead of bread, the king's captives received a few handfuls of olive pits with skins, from which the oil had been pressed. Even the king's house experienced food shortages, although no one died of hunger there. [. . .]

{67} [. . .] My husband, who had always been exempted [from labor] by [this] king, was then also put to work[38] with violence and blows. I could not endure this, so I seized the opportunity when the king was outside of his palace and went to him with my husband and child. However, I did not manage to present myself, as the king had already gone inside his palace and the gates had been shut. I had no intention of going home before I had presented myself before the king, but this did not succeed. Notwithstanding this, I arranged to be summoned by the king with my husband and child the following day. We arrived at the palace, where one of his envoys led me and my child inside to the king and his women. There, I was received with exceptional kindness, and the king asked me what I desired. I said to the king that I begged of him that my husband would be freed from labor and that he would be allowed to earn a living for me and the child, just like when [the king's] {68} father and brothers had been king.[39] The king, hearing that my husband had been put to work without his orders, was very angry about this and asked why I had not come to tell him this sooner. So I said to the king that I would have come before him when the Spanish [slaves] departed to freedom[40] if I had not been prevented, as I would have asked the king for the house of the Spanish woman. It had been bought for the married Christians by the king's father. He had given it to her to run her business in, for it was not right for married [Christians] to live in the *cnoy*[41] with the other Christians. [I also said to the king] that the house which I had received from the queen had collapsed and that I was now forced to live with the [other] Christians. The king answered me very favorably by giving me a house in the city—whichever one I liked best.

---

38. *also put to work*: since 120 French slaves had recently been ransomed (on 10 August 1737), the supply of Christian slaves who could be put to work was running low.

39. *father and brothers had been king*: Pieter Jansz Iede, who had been in Morocco for twelve years already before Ter Meetelen was brought there, experienced the rule of Moulay Ismail (ruled 1672–1727). Under his rule, Morocco's political power reached a high point, but Moulay Ismail was notoriously cruel, particularly later in his reign. He was the father of the various brothers fighting for power during Ter Meetelen's time in Morocco.

40. *when the Spanish [slaves] departed to freedom*: Moulay Mohammed ben Arbiya released over fifty Spanish slaves in 1736 (Van den Broek and Jacobs, *Christenslaven*, 292n156).

41. *cnoy*: the *bagnio* or prison where the Christian slaves lived.

He [also said that] my husband would not be maltreated and that whoever spoke ill to me or to my husband or child could be certain of falling into the king's bad grace. I was not a little surprised by such a friendly and favorable reception. The king gave me to one of his real wives as a slave and ordered me to come to the palace daily, which I said I would do.

After having filled my hands and those of my child, the king then sent me to town with two messenger women with the order that {69} nobody should hurt my husband or my child in any way. The governor of the city had to give me the house that pleased me most and, on top of that, also a *torseman*,[42] which is to say a language expert. [She had] to go with me daily to the king as an interpreter, because I did not speak the language yet. So I was given an Irish renegada[43] who had turned Turk after many torments, and I chose the house of a basha, which I moved into with my [family]. The king's orders were so strict that no one dared say a bad word to us. At that time, I had to go to the king's house daily with my interpreter. I was sometimes with the king for a good hour or two along with my mistress and interpreter and spoke of all sorts of rare plants and of all kinds of things which come from foreign lands, and of landscapes, kingdoms, and cities. I instructed the king well, since I had a lot of experience in these things due to my travels and [since I] knew everything. This pleased the king a great deal and brought me more into the king's favor every day.

Finding myself now in the king's favor during such a grievously expensive period, during which the king did not give the Christians any rations, I thought of my fellowmen. [I wanted to] free them from the king's labor, which I achieved on 14 September, after the king had also doubly provided me and my husband and child with valuable clothes and linen. With my husband {70} now being well clothed, I took the rest to the other slaves in the royal palace. I fetched the king from his palace, who then examined the Christian slaves and exempted them all from work. The rumor that I had so much influence over the king spread so far across the country that people of the land who had any claim to make of the king came to me with gifts so that I would settle the matter with the king. But God guided my heart to consider that I was a slave. I directed them to the bashas, so that they found no consolation with me. I was also so tied to going to the palace daily that I grew tired of it. I then played truant and pretended to be ill in order to

---

42. *torseman*: from the Arabic *turjumān*, meaning "translator."
43. *renegada*: a female renegade, i.e., a Christian woman who has converted to Islam.

stay at home for a bit. However, then I had about three messengers coming daily from the king to ask about my well-being, who brought a sheep or some chickens or sweetmeats from the king.

I had hardly got home and remained there for three days when there was mourning in the whole palace among the women because the women were always being abused or strangled. One evening, I was fetched by the king's bodyguard. When I arrived at the royal palace, the king had killed two of his concubines. He was very angry and had also abused one of his secondary wives very badly. He had banished his main wife, so my mistress was in deadly fear, as well as a black woman whom he would have {71} strangled. The king had been hunting that day and had hunted a wild boar and brought it back alive. This was the reason why he had had me summoned—so that I would see it. As it was late, I could not see it due to the darkness of the night, but the king charged me to come the following day to see the boar fight with the dogs, which I did. [. . .]

[*Due to the famine, Moulay Mohammed ben Arbiya decided that he would free his slaves if he could get ransom money for them. On 5 November 1737, Maria ter Meetelen's husband departed for Tangier, a coastal city in northwestern Morocco near the Strait of Gibraltar, in order to negotiate their ransom.*]

{76} [. . .] My husband had hardly departed when I asked the king for rations, which he granted me and his real wives: four pounds of wheat flour per day. I had a Jewess as {77} a maid as well as a Christian [servant]. I dismissed my maid and asked the king for about four Christians for my house, because I lived in the city and, times being so expensive, it was a bit dangerous to live there. My house would then be protected against all evildoers, for all [they] did was plunder and steal. The king gave me permission to choose this number of Christians from the group, which I did. I provided them with food and clothing. I continued to go to the royal palace daily to attend all amusements with the king and his wives and to stroll through the courts every day. I sometimes stayed there overnight with my child, who was dearly loved by the king—more so than his own [children]. [. . .]

{88} [. . .] In the meantime, I was with the king every day, philosophizing extensively about astrology. I had taught [the king] so much about it that he considered me the greatest scholar in his whole country. Therefore, he had some of his greatest and most eminent summoned by writing, in order to discuss astrology with me. A Jewish rabbi—[rabbis] were considered more proficient in that science than the Turks—was also summoned before the king. It was on 8 April 1738 that eight of the king's scholars and the Jewish rabbi came before the king. I had to debate the course of the sun and moon and stars with them, and the movement of the whole earth, which I explained to them clearly. The king, having sharper wits than any of them, understood the matter, and they did not know how to refute it. They excused themselves by saying that it went against their religion, but the king answered them that it was not against their religion; they should rather say "we do not understand it." So they left, embarrassed.

Meanwhile, our long-awaited ambassador, Captain Joost Sels, came, with whom the king entered into negotiations. However, they could not {89} come to an agreement, as the king wanted to take the money given [for the ransom] himself, and the blacks,[44] on the other hand, wanted it too, so that [their interests] conflicted. The king dearly wanted to free us but did not know how to get the gold, so he came to me continuously for advice. However, I saw no solution, as the king was in the power of the blacks. Every year, they received their *retep*[45] or salary from the king, but the king's treasury was empty [and he was unable] to give them anything, so the king had doubts about what to do.

In the end, the king decided to free me[46] and my husband and children. The king would have given me some valuables as gifts to take along—some tiger skins[47] and lion skins and valuable carpets and silk clothing and handkerchiefs, the like of which are not to be found in Europe. This would have happened had there not been spies who reported all this to the blacks. For this reason, the king's most loyal friend, the governor of Salé, was deposed and another put in his place by the blacks. He then came to the city, where he negotiated our freedom with our people. [They] promised him two hundred ducats if we were freed and that the fathers would then pay him this sum. This governor so persuaded the king that the king decided to send us away and give the money to the blacks. {90} [The blacks] were in the field with their army in order to go campaigning with the king.

---

44. *blacks*: by "blacks" Ter Meetelen means the "Black Guard" or the Abid al-Bukhari, which was a corps of forcibly recruited, mostly sub-Saharan slave soldiers that had been created by Moulay Ismail (ruled 1672–1727). After his death, however, the army became a destabilizing force and was frequently involved in intrigues and coups. For more information, see chaps. 5 and 6 of Chouki el Hamel, *Black Morocco: A History of Slavery, Race, and Islam* (Cambridge: Cambridge University Press, 2014).

45. *retep*: from the Arabic *rātib*, meaning "salary."

46. *the king decided to free me*: the 1748 Dutch edition contains a negative ("om niet in vryheyt te stuuren," i.e., "not to free me"). However, this does not make sense in context.

47. *tiger skins*: there are no tigers in North Africa. Ter Meetelen probably means leopard or cheetah skins.

They were stationed two hours away from the city. On the same day, 22 June, they announced a directive that anyone who wanted grain could come and buy or fetch it from them in the camp. It cost only two *dubbeltjies*[48] per ten-pound measure. Sixty dubbeltjies were given for it that day still. That same evening, I presented myself before the king to report this and [to get his] seal on the passport, so that we could get ready to leave the following day. But the king was not in a good mood and ordered me to return again in the morning. In the morning, I accordingly readied myself to go to there. [However], on going out, my interpreter was almost robbed, but she escaped, and the king had been taken prisoner at midnight and put in chains, so we found ourselves without a king.[49] [. . .]

[*In the resulting political turmoil and as a favorite of the deposed king, Maria ter Meetelen had to place herself under the protection of a basha.*]

{93} [. . .] Early in the morning, I was taken to the basha with my husband and children. [We were] escorted by some of our nation with gleeful shouts of, "Now the king's whore will be burned! Even if she does not want to hand over the money and precious stones,[50] she will have to! Burn her! Burn her! Burn her!" One of them spat after me. I remained patient and thought, "God will avenge this," and indeed they {94} got their deserts. Thus he who can suffer and endure will find his enemies defeated.

In the afternoon, we came before the basha, and my husband remained with our belongings and animals. My children and I were taken into the house and brought before the basha and his women. They received me very kindly and wished that God would hasten my deliverance. I thanked the basha for this. He sent me to his wife, where all the important people's wives were gathered to see me. They were all very friendly to me and did not speak of any negative things. They gave me food and drink. In the meantime, the converted Jewess[51] came to me and said to me in Spanish, "Tell me where you have left the money and the precious stones. Your husband has already confessed and they have punished him severely. They are busy skinning him and if you do not tell me, they will immediately come

---

48. *dubbeltjie*: a relatively small denomination of silver coin.

49. *without a king*: Ter Meetelen may have misremembered the date when the king was deposed, as she implies here that this happened after 22 June 1738. However, Van den Broek and Jacobs, *Christenslaven*, point out that, in a letter dated 10 June 1738, the Dutch consul in Cádiz reported that the king had been deposed (307n201).

50. *money and precious stones*: these were purportedly gifts from Moulay Mohammed ben Arbiya. Ter Meetelen states that she did not have such valuables in her possession.

51. *converted Jewess*: a member of the basha's household.

for you and do the same to you." When I heard this, my heart plummeted so much that I could hardly say a word. My tears streamed from my eyes. I answered thus, "Oh, they should leave my husband, who is as innocent as a child, alone. Let me die in his place; I have nothing though." I could not say more. I sat a good few hours in this state with my children on my lap, who were weeping bitterly with me. And the Jewess continually came {95} to trouble me with new complaints, so that it seemed that my husband was already dead. I pulled myself together somewhat and prepared to die, committing my children to God's care. I thought about how God had saved me from so many dangers and had been father and mother to me from the time I was thirteen and had always taken care of me. I said, "Oh God, You are still the same God and I know that nothing happens without Your knowledge. You arrange everything for the best and if You take me away from my children, Lord, You will be their father and protector. I commit them to Your protection." I found solace in God and took heart and was ready to die.

I sought an opportunity to present myself before the basha to tell him that my husband was innocent, but I was prevented. Toward evening, the converted Jewess came and said that I would now be brought before the basha, but I should cry as I went there. I then noticed the falseness of this female. I subsequently went to the basha, who received me with no less kindness than before and showed me much respect, as if I were not a slave. In the meantime, my husband had also come there. He spoke to the basha and I, looking around and seeing that no harm had befallen him, felt as one reborn and my heart leapt with joy. After having taken leave of the basha, who wished me many blessings and freedom and hoped to reach {96} an agreement with our ambassador, we left and went to the place where they took us to spend the night. I asked my husband whether anyone had hurt him, but no one had spoken either good or ill to him. [. . .]

After four days, we were brought back to Mehdya.[52] Our people, thinking that we had been executed, were thoroughly astonished. We were not there for long, because the king, who had made his entry into the palace as king on 14 August,[53] immediately summoned the Christians. As many mules as [there were Christians] were sent to fetch us. We, who had thought we

---

52. *Mehdya*: a Moroccan coastal town. "Mamooren" in the 1748 Dutch edition (it was known as La Mamora under Spanish occupation in the seventeenth century). The Dutch slaves had traveled to Mehdya in July 1738 for ransom negotiations.

53. *king on 14 August*: in 1738, Moulay al-Mustadi, another half-brother of Moulay Abdallah, succeeded in taking power for the first time.

would return to freedom, went into renewed slavery with nothing. There [in Meknès], on 21 August, we found that we had been robbed of what we had left there by the three Portuguese who had remained.[54] We did get our beds back as well as a table and a few benches; no more than that.

{97} On the 22nd of the same month, we were then brought before the king, who gave each of us Christians a modest place in the palace [in order] to guard the storehouse. [The Christians] were also put to work, but my husband was exempted from work. At that time, we had nothing to eat and no way to start anything. So, I had to get to work again, as I did not want to die of hunger with my husband and children. In that year, there was a good grape harvest, but money was lacking. Now, the merchants of Salé had come with a gift for the king to congratulate him on his accession to the throne. With great difficulty, I borrowed twenty ducats from them in order to be able to do my *vendimi*[55] or wine harvest. Grapes were cheap then, and we paid only twelve to fourteen *stuyvers*[56] per hundred pounds. My husband distilled the harvest as far as the money would go and immediately stocked up the inn with new mustum[57] and brandy distilled from grapes, so that we were able to earn our living again within eight to ten days.

Our inn was separate from the house we lived in. At night, a Christian who worked in the royal storehouse during the day stayed there, and by day, my husband was there. The inn had scarcely been set up when my husband caught a serious eye disease that laid him up for a good two months. As a result, the inn had to remain closed. My {98} heart could not let this time pass in which we could have earned before the king went to the army. Both my children were also very unwell and I also had only one good eye. In addition, it was almost time for the royal fast when no alcohol could be sold. My husband did not want me to go to the inn. I let others talk him round and convinced him [to let me] go there with my entire household. I had to make do with very little, as there was little accommodation. I ran everything—the housekeeping and the inn—and God strengthened me wonderfully and blessed me beyond measure with business. I earned so much in a month that I could make as much wine and brandy as I had made before.

---

54. *the three Portuguese who had remained*: like the Dutch slaves, these three slaves had not been freed when the previous sultan, Moulay Mohammed ben Arbiya, freed his French slaves in August 1737 (Van den Broek and Jacobs, *Christenslaven*, 60).

55. *vendimi*: from the Spanish *vendimia*, meaning "harvest."

56. *stuyvers*: more commonly known as a *stuiver*, this early modern Dutch coin dates back to the sixteenth century.

57. *mustum*: grape juice with a very low alcohol percentage.

In addition to this, we saved enough cash to be able to eat during the fast. I could then estimate my capital to be about one hundred ducats again.

At that time, I had some peace from the Christians, but this did not last long, for when they returned from the army with the king, they did everything they could to take away my inn or to have it forbidden. This again caused great daily trouble. Since I did not know yet whether the king was well disposed toward us Christians or not, I took a chance and presented myself before the king. I asked for a house in the city in order to {99} run an inn there. The king was very pleased with the way I addressed him and showed his pleasure by granting my request. However, the Moors and his bashas advised him against it, as it was somewhat dangerous for my household to be alone in the city and I had a house in the *bagnio*.[58] They reckoned that I could just as well run my inn there, but my fellowmen were opposed to this and prevented me. I was blameless and had not complained of them to the king, for then it would have gone badly for them.

The king told me to go to the bagnio with my husband and children and [said that] I should run my inn there. And if anyone tried to hinder me, I should come and complain to him and he would cut their heads off. So I went to my house and ran my inn, but they would still not stop sabotaging my husband and me. So I sought an opportunity to present myself to the king's mother at the palace. I achieved this without too much trouble and went to her daily and to her sister, whose liking for my sincerity grew so great that I had total influence over her and never went home emptyhanded—I would receive a bag of flour or meat or money or fruit. I was a favorite with the king's entire family.

So it came to pass that the king had been king for a year and {100} we did not know of the misfortune that the king was going to be deposed. [. . .]

[*In the early 1740s, Moulay Abdallah saw yet another return to power, followed by more political turmoil. In 1742, Moulay al-Mustadi seized power for the second time. Maria ter Meetelen demonstrated her remarkable ability to ingratiate herself with the ruling family yet again. Under Moulay al-Mustadi, Ter Meetelen's long hoped-for freedom finally became reality.*]

{107} [. . .] The friendship of the king's mother and sister toward me, as well as that of the king himself, increased day by day, with the result that I had a great deal of influence over them. Consequently, I did my best

---

58. *bagnio*: the prison or slave quarters where the slaves lived.

to win our freedom and that of my fellowmen. The king did not seem to be opposed to this. He sought to send me and my husband and children to his {108} brother, who was viceroy in Marrakech,⁵⁹ until the arrival of an ambassador at Agadir,⁶⁰ who would send me and my husband and children to freedom. [He did this] because he did not know how long he would remain king, and [if he was deposed], the Christians would have to return to the storehouse, [whereas] if we were with his brother, we would be safe.

So the date for our departure was already fixed and our things were packed, but my husband was completely against it, as it was such a long journey and we would have had to be on the road for a good month in terrible heat and with two children. Therefore, I was obliged to ask the king for permission to stay, which I was granted by the king. The king's mother and sister often badgered me to turn Turk, [saying] that it was a sin that I was an unbeliever. However, I always answered that it had not yet pleased Heaven, and kissed the ground. When they saw that they could not succeed with me, they asked me to raise my little girl, who was not even a year old, for the son of her son.⁶¹ To this, I replied that if this should happen, I would not be able to prevent it. They were very pleased with this and thereafter never called my daughter anything other than Larossa ta Sidi Magomet,⁶² that is to say, the bride of Sidi Magomet. That was the name of the king's son. I did not let this to-do bother me at all, {109} for I was sure that God would deliver me from their hands, which I do not want to record here for reasons of my own. I did not tell my husband everything that happened to me with the king and his mother and sister, for he would probably have forbidden my going to the palace. He could not stand the Moors, for he had suffered much under them before my arrival in Barbary. [. . .]

[*An outbreak of the plague swept over Morocco, but the ransom negotiations for the Dutch community, including Ter Meetelen and her family, continued.*]

---

59. *Marrakech*: "Marokken" in the 1748 Dutch edition.

60. *Agadir*: a Moroccan coastal city. "Santa Cruys" in the 1748 Dutch edition. It was known as Santa Cruz do Cabo de Gue under the Portuguese in the sixteenth century.

61. *son of her son*: Bekkaoui identifies him as Prince Sidi Muhammad (ruled 1757–1790), who was interested in Elizabeth Marsh (compare "Narrative of Elizabeth Marsh's Captivity in Barbary" in chapter 12, this volume). See Khalid Bekkaoui, ed., *White Women Captives in North Africa: Narratives of Enslavement, 1735–1830* (Basingstoke, UK: Palgrave Macmillan, 2011), 287n79.

62. *Larossa ta Sidi Magomet*: probably from the Arabic: al-ʿarūsa tāʿ Sīdī Muḥammad; literally: "the bride belonging to Sidi Muhammad."

{111} [. . .] About five weeks later, on 9 November,[63] I and my husband and both children were summoned before the king, who freed all four of us and handed us over to the envoy of the basha of Tangier. The king freed us gladly, but he would rather have kept the others, if the envoy had not insisted strongly on getting them also. The following day, the king summoned all the Christian {112} slaves and chose a further nine of them, whom he freed. At the insistence of the envoy of the basha, he summoned the remaining ones, from among whom we thirteen were selected. After a great deal of effort, the king made a further arrangement after the basha sent him ten Christian slaves so that [the king] would free the remainder, who were ten in number. So the fourteen of us were freed.[64] As soon as the king had freed us, he summoned my husband and my little daughter, whom he loved beyond measure and had played with many a time. My husband could not speak before the king for joy. I was proficient in complimenting after the Turkish fashion. My compliments were exceptionally charming, so that the king took great delight in them and exclaimed, "As true as I live, this Christian woman is worthy of being a princess!" With this honor, I took my leave of the king.

The day thereafter, I bid farewell to the king's mother and sister, who were more tender toward me than any parents could have been toward their child. They both wept and gave me two ducats for the trip. They wished that they could have kept me, but this could not be, for the king had an obligation toward the basha. The king had too few men and Moulay Abdallah was stationed in Fez. [Moulay Abdallah] would have to be driven away from there if the caravan was to reach his kingdom regularly, wherefore the basha came with a considerable army {113} to assist the king in defeating his enemies.

So, on 16 December, we set off on our journey and, for safety reasons, had to make extensive detours. Otherwise, we would have fallen into the hands of Moulay Abdallah and would then have remained in slavery to this day, together with the rest who had remained behind. [. . .]

[*The Dutch slaves made a difficult journey to Tétouan, a port city in northern Morocco, where they had to remain for several months for want of a ship. Foreign ships were avoiding Morocco at the time due to an outbreak of the plague there.*

---

63. *9 November*: in the year 1742.

64. *The following day [. . .] the fourteen of us were freed*: Ter Meetelen is unclear in her description of this negotiation.

Only on 11 April 1743 were the former slaves able to board a ship and, after numerous delays, they arrived in Lisbon on 20 June 1743. From Lisbon, they took a ship to Holland, but due to unfavorable weather, they had to stop in Portsmouth, England.]

{126} [. . .] Then we set sail but had unfavorable conditions for our journey, as we had to go against the wind. Consequently, we had to stop at Portsmouth in England, where we got fresh supplies. We had already been on rations for several days, as our food supplies had run out due to our long journey. We left Portsmouth on 14 September[65] and arrived safe and sound in Texel[66] on the 18th. On the 21st we arrived in Amsterdam, where I had not been for twenty years. I immediately sought out my parents and friends, but they had all died, and I found no one other than a half-brother.[67] I stayed at his house for about fourteen days, until I went with my husband to his birthplace in Medemblik.[68] Here, I settled down, and I still live here. I do not complain that I have fallen so far in this world, nor about my twelve years of slavery, nor of the sufferings the Turks inflicted on me—I can tolerate all this. But the scorn and derision my fellowmen inflicted on my husband and me, which is impossible to record here in writing—this cannot be forgotten.

I thank the Lord from the bottom of my heart for His mercy and [I] praise Him for liberating us from our slavery with our children; and that our children and children's children will still speak of [our adventures] in the land of the Turks, wherefore I thought it good to have this printed. {127} For everyone should see and read how wonderfully God protects His own, who put their faith in Him, and how He can vanquish his enemies and preserve [His people]; and all the things that can happen to one, which I personally have written down here truthfully, hoping that the beloved reader will find it satisfactory. I remain the beloved reader's humble servant,

Maria ter Meetelen

Written in Medemblik,

on 14 June 1748.

THE END

---

65. *14 September*: in the year 1743.

66. *Texel*: an island in the province of North Holland, the Netherlands.

67. *half-brother*: this was Jan ter Meetelen (1712–1788). In addition, a sister and two half-sisters of Maria ter Meetelen were still alive. It is not clear why she does not mention them. See Van den Broek and Jacobs, *Christenslaven*, 331n284.

68. *Medemblik*: a town in North Holland, the Netherlands. "Medenblik" in the 1748 Dutch edition.

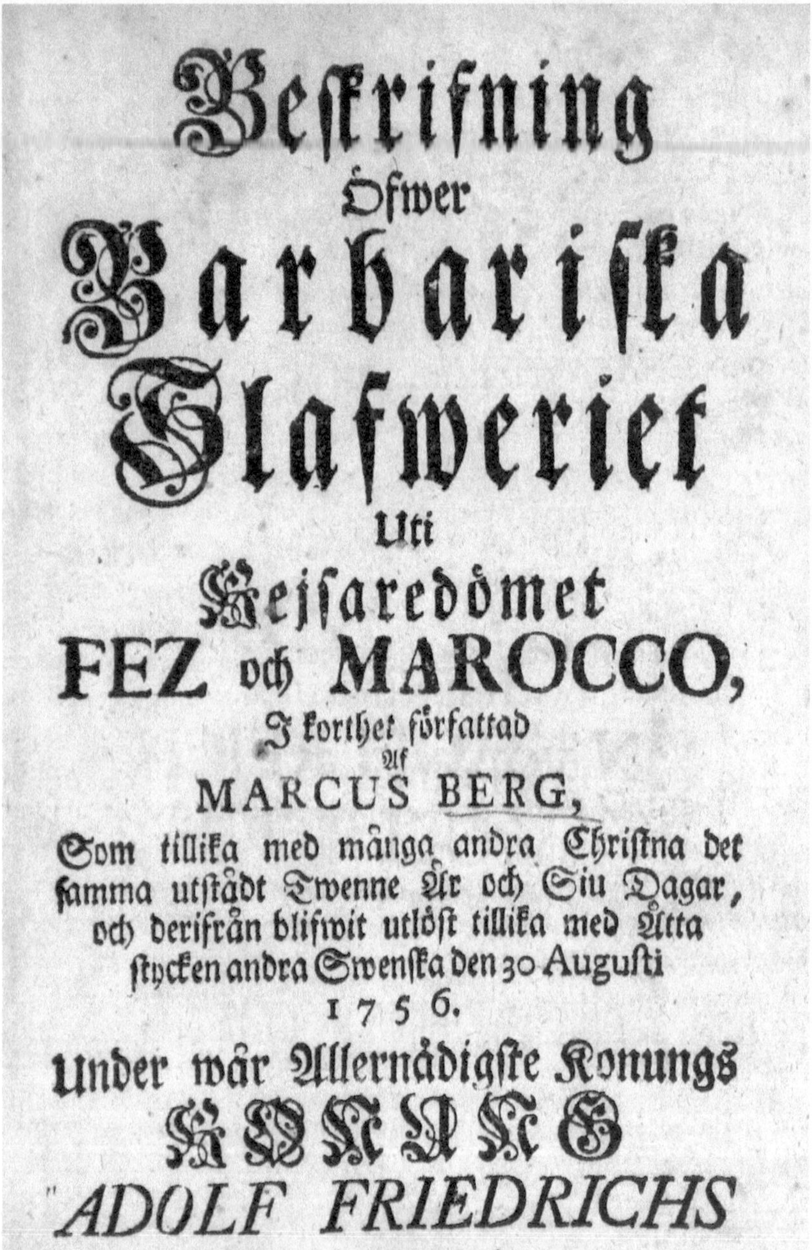

Beskrifning öfwer Barbariska Slafweriet

Uti

Kejsaredömet FEZ och MAROCCO,

I korthet författad

Af

MARCUS BERG,

Som tillika med många andra Christna det samma utstådt Twenne År och Siu Dagar, och derifrån blifwit utlöst tillika med Åtta stycken andra Swenska den 30 Augusti

1756.

Under wår Allernådigste Konungs

KONUNGS

ADOLF FRIEDRICHS

Milda Regering.

Stockholm,

Tryckt hos LOR. LUDV. GREFING, 1757.

Figure 11.1 Title page of Marcus Berg's narrative

Source: Marcus Berg, *Beskrifning öfwer barbariska slafweriet uti kejsaredömet Fez och Marocco* [. . .] (Stockholm, 1757); Lund University Library, Äldre Samlingen Sv Res Afr.

CHAPTER XI

MARCUS BERG, *DESCRIPTION OF THE BARBARIC SLAVERY IN THE KINGDOM OF FEZ AND MOROCCO*

1757 Swedish print edition; selection

Captivity in Morocco 1754–1756

The only authentic Swedish Barbary captivity narrative that made it into print is Marcus Berg's *Description of the Barbaric Slavery in the Kingdom of Fez and Morocco* (1757), which records Captain Berg's experiences as a slave in Morocco from 1754 to 1756.[1] What is surprising about this text is that it was preceded by a fictitious Swedish Robinsonade, attributed to Gustav Landcronas and published in 1740, which is, in turn, based on a German text published in 1724. Both versions of Landcronas's adventures follow the lead of the novel *Robinson Crusoe*, embedding episodes of Barbary captivity in a Robinsonesque conglomerate plot. When Marcus Berg's authentic narrative appeared in print in 1757, Swedish readers knew the genre of the Barbary captivity narrative solely through these fictional specimens. Berg's account follows in the footsteps of older, authentic European Barbary narratives by describing the struggle against pirates at sea, the journey to North Africa, various episodes of the captive's life, and, finally, the ransom and return of the captive. During his stay in Morocco, Berg communicated with Swedish consuls to receive economic support for the crew. In an appendix to his actual narrative, Berg also provided useful information on Morocco for Swedish authorities. It included

---

1. On Marcus Berg, see Joachim Östlund, "Swedish Barbary Captivity Tales: From Letters to Literature (1650–1770)," in *Mediterranean Slavery and World Literature: Captivity Genres from Cervantes to Rousseau*, ed. Mario Klarer (London, New York: Routledge, 2020), 69–92, esp. 85–88.

a detailed report about the country that counts as the first written description of Morocco in Swedish.

Berg, born in 1726, was the captain of the ship *Mercurius* when he and his crew of nine sailors were seized near Cartagena in Spain in 1754 by Moroccan corsairs sailing under an Algerian flag. This deceptive maneuver made the crew believe that the corsairs posed no threat to them, since Sweden had concluded a peace treaty with Algiers in 1729. Locals in Tétouan celebrated the arrival of the Swedes by parading the captives through the streets while insulting them: Berg was riding a donkey and one of his younger seamen had to hold the tail of the donkey, with the rest of the crew following hand in hand (5–8).[2] The subsequent narrative goes into a great deal of detail about the long-winded and confusing ransom process and the sufferings Berg experienced during his two-year captivity, including Berg's life in the *bagnios* (prisons). Not unlike other Europeans in Barbary captivity, Berg has to negotiate intra-Christian tensions between Protestants and Catholics in Muslim North Africa.

The most astonishing parts of the narrative contain psychological insights into the sadistic psyche of the Moroccan sultan. Berg's descriptions of the ruler's unpredictable rage and self-aggrandizing demeanor paint a picture of an erratic and cruel emperor. The impulsive ruler stands in contrast to the rational and caring Captain Berg, a difference that culminates in the final scene before the release of the Swedish captives. In the very last moment, the sultan decides to keep two of the youngest crew members: "The view of them on our departure, with tears in their eyes, and their desperation, could only leave us with compassion, since we were not given the chance to speak with them" (78). Berg is deeply affected by his inability to assist his fellow countrymen and immediately after his return undertakes various, ultimately futile, efforts to liberate them.[3] Two crew members had died in captivity already, while the two young boys whom the sultan had kept, Hans Lund and Marcus Österman, were never released.

In addition to being the only full-fledged Swedish Barbary captivity account in print, Berg's narrative stands out because of its firsthand description of the biggest earthquake in the eighteenth century. The disastrous force of this 1755 earthquake destroyed most of the city of Lisbon and caused the

---

2. Page numbers correspond to those in the original historical edition used for the translation in this anthology.

3. Joachim Östlund, *Saltets pris: Svenska slavar i Nordafrika och handeln med Nordafrika 1650–1770* (Lund: Tidskriften Respons, 2014), 304.

deaths of thousands of people. Numerous intellectuals at the time discussed this natural catastrophe in religious contexts of theodicy, that is, the question of why God would allow suffering and evil in the world. Marcus Berg was a witness to this natural catastrophe, whose epicenter was located off the coast of Morocco. From his prison roof, Berg gives an apocalyptic account of the earthquake: "The houses crumbled except for an almost completely ruined old fortress in Fez, and the water in the moats spilling from one side to the other. The color of the sky changed and the heavens seemed to open up in the southwest. Humans as well as animals were terrified" (43).[4]

Berg's captivity lasted from 23 August 1754 to 31 August 1756. It ended when Swedish authorities paid his ransom and those of his surviving crew members. Once back home, Berg and the other returnees gave a testimony of their experiences to the Swedish king and queen as well as the government. During his absence, Berg's wife had died, his property had been confiscated, and his nine-year-old daughter Maria had been placed in the care of friends. In 1757, a few months after his return, Berg published his book, titled *Beskrifning öfwer barbariska slafweriet uti kejsardömet Fez och Marocco*.

Notes on the Present Translation of Marcus Berg's *Description of the Barbaric Slavery in the Kingdom of Fez and Morocco*

This translation is based on the first edition: Marcus Berg, *Beskrifning öfwer barbariska slafweriet uti kejsaredömet Fez och Marocco, i korthet författad af Marcus Berg, som tillika med många andra christna det samma utstådt twenne år och siu dagar, och derifrån blifwit utlöst tillika med åtta stycken andra swenska den 30 Augusti 1756. Under wår allernådigste konungs konung Adolf Friedrichs milda regering* (Stockholm: tryckt hos Lor. Ludv. Grefing, 1757).

The selected passages span pages 20 to 50 of Berg's 143-page narrative. The numbers in brackets {} in the text always indicate the beginning of a page and refer to the original page numbers of the first edition. Because the narrative was written in eighteenth-century Swedish before the formation of the Swedish Academy, which introduced general rules of standardization,

---

4. On the 1755 earthquake and historical testimonies on the Moroccan situation, see P.-L. Blanc, "Earthquakes and Tsunami in November 1755 in Morocco: A Different Reading of Contemporaneous Documentary Sources," *Natural Hazards Earth System Science* 9 (2009): 725–38.

and because Berg was not an educated man or scholar, the narrative presents some unique challenges for the translator. This translation aims to be as faithful as possible to Berg's language while still providing a readable English text. Special thanks go to Devin Stewart and Khalid El Abdaoui for transliterations and translations pertaining to languages from the Islamic world, as well as to Almiria Wilhelm for her assistance with the preparation of the final translation.

Marcus Berg, *Description of the Barbaric Slavery in the Empire of Fez and Morocco, Briefly Authored by Marcus Berg, Who, Along with Many Other Christians, Suffered the Same for Two Years and Seven Days, and Thenceforth Was Released Together with Eight Other Swedes on August 30, 1756. Under the Benevolent Reign of Our Most Gracious King, King Adolf Friedrichs* (Stockholm: Printed by Lor. Ludv. Grafing, 1757)

Translated by Joachim Östlund

{20} After enduring many hardships, we arrived, totally exhausted, at the castle of the emperor,[5] located almost one German mile[6] from the city of Fez. On 26 September,[7] at three o'clock in the afternoon, we were lined up in front of the emperor, the first sight of whom caused us much dread and fear, convinced as we were of the severity with which slaves like us would be treated by such a cruel ruler. He came riding toward us with a rather threatening appearance, dressed in a large, wide coat, a Turkish hat on his head, and a spear in his hand. On one side of him walked a young Moor who carried a large parasol over [the emperor's] head, and on the other side a person who looked after his weapons. When he approached the place where we were lined up, we first had to fall to our knees and then reverently bow and kiss the earth. After being inspected by the emperor, all the young men were picked out to be servants at the castle, and later we were taken to the city of Fez, to Knuten,[8] where we found that there was a total of 104 Christian {21} slaves; twenty-six Spanish, two Spanish wives and a

---

5. *the emperor*: Moulay Abdallah (1694–1757), sultan of Morocco.
6. *German mile*: roughly 24,000 feet.
7. *26 September*: in the year 1754.
8. *Knuten*: Berg's name for the prison in Fez to which he is taken. Literally: "the knot."

five-year-old child, twenty-nine French, eleven Portuguese, six Englishmen, six [Englishmen] from Port Mahón,[9] and, with me, thirteen Swedes, and a Portuguese Jew. Knuten in Fez was built by the Christians at the command of the emperor and was surrounded by a forty-foot-high wall, and every nation had their own room, apart from the Swedes and the Danes. Until [our capture], of these nations' ships, no more than one Norwegian ship[10] had been taken, which was that of Captain Lars Didrichssen from Bergen and nine men. He was ransomed a few months before I got there, but only together with three men; the others had died. Nobody could imagine how miserably we were quartered in Knuten. We had to lie on the floor like cattle, together with so many different vermin such as lice, bedbugs, flies, rats, mice, scorpions, millipedes, and insects, that our bodies were sometimes covered with them, and we had to stand up and scrape them off and try to find another room to sleep in, but we were not there long before the same nuisance arose. Once, I found a dead scorpion under me after getting up from my wretched spot. It was a wonder that we were never poisoned to death by these creatures.

The day after our arrival in Fez, the Moors were celebrating one of their holidays, which they call Ei dilkebyr[11] and which is held with great hullabaloo, and we were free from work, but the following day, on 28 September, we were driven out to work. Even though I was in quite a bad state and exhausted from my sickness as well from the long and tiresome journey, I had to join the others in the work. When we arrived, our task was to build a new henhouse, which {22} was not so difficult. Later, we had to erect walls and dig pits, which was quite difficult [since] the earth had to be carried up from the pits in baskets, and then to be mixed with lime, sand, and water, together with small stones, to [form] a paste. The paste was then pounded solid with *margaetter* or clubs, inside a form or a frame made of planks to the height and width the wall was to be. When it began to harden, the planks were removed. It looks like a wall made of stone.

This place was not like Tétouan, where a distinction was made between those who were captains and the rest of the crew, and therefore we were

---

9. *Port Mahón*: Mahón, the capital of the island of Menorca, was British territory at the time.

10. *of these nations' ships [. . .] Norwegian ship*: at the time, Sweden (including Finland) and Denmark–Norway formed a political unit, of which Denmark was the dominant power.

11. *Ei dilkebyr*: in Arabic (Moroccan dialect): '*Īd-l-kebīr*. This is also known as Eid al-Adh or "the Festival of the Sacrifice."

given no more than one *blanquin*[12] each day for each one to live on, and not a single moment of rest from sunrise until five or six o'clock in the evening. Sometimes the emperor was in a good mood, which most often happened a long time after sunset. When the work was to stop, a flag was raised in the town, which commonly happened at four o'clock if the emperor did not impose some special task upon us. After handing in our tools at the castle, we had to walk almost one German mile before we arrived at Knuten in Fez, and then we first had to purchase and prepare food for dinner and supper at the same time. Therefore, our rest before the beginning of the next day, with hard work in the hot sun, was quite short, especially since we were so sick and weak most of the time that we could neither eat nor drink. Even so, we had to suffer the same slave labor as a healthy person.

Among us Swedes there was a lot of sickness and misery from the beginning of October until the end of this year. Often, five or six of us were so miserable that we could not do any work, but after much {23} begging and shedding of tears, the emperor allowed us to stay at home and be free from toil until we were better. Often, when I was sick but the *alcaides*[13] wanted to drive me to work, I was forced to visit the *bouscheven*,[14] begging on my bare knees and kissing his feet to ask for leave to stay at home until my health was restored, which was occasionally granted. Alcaides is the name here for those whom the emperor has given the authority to put the Christians to work, but it is quite unusual for them to escape from that service alive, since many of them are sacrificed to the wrath of the emperor. Bouscheven is the name of the person with the greatest power in Fez, and he is by extraction a black man, appointed by the emperor. Every time when one had to ask for leave, both the bouscheven and the alcaide had to be bribed, and often half a blanquin was enough. But a captain who has nothing to give is punished in an inhuman way compared to their more reasonable treatment of other people.

I did not seem to be getting better before I was forced to work and slave like the others; and moreover, to increase our torment, the emperor had put us under the charge not only of many Moors, but also of a Christian alcaide who is a Portuguese. He calls himself Paulus and because he has lived in Barbary for a fairly long time, he understands their language perfectly; but along with this he practices all possible vices and gross roguery that a

---

12. *blanquin*: a type of coin.
13. *alcaide*: from the Arabic *al-qā'id*, meaning "leader" or "captain."
14. *bouscheven*: it is not clear exactly what office Berg is referring to; in the next sentences, he explains only that this person is endowed with a large amount of power by the emperor.

Christian would dread even to mention. Although he had been ordered by the emperor to govern the Christians according to the laws and rules of their religion, he himself lived contrary to them. Together with other thoughtless Christians who sought his friendship and shared his ungodly ways {24}, they led a quite abominable and improper life with transgressions in sodomy. They often provoked discord and fights between their party and the rest of us, who in [spite] of our wretched state were trying to live as true Christians should, as true bearers of the cross, cast under the yoke of slavery for our sins. For this reason we often suffered more annoyance and sorrow from our fellow Christians' ungodly life and squabbling than from the brutality and wicked treatment of the barbarians. From this one can see that neither oppression nor freedom, slavery nor good days make one a good Christian, but only surrendering one's heart into the hands of God. Whether one lives among Christians or barbarians, [if one] only has worldly gains in mind, there is only the name "Christian" left and no greater chance to reach the Kingdom of Heaven than for the wickedest heathen. Praise be that God was even to be found in Barbary and did not forget any of His worshippers. Suffering is beneficial if the spirit of God can endure testing, but otherwise it does not achieve more than good days do.[15]

It would be futile to describe the cruel treatment of both Christians and Moors by the emperor when he gets angry, which often occurs without the slightest reason, and then his wrath can only be appeased by bloodshed or by tormenting and abusing all those involved. Every time we saw the emperor arrive at the place where we were working, we expected new torments, for as long as he was present, even when in a good mood, we had to carry our baskets on our bare heads and run as fast as we could up and down from the pit. The most difficult {25} thing was that, on our arrival in Fez, we had to shave all the hair from our heads and, according to the order of the emperor, we could not let our hair grow more than one finger long, otherwise it would be pulled out by the roots. But the beard was always supposed to grow. When the emperor was not out, hats and caps were allowed, but when he showed up, we had to bare our heads. And if he was worried, he immediately called out to the alcaides, "*Derrop serranij*,"[16]

---

15. *Suffering is beneficial [. . .] good days do*: Berg is probably referring to 1 Peter 2:20: "For what glory is it, if, when ye be buffeted for your faults, ye shall take it patiently? but if, when ye do well, and suffer for it, ye take it patiently, this is acceptable with God" (*King James Version* [hereafter *KJV*]).

16. *Derrop serranij*: from the Arabic (Moroccan dialect): *ḍrub sharrānī*; literally: "Beat the evil one" (i.e., the Christian).

or "beat the Christians." Then no mercy could be expected, but all those in charge ran after us, repeatedly hitting us with sticks, which usually lasted far into the evening until we were so exhausted that we could not stand up. But as long as the emperor was present, these beatings continued until we got up and began to run again with such heavy burdens on our bare heads that we could not lift them without someone else's help. On such unbearable occasions, we had not so much as a drop of water to quench our thirst the whole day, much less anything else to fortify ourselves with. The first time we experienced the emperor's severity in this way was on 30 October, when he also had three of our black alcaides beaten so that blood poured from them and we thought they would never survive. The emperor commanded them to lie down on the ground and then he commanded others to beat them with sticks until he told them to stop. A few days later, he had the alcaides beaten again, and the foremost of them had his head, arms, and legs crushed, so he only lived for a short while afterward. This inhumanity seemed only to delight the emperor.

At the same time he also inflicted a special tax on the Jews in the city of Fezvillie,[17] consisting of a sum of eleven thousand ducats,[18] that was to be paid to him immediately, and four thousand ducats to be paid to the citizens of Fez in {26} three days. And although the Jews came to him to ask for clemency, it was to no avail. Instead, the "Ludi,"[19] as they are called, who live in Fez, were ordered to enter the Jewish quarters, which was a closed part of the city, to extract money from each and every one according to his situation. Those who would not pay were treated badly, along with their women and children, causing a terrible wailing and lamentation among the Jews, some of whom fled from here shortly afterward to Meknès, a big city eight hours' journey from here.

Shortly after our arrival, five Spaniards and one from Port Mahón renounced the Christian religion and embraced the Muhammadan faith, for which they were released from slavery and were allowed to make a living in any way they wished. But they were not esteemed very highly by the Moors.

On 23 December, one of our Swedes by the name of Sven Stille, who had been rather ill since 23 October, died a blessed death, released from this

---

17. *Fezvillie*: from the Arabic (Moroccan dialect): Fās al-Bālī; literally: "Old Fez." Berg is most likely referring to the Jewish quarters of Fez.
18. *ducat*: a gold or silver European coin.
19. *Ludi*: this reference is not clear.

wretched slavery in which we others had to remain as long as it pleased the almighty God to give us strength to withstand the harsh treatment of the barbarians, [despite] the majority [of us] being very sick from gnawing sorrow. This Stille had been married in Kalmar[20] and left his wife and many small children in grief and in trouble. When a Christian dies it is permitted to bury him at a designated place outside the city, and the slaves have to carry the body themselves on a litter, sewn up in some old coat or whatever can be had.

{27} On 24 December, or Christmas Eve, we threw ourselves before the emperor and asked if we could be free to celebrate Christmas. He gave us three days during which, not without strange emotions, we considered the comforting birth of our Savior through which we have been liberated from eternal slavery and could also be freed in time from our worldly slavery. He has shown us precious examples of this. We could not help being reminded with reverence of the grace we had enjoyed, so many years before, as free Christians. With worldly pleasure we had survived years and the swift changes of time, on occasions when one has good fortune and little knows how to appreciate the priceless benefits one enjoys. We could thus acknowledge, not without humility, the righteous cross that we deserve to bear for the sake of our sins. We must submit to the gracious will of the Almighty.

We thus ended the old year in the name of our gentle savior Jesus, beginning the new year of 1755 with heartfelt pleasure in God and a firm hope in His limitless mercy, which is the sole comfort and refuge of our souls and the souls of all those in distress. We learned that there is no greater delight than simply knowing God, [which is] greater than knowing and possessing many benefits of good fortune. Knowing and serving God can so sweeten the harshest slavery that it is considered as a burden one bears gladly as long as it pleases Heaven. The whole world is far too insignificant and powerless to give either joy or torment to a soul in whose heart God dwells, because it scorns all torments, regarding them as mere trifles, puffs of wind, and shadows that fade quickly.

{28} The year 1755

The emperor, who since our arrival in Fez had been in a state of mental disturbance, continued to treat us badly with hard work at the beginning of this year. But the old slaves told us that he is not always enraged and sometimes treats his Christians with more compassion. This gave us hope

---

20. *Kalmar*: a coastal town in southeast Sweden. Berg writes it "Calmar" in the Swedish original.

[despite] our suffering and even made us fall down before him when he seemed to be in a good mood to ask for some money for clothes. He was very bountiful and gave each and every one of the Christian slaves four ducats to buy clothes. These coins are called "exchange-ducats" and their value corresponds to around twelve *daler kopparmynt*[21] each.

At the beginning of February, he gave us fifty baskets of apples, which made us forget his cruelty and made him [seem] more human, even if this only lasted for a short period. At the beginning of the year I was rather weak and sick. But there was no way to get any freedom from the hard work unless I could pay a daily sum of money to the bouscheven or the alcaides. {29} As soon as I could get money, I tried to avoid work, [since] I was afraid of getting worn out otherwise. If I had no money, neither ailment nor sickness allowed me to escape from constant slaving. Since our arrival, we had lived in very bad conditions here in Fez, because there was no way we could survive on what we were given daily by the emperor. All we had was the seven guineas[22] that I had managed to hide on the day of our capture, and fifty "exchange-ducats" that Consul Logie[23] in Algiers sent to us on 1 February 1755, even though no order was given from Sweden. Later, some Swedish merchant captains in Gibraltar, who were informed of our suffering, sent me eight ducats and sixteen blanquins. On 23 January, one of our Swedish boys died. His name was Gustav Lambrich, and after suffering from dropsy[24] for a long time, he died a terrible death. He died slowly and in pain while suffering from dropsy. He came from Öland and was the son of the late Vicar Lambrich and his now widowed and beloved mother. We, in great grief, buried him on the same day.

The uncontrollable temper of the emperor continued each day for the first months of the new year, although he treated his own officers much worse than us Christians. Sometimes he beat them with canes until we thought they would die, and sometimes he forced them to fight each other with biting and fencing, for the sake of his own amusement, until they seemed to die from their wounds. It is very frightful to watch when the emperor commands them to bite each other like wild dogs. {30} They fight

---

21. *daler kopparmynt*: a common currency in Sweden at the time.

22. *guinea*: a British gold coin.

23. *Consul Logie*: George Logie, the first Swedish consul to North Africa. He was appointed to Algiers in 1729 and remained there until 1758. See Gordon Boyce and Richard Gorski, *Resources and Infrastructures in the Maritime Economy, 1500–2000* (Oxford: Oxford University Press, 2017) 32, 32n31.

24. *dropsy*: edema, a buildup of fluid in the body that causes swelling.

naked and they bite big chunks of flesh from each other. Another [amusement of the emperor] is [to command] his subjects to hold onto each other's beards as they ride horses. When his servants beat the horses, each rider must keep hold of the other's beard.

Such horrible spectacles are his only amusement, and his temper shifts from clemency to cruelty. From being in a good temper he can suddenly turn into a tyrant, as he did on 1 March. On that day he gave baskets full of apples to twenty Christians, and shortly thereafter beat a Christian Portuguese who had been a slave for twenty-four years so badly that he looked almost dead. A Jew, captured together with Spaniards, struck a deal with the emperor for his ransom for three hundred pesos,[25] but a few days later he was forced to pay 560 ducats. You can never trust the emperor, since he often does the opposite [of what he has promised]. If one compares the highly dignified human, who asserts his gentleness, mercy, and justice, with the animal, [humankind] surpasses even the cruelest animal, because the human spares none of his own people if no upbringing or rules make the person docile. The barbarians are an example of how God's glorious people fell into horrible sin.

In March, the emperor was very good toward the Christians. When the weather was bad, with storms and rain, he even visited us while we were working and let us go back to Knuten. {31} He even gave us three days of freedom to celebrate Easter. Shortly afterward, however, his good mood turned to tyranny, and strangely enough, [this happened] after 13 April, which is the beginning of his Lent, or Ramadan. Ramadan is the Muhammadan name for Lent, which begins in April and continues for a three-month period, when the emperor fasts from dawn to dusk. But throughout the nights he drinks and rages like a madman together with his lords and officers. During this period he never visits any of his wives, because of his holiness. The Moors regard him as a saint and they believe that he holds conversations with Muhammad during this time. The Moors also celebrate this Lent, but only for one month.

During this time he went about murdering the majority of his highest-ranking officers, while others were whipped badly. The Christians were afflicted by even more hard work, and they were treated so badly by the alcaides, with beatings and blows, that they fell to the ground as if dead. We believed that we would never escape this situation, which continued

---

25. *peso*: a Spanish silver coin.

into the late hours, especially during the first fourteen days of their Lent, when the emperor was almost constantly present. But after a while, when he received a gift of red and blue cloth from the governor in Salé,[26] his mood became better. He immediately sent the gift to the Jews and ordered them to pay three thousand ducats for it, even though it was worth only three hundred ducats. By the end of April, news arrived of the coming of a huge party of "Brevers,"[27] which {32} worried the emperor a great deal, since he was not sure whether they came as friends or as foes. Brevers is the name of the people living in the countryside or in the mountains, and they travel through the country in their thousands. They travel with their women, children, cattle, and everything they own, and when they find a suitable spot, they set up their tents to farm the land. But after salvaging the harvest, they leave for another place, and since these parties challenge each other, they wage constant war. The victorious [group] confiscates the belongings of the other and scatters those who survive. They have constant hostilities with the cities, taking their cattle and possessions, which [the cities] also do in return. The emperor wished to have peace with the Brevers since he had lost so much due to their enmity. Seven times they took away his title as emperor and crowned his brother Mulli Gedris in his place, and for this reason the emperor feared their arrival, even if under other circumstances they would be considered his subjects.

On the morning of 30 April, we could see the Brevers from a long way away as they marched toward the castle. Their army had been told to gather sixteen thousand men, a number much greater than the emperor could summon. The emperor only had eight thousand blacks in Meknès, who were good soldiers, but whom he could not summon at such short notice. Even so, he deployed the blacks in his guard, consisting of 1,500 men, as well as half the Christians from the castle, [while] the other half manned the cannons in the city of Fez. In the castle, the emperor has twelve cannons of four pounds each, being six cannons of metal and six of bronze, {33} which were positioned on the field and manned by Christians, since the Moors did not understand how to use them, while on the city walls there were only eight iron cannons, damaged by rust, and also manned by us. The emperor rode on horseback in front of his blacks, armed with a lance and awaiting the arrival of the Brevers. When they were almost within

26. *Salé*: the base of the feared Sallee pirates. Berg spells it "Saleé" in the Swedish original.
27. *Brevers*: Berbers; pre-Arab inhabitants of North Africa.

firing range of the castle's cannons, they halted, sending forward the highest-ranking officers and eight hundred sheep, which the emperor considered to be a sign of peace. Therefore, he rode toward them alone and commanded that two donkeys, which could carry heavy loads, should follow him. They were loaded with powder and cannonballs. The emperor greeted the officers and received the eight hundred sheep in exchange for the ammunition, thereby confirming the peace agreement. Then he returned to his tent outside the castle, while the Brevers raised their tents on the area where they had stopped. After a while, the noblest Brever came to the emperor in his tent, telling him of their need of money and hoping that he, as their friend, could help. But [the emperor] answered that they had more riches then he had and that he would only receive money after ransoming his Christians. Instead, he asked them to live like brothers and assured them of his friendship. But without taking notice of his imperial assurance, they pushed him hard and forced him to hand over his own coat to one of the envoys. His nobles also had to give up their coats to others, who then finally left him in peace. {34} He had to repeat this compensation for four days during their stay, and when they finally left on 3 May, they took with them all his cattle, such as sheep and camels. He lost much of value during their stay, but even so, he was satisfied to get off cheaply, since they had actually dethroned him a number of times before.

The eight hundred sheep that the Brevers had offered the emperor were given to the blacks. They fell on them like wolves, but since the number of blacks was almost double that of the sheep, they pulled their big knives out and started to cut the living sheep in two, and then ran away with half a sheep on their backs. When those who did not get their share ran after them, they cut the other half in two. It was quite horrible to see how badly they treated the poor animals when they cut them into pieces.

Every day, the emperor was visited by other Brevers, whom he gave ten pesos each. Because of so many visitors, he was forced to leave his tent and enter his castle, and thus fewer of them could put pressure him. On 10 May, all the Christians were given ten blanquins each by the emperor with which to buy shoes or babouches.[28] The blacks were given five pesos each, and the Ludi ten pesos each, thereby demonstrating his unusually good mood. This lasted until the end of May.

---

28. *babouches:* a soft Moroccan slipper.

In June, the emperor started to treat the Christians badly again and murdered many of his own people, causing us to fear that we would be released from our slavery in a brutal manner. A Portuguese, who was alcaide over the Christians boys that attended {35} the emperor's horses, had beaten [the horses]. This information reached the emperor, who immediately called the Portuguese to him, asking him if he was a pig, which he was forced to answer with a "yes." Then the emperor said, "You can beat donkeys and carriers, but not horses, and therefore you shall no longer be my alcaide." After that he gathered together all the boys of the castle and commanded them to point their fingers at the Portuguese and yell: "He is a pig." Later, a Frenchman was appointed as the new horse alcaide, and the denounced Portuguese had to join us in our work. On 15 June, the emperor shot dead his own chef and one of his officers, while others were punished and whipped as usual. Not a single day passed without him enjoying some tyrannical act, as mentioned previously.

The emperor seemed to be in a better mood at the beginning of July, when he offered us thirty-nine baskets of apples, and on the twelfth of the same month, when Ramadan ended, we were given freedom from work as he celebrated his Easter, which they call Eidiseér.[29] But his clemency soon ended when he received information that the governor in Salé had given free passage to an English ship with a Turkish passport. This enraged him so much, even though he had ordered this, that he seized the brother of the governor and [had him] undressed and chained. On 18 June, the emperor himself cut at his head with five slashes of his saber. Because of this, there was great discord between Salé and the emperor, and also with his son, the prince of Morocco.

In the same period, around two hundred Brevers arrived and demanded to speak to the emperor, {36} who was riding his horse at that moment and had stopped by the pit where we were working. When the calls from the Brevers were not answered, they became very angry and started to yell "*Hamacca, Harrami, Karran*,"[30] which in their language are obscene taunts unfit for Christians and legally punishable, and tried to get to the emperor. But they could not reach him quickly enough, because the emperor charged

---

29. *Eidiseér*: in Arabic (Moroccan dialect): ʻ*Id-ṣ-ṣġīr*. This is also known as Eid al-Fitr or "the Festival of the Breaking of the Fast."

30. "*Hamacca, Harrami, Karran*": from the Arabic (Moroccan dialect): *Hamacca* = *Aḥmaq*, meaning "moron"; *Harrami* = *Harāmī*, meaning "bastard"; *Karran* = *Qarrān*, meaning "cuckold."

at full gallop toward his castle. None of those who had been enslaved for many years could remember seeing him ride as fast as he did that time. But they continued yelling and calling him obscene names and also asked us Christians how we could work for a person like Mulli Abdulla.[31] We answered that we were forced to do this. Then they asked us if we wanted to follow them and also promised us more freedom, but the old slaves who knew these Brevers assured us that they were much worse than the emperor. Therefore we refused their proposal. They rode away quite bitterly, wishing that they could have caught the emperor, and explaining that they would soon reduce his power.

On 20 June, the number of Christian slaves increased by twenty Frenchmen, not including twelve more who stayed in Tétouan, that had been taken from three French ships. The day after, another eight French slaves arrived from Morocco who praised our Swedish consul in Algiers, Mr. Logie, saying that he had helped them with food and money while the French consul had done nothing. {37} These eight arrived here because of the capture of the French captain, Mons. Calliou from Nantes, who was driven toward Algiers by a storm. The privateer[32] [who had captured Captain Calliou] brought him back to Salé and from there to Morocco. Since the prince of Morocco and the emperor of Fez owned one half of Salé each, the prince kept eight [of the crew], but not the captain, while the remaining eight were sent here. The privateer sailed a ship with three masts and armed with twelve cannons, and that was in the year 1756. Two three-masted privateers would be replaced by two new ones, equipped with eighteen and twenty cannons, meaning that there would be three ships in Salé and not more.

During the remainder of July, we were burdened with very heavy work clearing the ditches surrounding the castle and digging a deep well around which we built a high wall. Also, we had to raise a high pile of earth using the soil taken from the ditches. This pile was made for the emperor to sit upon, giving him a view over the flat land and thereby forcing us to work much longer than usual, especially on 26 July, when the emperor stayed with us the whole day. In a bitter mood, mounted on his horse with his hands over his head or on the pommel, he yelled constantly *"Derrup ferrani helluf,"*[33]

31. *Mulli Abdulla*: Moulay Abdallah.
32. *privateer*: a privately owned, armed vessel licensed to attack enemy ships, or the commander of such a vessel.
33. *Derrup ferrani helluf*: from the Arabic (Moroccan dialect): *ḍrub neṣrānī hallūf*; literally: "Beat the Christian swine." Note that Berg was very inconsistent with his spelling (see note 16).

meaning "Beat the Christian swine." While the froth from his mouth floated down onto his clothes, the alcaides beat the Christians until they were blue, and many of us were so badly beaten that we had to be carried home on litters when our work finally ended at eleven o'clock at night. Each and every one can imagine {38} the pain we suffered that night and how little rest we were given before the next day of work. Our bodies were so sore that we could not get any sleep. We feared that the emperor would be in the same bad mood the following day, but to our relief he was not. Instead, he gave all the Christians a red cloth for a garment, while the French, whom he liked more, were also given trousers. His good temper continued until the end of the month. At that time, he organized a huge banquet and meant to invite the noblest people from the city of Fez and Fezvillie, but when everything was in order and the food was taken to his tent, he assembled all the Christians and ordered them to position themselves away from the tent. After that, the meal was taken to us with the order to eat it. We expected this to be organized properly, but when we discovered that those first in line not only started to eat with great appetite but also hid huge chunks of food, the situation changed so that the strongest also got the best food. The dinner was really good and cooked in the Spanish manner by the wives of the emperor. We saw this good treatment as a sign of the emperor's positive mood, but things soon changed, and the emperor forced us to pay for the dinner with work and beatings once more.

At the beginning of August we received favorable news in a letter from Captain Weilli[34] in Tétouan, saying that Consul Bellman[35] in Cádiz had been informed by our Royal Highness the King that he would graciously pay our ransom. This was {39} delightful, even if [we] could only [express ourselves] with faithful and fervent prayers to the almighty God, the ruler of everything, that He would give strength to His anointed, and also confer on [the Swedish king] every royal bliss, [which would bring] joy to the subjects under his rule. Our own suffering continued on a daily basis, but with better hope, which gave us more steadfastness and patience to withstand all cruelties.

---

34. *Captain Weilli*: captain of the ship *Concordia* from Kalmar.
35. *Consul Bellman*: Jacob Martin Bellman, the Swedish consul at Cádiz from 1744 to 1766. He regularly cooperated with Consul Logie to release Swedish prisoners from Barbary. See Leos Müller, *Consuls, Corsairs, and Commerce: The Swedish Consular Service and Long-Distance Shipping, 1720–1815* (Stockholm: Elanders Gotab, 2004), 107.

On 12 August, one of the holy Muhammadans arrived from Mecca to pay a visit to the emperor, carrying with him the flag of Muhammad, which is white. The emperor intercepted him on a horse and [greeted him by] dismounting. They hugged and kissed each other in a friendly manner. Thereafter, the emperor kissed the flag and rode back. The holy flag was taken into the castle to be kissed by all of the emperor's wives, which was a very honorable act. The month of August ended in ordinary hardship and without any news about our time of release. September started with similar doubts, but because of the new situation, the emperor was quite balanced and [showed] goodwill at this time as well as at the end of the previous month.

On 12 September, all the emperor's blacks[36] arrived from Meknès, consisting of eight thousand men on horseback. They are given no salary, but instead are supposed to be happy with the gifts they are given by the emperor when they meet him once a year. This is because they are slaves, not free men.

{40} This time they received 50,000 pieces of eight[37] together with orders to travel back home to their relatives, and then immediately to return to follow the Emperor on a planned journey to Tétouan or Salé. But this was canceled because his son, the prince of Morocco, traveled to Salé [instead].

During this time, Brevers arrived in large numbers to greet the emperor, but they left disappointed, since he had few resources and they received nothing from him. News from Salé reported that the prince of Morocco had enforced on the Christian merchants and the Moors an unusual tax that exceeded 200,000 ducats and that he had killed an Englishman named Master Mouhntens because of his refusal to pay the money.

On 17 September, a letter from Alcaide Lucas in Tétouan eventually reached the emperor regarding the ransom for thirteen Swedes and nine of the French. However, two of our own were dead, and therefore we were [only] eleven Swedes. For this reason, the emperor added us to the French and replied that he wanted one hundred cannonballs for each and every one

---

36. *the Emperor's blacks*: the "Black Guard" or the Abid al-Bukhari, which was a corps of forcibly recruited, mostly sub-Saharan slave soldiers that had been created by Moulay Ismail (ruled 1672–1727). After his death, however, the army became a destabilizing force and was frequently involved in intrigues and coups. For more information, see chaps. 5 and 6 of Chouki el Hamel, *Black Morocco: A History of Slavery, Race, and Islam* (Cambridge: Cambridge University Press, 2014).

37. *piece of eight*: a Spanish silver coin also known as the Spanish dollar or peso.

of the twenty Christians. The agreement said that he would not let any of them leave until all the Christians were ransomed, since he was afraid of losing the French. Three of them served him constantly at the castle and were responsible for all of his communications. Therefore, he wrote to Demetrii in Tétouan regarding the question of ransoming all the Christians, and our release was in God's hand. We lived in good hope, praising God and our compassionate ruler for giving {41} thought to our misery. Even so, we felt abandoned and forgotten by all our former friends and relatives in Sweden, since we never received any letters or news from home during our long time here, even though we had written to Sweden a number of times. We did not know whether any of our letters had arrived or not.

On 17 September there was a Moorish holiday called Eidilkebir,[38] when all the Christians were free from work.

On 18 September, a *marquet* arrived from Tétouan. That is the name for a band of traders who travel from one city to another, like a caravan. They try to stay together and [the group] usually consists of one hundred mules or camels. With this marquet, one thousand cannonballs were brought to the emperor as a gift for the nine French, which made him ask why the entire sum had not been paid as [he had] demanded for the twenty Christians, since he counted us, the Swedes, together with them.

By the end of September, I was very sick, but even so, I was forced to work. My mate Cornelius Helm and the boy Hans Lund were both sick with fever.

At the beginning of October, there was sickness among many of us Swedes, worsening our situation even more.

{42} On 16 October, a *caffilie* arrived, which is almost the same as a marquet, but consisting of not more than forty to fifty mules or camels, bringing all the Christian slaves from Tétouan except the Swedes. [The Swedes] consisted of Captain Weilli and five of our crew, who worked as carpenters finishing galleys. The number of Christian slaves who arrived from Tétouan amounted to twenty, namely twelve Spaniards and eight Frenchmen. No Frenchman, even if he is a carpenter, is prepared to agree to

---

38. *Eidilkebir*: in Arabic (Moroccan dialect): ʿĪd-l-kebir. This is also known as Eid al-Adh or "the Festival of the Sacrifice." Berg is inconsistent with his spelling, writing it *Ei dilkebyr* earlier in the text (see note 11).

work [at building galleys]. Instead, they say that they are more willing to suffer than to contribute to the making of tools[39] for the persecution of Christians. Even so, letters arrived from Alcaide Lucas in Tétouan, confirming our ransom [as well as that of] the nine French and the eleven Portuguese. But since the emperor received no information from the agent Demetrii, who was responsible for our affairs and who was supposed to communicate with the emperor on behalf of the Europeans, the emperor did not believe the alcaide. Instead, he sent one of his men to Tétouan on 20 October to gather information about the ransom negotiations for the Christians. The emperor told his men that if they brought good news back on the issue, then all the Christian slaves would leave for Tétouan. But these thoughts, advantageous for us, did not prevail for long. Because almost at the moment when he spoke them, [his thoughts] changed.

On 1 November at half past ten, we had a huge and terrible earthquake[40] which continued for ten minutes. The earth trembled and moved up and down, {43} making people unable to stand and causing them to fall. A loud rumbling and churning sound came from the ground, [which] cracked and spilled huge amounts of water in different places. In some places the water was completely red, and in other places all yellow. A huge section of the wall around our prison fell. The houses crumbled, except for an almost completely ruined old fortress in Fez, and the water in the moats spilled from one side to the other. The color of the sky changed and the heavens seemed to open up in the southwest. Humans as well as animals were terrified; barbarians pointed toward the heavens with their fingers, took off their turbans, shouting *Arbia*,[41] which means "God." Because of my sickness, I stayed in Knuten that day and therefore had more freedom to watch the miracles and the supreme power of the Almighty. This moment made me reflect on our merciful Savior's gracious prophecy on the release of man according to the Gospel of Luke, chapter 21, verse 25. This would occur with signs in the sun and in the moon and in the stars; on Earth, humans would be in anguish and they would despair; the sea and the waves would roar, and the people would languish in fear for the

---

39. *tools*: Berg is referring to the building of galleys.

40. *terrible earthquake*: Berg describes the seismic activity also responsible for the great Lisbon earthquake of 1 November 1755 that destroyed large parts of the city of Lisbon, killing thousands of its inhabitants.

41. *Arbia*: in Arabic (Moroccan dialect): *ā-rabbiya*, meaning "oh my Lord."

future of the earth.[42] What could resemble these prophecies of the end of the world better than this terrifying moment when the earth seemed to topple over, the sea rose, and animals trembled with fear? O Almighty, how little we express gratitude for Your compassion and how unprepared You will find Your people for Your terrible coming! Everlasting God, without Your unwarranted mercy, how could we escape Your righteousness? Lord, think of Your compassion and not of our trespasses! Fill our hearts with Your Holy Spirit for us to strengthen our faith in your beloved Son Jesus Christ. {44} From His example, His bitter suffering and innocent death, strengthen us in our suffering and make us raise our heads with joy while awaiting the release and the reward that our gentle Savior, on this great day of the holy gospel, has promised His patient bearer of the cross. Give His mercy to us and all the chosen saints. Pray to Him in front of the throne, upon our faces, and say: Amen! Praise, honor, wisdom, thanks, supremacy, and strength to our God for ever and ever. Amen. Book of Rev. 6:7.[43]

Over the course of the following days, we received news from different places about the saddening consequences of the terrible earthquake. The capital of Barbary, Meknès, crumbled completely, and more than one million Moors and Jews died. A marquet traveling from Salé to Morocco was engulfed completely in one of the cracks in the earth, resulting in the death of four hundred individuals and a large number of mules and camels loaded with merchant goods. In the city of Fezvillie, many houses collapsed and many citizens were killed. Twenty-two Moors and one woman completely lost their minds during this miserable event.

Only one house collapsed in Fez and for that reason large parties of Ludi visited the emperor, thanking him for his prayers to God and Muhammad and for thereby saving their city from destruction during the earthquake. For they think that the emperor, {45} through Muhammad, can do whatever he

---

42. *This would occur [. . .] future of the earth*: "And there shall be signs in the sun, and in the moon, and in the stars; and upon the earth distress of nations, with perplexity; the sea and the waves roaring; Men's hearts failing them for fear, and for looking after those things which are coming on the earth: for the powers of heaven shall be shaken. And then shall they see the Son of man coming in a cloud with power and great glory. And when these things begin to come to pass, then look up, and lift up your heads; for your redemption draweth nigh" (Luke 21:25–28, *KJV*).

43. *Book of Rev. 6:7*: Berg sometimes gets his biblical references wrong. He probably meant Revelations 7:11–12: "And all the angels stood round about the throne, and about the elders and the four beasts, and fell before the throne on their faces, and worshipped God, Saying, Amen: Blessing, and glory, and wisdom, and thanksgiving, and honor, and power, and might, be unto our God for ever and ever. Amen" (*KJV*).

wishes. They asked him about the reason for this terrible accident, and he answered that a great ox was traveling from sunset to sunrise and that the ox moved his horns from the left to the right side during the journey, thereby causing these movements of the elements.

At nine o'clock in the afternoon on 16 November, we felt a strong earthquake with terrible rumbling and cracking in the earth, continuing for three minutes. The houses shook and we feared that they would fall down upon us at any moment. At half past nine as well as at ten o'clock, we had two more earthquakes, which were fairly intense but not as strong. But within one hour, we had three more earthquakes, causing much surprise and fear among the Christians, since the great wall around Knuten started to fall down. This caused many Christians as well as the Catholic priests to leave Knuten and lie down under the open sky, since the weather was very good during the night.

Horror was also taking hold of the barbarians, and they ran out of the city in huge numbers to the tallest heights they could find to sing and call upon God and Muhammad. For eight days the emperor did not dare to leave his tent and enter the castle, because he had been in bed at the moment when the earthquake had started. He had been so horrified when the castle started to rumble and all his guns fell down that he ran out in such a hurry that they could not catch up with him and his horse until he was outside the courtyard. It is said that nobody had ever {46} seen the emperor run as fast as that time. The Jews were also terrified and did not dare to stay in their houses. Instead, they lived in tents for a long time and held ceremonies of penance and lamented the loss of the Jews in Meknès.

On 22 November, at seven o'clock in the morning, a strong rumble was heard with cracking, which also caused some tremors in the earth, but it only lasted for a minute.

On 23 November we were ordered to reduce [the height of] the high wall around Knuten by six ells,[44] while the remaining wall was still fourteen ells high.

---

44. *ell*: a unit of measurement based roughly on the length of a forearm and hand. The exact length differed by country. In Sweden from 1605 to 1863, this corresponded to 23.37 inches (59.38 cm).

For the rest of this month we were not burdened so badly with work as previously. The French captain and I enjoyed freedom, because the alcaide had treated me better since the news about our ransom had reached us in October, even though we still had no information on a date [for our release].

By the beginning of December, we had received news from different places about the horrible effects that the earthquake of 1 November had caused in Europe, and we were especially amazed at the destruction of the large and beautiful city of Lisbon and of the pitiful deaths of thousands of people. It was also told that Cádiz had suffered great damage when it was hit by water.[45]

Our hope of liberation from Barbary slavery was finally assured by a letter that I received on 1 December from the {47} Swedish consul in Cádiz, Mr. Jacob Bellman. He confirmed the decision by His Royal Highness our most gracious King regarding our ransom, which had been made a year ago already, and that [his orders] had been sent to Messrs. Colleti and Patissiati in Tétouan, who should have hastened our release, but did not care about it. During all the time we had been here, they never communicated with the emperor, thereby causing [the emperor] to doubt whether our rulers were interested in ransoming us.

Due to the good mood of the emperor, I asked one of his priests, who is called *Sanctos*, or holy, to write a supplication to him in the name of all the Christians with the request that he would allow us travel back to our countries in exchange for the ransom that was offered by our rulers, and also mentioning to him that our country was far away and that our nation had never caused him any harm. These together with many more arguments were presented by the *Sanctos*. My navigating officer, Cornelius Helm, delivered the letter to the emperor on 18 December, who immediately summoned the sanct who had written the letter to read it to him, since he could not read or write. When he had heard the [content of the] letter, he replied "*Bono svecus*,"[46] and added that, as soon as the messenger he had sent returned from Tétouan, the Christians from Sweden could take their leave. This made us very happy and we also wished that

---

45. *hit by water*: Berg is referring to the devastating tsunami caused by the earthquake, which, according to modern calculations, produced waves of "a height of 14 to 16.5 meters." See Blanc, "Earthquakes and Tsunami in November 1755 in Morocco," 726.

46. *Bono svecus*: Latin for "good Swedes."

the emperor was always in as good a temper as he had [then] been for more than a month. On 19 December he gave us seventeen baskets of dates and ordered us to sit down and eat them and if any Moor tried to take anything from us, [the emperor] would crush his head. During this {48} period we received even more kindness from the emperor. When all the Christian slaves fell down before him and complained that the Jews did not want to pay the blanquin that each and every [slave] should have had as a salary to live on, he [told] the Christians that if the Jews did not pay, the Christians should beat them and force them to pay. He also said that the Christians should not suffer, because he was their father and they had no one else. During this time he called us his Christians and ordered that no Moor should do us any harm. In this way the Almighty softens the tyrannical heart of the barbarian when He wants to aid someone. It is true that nobody can escape the powerful hand of the Lord. He softens the hard-hearted. Oh! We [are] miserable wretches who know the word of God and still abandon the source of all help.

On 22 December there was a big battle between the Brevers and the Ludi, who, with the [help of] the emperor's black [soldiers], won and took over six thousand beasts such as camels, horses, and a huge amount of sheep and goats from the Brevers. The battle took place so close to the castle that we were able to see the fighting. Their battles are fought in a rather confusing way. They are all mounted and they ride toward each other without any order. After the first volley is shot, they pull their sabers to challenge a man, and they are so mixed up that no one can separate friend from foe. The emperor was in his tent, coldheartedly watching the battle, but some of his men participated in the battle. {49} On the emperor's side, seven Ludi were killed in total and two wounded; on the other side, a huge number of Brevers were killed and badly wounded.

On 24 December, or Christmas Eve, we bowed in front of the emperor and asked leave to celebrate Christmas, which he granted by giving us three days of freedom. On the fourth day of Christmas, two Moors visited the emperor to complain about each other. Then the emperor ordered two loaded muskets [to be brought], with which he shot both of the Moors. He ordered that they should be taken to the Saint Sidi Grip's[47]

---

47. *Saint Sidi Grip*: Islam does not actually have saints. However, in Morocco, the tombs of numerous holy men and women are the object of pilgrimages. It is not clear exactly which "saint" Berg is referring to.

grave and said that tomorrow they would meet Muhammad, who would settle their quarrel. Such a quick execution, which is faster than [a legal dispute], terrifies the people [and creates] disunity. How unhappy are these people who have to expect both joy and unhappiness from the law spoken by such a spiteful and disordered mind that, at one moment, murders for a trifle and without reflection, while at the next, kills for a good reason.

During this time, the emperor was weak, engaging in a form of excess called *poulins*[48] by the French. He could neither walk nor ride, and therefore he used a small carriage pulled by his noblest men, which took him wherever he wished. He sent the Christian alcaide Paulus to the Catholic priests and demanded medication for his illness. When they went to cure him, which had a positive effect, he told the monks graciously that they are a humble kind who wished him well.

{50} The Catholic priests are always equipped with medicine and they understand a number of diseases better than any quack.

We celebrated Christmas as best we could under the circumstances, but unfortunately we experienced that there was not the mutual love and trust that there should have been between us Christians. With grief I have to confess that some of my own compatriots disagreed with me many times. May God forgive them for [these disagreements] and remind them of all the sound advice I shared with a good heart. [May God remind them] that many prayed for us in Sweden, [and that they should] not act immorally and hinder God's cause. But [since] everyone followed their lusts, a better way of life could not be expected. Many Christians despised any admonitions and anyone who tried to live quietly and decently was mocked. Instead, the one who drank, swore, and caroused was seen as a brave man and quickly won the respect of the malicious. [It is] wretched and miserable living among [such] Christians, who [do not] submit to the Christian law in a land without law. But may the Lord Almighty convert them from their evil ways and give us grace to put aside our old

---

48. *poulins*: Berg's reference is not clear.

selves and, with the coming of the New Year, renew our life according to His rules.

[*Berg was finally ransomed and able to leave Morocco on 6 September 1756, together with the surviving members of his crew, except for two young boys, who, contrary to the agreement, were not released.*]

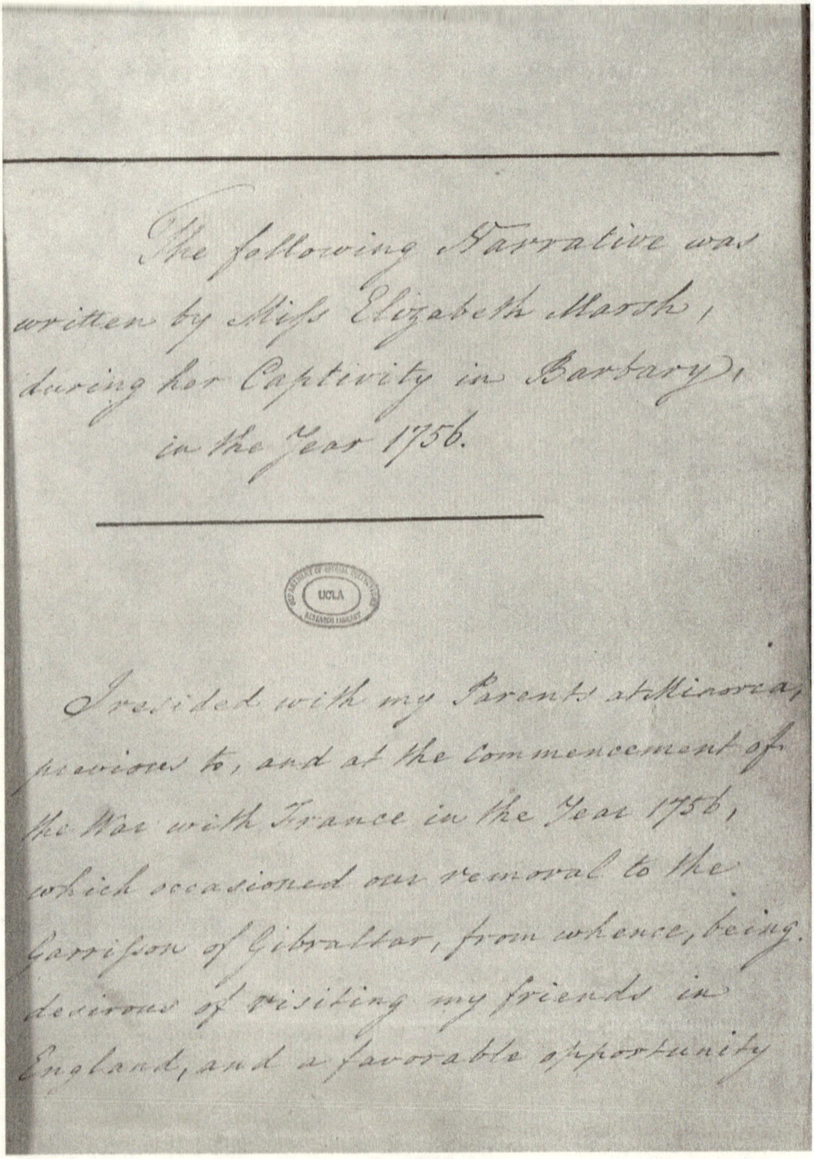
The following Narrative was written by Miss Elizabeth Marsh, during her Captivity in Barbary, in the Year 1756.

I resided with my Parents at Minorca, previous to, and at the commencement of the War with France in the Year 1756, which occasioned our removal to the Garrison of Gibraltar, from whence, being desirous of visiting my friends in England, and a favorable opportunity

Figure 12.1 Title page of Elizabeth Marsh's narrative

Source: Elizabeth Marsh, *Narrative of Her Captivity in Barbary* (1756); Bound Manuscripts Collection (Collection 170), Library Special Collections, Charles E. Young Research Library, University of California, Los Angeles.

CHAPTER XII

ELIZABETH MARSH, *NARRATIVE OF ELIZABETH MARSH'S CAPTIVITY IN BARBARY*

Undated British manuscript; complete captivity narrative

Captivity in Morocco 1756

The narrative by Elizabeth Marsh about her experiences in Morocco in 1756 is the oldest known British Barbary account by a female captive. The young Englishwoman was seized by Moroccan corsairs on a voyage from Gibraltar to England on 8 August 1756 and brought to Salé, Morocco, together with the rest of the ship's crew and passengers. In an arduous three hundred mile journey on the back of a mule, Marsh traveled to the Moroccan capital Meknès, where she was presented to Prince Sidi Muhammad. To protect herself from the advances of the prince, she pretended to be married to her fellow captive, James Crisp, a London merchant. After a comparatively short captivity of four months, Elizabeth Marsh was able to return to England, where she married James Crisp. In 1769, more than ten years after her liberation, she published her experiences in an anonymous print edition.

Marsh's description of her ordeals in North Africa distinguishes her narrative from earlier testimonies. Whereas most other Barbary narratives dwell on various aspects of the country, trying to describe the foreign culture in an ethnographic manner, Marsh is almost exclusively concerned with herself. Thus, her testimony becomes quite interesting in terms of narrative perspective. Also, her diction is revealing in this respect. It abounds with sensory impressions, bodily conditions, thirst, heat, hunger, noise, pain, etc. It seems as if we, as readers, experience her captivity solely through the eyes and body of Elizabeth Marsh herself. This subjective perspective, coupled with the strong introspective tendencies of the first-person narrator, introduces a new mode of representing Barbary captivity. This is not to say that older narratives did not communicate personal feelings. However, the intensity and the quantity of Marsh's sensory analysis and mental introspection is quite unusual when compared with older specimens of the genre, but very much in line with contemporary trends in the eighteenth-century novel.

Marsh's narrative is indebted to sentimental plots in eighteenth-century fiction, which centered on female characters whose virtue is challenged by the sexual advances of powerful men. Samuel Richardson's novel *Pamela; or, Virtue Rewarded* (1740) is a case in point. What we see in Richardson and his imitators is a curious amalgamation of voyeuristic descriptions of the sufferings of the female protagonists, coupled with sentimental pleas for empathy for their plight. All these ingredients are also at work in Elizabeth Marsh's narrative, in which she dwells on her own steadfastness in the face of sexual threat and the temptations of exotic luxury and power. This analysis of her testimony by no means intends to downplay the authenticity of Marsh's experiences and her personal suffering during her captivity. It does, however, aim to point out that authentic captivity accounts were invariably shaped by the larger trends of the time, especially literary trends.

With respect to themes of sentimentality and voyeurism, it is telling that the English philosopher Edmund Burke published his influential text *A Philosophical Enquiry into the Origin of Our Ideas of the Sublime and Beautiful* (1757) around the same time as Marsh released her narrative. Burke was interested in why humans enjoy being exposed to the sufferings of others. In other words, why do people experience voyeuristic pleasure when learning about the misery of others? Burke explains this innate human behavior as a humanitarian predisposition. He claims that humans are by nature inclined to want to watch the suffering of others, which in turn increases the likelihood that the observer takes action against the injustice that caused the pain of the one suffering.[1] While Burke's rationalization is general and not aimed particularly at explaining the logic of the sentimental novel, it does attempt to shed light on the fascination his contemporaries had with descriptions of human misery, whether fictional or authentic.

In addition to the printed text that was published anonymously in 1756, an undated handwritten manuscript that is most likely a copy of Marsh's

---

1. On Burke, see Mario Klarer, "Humanitarian Pornography: John Gabriel Stedman's *Narrative of a Five Years Expedition Against the Revolted Negroes of Surinam* (1796)," *New Literary History* 36, no. 4 (2005): 559–87.

autograph has survived. One would assume that the printed narrative would be tweaked by publishers or editors to fit the taste of a contemporary readership, especially with respect to the introspective focus on the first-person narrator and her suffering. However, when comparing the manuscript version, which is included in this anthology, with the print edition of 1769, the differences are less significant than one might expect. This means that Marsh intuitively internalized the logic of fictional narration that was popular at the time and allowed it to shape her authentic account of captivity in Morocco.

One can only speculate as to why Elizabeth Marsh decided to have her captivity narrative published. In the introduction to her printed edition, Marsh hints at the looming accusations against her: "that the Misfortunes I met with in Barbary have been more than equaled by those I have since experienced, in this Land of Civil and Religious Liberty."[2] As a female captive, Marsh had to defend herself against insinuations that she had not refrained from sexual contact with Muslim men, and the Moroccan ruler in particular. Another problem that arose for Marsh after her return to England was her pretended marriage to James Crisp. What seemed like a perfect way to ward off advances of Moroccan men backfired when her fake marriage in Morocco threatened to jeopardize Marsh's eligibility for marriage in England. This might be one of the reasons why Crisp and Marsh married after their return.

As the case of Elizabeth Marsh shows, female returnees from North African captivity were confronted with numerous direct and indirect accusations: Marsh had to demonstrate her religious steadfastness by refusing to convert to Islam as well as her sexual integrity with respect to both Muslim *and* Christian men during her captivity. This left Marsh in a very precarious situation. It is possible that the publication of the narrative was also her way to counter these insinuations via a straightforward and unwavering testimony that left no doubt about what happened in Morocco. *The Female Captive: A Narrative of Facts, which Happened in Barbary, in the Year 1756, Written by Herself* (London: C. Bathurst, 1769) was published anonymously, which would rather argue to the contrary: But despite the fact that her name was not on the title page of the first printed edition, rumors identifying her with the first-person narrator of the *The Female Captive* spread fast.

---

2. Khalid Bekkaoui (ed.), *White Women Captives in North Africa: Narrative of Enslavement, 1735–1830* (Basingstoke, UK: Palgrave Macmillan, 2011), 124.

Notes on the Present Edition of Elizabeth Marsh's *Narrative of Elizabeth Marsh's Captivity in Barbary*

The present edition has been transcribed from the manuscript held at the Charles E. Young Research Library: Elizabeth Marsh, "Narrative I: Narrative of Her Captivity in Barbary" (MS 170/604, Charles E. Young Research Library, Special Collections, University of California, Los Angeles). Only the first narrative ("Narrative I"), which relates Marsh's experience in Morocco, has been reproduced here (not the second part of the manuscript, which recounts her travels in India from 1774 to 1776). The manuscript is unpaginated; for ease of reference, page numbers have been assigned to the text and placed in square brackets, starting with the first page of the narrative. Pages are counted consecutively (not according to the recto/verso system). Elizabeth Marsh's spelling, punctuation, and capitalization have been standardized, and additional paragraph breaks have been added in order to enhance the readability of the narrative.

Elizabeth Marsh, *Narrative of Elizabeth Marsh's Captivity in Barbary* (Undated Manuscript; MS 170/604, Charles E. Young Research Library, Special Collections, University of California, Los Angeles)

[1] I resided with my parents at Minorca,[3] previous to, and at the commencement of the war with France in the year 1756,[4] which occasioned our removal to the garrison of Gibraltar, from whence, being desirous of visiting my friends in England, and a favourable opportunity [2] offering of a ship, in which a friend of my family (James Crisp Esqr.)[5] was going passenger, I embarked on the 29th of April.[6] The ship was under convoy of one of His

---

3. *Minorca*: also known as Menorca; one of the Balearic Islands in the Mediterranean that became British territory in the early eighteenth century.

4. *war with France [. . .] 1756*: the Seven Years' War, involving most of Europe, led by Britain on the one side and France on the other.

5. *James Crisp Esqr.*: a British merchant. See Linda Colley, *The Ordeal of Elizabeth Marsh: How a Remarkable Woman Crossed Seas and Empires to Become Part of World History* (London: Harper Perennial, 2014), 49. All subsequent references to Colley follow this edition.

6. *29th of April*: according to the present-day Gregorian calendar, this would be 27 July 1756 (Colley, *The Ordeal of Elizabeth Marsh*, 49).

Majesty's frigates, but we were unhappily deserted by her commander soon after losing sight of the garrison. When our captain perceived his intention of quitting his convoy, he carried all the sail he could in order to keep up with the king's ship, even to the danger of our lives.

On the 8th of May we were chased by a vessel which our captain, at first, imagined to be a French privateer,[7] but she proved to be [3] a Sallee rover,[8] which soon came up with us, and it was deemed more prudent to wait for her than, by endeavouring to escape, run a risk of being very ill-treated, if not put to death. The Moorish commander instantly came on board and enquired into the number of passengers, there being two others besides my friend, Mr. Crisp. He desired they would go with him on board his ship, promising not to detain them more than half an hour. They accordingly went and I made myself as easy as I could until night came on, when fear seized my spirits at their not returning. I [4] continued in that state until the morning, which brought on new affliction, for instead of seeing the gentlemen, boats crowded with Moors came on board our ship and the sailors were sent on board theirs.

In this unhappy situation I remained three days, when I had the pleasure to see my friend return, who informed me of his having with great difficulty obtained leave of the commander of the cruiser to visit me for a few hours, telling him I was his sister. After the time elapsed which had been granted, I was again thrown into great distress at this second separation, from the dread of being exposed to the Moors, who would [5] have behaved very ill to me had it not been for our ship's steward. Soon after the next day appeared, the Moorish commander and officers came on board, bringing with them an interpreter, who, in bad English, informed me I must go with them, at which, and the sea running very high, my mind was greatly terrified, for we were at a considerable distance from the cruiser. When I got on board, I saw our sailors tied together, but my friend and the other passengers were at liberty. A cabin was allotted for us which was so small as not to admit our standing upright. In this miserable place, four people were [6] to live, their provisions very bad, being a kind of paste resembling sago,[9] called by the Moors cuscussu.[10] This was served for dinner and supper. Almonds and raisins were my only support.

   7. *privateer*: a privately owned, armed vessel licensed to attack enemy ships.
   8. *Sallee rover*: a pirate ship from Sallee (now Salé, Morocco).
   9. *sago*: edible starch made from the pith of certain palms.
   10. *cuscussu*: couscous, a dish made by steaming crushed durum wheat (or other grains).

On the 14th, land was seen, and soon after [we] were near to a town called Mamora.[11] They fired two guns and hoisted the colours. At nine in the evening they came to an anchor in Sallee Road,[12] when a number of boats came off with drums and a sort of music which pleased those infidels, though it struck me with the greatest terrors imaginable. I found this rejoicing was, as customary with them, to make acclamations of joy upon [7] such occasions. We remained on board that night, and the next morning were ordered to our ship to take what necessaries we thought fit. I stayed in the boat while my friend endeavoured to get my clothes, but he was only allowed to bring away a small quantity for present use, and our bedding. We then left the ship, but the tide not permitting our going over the bar,[13] we were obliged to come to anchor and remain three hours exposed to a scorching sun, no fresh water, and my thirst intolerable. On crossing the bar, we were landed at a sandy beach, which was covered with thousands of Moors, shouting and hallooing, and [8] my friend and I put upon mules without saddles, with a man on each side to guard me from falling. In this manner we went two miles over a heavy sand, a band of music before us more dismal than a funeral drum, and repeated insults from the natives. The other passengers were on foot, and the sailors [were] dragged along and treated with great severity. We proceeded to the bashaw's,[14] who received us with seeming concern, ordered his guards to conduct us to a place half a mile farther, and all the way a great noise of women's voices from the tops of the houses, which I was informed was a testimony of joy on the arrival of a female [9] captive.

When we got to the habitation destined for us, a long passage presented itself to our view, at the end of which was a square ground floor with two rooms opposite each other and a gallery at the top, but no words can express the wretchedness of it. The best apartment was for me and the other passengers, the rest for our servants and the ship's crew, and a strong guard at the door. Soon after a slave brought some grapes, bread, and a pitcher of water. In the evening, I had a visit from the monster who brought me into that

11. *Mamora*: now Mehdya, Morocco. It was known as La Mamora while under Spanish rule (1614–1681).

12. *Sallee Road*: the port of Salé on the Atlantic coast of Morocco. They landed here on 15 August (Colley, *The Ordeal of Elizabeth Marsh*, 53).

13. *bar*: a hazardous sandbar in front of the Salé harbor.

14. *bashaw*: a high-ranking official in the Ottoman world. In Morocco, this was frequently used as the term for the governor of a city. In other texts in this anthology, the word has been translated as *basha*. However, in the case of texts originally written in English, "bashaw" has been retained.

country, attended by some principal Moors of the place. He assured me we should have our liberty as [10] soon as the emperor's[15] answer was returned from Morocco,[16] to the letter he had sent. On the next day, we had the pleasure of seeing two gentlemen, merchants of New Sallee,[17] one an Englishman, and therefore much concerned at our situation; the other French, who behaved with great civility to us all, and gave us hopes that His Imperial Highness's answer would be favourable and that he would undoubtedly order us to be set at liberty. When these gentlemen left us, my apartment was crowded with men, women, and children, among the number, a nephew of the Moorish captains, who endeavoured to separate us from our baggage [11] with a view to plunder but were prevented by my friend. Our friends, the merchants, advised our writing to Gibraltar, offering to provide a person who should safely convey our letters. We accordingly passed the night in writing to my father and to the governor of Gibraltar.

We had an invitation from the captain of the port, and on our waiting on him the next day, found him sitting on a carpet. He rose on our entering the apartment and handed me a cushion, conversed with my friend in Spanish, and then conducting me to the apartment of the ladies, introduced me to them and retired. One of them drew [12] my attention. She was very tall and stout with a broad flat face, very dark complexion, and long black hair. She wore a dress resembling a clergyman's gown, made of muslin and buttoned on the neck like the collar of a shirt, which reached her feet. She had bracelets on her arms and legs and was extremely inquisitive and curious in examining my dress. I was then conducted to the room where the captain of the port and my friend were sitting. Preparations were made for supper, which was after the Moorish taste and consisted of a dish of cuscussu and fowls, mixed with butter and sugar. The other dishes were of fruit and sweetmeats. This honest [13] Moor, for such I thought him, often expressed much concern at our misfortunes and I believe would readily have rendered us his service, but though he was a man in a high station, did not dare openly to pity our distresses. From his abode, we hastened to our place of confinement, where I passed the night with many afflicting thoughts

---

15. *the emperor*: Prince Sidi Muhammad (ca. 1710–1790), ruled from 1757 to 1790. While Moulay Abdallah was officially still the sultan of Morocco in 1756, in practice his son Sidi Muhammad was the absolute ruler (Colley, *The Ordeal of Elizabeth Marsh*, 58).

16. *Morocco*: Marsh is referring to the city of Marrakech, at the time an imperial city of Morocco (Colley, *The Ordeal of Elizabeth Marsh*, 62).

17. *New Sallee*: now Rabat, Morocco.

of what another day might produce. Indeed, my prepossessions were not groundless, for before I had breakfasted, the Moorish captain's nephew, with a great number of others, came and insisted on placing us in another apartment and leaving our baggage, under a guard, in the room we were in. This behaviour raised various [14] conjectures. My friend endeavoured to prevent their designs, but it only served to heighten their malice, and they redoubled their insults, which obliged us to acquiesce, and as every other means but patience was wrested from us, we had recourse to that sovereign remedy in all calamities of life.

The room appointed for us, as I have already observed, was much the best in the prison. That which they [subsequently] chose to place us in had one end of the ceiling open, occasioned by an earthquake, where I experienced great inconveniences from the dews, and besides this inhumanity, orders were given that none of our friends should be [15] admitted and our servants were hindered from going to procure such necessaries as we were in want of. At the same time, the rabble were permitted to enter our apartments at any hour. Being deprived of the company of our friends, who had shown us so many civilities, grieved me much. I tried what a bribe might do, which fortunately had the desired effect, and we were so happy to see them the same evening.

On the next morning, a Spanish *renegado*[18] came in great haste to inform us that he heard there was a person of consequence hourly expected from Morocco to conduct us safe on board our ship, [16] but the intelligence soon proved false by a letter from Monsieur Ray (the aforementioned French gentleman's name), acquainting us of a messenger being arrived from Morocco to attend us thither. We had but just got the information when his approach was announced, and with him, the governor of the place and several others, who told us we must prepare in five days for a journey to Morocco, and that he was one of the number to escort us; that his orders from His Imperial Highness were to travel gently on my account, resting in the day and proceeding on in the night that I might not be too much fatigued with the heat. But I was terrified [17] beyond expression, which the messenger perceiving, flattered me with hopes that as soon as the emperor had seen me (which I was made to believe was only what he wanted), I should be sent back immediately to Sallee, with liberty to leave Barbary. They then left us and the Almighty ordained that I should receive consolation from the fallacy

---

18. *renegado*: a renegade; one who had renounced his (Christian) faith in favor of Islam.

of this barbarian. But such is the human mind that where there is the least glimmering of hope, we love to cherish it.

A Minorqueen slave,[19] who was at Sallee trading for His Imperial Highness, was uncommonly affected at my situation and [18] of infinite service to us, both as an interpreter and a friend. He prevented our baggage from being plundered and our receiving many insults, which undoubtedly would have been offered but for his protection. This may appear strange to those unacquainted with Christian slaves in that country, but the Mahometans hold them as sacred as the tombs of their saints from the ill usage of any but their master, the prince.[20] He told my friend I should be in less danger of any injury at Morocco by his passing for my husband than my brother. Mr. Crisp replied [that] he imagined I should be entirely safe by his appearing in the [19] character he then did, and as he had been examined by the principal people at Sallee concerning the truth of it, it was then too late to alter. The conversation then dropped, and he left us, but his advice, and the manner in which he had given it, greatly alarmed me. Tears gave me some relief, but I remained in a melancholy condition until the dawn of the day, when a severe shock of the earth gave a turn to my thoughts and roused me from that state of despondence I had indulged the preceding night. We received a very kind invitation from Monsieur Ray to visit him at New Sallee before our departure, and we solicited [20] the Moorish admiral for a permission which he readily agreed to, and we then asked if he would indulge us with our baggage, to which he likewise consented. But on applying to his nephew, and offering him a handsome present, he refused to deliver them. However, by offering a more considerable gratuity, we succeeded.

Monsieur Ray and his friends provided us plentifully for the journey to Morocco, gave us a tent with the necessaries belonging to it, and had a man's saddle altered into a woman's, after the Spanish fashion, for me to ride on. On our quitting New Sallee, the gentlemen, attended by the governor, [21] walked out of the town with us to keep the crowd, which was very great, in order, and when we were a quarter of a mile from the place, we parted and mounted our mules: Mr. Crisp, the other passengers, the captain, and ship's company on pack saddles, myself on that Monsieur Ray had provided for me, but we had not proceeded many miles before I found it immensely uneasy.

19. *Minorqueen slave*: a Menorcan slave.
20. *the prince*: Marsh uses "prince" and "emperor" interchangeably for Prince Sidi Muhammad.

We stopped at seven in the evening on a large plain, when we were desired to fix our tent. Our trusty friend the slave accompanied us thus far, and I believe would gladly have remained with us, well knowing the many inconveniences we should be exposed to without his assistance. He [22] seemed remarkably pensive, and observant of me, which I was displeased with, and thought his behaviour very improper, until I overheard a conversation he had with Mr. Crisp, which was to the following effect:

I beg your excuse for the liberty I am going to take, and to be attentive to some advice I must offer you concerning this young lady. As a Christian, I cannot but be greatly afflicted at your misfortunes, but the danger this lady is exposed to gives me inexpressible concern. I therefore hope you will be persuaded to comply with my instructions. The anxiety I am under, on her account, induced me to accompany you as far [23] as this day's journey, and wish it were in my power to continue it with you, but, as that cannot be done, I have determined once more to represent to you how very necessary it is for her safety that you should pass for her husband. I have been a slave to Sidi Mahomet since the year 1750 and am not unacquainted with his temper and inclinations, and such, I assure you, is his despotic power that, if she is at all preserved from being detained in the seraglio,[21] it must be by the means above proposed."

Mr. Crisp argued the impossibility of his acting this part, as he had hitherto assumed the character of my brother, but [24] that difficulty was obviated by the slave's assuring him that he would undertake to settle the matter, namely, by writing a letter to John Arvona, a fellow slave at Morocco, and giving it to a Moor of confidence that was in the caravan, advising his being as expeditious as possible in order that he might be there a day or two before us. In his letter to the slave, he would desire him to acquaint the prince that we had been misrepresented, for we were married and going to settle in England, and he would give him, at the same time, instructions to spread that report in the palace and city of Morocco. Mr. Crisp, seeing me affected [25] by their conversation, prayed me to be assured of his friendship and that no conduct of his should ever give me the least cause of offence; that he only wished to preserve and deliver me safe to the arms of my afflicted parents,

21. *seraglio*: harem.

and, if I approved of what the slave advised, the other passengers and seamen should be made acquainted with it, that, in case of an examination, everyone might be in the same story. This sudden change shocked me greatly, and I could only answer with my tears. My heart was too deeply oppressed to give my opinion for or against it, indeed, I was unable to determine, but as the [26] arguments of the slave were very reasonable, I thought it most prudent to submit to their judgment in fixing on what they thought most expedient in the present extremity. We sat up the remainder of the night settling this affair, and very early in the morning, the slave took leave, recommending me to the protection of providence and the care of my friend. We mounted our mules and took the road to Morocco.

About noon we stopped at an old castle called Seria, where we were refreshed with eggs and milk, which were very acceptable. Soon after we left it, I had the [27] misfortune to be thrown from my mule, by which accident, though I was on the point of being killed, our conductors would not agree to stop a little time for me to recover myself but said we should pitch the tent early in the evening. My fall was occasioned by the fellow who led my mule, he owed me a grudge for complaining of him at Sallee while he was one of our guards. I was therefore again reseated, but in great pain. At night, our conductors, who were the principal people of near three hundred, left Mr. Crisp, myself, and a few sailors to the care of two men called muleteers.[22] What their intentions were [28] by doing so, we could never learn, but it exposed us to great dangers, as the wild Arabs often surrounded us. We travelled many hours over dangerous deserts, and the roarings of the different kinds of beasts in the mountains filled us with terror, though at length we reached the caravan, who were reposing themselves at the foot of a hill. They here permitted us to dismount, and I, being very ill, desired my friend to entreat them to consent that the tent might be pitched, but they would not allow it, as they should only rest an hour at that place and set off again. They [29] assured us, however, that they would stop for the night at a castle five miles farther, though no castle was seen, or so much as a house, or a track, where any human foot had ever been. When we lost our way, as was often the case, our muleteers fired a musquet,[23] which the others answered. By this means we were enabled to follow them, but the howlings in the mountains and dread of the Arabs alarmed us greatly. We travelled all

22. *muleteers*: drivers of mules.
23. *musquet*: musket.

that night, and at ten o'clock the next day, reached the caravan. They lifted me off my mule, but I could not stand, on account of the violence of the pain in the side on which I fell.

The [30] Moorish admiral, observing that I was ill, ordered the tent to be pitched and allowed me two hours to repose. When the time was expired, a messenger came to tell me I must proceed. I told him they acted contrary to the prince's orders and probably would kill me before they reached Morocco. Mr. Crisp asked the interpreter what was their reason for going at the rate they did. He answered that the feast of the Ramedam[24] was to begin in a few days, which occasioned their haste, and it being a high festival at Morocco, everyone was desirous of being present at the same. The [31] admiral who brought me into that detested country was applied to by Mr. Crisp, who entreated him to use his interest with the guards for leave to remain there that day. He promised to do everything to oblige us, but we soon received a message that our request could not be complied with, though I might depend upon their stopping at a duary, or town of tents, before night, where they would procure me such a machine as the Moorish women make use of instead of a saddle on the road. We accordingly set off and got to the town of tents, whereof we had been informed, and my saddle was changed for the [32] machine aforementioned. It was placed across my mule over a pack and held a small mattress. The Moorish women lie in it, as it may be covered close, but I sat with my feet on one side of the mule's neck and found it very proper to screen me from the Arabs, who would not now offer to come near me, imagining I was one of their own countrywomen going to Morocco. Without such a machine I could not have continued a journey of three hundred miles in that country.

At midnight we stopped. I suffered much for the want of good water, that [which] they had with them being extremely [33] nauseous from its being put into the hides of hogs, tarred on the inside, but bad as it was, I often accepted of it to moisten my mouth. The tent being pitched, I should have had some rest, but the noise which the camels made, by reason of the heavy burdens those poor creatures are constrained to carry, debarred me of the comfort. At daybreak the caravan began to stir. The heat of the sun, as the day advanced, was very great, which obliged our guards to stop at a large town of tents, where I purchased some water melons and distributed part of them among the sailors, but the crowd which [34] surrounded us shortened

---

24. *Ramedam*: Ramadan.

our stay, every one striving to get a sight of me. Though the day had been so very hot, we were not allowed to stop until eleven o'clock at night. However, it was an early hour for us and gave me an opportunity of having some rest. At three o'clock in the morning, we were ordered to get ready and set out at four. The roads were good 'til about noon, when we came to a large river, about two hundred yards over, and the water so deep and rapid that the mules often swam, having lost the causeway. When we reached the opposite side, our guards had a tent [35] pitched (in order to recover me from my fright and fatigue) at the foot of a prodigious mountain which we were to ascend, but the heat was too great for us to remain there the whole time our conductors intended. All the unfortunate captives, except myself, were constrained to climb up the mountain, leaving their mules with the Moors, who took care of the camels, and I had a man to lead my mule, one on each side and another behind. Three hours were spent in getting up to the top, and, as I was very faint, the guards permitted the tents to be pitched, being under a necessity of indulging me [36] with an hour's rest.

When they thought me sufficiently recovered, I was again seated on my mule. We set off immediately and did not stop until twelve that night, when, notwithstanding the fatigue I had suffered and the great dew that fell, our tent was not allowed to be pitched. We stayed 'til two o'clock and [then] proceeded to another town of tents, where we stopped and had our tent pitched in the midst of some hundreds of others, inhabited by Arabs, who instantly came tormenting us by their outrageous behaviour. Our guard finding them inclined to be rude to me, had the precaution to tell them I was going as a present to Sidi Mahomet, [37] and this, in some measure, protected me from those dangerous people. Our sailors surrounded me during our stay, which was not long. On account of the Arabs, who seemed determined to be mischievous, which extremely affrighting me, I entreated the admiral to leave that place, which he accordingly did. A large party followed our caravan for miles, but as the roads were very heavy, they returned.

The heat was almost intolerable and steep rocks, which we were obliged to pass over, continually presented themselves to our view. There was no appearance of a house or a tree, but a large tract of country abounding with high mountains. [38] At twelve o'clock that night, our guards informed us that they should not make a long stay and therefore would not pitch the tents, as they intended to be at Morocco the following day. We, however, prevailed on them to indulge us with two hours' respite, after which we proceeded over very rugged, narrow roads and between mountains which reached above the clouds, in which manner we travelled until eight in the morning.

When we arrived at the river of Morocco, we stopped there for an hour and a half, and then advanced nearer the capital, but we had a [39] severe trial of our fortitude before we reached it, for when we were within eight miles of the city, my tent was ordered to be pitched, and I received a message from the Moorish admiral to change my dress. The meaning of this, according to the interpreter's explanation, was, that I should make fine clothes, which I did not readily understand, but on further explanation, it was that they would have me dressed[25] in order to make some figure at going into Morocco. I entreated to be excused, acquainting them how very inconvenient it would be to unpack [40] my baggage and dress in such a place, but no entreaties had any effect, and I found it was their ambition to carry in, adorned in this manner, captives, who by appearance, seemed above the vulgar.[26] As I found it in vain to contend, I had a trunk opened and *they* fixed upon the clothes I was to put on, which were new, but I wrapped up my head in a night cap which almost covered my face, as I was told they did not intend to let me wear a hat. When I was ornamented, as they imagined, instead of being placed, as before, on my own [41] mule, I was seated before Mr. Crisp on his, and at the same time, one of the guards pulled off [Mr. Crisp's] hat and carried it away with him, which treatment amazed us extremely. But our astonishment increased when our fellow sufferers were made to dismount, and walk two and two, bareheaded, the sun being hotter than I had ever felt it. We had not proceeded far before we were met by John Arvona, a Minorqueen slave, who was the prince's treasurer and great confidant. He intended to have accompanied us into Morocco and had brought with him a horse [42] for Mr. Crisp to ride, but the admiral and cruiser's company would not permit him to leave the mule he was on, upon which the slave returned.

The multitude was computed at about twenty thousand horse and foot,[27] most of whom were armed and attended us with shouts and hallooings. Parties of them continually ran backwards and forwards, loading and firing their musquets in our faces. I was almost dead with grief and fatigue.

25. *dressed*: in the sense of "dressed up."
26. *to carry in [. . .] above the vulgar*: since Marsh is of a higher class, her captors wished to show this off.
27. *horse and foot*: horsemen and foot soldiers.

My friend every moment expected we should be thrown from the mule. The Almighty, however, whose watchful providence had defended [43] me from innumerable dangers, continued his goodness and supported me through the distresses of that dismal day. About noon we arrived at Morocco, when my friend and I were taken to an old castle, dropping to pieces with age, led up a number of stairs, and there left to our own reflections. We were seated on the floor lamenting our miserable fate when a French slave entered with some water, a loaf of bread, and melons.

We remained in that place 'til four o'clock in the afternoon, when the rest of the captives and their [44] guards assembled to take us from that horrible abode. I was so ill from fatigue that they were obliged to carry me down the stairs, but placed me, as before, on the mule, and we passed through the city, amidst a great concourse of people, to the palace, which was three miles beyond the castle we had left. When we came to the gates, they stopped, and after waiting near two hours, His Imperial Highness came out and received us in a public manner. He was mounted on a beautiful horse, with slaves on each side fanning off the flies, and guarded by a party of [45] the black regiment.[28] The Moorish admiral and his crew first presented themselves to him, falling on their knees and kissing the ground, and as they arose, did the same to his feet and retired. The prince, then addressing himself to us by means of his interpreter, informed us that the reason of our being taken was on account of Captain Parker's insolent behaviour, having treated him in a very disrespectful and rude manner, when [Captain Parker had been] ambassador, some little time before, from the king of Great Britain. He assured us, however, that we were not slaves, but that he should detain us [46] until the arrival of a consul, and then dismissed us, upon which we returned through the gates. We were thereupon conducted by a Jew to a house which had been provided for us in the Jewdery,[29] which afforded us a dismal prospect: It was a square ground floor, much like our place of confinement at Sallee, only with this addition, that the walls were covered with bugs and as black as soot. As soon as I perceived this, I begged that my tent might be pitched in the courtyard, which was accordingly

---

28. *the black regiment*: sometimes referred to as the "Black Guard," the Abid al-Bukhari was a corps of forcibly recruited black slave soldiers that had been created by Moulay Ismail (ruled 1672–1727). After his death, however, the army became a destabilizing force and was frequently involved in intrigues and coups. For more information, see chaps. 5 and 6 of Chouki el Hamel, *Black Morocco: A History of Slavery, Race, and Islam* (Cambridge: Cambridge University Press, 2014).

29. *Jewdery*: the Jewish quarter of Marrakech.

done, and I intended to go early to rest, but an order came [47] from the palace for me to attend on His Imperial Highness. I would gladly have been excused, but as a slave was sent to wait on me, I was constrained to comply. My friend, being very uneasy, was unwilling I should go with the man and intended to see me there himself, but the slave told him his orders were that none of the captives should accompany me.

We then set out and I was conveyed in at the garden door, which my companion locked and put the key in his pocket. We walked through a part of the garden, which contained a number of statues. The next place we came to was a gate [48] of curious workmanship, where stood two soldiers who stopped me as I was going in. They directed the slave to tell me I could not pass without pulling off my shoes. For a long time I refused to comply, but finding there could otherwise be no admittance, I threw my shoes from me, upon which the slave informed me that the prince was esteemed a saint and therefore no Christian, unless he was barefoot, could be admitted into his palace. Many more guards were to be passed before I could reach the apartment wherein His Imperial Highness was, but when I came there, I was received [49] by him with great attention. Four of his ladies were with him, who seemed as well pleased as he was himself at seeing me. Not that my appearance could prejudice them much in my favour, for I had put on my riding habit and my face had suffered extremely by the scorching morning sun, which the prince took notice of to the slave who attended me, saying that I had not been taken the care of which he had commanded, and he seemed highly offended. I should have been happy, could I have spoken Morisco, in acquainting him with the ill treatment I had experienced on the road. I entreated [50] the slave to mention it to the prince, but he begged I would not desire him to do me this service, for if he did, the Moors would never be satisfied until they had his life.

The ladies made many remarks on my dress, greatly recommended their own, and importuned me to put it on, but I declined. One of the most agreeable of them, and who showed me the greatest civility, was the daughter of an Englishman who became a renegado and had married a Moorish woman. She took her bracelets off her arms and put them on mine, desiring I would wear them. The [51] slave told me that I might now take my leave whenever I pleased, which I did immediately, being very glad to retire. But my conductor, instead of taking me to our lodgings, introduced me into another apartment, where I was soon followed by the prince, who, having seated himself on a cushion, inquired concerning the *reality* of my marriage with my friend. This inquiry was certainly unexpected, but though I positively affirmed that I was really married, I could perceive he much doubted it from his frequent interrogations as to the reality thereof. He likewise observed that it was customary for the [52] English wives to wear a wedding ring, which the slave informed me of, and I answered that it was packed up as I did not choose to travel with it. The prince, finding I persisted in my story, questioned me no further, but gave me assurances of his esteem and protection. He said he should take pleasure in obliging me and, ordering the slave to take particular care of me, he gave me leave to depart. We went with all haste to the garden gate, where I found my faithful friend, and we soon got to our dismal habitation. Amends, however, [were] speedily made for the [53] inconveniences of the place by the company of two gentlemen (merchants), who resided in that country and [who] had been so kind to leave their places of abode in order to meet us at Morocco.

John Arvona, the slave, soon after waited on me with a basket of fruit from His Imperial Highness, who had ordered him to enquire particularly concerning my health. It was strongly recommended to me by the gentlemen aforementioned not to expose myself to the view of the populace, as the prince had many spies to observe my actions, and if he should, by any unguarded event, discover the deceit I had made use of, I must [54] undoubtedly be confined to the seraglio and so lost to my family. I therefore flatter myself that great allowances will be made for my present character,[30] which though fictitious, gave me the greatest uneasiness, as it rendered me apprehensive that the ill-disposed part of the world would censure my conduct, but I had no reason to be under any apprehensions from the man whom providence had allotted to be my protector, for his behaviour would always bear the most accurate inspection, and the attention he paid me was as to a sister and friend.

Another basket of fruit [55] dressed with a variety of flowers was brought by Arvona from His Imperial Highness, with a message that he desired to see me, and had ordered [the slave] to wait on me to [sic] the palace. I dressed myself and attended the slave, when, at the first gate, I was obliged to leave my shoes under the care of the soldiers, and then hastened through the different apartments until we came to that where His Imperial Highness was.

---

30. *for my present character*: Marsh hints at the insinuations she had to face after her return home concerning her relationship with Crisp. Her alleged marriage in Morocco jeopardized her eligibility on the marriage "market" in England, leaving Crisp as the sole "candidate."

The slave then left me, and a French lad, who could be admitted into the apartments of the females, was sent for to interpret between us. The same ladies whom I had seen before were at the other end of [56] the room. He commanded a cushion to be placed near him and I was desired to be seated thereon. He was dressed in a loose robe of muslin with a train of at least two yards on the floor, and under that was a pink satin vest, buttoned with diamonds. He had a small cap of the same satin as his vest, with a diamond button, wore bracelets on his leg, and slippers wrought with gold; his figure, altogether not disagreeable, and his address civil and easy. [He was] tall, and of a tolerable good complexion, and appeared to be about five and twenty.[31]

A low table, covered with [57] a piece of muslin edged with silver, was placed before him, and on that was an elegant waiter,[32] containing a small teakettle and lamp and two cups and saucers, which were as light as tin, and curiously japanned[33] with green and gold. These, I was told, were presents from the Dutch. The tea was made in the kettle and he presented me with a cup of it, which, as it came from his hand, I ventured to drink, though I should have refused it from the ladies for very good reasons. When the table was removed, I was introduced to a young prince and princess, after which they retired and a slave brought a [58] great collection of rarities and showed them to me. I greatly admired everything I saw, which seemed to please the prince exceedingly, and he told me by means of the interpreter that he did not doubt of my preferring, in time, the palace to the confined way of life I was then in; that I might always depend on his favour and protection, and that the curiosities I had seen should be my own property. I thanked him for the honour he did me, but that, as I was very happy in a husband who was my equal in rank and fortune, I did not wish to change my situation in that respect, and, [59] whenever it was agreeable to him, I would take my leave. He looked very stern at my answer and made me no reply, but conversed a little while in Morisco, after which one of the ladies handed me to the other end of the room and seated me before them. One of them in particular observed me very much and seemed out of temper. She was a large woman, but low in stature, of a sallow complexion, thick lipped, and had a broad flat face with black eyes, the lashes whereof were painted of a deep red. Her hair was black, combed back to her head, and

---

31. *five and twenty*: Sidi Muhammad was actually in his midthirties.
32. *an elegant waiter*: a small tray.
33. *japanned*: covered with a hard varnish to give a smooth, glossy finish.

hung down a great length in various ringlets. She [60] had a large piece of muslin edged with silver round her head and raised high at the top. Her earrings were extremely large and the part which went through the ears was made hollow, for lightness. She wore a loose dress much like the captain of the port's wife at Sallee, only with the difference of a diamond button to the collar and its being made of the finest muslin. Her slippers were of blue satin, worked with silver, and she had bracelets on her arms and legs.

The lady whose father, as I have already mentioned, was an [61] Englishman, talked to me in Morisco, and was seemingly fond of me, and by her gestures, I imagined she wanted me to learn their language. I, however, asked the French boy what she was saying, who answered, "*Rien de consequence*,"[34] and I therefore concluded that what she said related only to common conversation, and being desirous of obliging her in trifles, I imprudently repeated some words after her, but found, when too late, that I had renounced the Christian religion (though innocently) by saying, "There is but one God, and Mahomet is his prophet." The palace was immediately in the utmost confusion, and [62] there was every sign of joy in all faces. I was surprised and affrighted (though I knew not the cause thereof), which the prince perceiving, ordered the noise to cease, and at the same time spoke to the ladies, who instantly left the room, taking me with them to an apartment remote from that wherein we had been. It was a large room and crowded with women, but mostly blacks. One of them spoke French. I asked her if the place we were in was the seraglio? She said it was a small part of it, and offered to show me farther, but I would not venture myself out [63] of sight of the door I had entered. An old slave brought me chocolate, but I declined taking it, for I had been cautioned against drinking anything they might offer me. After some time, I began to be impatient and uneasy at my being detained in that place and entreated them to permit my departure, but instead of granting my request, they endeavoured to remove my anxiety by assuring me that I should not remain much longer therein. I nevertheless continued my entreaties, though to no purpose, 'til a young lad came in who was one that attended on the women. I addressed him in French, which [64] fortunately for me, he understood, desiring him

---

34. *Rien de consequence*: "Nothing important."

to go with my respects to His Imperial Highness, and acquaint him that I besought him, as I was very ill, to give me leave to depart. The boy cheerfully complied, and in less than a quarter of an hour, an English renegado came with a message from the prince that I should attend him in a private apartment. I was shocked at the oddity of the message, but as it was my fate to be reduced to passive obedience and nonresistance, I followed the man through many squares, some of which were of white marble, and the pillars of mosaic work, with [a] variety [65] of fountains that fell into basins, and lattices at [the] top to keep out the sun, but such was my distressed situation that it was out of my power to make any material remarks on the objects presented to my view.

When we entered the apartment where the prince was waiting to receive me, I was amazed at the elegant figure he made, being seated under a canopy of crimson velvet, richly embellished with gold. The room was large, well decorated, and supported by pillars of mosaic work, and there was, at the other end, a range of cushions with gold tassels and a Persian carpet on the floor. He [66] commanded me and the English interpreter to draw near his person, when he conversed some time with the latter in Morisco, after which the man informed me that His Imperial Highness wished to know if I would become a Moor and remain in his palace, desiring me to be convinced of his esteem, hoping that I would properly consider the advantages resulting from doing as he desired, and promising me every indulgence that he could possibly show me. Though I was alarmed and even greatly terrified by these interrogations, I had the resolution to reply that it [67] was impossible for me to change my sentiments in religious matters, and that consideration was entirely unnecessary to me, who was peremptorily determined to remain a Christian, but that I should ever retain the highest sense of the honour he had done me and hoped for the continuance of His Highness's protection. I could easily perceive that he was disgusted with my answer from his remaining silent for some minutes. Throwing off the mask he had hitherto worn, he cruelly informed me that I had that very morning renounced the Christian faith, and turned Mahometan, and that no less a [68] punishment than burning, was, by their laws, inflicted on all who recanted from, or disclaimed their religion. The shock was so severe that it was with difficulty I supported myself from falling, and I invoked heaven for assistance in my distresses, they being excessively great, and nobody near me that I knew.

As soon as I was capable of making a reply, I assured the prince, if I was an apostate, it entirely proceeded from the fallacy of the French boy, and not from my own inclination, but that, however, if my death would give him any satisfaction, I no longer desired [69] to avoid the last remedy to all my misfortunes. For living on the terms he proposed would only add to my misery, and I therefore thought that the preservation of my life did not deserve my care and attention. He seemed greatly perplexed by my resolute declaration, and though he continued his importunity, yet it was more with the air of a supplicant than that of a sovereign, though he was still inflexible to everything I urged against what he proposed. I therefore, on my knees, implored his compassion, and besought him to permit me to leave him forever. My tears extremely [70] affected him, and raising me up and putting his hands before his face, he ordered that I should be instantly taken away. The man took me by the hand and, having hurried as fast as possible to the gates, found it no easy matter to pass a great crowd which had assembled there. My worthy friend was on the other side with his hair all loose and a distracted countenance, demanding me as his wife, but the guards beat him down for striving to get in, and the black women holding me and hallooing out, *no Christian, but a Moor,* tore all the plaits out of my clothes, and [71] my hair hung down about my ears. After a number of arguments he prevailed, and having forced me from the women, took me in his arms and got out of their sight.

On getting to our lodging, my friend sent for a French surgeon, a slave to His Imperial Highness, to bleed me, which news being carried to the palace, the prince, as we afterwards heard, was much concerned, [since] bleeding in that country [was] looked upon as very extraordinary and never practised but in cases of extremity. This was therefore a fortunate circumstance, as His Highness imagined it was occasioned [72] by his behaviour. Three people that day ran great risks of their lives on my account: one of them by acquainting my friend what they were doing with me at the palace; another, we were informed, was sent for by the prince, just after he had dismissed me, who ordered him, if I was not out of the gates, to bring me back to him, to which that good man answered that he had met me with my husband near our lodgings. I am under the greatest obligations to this worthy slave, who had substantial reasons for deceiving His Imperial Highness, as he well knew the fatal consequences [73] of my returning to the prince.

On the next morning, I got up very early to see our friends the merchants, who advised me to keep myself still, in appearance, ill, and not to admit any one to visit me but themselves. A visitor, however, presented himself to whom it would have been impolitic to have denied admittance. His name was Muli Dris, a prince of the blood. He was tall, of a sallow complexion and black eyes, and a great friend to the English. He conversed with my friend in Spanish and, when he went away, desired I would keep up my spirits, for he did not doubt that [74] all would end well. One of our [merchant] friends [was] breakfasting with me and Mr. Crisp, when the latter received a message from the palace, commanding him and the other two passengers, with the master and ship's crew, to attend, and the two merchants were likewise to be made acquainted with it, that they might, in like manner, give their attendance. They all waited upon His Imperial Highness, when he told them that the reason of his sending for them was to grant them liberty to proceed on their voyage, and that he would issue out proper orders for [75] their journey to Sallee. That notwithstanding the great indignities he had received from the late ambassador from the king of England (it is said that when he had his audience of the emperor, he was dressed quite *en déshabillé*, with boots and spurs on, and spoke in very haughty terms), and the further ill treatment he had met with from the English, who had furnished his rebellious subjects with arms and ammunition, he would set them an example of moderation as well as justice by permitting us to quit his dominions. The gentlemen, [76] on their return, told me what had passed, and I thought myself very happy at the appearance of once more seeing my dear and disconsolate parents. The next morning, information was brought us that the prince had altered his intention, who now determined we should go to Saffee,[35] and from thence to Sallee. This greatly surprised us, and we found he had not been sincere in his first proposal, which was a double mortification, he having obliged the gentlemen and the ship's crew to sign a letter to Lord Tyrawley, governor [77] of Gibraltar, wherein he promised to release us, and this was immediately sent by express. But we imagined he had only done this to deceive our friends and prevent their demanding our liberty.

---

35. *Saffee*: Safi, a port city situated on Morocco's Atlantic coast.

The next day, however, the long wished for dispatches were brought, with proper guards to attend us to Saffee. Our baggage was ready to set out at eight o'clock in the evening, we walked out of town and met with no interruption, as the Moors were obliged to retire into the city at sunset, and the Jews were easily kept at a distance by our guards. We mounted our mules and, [78] soon after, crossed the river of Morocco and there rested for the night. One of our friends the merchants had dispatched some of our attendants before, to prepare the tents and have our supper ready, which was a most comfortable change from that we had experienced on the road from Sallee. We set out early next morning, Mount Atlas, at the back of Morocco, with a chain of mountains about thirty miles before us. We stopped about noon, dined, and set off again in the evening, passed over a high [79] mountain, the top of which commanded a view of the Atlas, city of Morocco, and its extensive plains. We rested for the night, and at daybreak set out again, and pitched the tents, though not until late, near a salt lake three miles long and two broad, which from November to April is a river and the other months quite hard, esteemed a great curiosity, being fifty miles from the sea. On our journey, a number of wild Arabs alarmed us.

We were soon met by a governor, who, with a party of soldiers, was going to command at a place a few miles [80] distant. He accosted us in English, which he spoke well, having learnt that language whilst ambassador in England. He was very civil and ordered his people to fire, by way of salute, but my friend desired he would forbid it as I had not been well and he feared it might be too much for my spirits, which he immediately complied with. We stopped about three miles before we reached Saffee, where all the Christian merchants had assembled to meet us and brought some refreshments with them. A little time was here spent [81] in ceremony and then we proceeded to the gates of Saffee, where we dismounted on account of a great crowd, by mere curiosity there assembled, who obstructed our passage and gave us much uneasiness and interruption. Having at length entered the house of one of the gentlemen who, as I mentioned before, had left their abode to meet us at Morocco, my first thoughts were to return thanks to providence for the happiness I then enjoyed in being under the roof of those who professed the same faith as myself.

In the morning, the governor of the place paid us a visit and informed [82] us of his having received advices that our stay was to be only for fifteen days, during which we were to be treated as free people, and, in the interim, he was to receive further orders in relation to us. Part of this information was no way agreeable to me, who feared the prince was undetermined with regard to our liberty. Whilst we were at dinner, a number of Moors surrounded the table, but I found it was customary for them to enter the houses of Christians whenever they thought proper and the [83] owners could not prevent it. I put up all such letters as would have discovered my being a single woman and delivered them to the care of one of the gentlemen. Mr. Crisp procured me a plain gold ring from a Swedish captain, which I locked in a trunk, expecting a search to be made in order to know whether I was really married to him or only made a pretence thereof. Such precautions were necessary in order to guard against the dangers to which I was exposed. I desired my friend to write [84] to Arvona, at Morocco, to learn what had passed at the palace after my departure, for I was ever in dread that His Imperial Highness would again send for me, having heard from undoubted authority that I was not indifferent to him, and though he had discovered great condescension in permitting me to leave him, when it was in his power to detain me, yet I knew him to be an absolute prince and therefore had great reason to be extremely uneasy.

I had entertained great hopes [85] of letters from my friends, the disappointment of which made me very unhappy, who very well knew how much they would be afflicted on my account should they have heard the melancholy news of my being a prisoner in such a country. These and many other reflections kept me in perpetual misery, and I often wished to be taken from this world. We now received an unexpected visit from Arvona, who had been dispatched from Morocco, to guard some Spanish bulldogs which the friars, residing in Saffee, [86] had ordered to be sent from Cádiz as a present to His Imperial Highness. Arvona, in my hearing, told my friend, in Minorqueen, that the prince was very anxious on account of my health; that he had given orders for his being called up in the night, in order to talk with him concerning me, and that he frequently said he would have me [sent] again to Morocco, because Saffee did not agree with my constitution. The Minorqueen slave added that he much feared His Highness's resolution as to permitting me to leave [87] Barbary would be of no long continuance, notwithstanding his determination on the day I left Morocco. And the reason for his apprehensions was that the prince, being asked if he would not see the fair Christian before her departure, after a pause, replied, "No, lest I should be obliged to detain her." This honest man promised to supply us constantly with advices of what passed at the palace and then set out for Morocco. Arvona was no sooner gone than I acquainted my friend that I overheard their conversation, which [88] gave me the greatest uneasiness, but he, being equally concerned, entreated me to be as easy as possible, assuring me that he would spare no pains to lighten my afflictions and undergo any torments rather than I should return to the prince.

Another post came in that brought no letters from any of my family, which greatly increased my sorrow, who dreaded their being intercepted, as they would have discovered my real name. But a Swedish merchant of Saffee came to inform me that he could with certainty affirm that an [89] English admiral (Sir Edwd. Hawke)[36] was arrived at Gibraltar, from England, who had ordered that the *Portland* man-of-war, Captain Maplesden,[37] should be dispatched to demand us. This agreeable information, however, gained little credit with me, who had been accustomed to this sort of deception and even inured to disappointment. The gentleman, nevertheless, left me, to appearance well satisfied with his having been the messenger of glad tidings. The same day, I received a letter from one of our friends, the merchants, who had been so kind to us [90] at Morocco, of which the following is an extract:

> It is with great impatience I have waited, till now, in expectation that a courier might have offered for Saffee and have given me an opportunity of enquiring after your and your friend's health. When I reflect on the variety of events in the last month, they appear, at first, as a dream, though I am soon afterwards fully convinced of the reality of them. The fatal day at Morocco never occurs to my mind but with horror, and when I think [91] how near you were being lost forever, when the tyrant, to use Phocyas's expression in the Siege of Damascus,[38] would have sunk you down to infamy and perdition.

---

36. *Sir Edwd. Hawke*: Marsh is referring to Admiral Sir Edmund Hawk who, on 7 Oct 1756, dispatched the fifty-gun *Portland* to collect Marsh and her fellow captives (Colley, *The Ordeal of Elizabeth Marsh*, 82).
37. *the* Portland *man-of-war, Captain Maplesden*: Jervis Maplesden was the captain of the *Portland*.
38. *Siege of Damascus*: a 1720 tragedy by John Hughes.

It fixes a melancholy on me that I am not capable of shaking off for some time. Let me entreat you never to repeat a word in the language of the country, not even the most trifling, and always avoid the room when the governors or principal Moors enter. Excuse this advice, for I can with great truth affirm I shall be very uneasy until I hear you are gone from this country and happily [92] restored to your family and friends. In the meantime, while you are obliged to remain in Barbary, endeavour to reconcile yourself to it, reflect that it is a misfortune you have no way brought upon yourself, nor have it in your power to remedy. Have a firm trust in providence and be assured virtue and innocence will ever be the peculiar care of that Supreme Disposer of all events, who is capable of extricating you from your present distresses at a time when you may least expect it. You are, thank God, [93] in the house of a worthy, honest man, who, I am persuaded, will spare no pains to serve you. Let this, in some measure, alleviate your grief, by considering how much more dreadful your situation had been, had you remained at Morocco. I long for the arrival of the general post that I may hear if you had any letters from Gibraltar. Let me once more recommend to you to keep up your spirits and shed no useless tears. I will conclude with quoting you six lines from The Distressed Mother.[39]

[94] Though plung'd in Ills, and execis'd in care,
yet never let the noble mind despair:
When press'd by dangers, and beset with foes,
The gods their timely succour interpose;
And, when our virtue sinks o'erwhelm'd with grief,
By unforeseen expedients bring relief.

The friars, who had been some time in Saffee for the benefit of the Spanish slaves, desired to be admitted to see me, [95] as they were going to return to the garrison of Gibraltar. The superior of them stayed some time longer than the others, as he had a great deal to say, and he took great

---

39. *The Distressed Mother*: a 1712 tragedy by Ambrose Philips.

pains to encourage us to cheerfully submit to the Divine Will. He likewise assured me that he would see my family as soon as possible after his arrival and parted from us with tears. I had observed that one of his companions delivered a letter to my friend, whose countenance was extremely altered by the reading thereof, and therefore, when they were gone, I [96] desired to know its contents, as I was very certain it came from Morocco. I found it, however, a difficult matter to persuade him to grant my request, and he did not, at last, comply, until I promised not to afflict myself. The letter came from Arvona, which intimated that a Moor of some consequence (an enemy to the English) would shortly be sent by His Imperial Highness to Saffee. It appeared from his manner of writing that he was anxious for my preservation, as he entreated my friend to be particularly [97] attentive to the most effectual measures to secure my safety, but this advice was unnecessary, because the most affectionate parent could not have been more tenderly careful of me than he had ever been on all occasions. I endeavoured to conceal my apprehensions, but Arvona's letter was never out of my mind and produced many melancholy reflections which almost deprived me of hope, our greatest blessing, as they had already extremely interrupted my tranquillity.

A ship, a few days after, arrived from Holland, which brought two [98] gentlemen passengers, who, as soon as they heard of my distress, paid a visit to me. One of them was a merchant who had formerly resided in Santa Cruz and was going to Morocco with his companion to solicit the favour and protection of the prince in order to reestablish a house in the said city. The gentleman had, as it was reported, formerly traded with great success in this place, and to the surprise of all, the prospect of adding yet more to his fortune had so strange an effect upon him that the difficulties [99] a Christian is exposed to in that country were overlooked by him as matters of no importance or consideration. These gentlemen informed me that they had heard a messenger was come from Morocco whose aversion to the English was implacable, and they therefore advised me to keep my chamber, it being believed His Imperial Highness had sent him to inspect into the conduct of me and my friend. I was greatly obliged to them for their information and they set out for Morocco.

My room door was thrown open with great violence as I pensively sat [100] reflecting on the news I had heard and a most forbidding object presented itself to my view. He, for several minutes, fixed his eyes upon me without speaking a word and his aspect was as furious as can possibly be imagined. He afterwards narrowly inspected the room, muttering to himself in his own language, and then, giving me another terrifying look, he retired, pulling the door after him as he had opened it before. I was struck with great horror at his wild appearance and seemed riveted to my chair. My friend was ignorant of this [101] visit, who was walking with some gentlemen of the factory on the top of the house, and, when he returned, I was, for some time, incapable of acquainting him with what had happened to me. He immediately concluded that this person was the messenger who had been expected, and it was soon after confirmed by one of the gentlemen of the factory, who came to introduce the Danish consul, who was on the point of departing for Sallee and had desired to see me. This gentleman expressed great concern for my illness and, recommending a person who, in his opinion, had some knowledge of physic, [102] he obligingly sent him to me. My doctor advised my being bled, but as I was diffident of his skill, I chose to defer bleeding to another opportunity. He soon visited me again, when he found my complaint was a dejection of spirits, and therefore the intended operation was laid aside.

The pleasing news we afterwards heard from Monsieur Ray was the most successful physician, whose letter from Sallee speedily restored me to health, it being sent to congratulate us on the arrival of a man-of-war, but, the weather being bad, they [103] had not reached the shore. I now began to entertain favourable hopes of once more seeing my dear parents, and with these pleasing imaginations, I retired to rest, but my repose was interrupted in the night by two shocks of the earth, which continued a minute and a half. The fright I was in cannot be expressed, and before I was removed out of my room, a part of the ceiling was thrown down. The walls, though of a prodigious thickness, were cracked in many places, and the subsequent noise may be compared to a carriage going speedily over a rough [104] pavement, which ended with a tremendous explosion. The sky was serene, but the sea made a great roaring, and we afterwards heard the shipping had greatly suffered thereby.

The next morning, when I was at breakfast with my friend, a letter came from Arvona, at Morocco, enclosing a copy of that which had been sent from Captain Maplesden to the prince, and was to this purpose: That he was come there in the name of Admiral Sir Edward Hawke, to know the reason for taking, and detaining our ship, passengers etc. in [105] a time of peace, and it represented, in terms of respect, how much the king, his master, would esteem his justice in setting us at liberty, and that he might depend upon the treaty, which had been concluded, being inviolably maintained on the part of His Britannic Majesty. To this letter His Imperial Highness answered that at that juncture his cruiser was at sea and, consequently, his admiral was unacquainted with any peace being made, and on his return to Sallee, a report prevailed that his ambassador had failed in his negotiation, which [106] was the reason of his sending us to Morocco. That on our arrival, he (who always kept his word) had declared us free, as well as the ship and cargo, and likewise had ordered the crew back to Sallee in order to refit the ship. That in the interim, myself and other passengers were sent to Saffee to wait there until [she] was ready to proceed on her voyage. His Imperial Highness further declared that he would, on his part, duly adhere to the truce concluded, but if in the time stipulated, peace was not ratified by the court of England, [107] he should regard it as a declaration of war and order his cruisers to make reprisals and stop the communication between the garrison of Gibraltar and his dominions, ending his letter with complaints against the English for furnishing his rebellious subjects with arms and ammunition.

John Arvona, moreover, informed my friend that a Jew was to set out in a few days for Saffee with the answer to the captain of the man-of-war and to negotiate affairs with him. The prince, in his letter, said that we might either embark on board our [108] king's ship, or return to Sallee and continue our voyage in the merchantman, though he knew the latter was impossible, as she was almost pulled to pieces and his people were fitting out their cruisers with the materials, but had the case been otherwise, my strength was too much exhausted by illness and sorrow to be in a condition to take so fatiguing a journey. The Jew soon arrived from Morocco, and the very same day, the Portland man-of-war of fifty guns anchored in Saffee Road. A boat was immediately sent on shore with our letters, and [109] among the rest was one from my dear father, encouraging me to keep up my spirits. My friend received also a very obliging letter from Captain Maplesden, who advised our being in readiness, though we could not embark until the Jew went and returned from Morocco, entreating us to make ourselves easy, for he would do everything in his power to facilitate our enlargement.[40] In five days, the negotiator returned to Saffee with the joyful tidings that we were to embark the following day, but the badness of the weather prevented [110] any boats from going off, neither would any gratuity tempt the Moors to venture with us while the sea ran so high as it did.

Indeed I cannot say that I was much flattered that I should be permitted to quit the country, but providence was pleased to change the situation of affairs in my favour for, early the next morning, I was desired to get myself ready, as the weather would admit of our going. The sudden joy for this agreeable news oppressed my spirits, and it was with difficulty [that] my friends recovered me to a state of tranquillity. The gentlemen of the [111] house attended me to the strand, where I returned them my grateful thanks for their kindness, and we set off for the ship. I was in extreme dread until we reached the man-of-war, fearing a signal from the shore to order our return. I was received by Captain Maplesden with the greatest friendly attention and there were general expressions of joy at seeing me safe from the power of those who wished to detain me. Our conductors, after they were discharged and had received a handsome present, returned to their detested shore.

[112] Captain Maplesden was so good to resign his stateroom to me, and I cannot express the comfort I felt in having an apartment allotted to myself after the cruel restraint I had been under in Barbary and the uneasiness I had suffered on account of passing for what I really was not. I had, besides, an additional satisfaction, namely that of having it in my power to acquaint my parents to whom they were indebted (next to providence) for my preservation, as my friend had, in every respect, fulfilled the promise he had made [113] to them. We cruised several days and then arrived at Gibraltar, to the unspeakable joy of my distressed parents, and it is easy to be imagined how happy I was on this occasion.

It was not long after my return before my friend convinced me that his assiduity had proceeded from a stronger attachment than that of friendship by a declaration he made to myself and family of his love for me, and the unhappiness he was under at the thought of parting with me, but he flattered himself that the confidence they had already reposed in him by trusting me [114] to his care, with the esteem I had always professed for

---

40. *enlargement*: release (archaic).

him, would be a means of removing every obstacle which might prevent his future happiness. I was not surprised at this declaration, his general good character, the gratitude I owed him, and my father's desire overbalanced some other considerations, and we were married[41] and embarked shortly after for England.

---

41. *overbalanced [. . .] we were married*: Marsh had little choice but to marry James Crisp, since her reputation had been compromised by having masqueraded as his wife and spending so much time alone with him (see also note 30). In fact, her fiancé, Henry Towry, sent her father a letter soon after she was captured, indicating that he was no longer interested in her (Colley, *The Ordeal of Elizabeth Marsh*, 88–89).

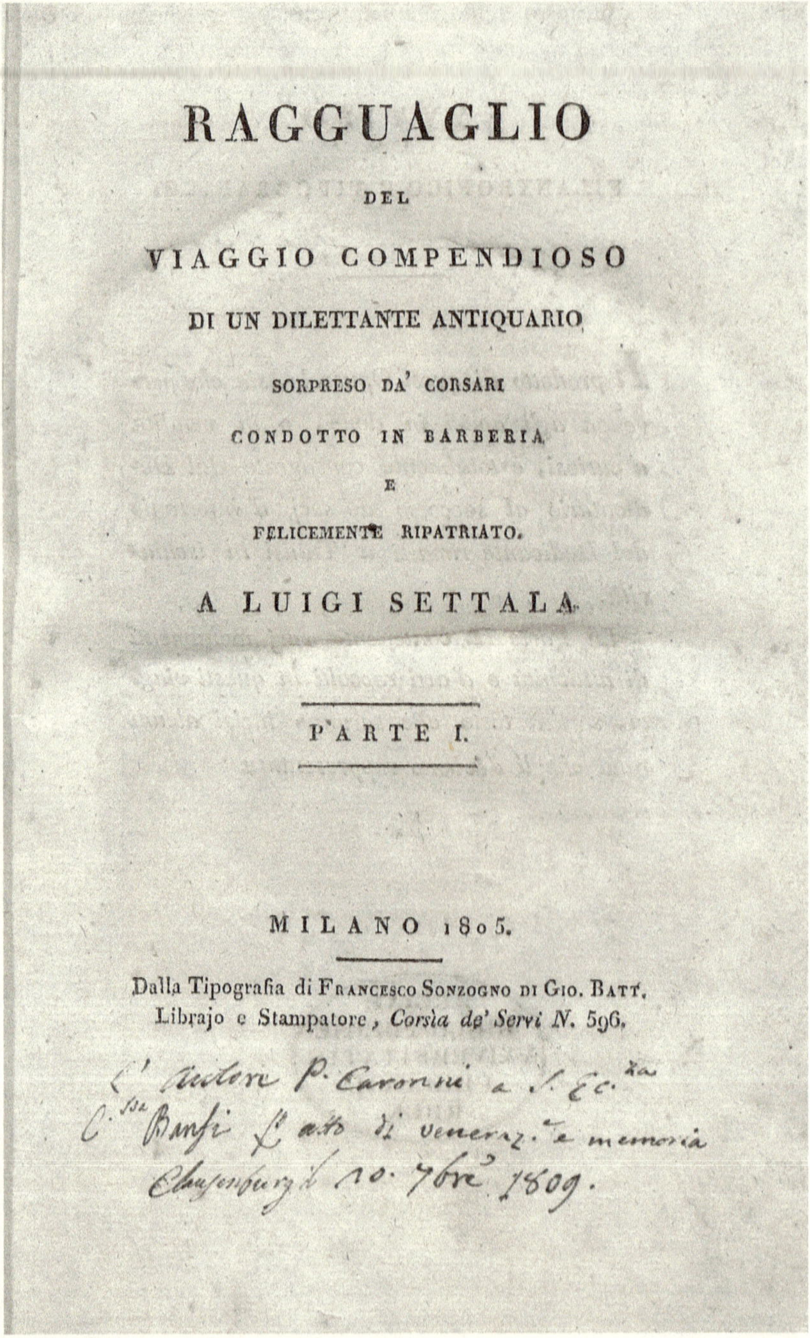

RAGGUAGLIO

DEL

VIAGGIO COMPENDIOSO

DI UN DILETTANTE ANTIQUARIO

SORPRESO DA' CORSARI

CONDOTTO IN BARBERIA

E

FELICEMENTE RIPATRIATO.

A LUIGI SETTALA

PARTE I.

MILANO 1805.

Dalla Tipografia di Francesco Sonzogno di Gio. Batt.
Librajo e Stampatore, *Corsìa de' Servi N.* 596.

L'Autore P. Caronni a S. Ecc.za
C.ssa Banfi l'atto di veneraz.e e memoria
Clausenburg li 10. 7bre 1809.

Figure 13.1 Title page of Felice Caronni's narrative
Source: Felice Caronni, *Ragguaglio del viaggio compendioso di un dilettante antiquario da'corsari condotto in Barberia e felicemente ripatriato: Parte 1* (Milan: Sonzogno, 1805); Signatur: N 559/1 (1.2), Shelfmark: N 559/1 (1.2); Hauptbibliothek Adenauerallee.

CHAPTER XIII

FELICE CARONNI, *THE ACCOUNT OF AN AMATEUR ANTIQUARIAN'S SHORT JOURNEY*

1805 Italian print edition; selection

Captivity in Tunis 1804

By the beginning of the nineteenth century, North African piracy had begun to decline and was soon to be ended by the intervention of the United States during the Barbary Wars and by European colonial maneuvers in North Africa. Published in two volumes in 1805 and 1806, Felice Caronni's account of events that took place in 1804 is one of the last surviving authentic Barbary captivity narratives and one of the very few Italian testimonies that made it into print. Because of the geographic proximity between Italy and North Africa, inhabitants of the peninsula had fallen prey to Barbary pirates for centuries. Given the high number of Italian slaves and returnees from the Barbary Coast, it is most surprising that we have so few Italian testimonies of slaves' experiences in North Africa. At the same time, the fact that Italians were very familiar with the concept of North African captivity might, in part, have been responsible for this lack of Italian slave narratives, given that such accounts would not have been a novelty for Italian audiences. Parts of Caronni's narrative are included in this anthology in order to give a voice to this otherwise underrepresented group.

As an educated Barnabite priest and collector of antiques, Felice Caronni (1747–1815) had a deep interest in the culture and heritage of North Africa. As a result, his text became a major reference work about Tunis at the time.[1]

---

1. "Carònni, Felice," *Treccani–Dizionario Bibliografico degli Italiani* (http://www.treccani.it/enciclopedia/felice-caronni).

[339]

Caronni's extensive narrative is divided into two parts: *Ragguaglio del viaggio compendioso di un dilettante antiquario, sorpreso da' corsari, condotto in Barberia e felicemente ripatriato: Parte 1* (Milan: Sonzogno, 1805) and *Ragguaglio di alcuni monumenti di antichità ed arti: Parte 2* (Milan: Sonzogno, 1806).[2] The first volume, of which selections are included in this anthology, describes Caronni's capture, abduction to Tunis, and return home to Milan. The second volume includes detailed depictions of the ancient monuments that Caronni visited, a treatise on the Tunisian writing system, and descriptions of artifacts that he collected and analyzed during his involuntary stay in North Africa.

Felice Caronni's fate as a captive was rather unusual: The priest, amateur classical scholar, and art collector was captured by Tunisian corsairs on 9 June 1804 while sailing from Palermo to Naples. As a citizen of Milan, which was part of the French Empire at the time, Caronni would have been protected by a treaty with Tunis, which should have guaranteed free passage for him. However, since Caronni's passport was lost during the pirates' attack, he was unable to prove his citizenship and was thus brought to Tunis together with the other captives. When his true identity as a Milanese citizen became apparent soon after his arrival in North Africa, he received special treatment and was able to move relatively freely in and around the city of Tunis. This provided the amateur classicist with ample opportunity to visit the ancient ruins of Carthage and to purchase coins, gems, and other classical Roman and Punic artifacts, detailed descriptions of which make up large parts of the second volume of his narrative. It is important to stress what a unique opportunity this forced stay in Tunis must have been for Caronni as an antiquarian. To purchase art as well as engage in sightseeing activities in a region with such an immense Roman heritage would have been impossible for him under normal circumstances.

Partly thanks to his status as a quasi-free person and partly because of his background as a learned man, Caronni was able to maintain contact with the upper echelons of Tunisian society. These exchanges included various official representatives of European nations as well as his own relatives, who facilitated his release. In addition, his former master regularly requested his presence at mealtimes in order to profit from Caronni's knowledge.

---

2. For a modern French translation of the first volume, see Felice Caronni, *Précis d'un voyage en Barbarie*, trans. Tatiana Cescutti, introduction and notes by Salvatore Bono (Paris: Bouchène, 2011).

The Tunisian bey himself took special interest in Caronni's liberation, which took place on 30 September, less than four months after his capture. This was unusually fast compared with the tenures of "regular" captives, who usually suffered in slavery for much longer before they were released—if, indeed, they were freed at all.

Notes on the Present Translation of Felice Caronni's *Account of an Amateur Antiquarian's Short Journey*

This translation is based on the following edition: Felice Caronni, *Ragguaglio del viaggio compendioso di un dilettante antiquario da'corsari condotto in Barberia e felicemente ripatriato: Parte 1* (Milan: Sonzogno, 1805).

The selection in this anthology focuses on those excerpts of Caronni's first volume that are most relevant for a better understanding of Barbary captivity in the early nineteenth century and Caronni's personal experiences as a collector of antiques. Caronni devotes a significant portion of his narrative to lengthy reports about his attempts to contact those who he hopes will be able to free him. These sections, which are of little interest to most modern readers, have been omitted. Caronni's secondhand descriptions of events and conversations that were reported to him, as well as his digressions on the subject of food, have also been cut. Omissions have been indicated with an ellipsis [. . .]. In case of longer omissions, short summaries in square brackets have been provided to bridge the gaps between different sections. The numbers in brackets {} in the text always indicate the beginning of a page and refer to the original page numbers of the 1805 edition. Paragraph breaks have been added to enhance the readability of the narrative. Special thanks go to Almiria Wilhelm for her assistance with the preparation of the final translation.

Felice Caronni, *The Account of an Amateur Antiquarian's Short Journey: Surprised by Corsairs, Taken to Barbary, and Happily Repatriated* (Milan: Sonzogno, 1805)

Translated by Erica Autelli and Isabella Miggitsch

{17} Because no neutral ship[3] could be found in Palermo that would sail to Naples, I had to adapt (because I could not delay my return) and board a Sicilian xebec,[4] which carried oranges for sale. After mass on Sunday 3 June,[5] we set sail, and our journey proceeded very slowly due to the calm wind conditions, so that after five tiresome days we still found ourselves drifting in the area of the volcanic islands between Stromboli and Lipari, which was halfway. As a matter of fact, I asked the crew to turn the ship, aided by the winds, to Messina, and consequently sail along Calabria with the added advantage of nocturnal land wind for acceleration and, in case of a frightening encounter, opportunities to retreat somewhere. I deeply regretted not being able to see this prestigious metropolis, which we passed so closely. I also offered {18} to pay all the expenses for the anchoring, but unfortunately they did not listen to me and stubbornly wanted to remain on the open sea. At least, because of the calm sea, I had the advantage of being able to digest food without the usual seafarer's nausea, to sleep calmly at night, and to occupy myself, with a pen in hand, at a small table during the day. No doubt the others were not as patient [as I], and the owners of the cargo could even less afford to be so, because in general, all goods diminish in value in case of a delay, but oranges are at still greater risk and are in more danger of rotting than other goods. The cargo's value amounted to nine hundred scudi[6] and was made up of two thousand oranges. Their unpleasant stench, which was ever increased, indicated that not a few of them were already moldy, and a substantial number already in full fermentation.

On Saturday morning 9 June, around sunrise, which was still fairly overcast, we found ourselves approximately thirty miles from Capri, an island

---

3. *neutral ship*: at the time, Italy was divided into the Kingdom of Italy (belonging to France), Naples, Sardinia, and Sicily. Caronni did not want to board a Sicilian or Neapolitan ship due to their lack of treaties with the Barbary states.
4. *xebec*: a three-masted Mediterranean sailing ship with long overhanging bow and stern.
5. *3 June*: in the year 1804.
6. *scudi*: Italian stamped coins.

rather notorious for its Tiberian orgies,[7] and worse, dangerously close to where pirates in their murky hideouts could capture us easily. I was woken by the noise of an unusual number of hasty footsteps and some [people] even reported the sighting of a ship, certainly of corsairs, approaching us from the coast of Salerno or Policastro. At that moment, I ascended to the upper deck and it appeared to me that I could really see the enemy, who headed directly our way. Meanwhile, the owner of our ship took out his national flag[8] and hoisted it at the stern, and I began to think that this signal must be enough to compel [their] respect. I could not imagine that [the owner] thought {19}—because of the current war between France and England[9]—that our assailants could belong to one of these nations, with whom the King of Naples was on good terms. Indeed, the Turkish galley did, in fact, come to a standstill, its oars suspended, like the wheel of Ixion[10] depicted in the inferno in Virgil's manuscript.[11] But the barbarians were not convinced [that the ship was from Naples], and as a result they were able to observe that the ship was Sicilian and defenseless. They could also see that roughly twenty people fled with the dinghy and that, consequently, they would not have encountered any resistance had they boarded the ship. Therefore they boldly resumed rowing briskly toward their prey.

I do not know how to recount the crew's convulsive rioting without reliving the horror. There were still eighteen individuals left on the xebec. Three of them were women whose screams pierced the air, and among others there were also two co-proprietors of the cargo, who were now inevitably afraid [of losing] their sole capital and berated themselves for having thoughtlessly risked fatherland, fortune, and liberty. Everyone ran about the ship, frantic and bewildered, not able to bear the thought of the imminent horrors of slavery. During his escape, one of the fleeing sailors lost sight of one of his sons, who was maybe eight years old, and subsequently climbed halfway back up the ship's side to pull him from the ship into his arms and take him along. Then one of the passengers saved himself by seizing the moment, quickly throwing his suitcase onto the swiftly retreating dinghy

---

7. *Tiberian orgies*: the Roman emperor Tiberius (42 BCE–37 CE) spent the later part of his life on the island of Capri, reportedly living a life of dissipation and cruelty.

8. *national flag*: the Neapolitan one in this case.

9. *the current war between France and England*: Great Britain declared war on France in 1803.

10. *Ixion*: in Greek mythology, a Thessalian king who was bound on a perpetually revolving fiery wheel by Zeus. The wheel only came to a standstill briefly when Orpheus played his lyre in the Underworld.

11. *Virgil's manuscript*: the Vergilius Vaticanus (400 CE).

and jumping into the sea, and then climbing safely into it. Another tried to swim after him, until he almost drowned, and yet another was pushed back by the violent thrust of an oar {20} (because the dinghy was small and all the space already occupied by twenty-two people, including sixteen sailors and the owner), to suffer the very fate he had wanted to escape. I regretted to some extent that I, at the age of fifty-six, was not able to swim, [something] that I had tried to practice in vain thirty years ago. [But I saw] what was happening to the overloaded dinghy, which was in danger of sinking (due to the great distance to the mainland), especially as even more people would have followed my example and would have tried to get into it. As a consequence, the dinghy would have been in danger of capsizing due to the people clinging to the edge and their weight would have drawn it into the deep. It was clear to me in particular, because I was a frank Milanese, that it was more desirable to jeopardize one's liberty on the galley than one's life in that dinghy. Among other things, I struggled greatly to prevent a young Roman boy from throwing himself into the water. He wanted to venture into the waves just as he was—inexperienced and hindered by his coat. The rest of the men and women who remained on board were crowding in on me and turned to me for support in their mortal terror, with the result that I hardly had a chance to loudly demand the return of my passport[12] from the fleeing owner of the ship. The return of [this passport] would have been my only hope. If he had at least answered me that he had not taken it with him, or that he had it but could not hand it back due to the haste of this emergency! We will see how keen I was at the time on getting an answer, but he was completely focused on those who swam around the dinghy {21} and also on the advancing galley, or he did not hear my question, or—even though I adjured him by shouting and waving—he was afraid to lose time. And without caring about anyone other than himself, he put the oars in the water and pulled away with all his might. The dinghy disappeared and the corsairs appeared, and the sobs, the loss, and the screams of my upset companions started again. With their belief in religion, they imagined that I, as a priest, could achieve more than I actually could. They embraced me and prostrated themselves before me, beseeching me to help them, but I could not give them any other aid (I was not a little unsettled myself) than

12. *return of my passport*: the fact that the ship's captain thoughtlessly took Caronni's passport with him resulted in Caronni's captivity. As a citizen of Milan, Caronni would have been protected by a bilateral peace treaty with Tunis, but since he was unable to prove his citizenship, he remained a captive until his identity was confirmed.

evoking those Christian feelings in them which were necessary to bear this disaster more easily and to prepare them to face it with resignation to the immutable will of the greatest master of human events.

All eighteen of us were on the upper deck, immobile at our posts like sacrifices on the brink of being offered up, when the galley reached us effortlessly and halted alongside our xebec to enable the corsairs to board it. What disturbed me at this moment—I felt almost more like a detached spectator than an assaulted passenger—was the threatening posture of the *rais*,[13] who planted himself halfway up the ledge of the galley with a scimitar. He was on the point of striking and screeched in a language I could not understand, and all his *forzati*[14] were spurred on by a kind of frenzy and wanted to have a share of this booty, [although] they unfortunately knew that it could not be theirs. I instantly saw a dark-skinned boy, called Jakazum, who jumped first onto the ship and held fast to the rope {22} of the bowsprit.[15] He made way for the captain, called Babba-Ameth, a *buonavoglia*[16] called Jakmet, and another Maltese renegade named Sherif, who were the ones chosen to steer the ship. They looked over the deck and tried to calm our spirits by telling everyone: "Fear not, fear not." The rais was more enthusiastic than the others and he walked around and said, when he saw the Neapolitan flag flying, "Good catch, good catch." And he repeated honestly to everyone, "Fear not, fear not." He added, almost pleading, "Do not let the Moor enter, do not let the Moor enter." In the meantime, he struggled with four of his companions to move the galley away carefully by aiming their oars against the xebec. The galley contained approximately forty or more hungry slaves who were eager for a possible getaway route or at least for booty. Neither the men left on the galley nor the four who boarded the xebec seemed to suffice to stop the slaves. We feared for our lives and the corsair and his officers assured us that they had respect for our lives, but the real problem was the danger of losing the beautiful and valuable plunder. Indeed, in that moment I was hiding in the stern room and secretly hid money that I had removed from the suitcase in order to have it on me. I saw a rascal who shifted the table that was between us and the oranges. He stole into the chamber and meddled with our suitcases, in this moment stealing everything that fell into his hands.

13. *rais*: the ship's captain.
14. *forzati*: criminals who were forced to work on galleys as part of their punishment.
15. *bowsprit*: on a sailing vessel, a spar extending forward from the vessel's prow.
16. *buonavoglia*: paid galley rowers.

The crew was sent away to take care of the slaves, which contributed to the lessening of our fear. The rais came and asked everyone {23} presumptuously about their purses, tobacco pouches, and watches, and about the more valuable things that we had on ourselves. I was awaiting him in my room, to which he descended. He caught sight of me in my flawless religious uniform and he listened to me while I said that I was from the Italian Republic and therefore allied and honest. "Where is your passport?" he said to me. "It was in the hands of the owner [of the ship]," I replied, "but because he bolted, I do not know where it is." "Even better for me," he continued, "You are a good catch as well. In the meantime, give me the valuable things you have." As I was humbly apologizing for my missing passport and promising that I would recover it or at least show him a second one from Europe, Jakmet (the buonavoglia who had accompanied the rais) came and thought that he could frighten me with an *attagan*,[17] which is a scimitar. He was ready to hack off my head, but I felt certain that the corsairs valued our lives as much as we valued them ourselves, for ransom and servitude purposes. That is why I was not afraid of putting my neck on the line and preparing myself for the blow, which humiliated this subordinate and maybe made me look good in the eyes of the rais. Without arguing, I gave him my watch and my purse and emptied my pockets in order to show him that I did not have anything else in them other than the purse and a handkerchief. In the meantime, seventeen of our passengers were sent to the galley and among them was a young girl aged three called Rosalia, who could not escape them and who stubbornly held onto my neck as her only refuge. My clerical garment was the only reason why I was not suspected of rebellion and consequently I was spared and left on our xebec with the rais and four of his chosen confidants. [. . .]

[*Once they reached Tunis, Caronni and his fellow captives were taken to their master Bascì Amba. Caronni was allocated a room which he describes as clean, with a pleasant view. He managed to send a message to Father Settimio di Montalboldo, the vicar of the Capuchin mission involved in ransoming slaves. Caronni received the good news that the imperial French consul would assist him.*]

{60} [. . .] In those first days, the bey[18] and his entourage had much else to think about [apart from choosing slaves].[19] He was occupied with a very serious incident in which we would have wanted to take part instead of merely being spectators and which brought Tunis not only very close to

17. *attagan*: Caronni probably means a *yatagan*, a type of Ottoman saber.
18. *bey*: Hammuda ibn Ali (1759–1814), bey of Tunis from 1782 until 1814.
19. *choosing slaves*: the bey had first pick of any newly captured slaves.

giving up piracy, but also to losing its political existence altogether. At four o'clock in the afternoon of 26 June, we heard sudden cannon shots near La Goulette,[20] which drew all of us to the windows, from which we had a good view. Not only could we see the anchored ships in the bay, but we were also able to perceive (despite a distance of seven or eight miles) the nation involved in the action. All our Neapolitan comrades believed them {61} to be the ships of their sovereign and they quickly ascended to a higher point to get confirmation and to hope for success. It was indeed the corvette[21] which had been sighted by us several times near Gallibia and Solimano. She kept herself behind the [Neapolitan] royal battleship *Archimedes*, which I had seen four weeks before in Palermo. The aim of this fleet was to take the Tunisians by surprise to avenge the latest and also past outrages. That is why, up to now, they had sailed under a purportedly English flag, and they succeeded in reaching the roadstead[22] and getting close to the dangerous Tunisian frigate without being recognized. Some of the mariners said, "Look, these clumsy English are coming and positioning themselves at the hawser[23] of our anchor." "No," a voice could be heard from a nearby Ragusian[24] ship which was more interested in war strategies than in the common good, "Watch out, because it is Neapolitan." At that very moment, the English flag was pulled down and the Neapolitan one hoisted, followed by an unexpected burst of artillery from the frigate, and the crew all shot their muskets. Also, a casket of gunpowder was thrown on board, which would have been enough to set everything alight had the Turks not thrown it into the water due to their natural ignorance of its sudden effect. The cannon shots were recommenced and lasted for a quarter of an hour. Only sparse and late resistance arrived, but the expedition had ill luck and a fresh wind from the coast of Levante started to blow, which made the count of Thurn, the general commander, wary. {62} Signals of retreat were made by the battleship because the corvette was on the brink of running aground in the shallow waters of La Goulette and turning from predator to prey. Captain Staiti, who knew the situation very well due to many years of experience, felt certain that he was not in danger and hesitated to retreat, as he did not wish to lose this opportune moment. But first, the rais came to cut off the rope of

20. *La Goulette*: the port of Tunis. "Goletta" in the 1805 Italian edition.
21. *corvette*: a small, three-masted warship.
22. *roadstead*: a partially enclosed body of water outside a harbor where a ship can lie at anchor.
23. *hawser*: a rope used for towing or mooring a ship.
24. *Ragusian*: from the Sicilian city of Ragusa.

the frigate and let it collide with the troops farther down the narrow canal, which terminated there. Second, signals of urgent retreat were continuously made by the *Archimedes*, wherefore Captain Staiti had to leave his enterprise unaccomplished and retreat, so as not to be in danger of insubordination.

We watched this scene most attentively, it being easy to observe, though very far away. Our hearts were beating jubilantly as we were expecting the assault of the frigate, the rebellion of the four or five hundred slaves who worked at that port, the shackling of hundreds of renegades, their torturers, and as a consequence, our liberation. But the result of this attempt went up in smoke along with our hopes. The Neapolitan company retreated without further glory than a hundred killed or wounded Barbary pirates and some considerable damage to the masts and the frigate's main body, which could be subsequently repaired, however. It is easy to imagine that our spirits fell into deep sadness after we had been filled with such great expectations. Had one of the two royal ships arrived a few hours {63} earlier in these waters, we would have been saved. Or if a different wind had blown from the sea, the attack would have been accomplished and perhaps decided for good on the Tunisian beach. As it was, however, poor slaves were put in danger of suffering the consequences [of the Neapolitan attack] through the hands of their masters and a regency that was full of pride about the inefficacy of their enemies' attempt. A statement by the aforementioned count of Thurn was sent to some of the Christian consuls, in which he lamented, in the name of his sovereign, the excesses of the Barbary pirates' outrages through attacks on land and sea. He threatened (should the bey not consider restraining himself) with a revenge of greater proportions, not comparable with this first attack. The statement was communicated to the bey, but unfortunately he was well informed of the very limited powers of the King of Naples. He saw [the threat] as a sort of scarecrow, and he proved to be right, because the convoy did not show up again all summer. [. . .]

{64} [. . .] One morning, Bascì Amba arrived, accompanied by an Italian physician, in order to examine a slave's ear that was stinking due to eczema. During his visit, he asked me how I felt and how I happened to be there. I briefly provided him with information and quickly used the opportunity to talk about my national passport, through which I had to be acknowledged as a member of the treaty of the great nations' alliance[25] and consequently legitimized. [I told him] that I did not know whether my passport was left

---

25. *the great nations' alliance*: Napoleon concluded a peace agreement with the Ottoman Empire in 1802.

on board the proprietor Ferraro's ship and destroyed by the galley slaves or whether it had been taken away by him when he saved himself by boarding the dinghy. I also told him that I had not failed to ask [Ferraro] for it in front of the whole crew, with tears in my eyes and the voice that was still left within me. The others had meanwhile circled me and helped me with their testimony and called upon him by saying in unison, "So it is, so it is." I do not know whether he was more dissatisfied as a result of this unexpected discovery or more abashed by the mutual testimony, because he was moody instantly. "Be quiet," he shouted at me, "you are saying this in order to escape." He advanced with a threatening attitude. Without being disconcerted by this trait of obstinate despotism, {65} I retreated one step. "Sir," I added with humility, "The truth, in which I can calmly rest, wants to be revealed." The sacred proverb *responsio mollis frangit iras*[26] (Chapter 15) is indeed true! My attitude of tranquility disarmed him in this moment and he descended the stairs in the physician's company without saying anything else.

The physician helped as well. Because of his profession, he was a confidant of my cousin and had already heard from him about my case. He had accepted the commitment to help me as much as he could. Due to the latest conversations and my old letters from Italy, it was clear that I was who I claimed to be. "Let us carry out an experiment with the priest," he said to Bascì Amba and stopped him at the bottom of the stairs. "If he really is my friend's cousin, if he really is Milanese and consequently the one who wrote to him, we can test him and call him by his name with which he signs, which is Don Felice." This moment seemed to be suitable and thereupon he called out "Don Felice," wanting to find out [if this was truly my name]. I was only just able to hear something and to recognize my name. I listened carefully to be certain that I had not imagined it, but I clearly heard my name being repeated. "Who is it," I said, "Who is it that is calling me?" This must have been a harsh setback for the master,[27] who did not want to be ridiculed. But so it was, and he even heard the truth of my testimony confirmed by the biased consuls. From this point on, he showed himself softened in my presence and distinguished me from all others through clear signs of partiality. [. . .]

{66} [. . .] On Friday evening (which was going to be the last one[28]), the twenty-two slaves of my group wanted to confess {67} in order to be able

---

26. *responsio mollis frangit iras*: "A soft answer turneth away wrath" (Prov. 15:1, King James Version).
27. *master*: his owner Bascì Amba.
28. *the last one*: the last evening before they are presented to the bey, who will choose slaves for himself.

to face the destiny that awaited them with less fear. I had the huge privilege of honoring this night, as I was able to satisfy them spiritually by giving them some preliminary instructions and helping them begin their [spiritual] preparations. Dawn broke quickly on Saturday and Rais Hagy Amour,[29] who arrived from Gallibia where we had left him, appeared, looking for us. He was very happy to be welcomed by us with such affection and appreciation. He told us to follow him to Bardo,[30] where we had to be presented to the sovereign with him. Unfortunately, we anticipated this moment with the anxiety that precedes every uncertain situation and with a kind of impatience that is depicted in mythology: crowds of people in the dark, at the bank of the river Styx,[31] waiting to be taken by Charon[32] and dropped on the opposite bank, from which there is no return. And so we gathered around [Hagy Amour], who was riding a donkey, and were sent on a two-mile path to Sidi Almuda Pascià's[33] palace. This residence consisted of a kind of small, well-enclosed village and the walls of the elevated hall were fortified with plenty of artillery. Its entrance was guarded by armed men and weapons. Further inside were the well-guarded quarters of the diplomats and those of high status. In the center were the sovereign's living quarters, including the big hall of common law and audiences, which was fairly beautiful, built in three sections and supported by a double circle of columns. At the back, the bey was sitting on a decorated sofa, with legs crossed according to oriental custom. The crowd was large and {68} present for their own interest, because of [their] curiosity about the newly arrived slaves. My cousin was also there to meet me and, oh, what a delicious sensation for my heart to see and speak to such a close relative on the shores of Africa and in the midst of a crowd of Barbary pirates! He came closer and spoke with me as long as he wished. He also comforted me and assured me that both consuls had come that morning to assist me and that I should hope for the best.

Meanwhile, we were, I do not want to say presented, but rather pushed, one after the other, in front of the sovereign. I first left my shoes at the door, which is at the atrium. This was the correct etiquette for every house in

---

29. *Rais Hagy Amour*: the captain of the ship that captured Caronni and his companions.

30. *Bardo*: a city in the west of Tunisia.

31. *Styx*: in Greek mythology, the river that forms the boundary between the Underworld and the world of the living.

32. *Charon*: in Greek mythology, the ferryman who transports the souls of the deceased across the Styx.

33. *Sidi Almuda Pascià*: although Caronni does not make this clear, he is most likely referring to Hammuda ibn Ali (see note 18).

which carpets were rolled out. The ship owner Bascì Amba had presented our rais, who, while on his knees on the floor before [the bey], had notified him of the value of the cash and the plunder and had then retreated. I stood still and then he called me close to him. But instead of giving me time to tell him about myself and my reasonable complaint, he showed me a *pannonia lacta*,[34] which was coined in Hungary and depicted one of my designs for Ferdinand the Fourth and Carolina, ruler of the two Sicilies in the year 1790, and he asked me, "What is this?"

"A medallion of the king and queen of Naples."

"How valuable is it?"

"For the connoisseur, two pieces from Spain, but it does not have any market value because it is a kind of private luxury."

"And this?" he showed me one of my relics, a piece of wood from the holy cross, which was unfortunately edged with gilded silver.

"It is a Christian religious token."

Then he held a snuffbox in his hand with the image of a young cavalier {69} who was sent from Palermo in order to ingratiate himself in Naples.

"This," he started again, "who is this? Is it maybe a woman?"

"It is surely the master of the Roman servant near me."

And while I was saying so, two *aiducci*[35] who were next to me shoved me back to allow Luigi Cherubino to pass.

The trust with which we were presented, without at least our pockets having been searched, seemed entirely unusual to me. We were presented very close to the bey and nothing would have been easier (for desperate fellow slaves who met at Bardo and received a firearm or a blade) than to fire a lethal shot, whatever the cost. I was even more surprised by the Barbary pirates' trust in Christian loyalty. We knew that the bey and Zappi-Tappa— his first minister—had already been taught a terrible lesson of this sort by two black slaves. One had stabbed him in the throat with a dagger, from which a large scar was still left on his cheek, and the other had fired a shot from his pistol at the minister, which had almost cost him his life. Although these subordinates believed themselves to be mighty rivals, they saw the shot go amiss and retreated into the antechamber, where they fought yet another one in order to flee the investigation or a torturous death by [beating with] a stick or death at the stake. [. . .] {70} [. . .] After the personal interrogation

---

34. *pannonia lacta*: Caronni misspells "pannonia laeta," an antique medallion.

35. *aiducci*: possibly "guards."

was finished, I was led into the atrium, where I had to stay until the bey's order and until he had chosen those of us to whom he took a liking as his property. [. . .]

[*Caronni was sent back to Tunis and received the news that, thanks to the intervention of the consuls, he would not be considered a slave much longer. His former owner, Bascì Amba, wanted Caronni to remain with him for a few days, saying that he enjoyed Caronni's conversation and learning.*]

{75} The 2nd of July was one of those days which are very rare in the life of a man. Intense was the joy I felt within myself, intense was the joy over the consoling words that were addressed to me. After only eight days of having had the status of a slave in captivity, I became merely a simple hostage. I was released with goodwill from the house of the Turkish shipowner who could have imprisoned me, if he wanted to, sold me, forced me to labor, and beaten me. [I was taken in by] a French minister who tended to me, who had taken on all the obligations to reclaim my rights, and in whose house my reception was like a small triumph! After lunch was finished, which seemed to me to be a banquet for my happy release, I went to visit the imperial consul. We conversed and I received congratulations, embraces, and applause from the whole assembly. There was not one Christian, regardless of their nationality, who did not offer to support me with genuine friendship. They wished me to be with them more often, as did the Trinitarians who served the church and the hospital under auspices of the *Spagua*,[36] and also the Capuchins of the hospital, where {76} I started celebrating holy mass every day as a protégé of France.

During the first three weeks I was much occupied with new acquaintances and frequent kind invitations. My alleged master had not lost sight of me in the meantime, and in order to display his power over me, he occasionally sent me invitations, which the consuls advised me to accept. They consisted of several hours of conversation in the evenings during dinner. Afterward, he always sent me back with his guards, but never without some gifts of sweet pastry or sticks of delicious dates. [My master] sometimes lay down on his bed to smoke his pipe, wanting to hear accounts of the events in Europe and my own strokes of fate. I profited from these expressions of goodwill by making him realize that I had lost everything. Among other things, I mentioned some of my good books and the antique medals collected in Sicily, which luckily neither the rais nor his galley slaves had

---

36. *Spagua*: unclear; possibly "Spanish."

known how to profit from, especially after having thrown away my interpretation cards, despite my urgent requests. My misfortunes interested him the most, and I had to tell him about my last stay in Sicily, [which I had visited] not only out of curiosity, but in deference to the master of the arts, the Hungarian count Witzai. He sent me to collect important antiques at his expense to enrich the noble museum that had often been celebrated in the works of Eckhel[37] and for whom I had already undertaken many other successful trips. When rais Amour visited, I was so insistent that, within a few days, a portion {77} of the less showy copper medals, several books, and some other trifles were returned to me. The best had already been sold, partly on the market of Tunis (where I had to rebuy items that I recognized as my property at an exorbitant price) and partly dispatched to sell elsewhere to avoid possible liability.

On some of these days I walked past art enthusiasts who owned collections of cut jewels and antique coins that were partly Punic and partly Romanesque. I sorted out their poorly organized household goods with great pleasure and to my advantage and tried to convince them of the historical importance and rarity of many of those authentic artifacts and to separate out the apocrypha[38] which the Italians (due to their miserliness) had brought here in order to exploit the trust of the inexperienced. A philosophical and mutually useful trade developed between us that was advantageous for my knowledge and I also enriched myself with some rare pieces from their museum. [. . .]

I had not even been in Tunis for a month and had almost reached the coast of Mauretania,[39] when papers which were of greatest significance for my destiny arrived on a ship which came from Livorno[40] within ten days. {78} After the sailors and the few passengers who saved themselves had reached land with their dinghy on 10 June, the news of the capture of our xebec spread all over Naples. As a result, Brother Ferrara, head of the Barnabites[41] of R. Nuova, who had been waiting impatiently for me to return from Palermo, was immediately informed. He instantly sent letters to the superiors in Rome and elsewhere, so that [the letters] had

---

37. *Eckhel*: Joseph Hilarius von Eckhel, an eminent collector.
38. *apocrypha*: purportedly ancient items that are fake or of doubtful origin.
39. *Mauretania*: ancient name for a North African region corresponding to sections of present-day northern Morocco and western and central Algeria.
40. *Livorno*: a port city on the Ligurian sea in western Tuscany, Italy.
41. *Barnabites*: a Roman Catholic religious order.

already reached Milan on 23 June, while I was still at Cape Bon. They had been sent by my very caring Brother Giuseppe Antonio Carono and my good brother-in-law Giacomo Porchera to a shared friend in Livorno, Mr. Antonio Careno. My baptismal certificate was legally attested by the local magistrate of Monza in order to serve as justification for my liberation. On this occasion, pressing letters were sent to Mr. De-Voize[42] by the French ambassador in Naples, Cardinal Fesch in Rome, by Mr. Simeon, agent of the French minister in Florence, as well as by different consuls of these and other nations in Livorno that attested to the existence of my legally valid passport, mentioning the register and the date taken from the *libri mastri*.[43] They also ordered that I was immediately being claimed back and that this would be valid for the three regencies of Algiers, Tripoli, and Tunis. [. . .] All the Christians in Tunis congratulated me when they heard about the arrival of my documents, and it seemed almost unreal to me that such misery engendered such general commiseration and that everyone wanted to see me liberated. But due to a fatal incident, my happiness and that of the others' turned out to be premature. [. . .]

[*When the French consul presented Caronni's papers to the bey, the bey dismissed them as fake, claiming that they had arrived in Tunis suspiciously quickly. He refused to release Caronni until he had received more information about the ransom sum he would receive for Caronni.*]

{80} [. . .] When Mr. De-Voize returned from Bardo, I saw by the dismay showing on his face and his silence that the negotiations had not gone well that day. Religion and necessity were the only things which—due to this indiscretion, if not to say the Barbary injustice—gave me peace. {81} Usually, Mr. De-Voize was able to lift my spirits in order to render my situation more tolerable, and it was highly embarrassing when he showed me that he was more than just a little frustrated. An advantage and a great relief for me in these gloomy days was the letter of recommendation written by Mr. Lambruschini from Livorno to Mr. Holke, the Danish consul, for my benefit. As soon as [the Danish consul] had read it, he sent one of his illegitimate daughters to me to take me away from Tunis. We went to La Marsa,[44] which was ten miles away and which is situated at the foot of the famous,

---

42. *Mr. De-Voize*: the French consul Jacques-Philippe Devoize.
43. *libri mastri*: a register or ledger.
44. *La Marsa*: a coastal town near Tunis. "Marsa" in the 1805 Italian edition.

ruined, and unfortunately lost capital of the Punic Empire.[45] It even had a big aqueduct and was situated next to a lake and was surrounded by lovely hills with huge olive groves and vineyards, planted with many kinds of fruit. For a distance of eight miles we saw nothing but the houses and gardens of wealthy Moors, which were partly for their own pleasure and partly for the use of consuls who rented them at a cost of approximately one hundred sequins[46] per year. [. . .] For three weeks, I amused myself there a great deal with this very pleasant host, sometimes on foot, sometimes on horseback. The French consul also welcomed this, because now he had time to attend to more important matters that he had neglected because of me. But he never completely lost sight of my case [. . .].

I know that on 23 June, my brother managed to win Mr. Vice President Melzi over to my case, thanks to the effective intervention of Father Rossi. His Excellency wrote immediately to the Parisian cabinet in order [that they should] demand [my release] authoritatively. I knew that the physician Luigi Careno, my cousin in Vienna, was employed by several ministers of France and of Lombardy, Champigny, and Marescalchi. I knew that His Excellence Taillerand and His Excellence Cardinal Caprara, our archbishop and representative of the Pope, were very keen to see me released quickly. Our vice president's decision to write to Mr. De-Voize after hearing about the difficulties that had occurred was, however, very generous. He communicated to Mr. De-Voize that, regardless of the sum, he should settle every dispute with the bey before it could even arise, in order to remove any pretext for my detention. The distance between the locations, the embarkation delay, and the ship's slowness hindered the immediate effect of these attentions to me, because at the time when they were sending these invaluable messages to Africa, I had already arrived in Livorno. However, I will always be obliged to His Excellence Melzi, as well as to General Salimbeni, to Naval Commissioner Paolucci, to Councillor Carlotti, and to many others who had sent government letters to Tunis about this matter, including emphatic orders and urgent recommendations. {83} Upon my return to Tunis, I seized the moment for a private retreat in order to write down the little observations that I made in this location, in order to one day give anyone who might ask insight into them. In a different paragraph, I will describe some of the things

---

45. *capital of the Punic Empire*: Carthage, capital of the Carthaginian (Punic) Empire.
46. *sequin*: a common gold coin also known as a ducat.

I collected[47] during this short stay and leave it to those who want to know more about it to consult various historians and especially the more modern Shaw (edition of London 1757).[48] [...]

[*In the remainder of the first volume, Caronni includes extensive chapters on the history, religion, commerce, and culture of Tunis, as well as a description of his return voyage.*]

---

47. *the things I collected*: Caronni goes into detail about his antiquarian acquisitions in the second volume of his work.

48. *Shaw (edition of London 1757)*: Caronni is referring to Thomas Shaw, *Travels, Or, Observations Relating to Several Parts of Barbary and the Levant: Illustrated with Cuts* (London: A. Millar and W. Sandby, 1757).

APPENDIX

Selection of European and American Barbary Captivity Narratives

The following list makes no attempt to record all extant Barbary captivity narratives between the early sixteenth and early nineteenth century. However, it may serve as a useful starting point for readers interested in further exploring some of the major national or regional manifestations of this genre. Narratives are listed according to the language in which they were written or published.

AMERICAN

Adams, Robert. *The Narrative of Robert Adams: An American Sailor Who Was Wrecked on the Western Coast of Africa, in the Year 1810, Was Detained Three Years in Slavery by the Arabs of the Great Desert, and Resided Several Months in the City of Tombuctoo; with a Map, Notes and an Appendix*. London: Printed for J. Murray, 1816.

Bradley, Eliza. *An Authentic Narrative of the Shipwreck and Sufferings of Mrs. Eliza Bradley, the Wife of Capt. James Bradley, of Liverpool, England, Commander of the British Ship Sally, Which Was Wrecked on the Coast of Barbary*. Boston: J. Walden, 1823.

Carey, Matthew. *A Short Account of Algiers, Containing a Description of the Climate of That Country, of the Manners and Customs of the Inhabitants, and of Their Several Wars against Spain, France, England, Holland, Venice, and Other Powers of Europe [. . .]*. Philadelphia: J. Parker, 1794.

Cathcart, James Leander. *The Captives by James Leander Cathcart, Eleven Years a Prisoner in Algiers. Compiled by His Daughter, J.B. Newkirk*. La Porte, IN: Herald Print, [1899].

Cowdery, Jonathan. *American Captives in Tripoli; or, Dr. Cowdery's Journal in Miniature: Kept during His Late Captivity in Tripoli*. Boston: Belcher & Armstrong, 1806.

Foss, John D. *A Journal, of the Captivity and Sufferings of John Foss: Several Years a Prisoner in Algiers: together With Some Account of the Treatment of Christian Slaves When Sick: and Observations of the Manners and Customs of the Algerines*. Newburyport, MA: Angier March, [1798].

Gee, Joshua. *Narrative of Joshua Gee of Boston, Mass., While He Was Captive in Algeria of the Barbary Pirates, 1680–1687*, ed. Albert Carlos Bates. Hartford, CT: Wadsworth Atheneum, 1943.

Laranda, Viletta. *Neapolitan Captive: Interesting Narrative of the Captivity and Sufferings of Miss Viletta Laranda, a Native of Naples, Who, With a Brother, Was a Passenger on Board a Neapolitan Vessel Wrecked near Oran, on the Barbary Coast, September 1829 [. . .]*. New York: C.C. Henderson, 1830.

Mather, Cotton. *The Glory of Goodness: The Goodness of God Celebrated; in Remarkable Instances and Improvements Thereof: and More Particularly in the Redemption Remarkably Obtained for the English Captives, Which Have Been Languishing under the Tragical, and the Terrible and the Most Barbarous Cruelties of Barbary*. Boston: T. Green, 1703.

Nicholson, Thomas. *An Affecting Narrative of the Captivity and Sufferings of Thomas Nicholson, [a Native of New-Jersey,] Who Has Been Six Years a Prisoner among the Algerines [. . .]*. Boston: Printed for G. Walker, [181–?].

Paddock, Judah. *Narrative of the Shipwreck of the Ship Oswego, on the Coast of South Barbary: and of the Sufferings of the Master and the Crew While in Bondage among the Arabs: Interspersed with Numerous Remarks upon the Country and Its Inhabitants, and Concerning the Peculiar Perils of That Coast*. New York: Captain James Riley. J. Seymour, 1818.

Ray, William. *Horrors of Slavery: Or, the American Tars in Tripoli; Containing an Account of the Loss and Capture of the United States Frigate Philadelphia; Treatment and Sufferings of the Prisoners [. . .]*. Troy, NY: Oliver Lyon, 1808.

Riley, James. *An Authentic Narrative of the Loss of the American Brig Commerce: Wrecked on the Western Coast of Africa in the Month of August 1815: with an Account of the Sufferings of Her Surviving Officers and Crew [. . .]*. Hartford, CT, 1817.

Robbins, Archibald. *A Journal, Comprising an Account of the Loss of the Brig Commerce: of Hartford, Con., James Riley, Master, upon the Western Coast of Africa, August 28th, 1815: Also of the Slavery and Sufferings of the Author and the Rest of the Crew* [. . .]. Hartford, CT: Silas Andrus, 1818.

Saunders, Daniel. *A Journal of the Travels and Sufferings of Daniel Saunders, Jun.: A Mariner on Board the Ship Commerce, of Boston, Samuel Johnson, Commander Which Was Cast Away near Cape Morebet, on the Coast of Arabia, July 10, 1792*. Salem, MA: Thomas C. Cushing, 1794.

Shaw, Elijah. *A Short Sketch of the Life of Elijah Shaw: Who Served for Twenty-one Years in the U. S. Navy, Taking An Active Part in Four Different Wars between the United States & Foreign Powers* [. . .]. Rochester: E. Shepard, 1845.

Vandike, John. *Narrative of the Captivity of John, Who Was Taken by the Algierines in 1791: An Account of His Escape in 1791, Bringing With Him a Beautiful Young English Lady Who Was Taken in 1790; the Ill Usage She Received from Her Master: the Whole in a Letter to His Brother in Amsterdam*. Hanover, NH: Printed for the purchaser, 1799.

BRITISH

Brooks, Francis. *Barbarian Cruelty: Being a True History of the Distressed Condition of the Christian Captives under the Tyranny of Mully Ishmael, Emperor of Morocco, and King of Fez and Macqueness in Barbary* [. . .]. London: J. Salusbury and H. Newman, 1693.

Browne, Abraham. "A Book of Remembrance of God's Provydences Towards Me, A. B., throughout the Cours of my Life, Written for my Own Medytacion in New Engl." N.d. MS. Massachusetts Historical Society.

Coxere, Edward. "Adventures by Sea of Edward Coxere: A Relation of the Several Adventures by Sea with the Dangers, Difficulties and Hardships I Met for Several Years; as Also the Deliverances and Escapes through Them for Which I Have Cause to Give the Glory to God Forever." English: Journal of the English Association 6, no. 33 (1946): 152–53.

Elliot, Adam. *A True Narrative of the Life of Mr. George Elliot, Who Was Taken and Sold for a Slave; with his Travels, Captivity, and Miraculous Escape from Salle in the Kingdom of Fez*. London, [1770].

Fox, John. "The Woorthie Enterprise of John Foxe, in Delivering 266. Christians out of the Captivity of the Turks at Alexandria." In *The Principall Navigations, Voiages, and Discoveries of the English Nations* [. . .], ed. Richard Hakluyt. 1608.

Hasleton, Richard. *Strange and Wonderful Things Happened to Richard Hasleton, Borne at Braintree in Essex, in His Ten Yeares Trauailes in Many Forraine Countries. Penned as he Deliuered it from His Ovvne Mouth*. London: Printed by A I for William Barley, 1595.

Johnson, Richard. "The Casting Away of the Tobie neere Cape Espartel, without the Strait of Gibraltar on the Coast of Barbary, 1593." In The Principall Navigations, Voiages, and Discoveries of the English Nations [. . .], ed. Richard Hakluyt. 2nd ed. 3 vols. London, 1598–1600.

Knight, Francis. *A Relation of Seauen Yeares Slaverie under the Turkes of Argeire, Suffered by an English Captive Merchant Wherein is Also Conteined All Memorable Passages, Fights, and Accidents, Which Wappined in That Citie, and at Sea with Their Shippes and Gallies during That Time* [. . .]. London: T. Cotes, 1640.

Lawson, William, and Thomas Stewart Traill. *Account of the Captivity of Alexander Scott among the Wandering Arabs of the Great African Desert for a Period of Nearly Six Years*. The Literary Journal, vol. 1. American of the American Periodical Series, 1800–1850. Vol. 85. N.p.: E. Littel, 1821.

Lithgow, William. *The Totall Discourse of the Rare Aduentures, and Painefull Peregrinations of Long Nineteene Yeares Travailes from Scotland, to the Most Famous Kingdomes in Europe, Asia, and Affrica Perfited by Three Deare Bought Voyages* [. . .]. London: I. Okes, 1640.

Marsh, Elizabeth. *The Female Captive: A Narrative of Facts, Which Happened in Barbary, in the Year 1756*. N.p.: C. Bathurst, 1769.

Marsh, Elizabeth. "Narrative I: Narrative of Her Captivity in Barbary." MS 170/604. Charles E. Young Research Library, Special Collections, University of California, Los Angeles.

Middleton, Henry. *The Sixth Voyage, Set Forth by the East-Indian Company in Three Shippes* [. . .]. Purchas His Pilgrims. Ed. Samuel Purchas. London: William Stansby, 1625. 247–66.

News from Sally of a Strange Delivery of Four English Captives from the Slavery of Turks. London, 1642.

Nixon, Anthony. *The Three English Brothers: Sir Thomas Sherley His Trauels, with his Three Yeares Imprisonment in Turkie: Hhis Inlargement by his Maiesties Letters to the Great Turke: and Lastly, His Safe Returne into England This Present Yeare, 1607* [. . .]. London, 1607.

Ockley, Simon. *An Account of South-West Barbary: Containing What is Most Remarkable in the Territories of the King of Fez and Morocco. Written by a Person Who Had Been a Slave There a Considerable Time* [. . .]. London: Printed for J. Bowyer, 1713.

Okeley, William. *Eben-ezer, or, A Small Monument of Great Mercy: Appearing in the Miraculous Deliverance of William Okeley, Williams Adams, John Anthony, John Jephs, John—, Carpenter, from the Miserable Slavery of Algiers, with the Wonderful Means of Their Escape in a Boat of Canvas* [. . .]. London: Printed for Nat. Ponder, 1675.

Pellow, Thomas. *The History of the Long Captivity and Adventures of Thomas Pellow, in South Barbary: Giving an Account of His Being Taken by Two Sallee Rovers, and Carry'd a Slave to Mequinez, at Eleven Years of Age: His Various Adventures in that Country for the Space of Twenty-three Years: Escape, and Return Home. In Which is Introduced, a Particular Account of the Manners and Customs of the Moors; the Astonishing Tyranny and Cruelty of Their Emperors, and a Relation of All Those Great Revolutions and Bloody Wars which Happen'd in the Kingdoms of Fez and Morocco, Between the Years 1720 and 1736. Together with a Description of the Cities, Towns, and Publick Buildings in Those Kingdoms; Miseries of the Christian Slaves; and Many Other Curious Particulars.* 2nd ed. London: Printed for R. Goadby, and sold by W. Owen, [1740?].

Phelps, Thomas. *A True Account of the Captivity of Thomas Phelps at Machaness in Barbary and of His Strange Escape in Company of Edmund Baxter and Others* [. . .]. London: H. Hills jun., 1685.

Pitts, Joseph. *A True and Faithful Account of the Religion and Manners of the Mohammetans in Which is a Particular Relation of Their Pilgrimage to Mecca* [. . .]. Exon [Exeter]: S. Farley, 1704.

Rawlins, John. *The Famous and Wonderful Recovery of a Ship of Bristol, Called the Exchange, from the Turkish Pirates of Argier* [. . .]. London, 1622.

A Relation Strange and True, of a Ship of Bristol named the Jacob, of 120 Tunnes, Which Was about the End of Octob. Last 1621 Taken by the Turkish Pirats of Argier [. . .]. London, 1622.

Saunders, Thomas. *A True Discription and Breefe Discourse, of a Most Lamentable Voiage, made Latelie to Tripolie in Barbarie, in a Ship Named the Iesus* [. . .]. London: Richard Iones, 1587.

Smith, John. *The True Travels, Adventures and Observations of Captaine Iohn Smith, in Europe, Asia, Africke, and America: Beginning about the Yeere 1593, and Continued to This Present 1629.* London, 1630.

S[mith], T[homas]. *The Adventures of (Mr T. S.) an English Merchant, Taken Prisoner by the Turks of Argiers and Carried into the Inland Countries of Africa* [. . .]. London, 1630.

Spratt, Devereux. "The Capture of a Protestant Divine, by an Algerine Corsair, in the Seventeenth Century." In *Travels and Researches in Crete*, ed. T. A. B. Spratt. 2 vols., 1384–87. N.p., 1865.

A True and Perfect Account of the Examination, Confession, and Execution of Joan Perry and her Two Sons, John and Richard Perry, for the Supposed Murder of Will. Harrison [. . .]. London: Printed for John Atkinson, [1676].

Wadsworth, James. *The English Spanish Pilgrime; or, A New Discouerie of Spanish Popery, and Iesuiticall Stratagems* [. . .]. London: T[homas] C[otes], 1629.

Webbe, Edward. *The Rare and Most Wonderfvll Things which Edw. Webbe an Englishman Borne, Hath Seene and Passed in His Troublesome Trauailes* [. . .]. London: Printed for William Wright, 1590.

Whitehead, John. "John Whitehead his Relation of Barbary." 1697. MS Sloane. British Library.

DANISH

Olufs, Hark. *Harck Olufs, fød paa Øen Amrom udi Riber-Stift i Jydland, besynderlige Avantures, som have tildraget sig med ham især til Constantine og paa andre Steder i Africa, for deres Merkværdigheds skyld i Trykken udgivne.* 1747.

Olufs, Hark. *Harck Olufs aus der Insul Amron im Stifte Ripen in Jütland gebürtig, sonderbare Avanturen, so sich mit ihm insonderheit zu Constantine und an andern Orten in Africa zugetragen. Ihrer Merkwürdigkeit wegen in Dänischer Sprache zum Drucke befördert, itzo aber ins Deutsche übersetzet.* Flensburg: Johann Christoph Kortens, 1751.

DANISH/NORWEGIAN

Diderich, Lars. *Sandfærdig Fortællelse om de Christnes ynkværdig Slaverie udi Barbariet, forfattet for enhver Christen, som et opbyggeligt Speyl, ved en Samtale imellem Theophilum og Timotheum.* 1756.

DUTCH

d'Aranda, Emanuel. *Historie vande Turckse slavernie, beschreven door Emanuel De Airanda.* s'Graven-Haghe: Christoffel en Iasper Doll, 1657.

d'Aranda, Emanuel. *The History of Algiers and It's Slavery, with Many Remarkable Particularities of Africk, Written by the Sieur Emanuel D'Aranda, Sometime a Slave There.* Trans. John Davies. London: Printed for John Starkey, 1666.

d'Aranda, Emanuel. *Relation de la Captivité en Algérie de Emmanuel de Aranda 1640.1642.* N. d. MS. Castle Van Loppem Foundation, West Flanders, Belgium.

d'Aranda, Emanuel. *Relation de la captivité et liberté du Sieur Emanuel de Aranda, mené esclave a Alger en l'an 1640 & mis en liberté l'an 1642*. Brussels: Jean Mommaert, 1656.

de Vries, Simon. *Handelingen en Geschiedenissen, Voorgevallen tusschen den Staet der Vereenighde Nederlanden En dien van de Zee-Roovers in Barbaryen*. Amsterdam: Hoorn, 1684.

ter Meetelen, Maria. *Wonderbaarlyke en merkwaardige gevallen van een twaalf jarige slaverny, van een vrouspersoon. Genaemt Maria ter Meetelen, woonagtig tot Medenblik*. Hoorn: Jacob Duyn, 1748.

FRENCH

Brassard, Isaac. "Relation de la captivité de M. Brassard à Alger." Ed. H. de France. *Bulletin de la Société de Histoire du Protestantisme Français* 27 (1878): 349–55.

Chastelet des Boys, René. *L'Odyssée ou Diversité d'Avantures encontres et voyages en Europe, Asie et Affrique, divisée en quatre parties*. La Flèche: G. Laboe, 1665.

Cochelet, Charles. *Naufrage du brick français, La Sophie perdu le 30 mai 1819 sur la côte occidentale d'Afrique, et captivité d'une partie des naufragés dans le désert du Sahara [. . .]*. Paris: P. Mongie aîné, 1821.

Comelin, François. *Voyage pour la Redemption des captifs aux royaumes d'Alger et de Tunis. Fait en 1720 [. . .]*. Paris, 1721.

Dard, Charlotte-Adelaïde. *La Chaumière africaine, ou, Histoire d'une famille française jetée sur la côte occidentale de l'Afrique à la suite du naufragee la frégate La Méduse*. Dijon, 1824.

de Arreger, Jean-Victor-Laurent. *Un Captif à Alger au XVIIIe siècle*. Ed. L. Pingaud. Revue Historique T. 13 Fasc. 2 (1880): 325–39.

de Brisson, Pierre-Raymond. *Histoire du Naufrage et de la captivité de M. de Brisson [. . .]*. Paris: Chez Royez, 1789.

de Fercourt, Claude Auxcousteaux. *Relation de l'esclavage des sieurs De Fercourt et Regnard, pris sur mer par les corsaires d'Alger (1678–79)*. Toulouse: E. Privat, 1905.

de la Motte, La Philémon. *Voyage pour la redemption des captifs, aux royaumes d'Alger et de Tunis*. Paris, 1721.

de Maurville, Bidé, and François Joseph Hippolyte. *Relation de l'affaire de Larache*. Amsterdam, 1775.

du Lisdam, Henry. *L'Esclavage du brave chevalier François de Vintimille des comtes de Marseille & Olieule, à présent commandeur du Planté & Cadillan: où l'on peut voir plusieurs rencontres de guerre dignes de remarque, par Henry Du Lisdam*. Lyon: C. Morillon, 1608.

Dumont, Pierre Joseph. *Histoire de l'esclavage en Afrique (pendant trente-quatre ans) de P.J. Dumont, natif de Paris: maintenant a l'Hospice Royal des Incurables.* 2nd ed. Paris: Pillet Aîné, 1819.

Dumont, Pierre Joseph. *Narrative of Thirty-Four Years Slavery and Travels in Africa by P.J. Dumont; Collected from the Account Delivered by Himself by J.S. Quesne.* London: Printed for Sir. R. Phillips, 1819.

Durand, Jean-Baptiste-Léonard. *Voyage au Sénégal ou Mémoires historiques, philosophiques et politiques sur les découvertes, les établissemens et le commerce des Européens dans les mers de l'Océan atlantique* [. . .]. Paris: Agasse X, [1802].

Follie, Adrien Jacques. *Mémoire d'un françois qui sort de l'Esclavage.* Amsterdam: Laporte, 1785.

Foucques, Guillaume. *Mémoires portants plusieurs advertissemens presentez au Roy par le cappitaine Foucques, capitaine ordinaire de sa Mjesté en la marine du Ponant. Après estre délivré de la captivité des Turcs* [. . .]. Paris: G. Marette, 1609.

Galland, Antoine. *Histoire de l'esclavage d'un marchand de la ville de Cassis, à Tunis.* Ed. Catherine Guénot and Nadia Vasquez. Paris: Editions de la Bibliothèque, 1992.

Gallonyé, Jean. *Histoire d'une esclave qui a esté quatre années dans les Prisons de Sallé en Afrique. Avec un abregé de la Vie du Roy Taffilette.* Lyon: Rolin Glaize, 1679.

Girard, Francois. *Histoire abrégée des officiers suisses, que se sont distingués aux services étrangers dans des grades supérieurs* [. . .]. Fribourg: Piller, 1781.

Gramaye, Jean-Baptiste. *Alger XVIe-XVIIe siècle: journal de Jean-Baptiste Gramaye* [. . .]. Ed. Abd El Hadi Ben Mansour. Paris: Les Éd. du Cerf, 1998.

Lettre d'un comédien, à un de ses amis, touchant sa captivité et celle de vingt-six de ses camarades, chez les corsaires de Tunis [. . .]. Paris: Chez Pierre Clément, 1741.

Lomon, Alexandre-Martin. *Souvenirs de l'Algérie: Captivité de l'Amiral Bonard et de l'Amiral Bruat.* Paris: J. Hetzel et Claye, 1863.

Marot, Louis. *Relation de quelques aventures maritimes de L.M.P.R.D.G.F.* Paris: Gervais Clouzier, 1673.

Mollien, Gaspard-Théodore. *Découverte des sources du Sénégal et de la Gambie en 1818* [. . .]. Paris: C. Delagrave, 1889.

Moüette, Germain. *Relation de la captivité du Sr Moüette dans les royaumes de Fez et de Maroc: où il a demeuré pendant onze ans.* Paris: Jean Cochart, 1683.

Quartier, Antoine. *L'esclave religieux, et ses avantures.* Paris: Daniel Hortemels, 1690.

Regnard, Jean-François. "La Provençale." 1731. *Théatre de Regnard: Suivi de ses voyages en Laponie, en Pologne, etc. et de La Provençale*, 475–519. Paris: Librairie de Firmin Didot Frères, 1843.

Rocqueville, [François] le sieur de. *Relations des moeurs et du gouvernement des Turcs d'Alger.* Saint-Denis: Bouchene, 1675.

[Saint-Sauveur, Jacques Grasset de]. *La Belle captive, ou Histoire véritable du naufrage & de la captivité de Mlle. Adeline, comtesse de St.-Fargel, âgée de 16 ans, dans une des parties du royaume d'Alger, en 1782.* Paris: J.B.G. Musier, 1786.

Saugnier. *Relations de plusieurs voyages à la côte d'Afrique à Maroc, au Sénégal, à Gorée, à Galam, etc.* [. . .]. Paris: Gueffier jeune, 1791.

Savigny, Jean Baptiste Henri, and Alexandre Corréard. *Naufrage de la frégate la Méduse faisant partie de l'expédition du Sénégal en 1816* [. . .]. Paris: Hocquet et al., 1817.

Thédenat, [Pierre-Paul]. *Les Aventures de Thédenat, esclave et ministre d'un bey d'Afrique, 18e siècle* [. . .]. Ed. Marcel Emerit. Alger: Jules Carbonel, 1948.

Voyage dans les états barbaresques de Maroc, Alger, Tunis et Tripoly, ou lettres d'un des Captifs qui viennent d'être rachetés par MM. les chanoines réguliers de la Sainte-Trinité. Paris: Guillot, 1785.

GERMAN

Eisenschmied, Leonhard. *Leonhard Eisenschmieds, eines österreichischen Unterthans merkwürdige Land- und Seereisen durch Europa, Africa und Asien.* 2 vols. Grätz: Tanzer, 1807.

Frisch, Johann. *Der Schauplatz Barbarischer Schlaverey.* Altona: Wolfenbüttel, 1666.

Frisch, Johann. *Schauplatz Barbarischer Sclaverey: Worauff unter Beschreibung der 4 vornehmsten Raub-Städte: Algiers, Thunis, Tripoli und Salee. Derselben Regierung, Raubereyen, Sitten, Gewohnheiten und andere seltzame Begebenheiten und Zufälle vorgestellet warden.* Hamburg: Thomas von Wiering, 1694.

Geißler, Andreas. *Der österreichische Robinson, oder: Leben, und merkwürdige Reisen Andreas Geißlers, eines gebohrnen Wieners, von ihm selbst beschrieben.* Frankfurt and Leipzig, 1791.

Jacobsen, Jürgen. *Beschreibung meiner unglüklichen Seefahrten in einer Zeit von 17 Jahren, meiner Schiksale während vierjähriger Gefangenschaft in Afrika: nebst Bemerkungen über Afrika's Einwohner und deren Sitten, von mir selbst geshrieben und herausgegeben.* Flensburg: Gedrukt bey Gerhard Christoph Jäger, 1821.

Keßler, Johann Friedrich. *Reisen zu Wasser und zu Lande.* Leipzig: Erdmann Ferdinand Steinacker, 1805.

[Kühn, Johann Michael]. *Johann Michael Kühns merkwürdige Lebens- und Reise-Beschreibung, worinnen nicht nur Dessen Schiffahrten nach Grönland und Spitzbergen* [. . .]. Gotha: Mevius, 1741.

Pfeiffer, Simon Friedrich. *Meine Reisen und meine fünfjährige Gefangenschaft in Algier mit einer Vorrede von Herrn Professor Dr. Schmitthenner.* Gießen, 1832.

Pfeiffer, Simon Friedrich. *The Voyages and Five Years' Captivity in Algiers of Doctor G.S.F. Pfeiffer: with an Appendix, Giving a True Description of the Customs, Manners, and Habits of the Different Inhabitants of the County of Algiers* [. . .]. Harrisburg, PA: J. Winebrenner, 1836.

Ravn, Wilhelm F. *Wilhelm Fridrich Ravns des mit den Königlich-Dänischen Schiffen im Jahr 1751 nach der Stadt Saphia im Marockanischen abgegangenen Cassirers zuverläßiger Bericht* [. . .]. Copenhagen and Leipzig: Ackermann, 1754.

Schiltberger, Hans. *Reisetagebuch.* Augsburg: Anton Sorg, [1476].

Sturmer, Balthasar. *Verzeichnüs der Reise Herrn Balthasar Sturmers. Vonn Marienburg aus Preussenn gebürtig, von Dantzigk ab nach Lisbona in Portugal, Sicilien vndtt in andere Öertter. Wie er von den Turcken vndtt Mooren gefangen vndtt entlichen wunderbarlicher Weise erlösett worden. Von ihme selber auffs fleisigste verzeichnett vndt beschrieben.* 1558. MS germ. Quart. 1014, Berlin State Library. Digitized collection: http://digital.staatsbibliothek-berlin.de/werkansicht?PPN=PPN737576820&PHYSID=P HYS_0001.

Verwunderlicher Seehafen Krieg. Das ist: Warhaffte Newe Zeitung / Was massen ein geborner Polack / aber gefangner Sclaf vnd Ruderknecht / ein Türckische Haupt-Galleen / durch sein kühn vnd tapfferkeit / wunderbarlicher weiß übergwältigt / vnd dieselb mit grossem Gut vnd Reichthumb in die Christenheit gebracht. Auß dem Welschen in die Teutsche Sprach übersetzt / vnd Getruckt im Jahr 1628. 1628.

[Wolffgang, Andreas Matthäus and Johann Georg Wolffgang]. *Reisen und wunderbare Schicksale zweyer in die Algierische Leibeigenschaft gerathenen Brüder Andreas Matthaeus und Johann Georg Wolffgang, Kupferstecher in Augsburg.* [Augsburg], 1767.

ICELANDIC

Egilsson, Ólafur. *Tyrkjaránið á Íslandi 1627 (The Turkish Raid on Iceland 1627).* Ed. Þorkelsson, Jón. Reykjavik: Prentsmiðjan Gutenberg, 1906–1909.

The Travels of Reverend Ólafur Egilsson: The Story of the Barbary Corsair Raid on Iceland in 1627. Ed. and trans. Karl S. Hreinsson and Adam Nichols. Washington, DC: Catholic University of America Press, 2016.

ITALIAN

Caronni, Felice. *Ragguaglio del viaggio compendioso di un dilettante antiquario da'corsari condotto in Barberia e felicemente ripatriato: Parte 1.* Milan: Sonzogno, 1805.

Caronni, Felice. *Ragguaglio di alcuni monumenti di antichità ed arti: Parte 2.* Milan: Sonzogno, 1806.

Daldini, Santino. *Viaggio di Terra Santa nell'anno 1819, e prigionia dell'autore coi compagni in Tripoli di Barberia.* Milan, 1829.

Marnavitio, Marco Thomeo. *Relatione della conquista fatta della Galera Capitana d'Alessandria* [. . .]. Rome: Lodovico Grignani, 1628.

Pananti, Filippo. *Avventure et osservazioni di Filippo Pananti sopra la coste di Barberia.* Milan: Presso A.F. Stella, 1817.

Pananti, Filippo. *Narrative of a residence in Algiers: Comprising a Geographical and Historical Account of the Regency, Biographical Sketches of the Dey and His Ministers.* London, 1818.

Pananti, Filippo. *Relation d'un séjour à Alger* [. . .]. Paris: Le Normant, 1820.

PORTUGUESE

Mascarenhas, João de Carvalho. *Memoravel relaçam da perda da nao Conceiçam que os turcos queymàraõ à vista da barra de Lisboa; varios successos das pessoas, que nella cativàraõ. E descripçaõ nova da cidade de Argel, & de seu governo; & cousas muy notaveis acontecidas nestes ultimos annos de 1621. atè 1626.* Lisbon: Na Officina de Antonio Alvares, 1627.

Saldanha, António de. *Crónica de Almançor, Sultão de Marrocos (1578–1603).* Lisbon: Instituto de Investigação Científica e Tropical, 1997.

SPANISH

Cautiverio y trabajos de Diego Galán, natural de Consuegra y vecino de Toledo [. . .]. MS. Toledo: Biblioteca de Castilla-La Mancha-Biblioteca Pública del Estado, MS. R(MS) 267.

Cautiverio y trabajos de Diego Galán, natural de Consuegra y vecino de Toledo (1589 a 1600). Ed. Manuel Serrano y Sanz. Madrid: Sociedad de Bibliófilos Españoles, 1913.

Del Mármol, Luis. *Libro Tercero y segundo volumen dela Primera parte de la description general de Affrica*. Granada: Rene Rabut, 1573.

de Sosa, Antonio [Diego de Haedo]. *Topographia e historia general de Argel, repartida en cinco tradados, do se verán cosas estraños, muertes espantosas, y tormentos exquisitos, que conviene se entiendan en la Christiandad* [. . .]. Valladolid, 1612.

de Torres, Diego. *Relacion del origen y sucesso de los xarifes, y del estado de los reinos de Marruecos, Fez Tarudante* [. . .]. Seville, 1586.

Relación de el cautiverio i libertad de Diego Galán de Escobar: Natural de la Villa de Consuegra y Veçino de la Çiudad de Toledo. [1620]. MS. Biblioteca del Real Monasterio de El Escorial, MS. I.III.27.

Relación del cautiverio y libertad de Diego Galán. Ed. M. Á de Bunes and Matías Barchino. Toledo: Diputación Provincial, 2001; Seville: Renacimiento-Escuela de Plata, 2008.

SWEDISH

Berg, Marcus. *Beskrifning öfwer barbariska slafweriet uti kejsaredömet Fez och Marocco, i korthet författad af Marcus Berg, som tillika med många andra christna det samma utstådt twenne år och siu dagar, och derifrån blifwit utlöst tillika med åtta stycken andra swenska den 30 Augusti 1756. Under wår allernådigste konungs konung Adolf Friedrichs milda regering.* Stockholm: tryckt hos Lor. Ludv. Grefing, 1757.

List of Works Cited and General Works on North African Piracy and Captivity

Primary Texts Anthologized in This Volume

Berg, Marcus. *Beskrifning öfwer barbariska slafweriet uti kejsaredömet Fez och Marocco, i korthet författad af Marcus Berg, som tillika med många andra christna det samma utstådt twenne år och siu dagar, och derifrån blifwit utlöst tillika med åtta stycken andra swenska den 30 Augusti 1756. Under wår allernådigste konungs konung Adolf Friedrichs milda regering.* Stockholm: tryckt hos Lor. Ludv. Grefing, 1757.

Brassard, Isaac. "Relation de la captivité de M. Brassard à Alger." Ed. H. de France. *Bulletin de la Société de Histoire du Protestantisme Français* 27 (1878): 349–55.

Caronni, Felice. *Ragguaglio del viaggio compendioso di un dilettante antiquario da'corsari condotto in Barberia e felicemente ripatriato: Parte 1.* Milan: Sonzogno, 1805.

d'Aranda, Emanuel. *Relation de la Captivité en Algérie de Emmanuel de Aranda 1640.1642.* N.d. MS. Castle Van Loppem Foundation, West Flanders, Belgium.

de Sosa, Antonio [Diego de Haedo]. "Dialogo segvndo, de los martyres de Argel." *Topographia e historia general de Argel, repartida en cinco tratados, do se veran casos estraños, muertes espantosas y tormentos exquisitos, que conviene se entiendan en la Christiandad: con mucha doctrina, y elegancia curiosa.* Valladolid: Diego Fernandez de Cordova y Oviedo, 1612. Digitized collection: http://bdh-rd.bne.es/viewer.vm?id=0000079195. 144r-191v.

Einarsson, Sighvatur. *Reisubók séra Ólafs Egilssonar.* Skógar MS., Skógar Museum, Iceland.

Krinstjánsson, Sverrir. *Reisubók séra Ólafs Egilssonar.* Reykjavík: Almenna Bókafélagið, 1969.

Marsh, Elizabeth. "Narrative I: Narrative of Her Captivity in Barbary." MS 170/604. Charles E. Young Research Library, Special Collections, University of California, Los Angeles.

Olufs, Hark. *Harck Olufs aus der Insul Amron im Stifte Ripen in Jütland gebürtig, sonderbare Avanturen, so sich mit ihm insonderheit zu Constantine und an andern Orten in Africa zugetragen. Ihrer Merkwürdigkeit wegen in Dänischer Sprache zum Drucke befördert, itzo aber ins Deutsche übersetzet.* Flensburg: Johann Christoph Kortens, 1751.

Pellow, Thomas. *The History of the Long Captivity and Adventures of Thomas Pellow, in South Barbary: Giving an Account of His Being Taken by Two Sallee Rovers, and Carry'd a Slave to Mequinez, at Eleven Years of Age: His Various Adventures in that Country for the Space of Twenty-three Years: Escape, and Return Home. In Which is Introduced, a Particular Account of the Manners and Customs of the Moors; the Astonishing Tyranny and Cruelty of Their Emperors, and a Relation of All Those Great Revolutions and Bloody Wars which Happen'd in the Kingdoms of Fez and Morocco, Between the Years 1720 and 1736. Together with a Description of the Cities, Towns, and Publick Buildings in Those Kingdoms; Miseries of the Christian Slaves; and Many Other Curious Particulars.* 2nd ed. London: Printed for R. Goadby, and sold by W. Owen, [1740?].

Pétursson, Hannes. *Reisubók séra Ólafs Egilssonar.* MS. Thott 514, Thott Collection, Copenhagen.

Quartier, Antoine. *L'esclave religieux, et ses avantures.* Paris: Daniel Hortemels, 1690. Digitized edition: https://gallica.bnf.fr/ark:/12148/bpt6k104958t.

Reisubók séra Ólafs Egilssonar. MS. Borealis 56, Bodleian Library, Oxford.

Reisubók séra Ólafs Egilssonar. MS. Landsbókasafn 153, National Archive of Iceland, Reykjavík.

Sturmer, Balthasar. "Der Bericht des Balthasar Sturmer." In *Verschleppt, Verkauft, Versklavt: Deutschsprachige Sklavenberichte aus Nordafrika (1550–1800),* ed. Mario Klarer, 49–80. Vienna: Böhlau, 2019.

Sturmer, Balthasar. *Verzeichnüs der Reise Herrn Balthasar Sturmers. Vonn Marienburg aus Preussenn gebürtig, von Dantzigk ab nach Lisbona in Portugal, Sicilien vndtt in andere Öertter. Wie er von den Turcken vndtt Mooren gefangen vndtt entlichen wunderbarlicher Weise erlösett worden. Von ihme selber auffs fleisigste verzeichnett vndt beschrieben.* 1558. MS germ. Quart. 1014. Berlin State Library. Digitized collection: http://digital.staatsbibliothek-berlin.de/werkansicht?PPN=PPN737576820&PHYSID=PHYS_0001.

ter Meetelen, Maria. *Wonderbaarlyke en merkwaardige gevallen van een twaalf jarige slaverny, van een vrouspersoon. Genaemt Maria ter Meetelen, woonagtig tot Medenblik.* Hoorn: Jacob Duyn, 1748.

Þorkelsson, Jón. *Tyrkjaránið á Íslandi 1627.* Reykjavik: Prentsmiðjan Gutenberg, 1906–1909.

[Wolffgang, Andreas Matthäus, and Johann Georg Wolffgang]. *Reisen und merkwürdige Schicksale zweyer in die Algierische Leibeigenschaft gerathenen Brüder Andreas Matthäus und Johann Georg Wolffgang, Kupferstecher in Augsburg, samt einer Nachricht von der Wolfgangischen Künstler-Familie.* 2nd ed. Augsburg: Conrad Heinrich Stage, 1769.

[Wolffgang, Andreas Matthäus, and Johann Georg Wolffgang]. *Reisen und wunderbare Schicksale zweyer in die Algierische Leibeigenschaft gerathenen Brüder Andreas Matthaeus und Johann Georg Wolffgang, Kupferstecher in Augsburg.* [Augsburg]: [Conrad Heinrich Stage], 1767.

Works Cited and Select Publications on Mediterranean Piracy and Slavery

Allison, Robert J. *The Crescent Obscured: The United States and the Muslim World, 1776–1815.* New York: Oxford University Press, 1995.

à Kempis, Thomas. *The Imitation of Christ.* Trans. Richard Challoner. Rockford, IL: Tan, 1989.

Amelang, James. "Writing Chains: Slave Autobiography from the Mediterranean to the Atlantic." In *Mediterranean Slavery Revisited, 500–1800/Neue Perspektiven auf mediterraner Sklaverei, 500–1800,* ed. Stefan Hanß and Juliane Schiel, 541–56. Zurich: Chronos, 2014.

Baepler, Paul M. "The Barbary Captivity Narrative in American Culture." *Early American Literature* 39, no. 2 (2004): 217–46.

Baepler, Paul M., ed. *White Slaves, African Masters: An Anthology of American Barbary Captivity Narratives.* Chicago: University of Chicago Press, 1999.

Barnby, Henry. "The Sack of Baltimore." *Journal of the Cork Historical and Archaeological Society* 74, no. 220 (1969): 101–29.

Bashan, Eliezer. "Rachat des captifs dans la société juive meditéranéenne du XIVe au XIXe siècle." In *La société juive à travers l'histoire,* vol. 4, ed. Shmuel Trigano, 463–472. Paris: Fayard, 1993.

Beach, Adam. "African Slaves, English Slave Narratives, and Early Modern Morocco." *Eighteenth-Century Studies* 46, no. 4 (2013): 333–48.

Bekkaoui, Khalid. "Piracy, Diplomacy, and Cultural Circulations in the Mediterranean." In *Piracy and Captivity in the Mediterranean: 1550–1810,* ed. Mario Klarer, 186–98. London: Routledge, 2019.

Bekkaoui, Khalid, ed. *White Women Captives in North Africa: Narratives of Enslavement, 1735–1830.* Basingstoke, UK: Palgrave Macmillan, 2011.

Bennassar, Bartolomé, and Lucile Bennassar. *Les chrétiens d'Allah. L'histoire extraordinaire des renégats XVIe–XVIIe siècles.* Paris: Perrin, 2006.

Berg, Marcus. *Beskrifning öfwer barbariska slafweriet uti kejsaredömet Fez och Marocco, i korthet författad af Marcus Berg, som tillika med många andra christna det samma utstådt twenne år och siu dagar, och derifrån blifwit utlöst tillika med åtta stycken andra swenska* den 30 Augusti 1756. Under wår allernådigste konungs konung Adolf Friedrichs milda regering. Stockholm: tryckt hos Lor. Ludv. Grefing, 1757.

Bhabha, Homi K. *The Location of Culture.* London: Routledge, 1994.

Bietenholz, Peter G., and Thomas B. Deutscher. *Contemporaries of Erasmus: A Bibliographical Register of the Renaissance and Reformation.* Toronto: University of Toronto Press, 1985.

Blanc, P.-L. "Earthquakes and Tsunami in November 1755 in Morocco: A Different Reading of Contemporaneous Documentary Sources." *Natural Hazards Earth System Science* 9 (2009): 725–38.

Bono, Salvatore. *Piraten und Korsaren im Mittelmeer: Seekrieg, Handel und Sklaverei vom 16. bis 19. Jahrhundert.* Stuttgart: Klett-Cotta, 2009.

Bono, Salvatore. *Schiavi Musulmani Nell'Italia Moderna: Galeotti, vu' Cumpra', Domestici.* Perugia: Universitá degli Studii, 1999.

Bono, Salvatore. *Schiavi. Una storia mediterranea (XVI–XIX secolo).* Bologna: Société Editrice il mulino, 2016.

Bono, Salvatore. "Slave Histories and Memoirs in the Mediterranean World: A Study of the Sources (Sixteenth–Eighteenth Centuries)." In *Trade and Cultural Exchange in the Early Modern Mediterranean, Braudel's Maritime Legacy,* ed. Maria Fusaro, Colin Heywood, and Mohamed-Salah Omro, 97–115. New York: Tauris, 2010.

Boyce, Gordon, and Richard Gorski. *Resources and Infrastructures in the Maritime Economy, 1500–2000.* Oxford: Oxford University Press, 2017.

Brassard, Isaac. "Relation de la captivité de M. Brassard à Alger." Ed. H. de France. *Bulletin de la Société de Histoire du Protestantisme Français* 27 (1878): 349–55.

Braudel, Fernand. *The Mediterranean and the Mediterranean World in the Age of Philip II.* London: Collins, 1972.

Brown, Robert, ed. *The Adventures of Thomas Pellow, of Penryn, Mariner: Three and Twenty Years in Captivity Among the Moors. Written by Himself, and Edited with an Introduction and Notes by Dr. Robert Brown.* By Thomas Pellow. London: T. F. Unwin, 1890.

Camus, Albert. *La peste.* Paris: Gallimard, 1947.

Caronni, Felice. *Précis d'un voyage en Barbarie.* Trans. Tatiana Cescutti. Introduction and notes by Salvatore Bono. Paris: Bouchène, 2011.

Caronni, Felice. *Ragguaglio del viaggio compendioso di un dilettante antiquario da'corsari condotto in Barberia e felicemente ripatriato: Parte 1.* Milan: Sonzogno, 1805.

"Carònni, Felice." *Treccani–Dizionario Bibliografico degli Italiani.* https://www.treccani.it/enciclopedia/felice-caronni. Accessed July 17, 2019.

Casale, Giancarlo. *The Ottoman Age of Exploration.* Oxford: Oxford University Press, 2010.

Chevallier, Jim. *A History of the Food of Paris: From Roast Mammoth to Steak Frites.* Lanham, MD: Rowman and Littlefield, 2018.

Clissold, Stephen. *The Barbary Slaves.* Totowa, NJ: Rowman and Littlefield, 1977.

Clodfelter, Michael. *Warfare and Armed Conflicts: A Statistical Encyclopedia of Casualty and Other Figures, 1492–2015.* Jefferson, NC: McFarland, 2017.

Colley, Linda. *Captives: Britain, Empire and the World 1600–1850.* London: Vintage Digital, 2010.

Colley, Linda. "Going Native, Telling Tales: Captivity, Collaborations and Empire." *Past & Present* 168 (2000): 170–93.

Colley, Linda. *The Ordeal of Elizabeth Marsh: How a Remarkable Woman Crossed Seas and Empires to Become a Part of World History.* London: Harper Perennial, 2014.

Corbett, Julian. *England in the Mediterranean: A Study of the Rise and Influence of British Power Within the Straits, 1603–1713.* London: Longmans, Green, 1904.

d'Aranda, Emanuel. *Relation de la Captivité en Algérie de Emmanuel de Aranda 1640.1642.* N. d. MS Castle Van Loppem Foundation, West Flanders, Belgium.

Dan, Pierre. *Historie van Barbaryen, En des zelfs Zee-Roovers: Behelzende een beschrijving van de Koningrijken en Steden Algiers, Tunis, Salé, en Tripoli,* with S. Vries and G. Broekhuizen. Amsterdam: Jan ten Hoorn, 1684.

Davis, Robert C. *Christian Slaves, Muslim Masters: White Slavery in the Mediterranean, the Barbary Coast, and Italy, 1500–1800.* Basingstoke, UK: Palgrave Macmillan, 2003.

Davis, Robert C. "Counting European Slaves on the Barbary Coast." *Past & Present* 172, no. 1 (2001): 87–124.

Davis, Robert C. *Holy War and Human Bondage: Tales of Christian–Muslim Slavery in the Early-Modern Mediterranean.* Santa Barbara, CA: Praeger/ABC-CLIO, 2009.

David, Robert C. "Rural Slavery in the Early Modern Mediterranean: The Significance of Algiers." In *Human Bondage in the Cultural Contact Zone. Transdisciplinary Perspectives on Slavery and Its Discourses,* ed. Raphael Hörmann and Gesa Mackenthun, 81–94. Münster: Waxmann, 2010.

de Armas Wilson, Diana. "Khayr al-Din Barbarossa: Clashing Portraits of a Corsair-King." In *Piracy and Captivity in the Mediterranean: 1550–1810,* ed. Mario Klarer. London: Routledge, 2019.

de Cervantes Saavedra, Miguel. *"The Bagnios of Algiers" and "The Great Sultana": Two Plays of Captivity,* ed. and trans. Barbara Fuchs and Aaron Ilika. 1615. Philadelphia: University of Pennsylvania Press, 2010.

De Illescas, Gonçalo. *Segvnda parte dela historia pontifical y catholica.* Barcelona: Emprenta de Jaime Cendrat, 1606.

del Mármol Carvajal, Luis. *Descripción general de África.* Granada, 1573.

de Sosa, Antonio [Diego de Haedo]. "Dialogo segvndo, de los martyres de Argel." *Topographia e historia general de Argel, repartida en cinco tratados, do se veran casos estraños, muertes espantosas y tormentos exquisitos, que conviene se entiendan en la Christiandad: con mucha doctrina, y elegancia curiosa.* Valladolid: Diego Fernandez de Cordova y Oviedo, 1612. Digitized collection: http://bdh-rd.bne.es/viewer.vm?id=0000079195. 144r–191v.

de Torres, Diego. *Relación del origen y suceso de los xarifes y del estado de los reinos de Marruecos*. 1586.

Devoulx, Albert. "Le Register des Prises Maritimes." *Revue Africaine: Journal des Travaux de la Société Historique Algérienne*, quinzième année, 85 (1871): 77–79.

Döring, Detlef. "Die sächsische Afrikaexpedition von 1731 bis 1733. Ihre Planung, ihre Teilnehmer, ihre Ergebnisse." In *Eine Afrikareise im Auftrag des Stadtgründers: Das Tagebuch des Karlsruher Hofgärtners Christian Thrann 1731–1733*, ed. Stadtarchiv Karlsruhe, Peter Pretsch, and Volker Steck, 42–56. Karlsruhe: Info Verlag, 2008.

Duprat, Anne, ed. *La guerre de course en récits: Terrains, corpus, séries*. Dossier en ligne du Projet ANR CORSO, novembre 2010. www.oroc-crlc.paris-sorbonne.fr/index.php?/visiteur/Projet-CORSO/Ressources/La-guerre-de-course-en-recits. Accessed March 29, 2020.

Duprat, Anne, and Emilie Picherot, eds. *Récits d'Orient dans les littératures d'Europe: XVIe–XVIIe siècles*. Paris: Presses de l'Université Paris-Sorbonne, 2008.

Einarsson, Sighvatur. *Reisubók séra Ólafs Egilssonar*. Skógar MS., Skógar Museum, Iceland.

El Abdaoui, Khalid. "Murat Reis." In *Piraten und Sklaven im Mittelmeer: Eine Ausstellung in Schloss Ambras Innsbruck 20. Juni bis 6. Oktober 2019*, ed. Mario Klarer, Sabine Haag, and Veronika Sandbichler, 37–9. Vienna: Kunsthistorisches Museum, 2019.

el Hamel, Chouki. *Black Morocco: A History of Slavery, Race, and Islam*. Cambridge: Cambridge University Press, 2014.

Emiralioğlu, Pınar. *Geographical Knowledge and Imperial Culture in the Early Modern Ottoman Empire*. New York: Routledge, 2016.

Ewan, Elizabeth, Rosemary J. Pipes, Jane Rendall, and Siân Reynolds. *The New Biographical Dictionary of Scottish Women*. Edinburgh: Edinburgh University Press, 2018.

Fendri, Mounir. "'Barbaresken'—Das Bild des Maghrebiners in der deutschen Literatur im 18. und bis Mitte des 19. Jahrhunderts: Imagologie und kultureller Wandel im deutsch/europäisch-arabischen Verhältnis." In *Praxis interkultureller Germanistik. Forschung—Bildung—Politik: Beiträge zum II. Internationalen Kongreß der Gesellschaft für interkulturelle Germanistik, Straßburg 1991*, ed. Bernd Thum and Gonthier-Louis Fink, 669–83. Publikationen der Gesellschaft für interkulturelle Germanistik 4. Munich: Iudicium, 1993.

Féraud, M. Louis. "Entre Setif et Biskara." *Revue Africaine: Journal des Travaux de la Société Historique Algerienne*, quatrième année, 22 (1860): 187–200.

Fischer, Frattarelli. Lucia. *Vivere fuori dal ghetto: Ebrei a Pisa e Livorno (secoli XVI–XVIII)*. Torino: Zamorani, 2008.

Fisher, Godfrey. *Barbary Legend: War, Trade and Piracy in North Africa, 1415–1830*. Oxford: Clarendon Press, 1957.

Fontana, Fulvio. *I pregi della Toscana nell'imprese più segnalate de' cavalieri di Santo Stefano: opera data in luce da Fulvio Fontana della compagnia di Gesù dedicata all'altezza reale di Cosimo III, gran duca di Toscana e gran maestro dell'ordine*. Firenze: Per Pier Mattia Miccioni, e Michele Nestenus, 1701.

Fontenay, Michel. "Il mercato maltese degli schiavi al tempo dei Cavalieri di San Giovanni (1530–1798)." *Quaderni Storici* 107 (2001): 391–413.

Fontenay, Michel. "La place de la course dans l'économie portuaire: L'exemple de Malte et des ports barbaresques." *Annales. Économies, Sociétés, Civilisations* 43, no. 6 (1988): 1321–47.

Franklin, Benjamin. ["Sidi Mehemet Ibrahim on the Slave Trade."] "To the Editor of the Federal Gazette." *Federal Gazette and Philadelphia Evening Post*, March 25, 1790, 3. American Antiquarian Society.

Frey, Albert R. *A Dictionary of Numismatic Names: Their Official and Popular Designations*. New York: American Numismatic Society, 1917.

Fricke, Stefanie. "Female Captivity in Penelope Aubin's *The Noble Slaves* (1722) and Elizabeth Marsh's *The Female Captive* (1769)." In *Mediterranean Slavery and World Literature: Captivity Genres from Cervantes to Rousseau*, ed. Mario Klarer, 111–31. London: Routledge, 2020.

Frisch, Johann. *Schauplatz Barbarischer Sclaverey: Worauff unter Beschreibung der 4 vornehmsten Raub-Städte: Algiers, Thunis, Tripoli und Salee. Derselben Regierung, Raubereyen, Sitten, Gewohnheiten und andere seltzame Begebenheiten und Zufälle vorgestellet warden*. Hamburg: Thomas von Wiering, 1694.

Fuchs, Barbara. *Passing for Spain: Cervantes and the Fictions of Identity*. Champaign, IL: University of Illinois Press, 2002.

Funk, Elisabeth Paling, and Martha Dickinson Shattuck. *A Beautiful and Fruitful Place: Selected Rensselaerwijck Papers*. Vol. 2. Albany, NY: Excelsior Editions/State University of New York Press, 2011.

Gallagher, John. "Language-Learning, Orality, and Multilingualism in Early Modern Anglophone Narratives of Mediterranean Captivity." In *Renaissance and Early Modern Travel: Practice and Experience, 1500–1700*, ed. Eva Johanna Holmberg. Special issue, *Journal of the Society for Renaissance Studies* 33, no. 4 (2019): 639–61.

Gallotta, Aldo. "Il ġazavāt-I Ḫayreddīn Paša di Seyyid Murād: Edito in Facsimile Secondo il Ms. 1663 dell'Escurial di Madrid con le Varianti dei Mss." *Studi Magrebini* 13 (1983): entire issue.

Gallotta, Aldo. "Le ġazavāt di Khayreddīn Barbarossa." *Studi Magrebini* 3 (1970): 79–160.

Garcés, María A. *Cervantes in Algiers: A Captive's Tale*. Nashville, TN: Vanderbilt University Press, 2002.

Garcés, María Antonia, ed. *An Early Modern Dialogue with Islam: Antonio De Sosa's Topography of Algiers (1612)*. Trans. Diana de Armas Wilson. Notre Dame, IN: University of Notre Dame Press, 2011.

García-Arenal, Mercedes. "Spanish Literature on North Africa in the XVI Century: Diego Torres." *Maghreb Review* 1–2 (1983): 53–59.

Gesta Romanorum: Lateinisch/Deutsch. Ed. and trans. Rainer Nickel. Stuttgart: Reclam, 2003.

Goodin, Brett. *From Captives to Consuls: Three Sailors in Barbary and Their Self-Making Across the Early American Republic, 1770–1840.* Baltimore, MD: Johns Hopkins University Press, 2020.

Gordon, Michael Ross. "Cervantes' Algerian Swan Song: The Birth of *Los baños de Argel* and Its Positive Portrayal of Jews." In *Mediterranean Slavery and World Literature: Captivity Genres from Cervantes to Rousseau*, ed. Mario Klarer, 96–110. London: Routledge, 2020.

Goridis, Philippe. *Gefangen im Heiligen Land: Verarbeitung und Bewältigung christlicher Gefangenschaft zur Zeit der Kreuzzüge.* Ostfildern: Thorbecke, 2015.

Grammont, H. D. *Histoire d'Alger Sous la Domination Turque (1515–1830).* Paris: E. Leroux, 1887.

Greene, Molly. *Catholic Pirates and Greek Merchants: A Maritime History of the Mediterranean.* Princeton, NJ: Princeton University Press, 2010.

Guiley, Rosemary. *The Encyclopedia of Saints.* New York: Facts on File, 2001.

Gurkan, Emrah Safa. "The Centre and the Frontier: Ottoman Cooperation with the North African Corsairs in the Sixteenth Century." *Turkish Historical Review* 1 (2010): 125–63.

Hanß, Stefan, and Juliane Schiel, eds. *Mediterranean Slavery Revisited (500–1800)—Neue Perspektiven auf mediterrane Sklaverei (500–1800).* Zürich: Chronos, 2014.

Hartner, Marcus. "Pirates, Captives, and Conversions: Rereading British Stories of White Slavery in the Early Modern Mediterranean." *Anglia—Zeitschrift für englische Philologie* 135, no. 3: 417–39.

Hartner, Marcus. "Toward a New Literary History of Captivity: Adventure and Generic Hybridity in the Late Sixteenth Century." In *Mediterranean Slavery and World Literature: Captivity Genres from Cervantes to Rousseau*, ed. Mario Klarer, 47–68. London: Routledge, 2020.

Hasleton, Richard. *A discovrse of the miserable captiuitie of an Englishman, named Richard Hasleton: borne in Braintree in Essex, declaring also his cruell moments during ten years of space, and his vvonderfull deliuerance: being a very strange thing to such as shall reade the same, he being now by Gods prouidence safelie arriued in his ovvne countrie, no doubt to his great comfort. Penned as he delivered it from his owne mouth.* London: Abell Ieffes, 1595.

Heers, Jacques. *Les Barbaresques: La course et la guerre en Méditerranée, XIVe–XVIe siècle.* Paris: Perrin, 2001.

Heinsen-Roach, Erica. *Consuls and Captives: Dutch–North African Diplomacy in the Early Modern Mediterranean.* Rochester, NY: University of Rochester Press, 2019.

Helgason, Þorsteinn. "Historical Narrative as Collective Therapy: The Case of the Turkish Raid in Iceland." *Scandinavian Journal of History* 22, no. 4 (1997): 275–89.

Hershenzon, Daniel. *The Captive Sea: Slavery, Communication, and Commerce in Early Modern Spain and the Mediterranean.* Philadelphia: University of Pennsylvania Press, 2018.

Hershenzon, Daniel. "'[P]ara que me saque cabesa por cabesa ...': Exchanging Muslim and Christian Slaves Across the Western Mediterranean." *African Economic History* 42 (2014): 11–36.

Hershenzon, Daniel. "The Political Economy of Ransom in the Early Modern Mediterranean." *Past & Present* 231, no. 1 (2016): 61–95.

Hirschberg, Haim Zeev, Eliezer Bashan, and Robert Attal. *A History of the Jews in North Africa. From the Ottoman Conquests to the Present Time.* Leiden: Brill, 1981.

History of the Captivity and Sufferings of Mrs. Maria Martin: Who Was Six Years a Slave in Algiers, Two of Which She Was Confined in a Dark and Dismal Dungeon, Loaded with Irons for Refusing to Comply with the Brutal Request of a Turkish Officer. Boston: Crary, 1807.

Horden, Peregrine, and Nicholas Purcell. *The Corrupting Sea: A Study of Mediterranean History.* Oxford: Blackwell, 2000.

Hötte, Hans H. A. *Atlas of Southeast Europe. Geopolitics and History.* Vol. 1, *1521–1699.* Leiden: Koninklijke Brill NV, 2014.

Hreinsson, Karl Smári, and Adam Nichols, eds. and trans. "The Chronicle of Kláus Eyjólfsson," In *The Travels of Reverend Ólafur Egilsson: The Story of the Barbary Corsair Raid on Iceland in 1627*, 96–106. Washington, DC: Catholic University of America Press, 2016.

Hreinsson, Karl Smári, and Adam Nichols, eds. and trans. *The Travels of Reverend Ólafur Egilsson: The Story of the Barbary Corsair Raid on Iceland in* 1627. Washington, DC: Catholic University of America Press, 2016.

Isom-Verhaaren, Christine. *Allies with the Infidels: Ottoman and French Views of Their Early Modern Encounter.* London: Tauris, 2011.

Jaspert, Nikolas, and Sebastian Kolditz. *Seeraub im Mittelmeerraum.* Mittelmeerstudien 3. Paderborn, Germany: Schöningh, 2013.

Jenkins, Hester D. *Ibrahim Pasha, Grand Vizir of Suleiman the Magnificent.* New York: Columbia University Press, 1911.

Jónsson, Björn. *Tyrkjaráns-Saga.* Reykjavík: í Prentsmiðju Íslands, 1866.

Junker, Carsten. "Of Cross and Crescent: Analogies of Violence and the Topos of 'Barbary Captivity' in Samuel Sewall's *The Selling of Joseph* (1700), with a Postscript on Benjamin Franklin." In *Mediterranean Slavery and World Literature: Captivity Genres from Cervantes to Rousseau*, ed. Mario Klarer, 259–76. London: Routledge, 2020.

Kaiser, Wolfgang. *Le commerce des captifs: Les intermédiaires dans l'échange et le rachat des prisonniers en Méditerranée, XVe–XVIIIe siècle.* Rome: École française de Rome, 2008.

Kaiser, Wolfgang. "Sprechende Ware. Gefangenenfreikauf und Sklavenhandel im frühneuzeitlichen Mittelmeerraum." *Zeitschrift für Ideengeschichte* 3, no. 2 (2009): 29–39.

Kattenberg, Lisa F. "The Free Slave: Morality, Neostoicism, and Publishing Strategy in Emanuel d'Aranda's *Algiers and It's Slavery* (1640–82)." In *Mediterranean Slavery and World Literature: Captivity Genres from Cervantes to Rousseau*, ed. Mario Klarer, 153–74. London: Routledge, 2019.

Klaar, Karl. "Georg Kleubenschedl von Stams, Sklave in Tunis und seine Befreiung 1612–1636." *Tiroler Heimat* 1 (1928): 182–85.

Klarer, Mario. "Before Barbary Captivity Narratives: Slavery, Ransom, and the Economy of Christian Virtue in *The Good Gerhard* (c. 1220) by Rudolf of Ems." In *Mediterranean Slavery and World Literature: Captivity Genres from Cervantes to Rousseau*, ed. Mario Klarer, 23–48. London: Routledge, 2020.

Klarer, Mario. "Humanitarian Pornography: John Gabriel Stedman's *Narrative of a Five Years Expedition Against the Revolted Negroes of Surinam* (1796)." *New Literary History* 36, no. 4 (2005): 559–87.

Klarer, Mario, ed. *Mediterranean Slavery and World Literature: Captivity Genres from Cervantes to Rousseau*. London: Routledge, 2020.

Klarer, Mario, ed. *Piracy and Captivity in the Mediterranean: 1550–1810*. London: Routledge, 2019.

Klarer, Mario. "Regionale Verflechtungen transmediterraner Piraterie und Sklaverei: Tunis, Danzig und Innsbruck." In *Piraten und Sklaven im Mittelmeer. Eine Ausstellung in Schloss Ambras Innsbruck 20. Juni bis 6. Oktober 2019*, ed. Mario Klarer, Sabine Haag, and Veronika Sandbichler, 49–55. Vienna: Kunsthistorisches Museum, 2019.

Klarer, Mario. "Trading Identities: Balthasar Sturmer's *Verzeichnis der Reise* (1558) and the Making of the European Barbary Captivity Narrative." In *Piracy and Captivity in the Mediterranean: 1550–1810*, ed. Mario Klarer, 25–55. London: Routledge, 2019.

Klarer, Mario, ed. *Verschleppt, Verkauft, Versklavt: Deutschsprachige Sklavenberichte aus Nordafrika (1550–1800)*. Vienna: Böhlau, 2019.

Klarer, Mario, Sabine Haag, and Veronika Sandbichler, eds. *Piraten und Sklaven im Mittelmeer: Eine Ausstellung in Schloss Ambras Innsbruck 20. Juni bis 6. Oktober 2019*. Vienna: Kunsthistorisches Museum, 2019.

Krinstjánsson, Sverrir. *Reisubóók séra Ólafs Egilssonar*. Reykjavík: Almenna Bókafélagið, 1969.

Kühn, Michael. *Johann Michael Kühns merckwürdige Lebens- und Reise-Beschreibung*. Gotha: Mevius, 1741.

Leiner, Frederic C. *The End of Barbary Terror, America's 1815 War Against the Pirates of North Africa*. New York: Oxford University Press, 2007.

Letters from Italy describing the Manners, Customs, Antiquities, Painting, etc. of That Country in the Years MDCCLXX and MDCCLXXI by an English Woman to a Friend Residing in France. 3 vols. London: Edward and Charles Dilly, 1776.

Lunsford, Virginia W. *Piracy and Privateering in the Golden Age Netherlands*. Basingstoke, UK: Palgrave Macmillan, 2005.

MacLean, Gerald. "Slavery and Sensibility: A Historical Dilemma." In *Slavery and the Cultures of Abolition: Essays Marking the Bicentennial of the British Abolition Act of 1807*, ed. Brycchan Carey and Peter J. Kitson, 173–94. Cambridge: Brewer, 2007.

Mahaffy, Robert Pentland, ed. *Calendar of State Papers, Ireland, 1625–1632*. London: Eyre and Spottiswoode, 1900.

Mark, Peter. " 'Free, Unfree, Captive, Slave': António de Saldanha, a Late Sixteenth-Century Captive in Marrakesh." In *Piracy and Captivity in the Mediterranean*, ed. Mario Klarer, 99–110. London: Routledge, 2010.

Marr, Timothy. *The Cultural Roots of American Islamicism*. Cambridge: Cambridge University Press, 2006.

Marsh, Elizabeth. *The Female Captive: A Narrative of Facts, Which Happened in Barbary, in the Year 1756, Written by Herself*. London: C. Bathurst, 1769.

Marsh, Elizabeth. "Narrative I: Narrative of Her Captivity in Barbary." MS 170/604. Charles E. Young Research Library, Special Collections, University of California, Los Angeles.

Marteilhe, Jean. *The Huguenot Galley-Slave: Being the Autobiography of a French Protestant Condemned to the Galleys for the Sake of his Religion*. New York: Leypoldt and Holt, 1867.

Martin, Meredith, and Gillian Weiss. *The Sun King at Sea: Maritime Art and Galley Slavery in Louis XIV's France*. Los Angeles: Getty Publications, forthcoming 2022.

Mascarenhas, João Carvalho. *Memoravel relaçam da perda da nao Conceiçam que os turcos queymaraõ à vista da barra de Lisboa; varios successos das pessoas, que nella cativaraõ. E descripçaõ nova da cidade de Argel, & de seu governo; & cousas muy notaveis acontecidas nestes ultimos annos de 1621. atè 1626*. Lisbon: Na Officina de Antonio Alvares, 1627.

Matar, Nabil. *An Arab Ambassador in the Mediterranean World: Muhammad Ibn Othman Al-Miknasi*. London: Routledge, 2014.

Matar, Nabil. *Britain and Barbary, 1589–1689*. Gainesville: University Press of Florida, 2005.

Matar, Nabil. *British Captives from the Mediterranean to the Atlantic, 1563–1760*. Leiden: Brill, 2014.

Matar, Nabil. *Islam in Britain, 1558–1685*. Cambridge: Cambridge University Press, 1998.

Matar, Nabil. *Mediterranean Captivity Through Arab Eyes, 1517–1798*. Boston: Brill, 2020.

Matar, Nabil. *Turks, Moors and Englishmen in the Age of Discovery*. New York: Columbia University Press, 1999.

Matar, Nabil. "Two Arabic Accounts of Captivity in Malta: Texts and Contexts." In *Piracy and Captivity in the Mediterranean: 1550–1810*, ed. Mario Klarer, 235–76. London: Routledge, 2019.

Milton, Giles. *White Gold: The Extraordinary Story of Thomas Pellow and North Africa's One Million European Slaves*. London: Hodder & Stoughton, 2004.

Morsy, Magali. *La Relation de Thomas Pellow: Une lecture du Maroc au 18e siècle*. Paris: Ed. Recherche sur les civilisations, 1983.

Müller, Leos. *Consuls, Corsairs, and Commerce: The Swedish Consular Service and Long-Distance Shipping, 1720–1815*. Stockholm: Elanders Gotab, 2004.

Naylor, Phillip C. *Historical Dictionary of Algeria*. Lanham, MD: Scarecrow Press, 2006.

Netton, Ian Richard. *Encyclopedia of Islamic Civilization and Religion*. Abingdon, UK: Routledge, 2008.

Nolan, Joanna. *The Elusive Case of Lingua Franca: Fact and Fiction*. London: Palgrave Macmillan, 2021.

Oberösterreichische Regierung, Kopialbücher, Parteibücher 1636.Vol. 94. Tiroler Landesarchiv.

Olufs, Hark. *Harck Olufs aus der Insul Amron im Stifte Ripen in Jütland gebürtig, sonderbare Avanturen, so sich mit ihm insonderheit zu Constantine und an andern Orten in Africa zugetragen. Ihrer Merkwürdigkeit wegen in Dänischer Sprache zum Drucke befördert, itzo aber ins Deutsche übersetzet*. Flensburg, Germany: Johann Christoph Kortens, 1751.

Östlund, Joachim. *Saltets pris: Svenska slavar i Nordafrika och handeln med Nordafrika 1650–1770*. Lund: Tidskriften Respons, 2014.

Östlund, Joachim. "Swedish Barbary Captivity Tales: From Letters to Literature (1650–1770)." In *Mediterranean Slavery and World Literature: Captivity Genres from Cervantes to Rousseau*, ed. Mario Klarer, 69–92. London: Routledge, 2020.

Owens, W. R. "Defoe, Robinson Crusoe, and the Barbary Pirates." *English* 62, no. 236 (2013): 51–66.

Palm, Kurt. "Mozart, Islam, and the Hangman of Salzburg." In *Mediterranean Slavery and World Literature: Captivity Genres from Cervantes to Rousseau*, ed. Mario Klarer, 197–211. London: Routledge, 2020.

Panzac, Daniel. *Les corsaires barbaresques: La fin d'une épopée, 1800–1820*. Paris: CNRS Editions, 1999.

Pelizza, Andrea. "Confraternity Models in the 'Redemption of Slaves' in Europe: The *Broederschap der alderheylighste Dryvuldigheyt* of Bruges (Brugge) and the *Scuola della Santissima Trinità* of Venice." In *Piracy and Captivity in the Mediterranean: 1550–1810*, ed. Mario Klarer, 199–219. London: Routledge, 2019.

Pellow, Thomas. *The Adventures of Thomas Pellow, of Penryn, Mariner: Three and Twenty Years in Captivity Among the Moors. Written by Himself, and Edited with an Introduction and Notes by Dr. Robert Brown*, ed. Robert Brown. London: T. F. Unwin, 1890.

Pellow, Thomas. *The History of the Long Captivity and Adventures of Thomas Pellow, in South Barbary: Giving an Account of His Being Taken by Two Sallee Rovers, and Carry'd a Slave to Mequinez, at Eleven Years of Age: His Various Adventures in that Country for the Space of Twenty-three Years: Escape, and Return Home. In Which is Introduced, a Particular Account of the Manners and Customs of the Moors; the Astonishing Tyranny and Cruelty of Their Emperors, and a Relation of All Those Great Revolutions and Bloody Wars which Happen'd in the Kingdoms of Fez and Morocco, Between the Years 1720 and 1736. Together with a Description of the Cities, Towns, and Publick Buildings in Those Kingdoms; Miseries of the Christian Slaves; and Many Other Curious Particulars*. 2nd ed. London: Printed for R. Goadby, and sold by W. Owen, [1740?].

Pellow, Thomas. *The History of the Long Captivity and Adventures of Thomas Pellow, in South Barbary*, ed. Josephine Grieder. New York: Garland, 1973.

Pertz, Georg Heinrich. *Monumenta Germaniae Historica, inde ab anno Christi quingentesimo usque ad annum millesimum et quingentesimum.* Vol. 16, *Annales aevi Suevici.* Stuttgart, 1859.

Peskin, Lawrence A. *Captives and Countrymen: Barbary Slavery and the American Public, 1785–1816.* Baltimore, MD: Johns Hopkins University Press, 2009.

Pétursson, Hannes. *Reisubók séra Ólafs Egilssonar.* MS. Thott 514, Thott Collection, Copenhagen.

Playfair, Lambert. *The Bibliography of the Barbary States.* Westmead: Gregg International Publishers, 1971.

Popkin, Jeremy D. "*Émile* in Chains: A New Perspective on Rousseau, Slavery, and Hegel's *Phenomenology*." In *Mediterranean Slavery and World Literature: Captivity Genres from Cervantes to Rousseau,* ed. Mario Klarer, 294–310. London: Routledge, 2020.

Porter, Whitworth. *Malta and Its Knights.* London: Pardon and Son, 1871.

Pretsch, Peter. "Christian Thrann—Hofgärtner, Entdecker, Unternehmer." In *Eine Afrikareise im Auftrag des Stadtgründers: Das Tagebuch des Karlsruher Hofgärtners Christian Thrann 1731–1733,* ed. Peter Pretsch and Volker Steck, 29–41. Karlsruhe: Info Verlag, 2008.

Quartier, Antoine. *L'Esclave religieux, et ses avantures.* Paris: Daniel Hortemels, 1690. Digitized edition: https://gallica.bnf.fr/ark:/12148/bpt6k104958t.

Rech, Walter. "Ambivalences of Recognition: The Position of the Barbary Corsairs in Early Modern International Law and International Politics." In *Piracy and Captivity in the Mediterranean: 1550–1810,* ed. Mario Klarer, 76–98. London: Routledge, 2019.

Reisubók séra Ólafs Egilssonar. MS. Borealis 56, Bodleian Library, Oxford, UK.

Reisubók séra Ólafs Egilssonar. MS. Landsbókasafn 153, National Archive of Iceland, Reykjavík.

Rejeb, Lotfi Ben. "Jonathan Cowdery's *American Captives in Tripoli* (1806): Experience of the Frigate *Philadelphia* Officers (1803–05)." In *Mediterranean Slavery and World Literature: Captivity Genres from Cervantes to Rousseau,* ed. Mario Klarer, 241–56. London: Routledge, 2020.

Requemora, Sylvie, and Sophie Linon-Chipon, eds. *Les tyrans de la mer: Pirates, corsaires et flibustiers.* Paris: Presses de l'Université de Paris–Sorbonne, 2002.

Ressel, Magnus. "A Dystopia as Utopia: The Algerian City of Oran and Annette von Droste-Hülshoff's *The Jew's Beech Tree (Die Judenbuche).*" In *Mediterranean Slavery and World Literature: Captivity Genres from Cervantes to Rousseau,* ed. Mario Klarer, 132–50. London: Routledge, 2020.

Ressel, Magnus. *Zwischen Sklavenkassen und Türkenpässen. Nordeuropa und die Barbaresken in der Frühen Neuzeit.* Berlin: de Gruyter, 2012.

Rheinheimer, Martin. *Der fremde Sohn. Hark Olufs' Wiederkehr aus der Sklaverei.* Neumünster: Wachholtz, 2001.

Rheinheimer, Martin. "From Amrum to Algiers and Back: The Reintegration of a Renegade in the Eighteenth Century," *Central European History* 36 (2003): 209–33.

Rheinheimer, Martin. "Sklave in Algier: Die Kaperei der Barbaresken in Atlantik und Nordsee." In *Strandungen, Havarien, Kaperungen: Beiträge zur Seefahrtsgeschichte Nordfrieslands*, ed. Robert Bohn and Sebastian Lehmann, 36–60. Amsterdam: De Bataafsche Leeuw, 2004.

Rhoads, Murphey. "Seyyid Muradi's Prose Biography of Hizir ibn Yakub, Alias Hayreddin Barbarossa: Ottoman Folk Narrative as an Under-Exploited Source for Historical Reconstruction." *Acta Orientalia Academiae Scientiarum Hungaricae* 54 (2001): 519–32.

Ritter, Anne-Barbara. "Ein deutscher Sklave als Augenzeuge bei der Eroberung von Tunis (1535). Untersuchung und Edition eines unbekannten Reiseberichts aus dem Jahr 1558." In *Europas islamische Nachbarn. Studien zur Literatur und Geschichte des Maghreb*, ed. Ernstpeter Ruhe, 187–231. Würzburg: Königshausen & Neumann, 1993.

Rodríguez-Rodríguez, Ana María. *Letras liberadas. Cautiverio, escritura y subjetividad en el de la época imperial española*. Madrid: Visor Libros, 2013.

Rogerson, Barnaby. *The Last Crusaders: The Hundred-Year Battle for the Centre of the World*. London: Little, Brown, 2009.

Rowson, Jennifer Margulis, and Karen Poremski, eds. *Slaves in Algiers, or, A Struggle for Freedom*. Acton, MA: Copley, 2000.

Ruhe, Ernstpeter. *Aus Barbareÿen Erlösett*. Würzburg, Germany: Königshausen & Neumann, 2020.

Ruhe, Ernstpeter. "L'aire du soupçon: Les récits de captivité en langue allemande (XVIe–XIXe siècles)." In *Récits d'Orient dans les littératures d'Europe (XVIe–XVIIe siècles)*, ed. Anne Duprat and Emilie Picherot, 185–200. Paris: Presses de l'Université Paris–Sorbonne, 2008.

Ruhe, Ernstpeter. "Christensklaven als Beute nordafrikanischer Piraten: Das Bild des Maghreb im Europa des 16.–19. Jahrhunderts." In *Europas islamische Nachbarn*, ed. Ernstpeter Ruhe. Studien zur Literatur und Geschichte des Maghreb 1, 159–86. Würzburg: Königshausen & Neumann, 1993.

Ruhe, Ernstpeter. "Dire et ne pas dire: Les récits de captifs germanophones et les cérémonies de retour." In *Captifs en Méditerranée: Histoires, récits et légendes*, ed. François Moureau, 119–36. Paris: Presses de l'Université Paris–Sorbonne, 2008.

Ruhe, Ernstpeter, ed. *Europas islamische Nachbarn. Studien zur Literatur und Geschichte des Maghreb 1*. Würzburg: Königshausen & Neumann, 1993.

Ruhe, Ernstpeter. "Images from the Dey's Court: The Artist as Slave in Algiers (1684–88)." In *Mediterranean Slavery and World Literature: Captivity Genres from Cervantes to Rousseau*, ed. Mario Klarer, 212–40. London: Routledge, 2020.

Ruhe, Ernstpeter. *Porträt des Künstlers als Sklave: Zwei Augsburger Kupferstecher als Gefangene in Algier (1684–1688)*. Würzburg: Königshausen & Neumann, 2017.

Ruhe, Ernstpeter. "Zwei Augsburger Künstler in 'Algierischer Leibeigenschaft': Die 'Wunderbaren Schicksale' der Brüder Wolfgang." *Oriente Moderno* 91 (2011): 1–17.

Sabatos, Charles. *Frontier Orientalism and the Turkish Image in Central European Literature*. Lanham, MD: Lexington, 2020.

Said, Edward W. *Orientalism*. New York: Random House, 1979.

Saldanha, António, António D. Farinha, and Léon Bourdon. *Crónica de Almançor, Sultão de Marrocos (1578–1603)*. Lisbon: Instituto de Investigação Científica Tropical, 1997.

Salzmann, Ariel. "Migrants in Chains: On the Enslavement of Muslims in Renaissance and Enlightenment Europe." *Religions* 4, no. 3 (2013): 391–411.

Sarti, Raffaella. "Bolognesi schiavi dei 'turchi' e schiavi 'turchi' a Bologna tra cinque e settecento: alterità etnico-religiosa e riduzione in schiavitù." *Quaderni Storici* 107 (2001): 437–73.

Schmitz-von Ledebur, Katja. "Emperor Charles V Captures Tunis: A Unique Set of Tapestry Cartoons." *Studia Bruxellae* 13, no. 1 (2019): 387–404.

Schmitz-von Ledebur, Katja. "Der Tunis-Kriegszug Kaiser Karls V. Eine Dokumentation in Kartons und Tapisserien." In *Piraten und Sklaven im Mittelmeer: Eine Ausstellung in Schloss Ambras Innsbruck 20. Juni bis 6. Oktober 2019*, ed. Mario Klarer, Sabine Haag, and Veronika Sandbichler, 57–63. Vienna: Kunsthistorisches Museum, 2019.

Schmitz-von Ledebur, Katja, and Sabine Haag. *Fäden der Macht: Tapisserien des 16. Jahrhunderts aus dem Kunsthistorischen Museum Wien: Eine Ausstellung des Kunsthistorischen Museums Wien 14. Juli bis 20. September 2015*. Vienna: Kunsthistorisches Museum, 2015.

Schneider, Manfred. "Poesie der Piraterie: Lord Byrons 'The Corsair' und das Auftauchen des *communis amicus omnium*." In *Seeraub im Mittelmeerraum: Piraterie, Korsarentum und Maritime Gewalt von der Antike bis zur Neuzeit*, ed. Nikolas Jaspert and Sebastian Kolditz. Mittelmeerstudien 4, 115–29. Paderborn: Ferdinand Schöningh, 2013.

Setton, Kenneth Meyer. *The Papacy and the Levant, 1204–1571*. Philadelphia: American Philosophical Society, 1976.

Sha'ban, Fuad. *Islam and Arabs in Early American Thought: Roots of Orientalism in America*. Durham, NC: Acorn, 1991.

Shaw, Thomas. *Travels, Or, Observations Relating to Several Parts of Barbary and the Levant: Illustrated with Cuts*. London: A. Millar and W. Sandby, 1757.

Smiley, Will. *From Slaves to Prisoners of War: The Ottoman Empire, Russia, and International Law*. Oxford: Oxford University Press, 2018.

Snader, Joe. *Caught Between Worlds: British Captivity Narratives in Fact and Fiction.* Lexington: University Press of Kentucky, 2000.

Snader, Joe. "The Oriental Captivity Narrative and Early English Fiction." *Eighteenth Century Fiction* 9, no. 3 (1997): 267–98.

Sobers-Khan, Nur. *Slaves Without Shackles: Forced Labor and Manumission in the Galata Court Registers, 1560–1572.* Berlin: Klaus Schwartz, 2014.

Spindler, Robert. "Benevolent Masters, Despicable *Renegados*: Relativizing Portrayals of Muslims in British Barbary Captivity Narratives, 1595–1739." *Anglistik: International Journal of English Studies* 30, no. 3 (2019): 141–56.

Spindler, Robert. *Corsairs, Captives, Converts in Early Modernity: Narrating Barbary Captivity in German-Speaking Europe and the World, 1558–1807.* Würzburg: Königshausen & Neumann, 2020.

Spindler, Robert. "An Early 'Schelmenroman': The Picaresque Elements in the German Barbary Narrative 'Verzeichnis der Reise' (1558) by Balthasar Sturmer." *Germanisch-Romanische Monatsschrift* 69, no. 1 (2019): 1–20.

Spindler, Robert. "Identity Crises of Homecomers from the Barbary Coast." In *Piracy and Captivity in the Mediterranean: 1550–1810*, ed. Mario Klarer, 128–43. London: Routledge, 2019.

Spindler, Robert. "The Robinsonade as a Literary Avatar of Early Nineteenth-Century Barbary Captivity Narration." In *Mediterranean Slavery and World Literature: Captivity Genres from Cervantes to Rousseau*, ed. Mario Klarer, 175–94. London: Routledge, 2020.

Starr, G. A. "Defoe, Slavery, and Barbary." In *Mediterranean Slavery and World Literature: Captivity Genres from Cervantes to Rousseau*, ed. Mario Klarer, 277–93. London: Routledge, 2020.

Starr, G. A. "Escape from Barbary: A Seventeenth-Century Genre." *Huntington Library Quarterly* 29 (1965): 35–52.

Stella, Alessandro. *Histoires d'Esclaves dans la Péninsule Ibérique.* Paris: Éditions EHESS, 2000.

Stevens, James Wilson. *An Historical and Geographical Account of Algiers: Comprehending a Novel and Interesting Detail of Events Relative to the American Captives.* Philadelphia: Hogan & M'Elroy, 1797.

Stone, Caroline, and Karen Johnson, trans. *The Curious and Amazing Adventures of Maria ter Meetelen: Twelve Years a Slave (1731–43).* Kilkerran, Scotland: Hardinge Simpole, 2010.

Sturmer, Balthasar. "Der Bericht des Balthasar Sturmer." In *Verschleppt, Verkauft, Versklavt: Deutschsprachige Sklavenberichte aus Nordafrika (1550–1800)*, ed. Mario Klarer, 49–80. Vienna: Böhlau, 2019.

Sturmer, Balthasar. *Verzeichnüs der Reise Herrn Balthasar Sturmers. Vonn Marienburg aus Preussenn gebürtig, von Dantzigk ab nach Lisbona in Portugal, Sicilien vndtt in andere Öertter. Wie er von den Turcken vndtt Mooren gefangen vndtt entlichen wunderbarlicher*

Weise erlösett worden. Von ihme selber auffs fleisigste verzeichnett vndt beschrieben. 1558. MS germ. Quart. 1014. Berlin State Library. Digitized collection: http: // digital .staatsbibliothek-berlin.de/werkansicht?PPN=PPN737576820&PHYSID=P HYS_0001.

Sumner, Charles. *White Slavery in the Barbary States: A Lecture Before the Boston Mercantile Library Association, Feb. 17, 1847.* Boston, 1853.

ter Meetelen, Maria. *Wonderbaarlyke en merkwaardige gevallen van een twaalf jarige slaverny, van een vrouspersoon. Genaemt Maria ter Meetelen, woonagtig tot Medenblik.* Hoorn: Jacob Duyn, 1748.

Þorkelsson, Jón, ed. *Tyrkjaránið á Íslandi 1627*. Reykjavik: Prentsmiðjan Gutenberg, 1906–1909.

Þorsteinn, Helgason. *The Corsairs' Longest Voyage: The Turkish Raid in Iceland 1627*. Boston: Brill, 2018.

Toaff, Renzo. *La nazione ebrea a Livorno e a Pisa: 1591–1700*. Florence: Olshki, 1990.

Trigeiros, António Miguel. "Portuguese Coins in the Age of Discovery." *The Numismatist* 104, no. 11 (1991): 1728–35.

Tucker, Spencer, ed. *A Global Chronology of Conflict: From the Ancient World to the Modern Middle East*. Santa Barbara, CA: ABC-CLIO, 2010.

Turbet-Delof, Guy. "Le père mercedaire Antoine Quartier et sa chronique tripoline des années 1660–1668." *Les Cahiers de Tunisie* 8, nos. 77–78 (1972): 51–58.

van den Broek, Laura, and Maaike Jacobs, eds. *Christenslaven: De slavernij-ervaringen van Cornelis Stout in Algiers (1678–1680) en Maria ter Meetelen in Marokko (1731–1743)*. Zutphen: Walburg Pers, 2006.

van Donzel, E. J. *Islamic Desk Reference*. New York: Brill, 1994.

von Droste-Hülshoff, Annette. *The Jews' Beech Tree: A Moral Portrait from Mountainous Westphalia. New Biographical Findings, a Critical Introduction, and a Translation of the Original Work*, ed. Jolyon Timothy Hughes. Lanham, MD: University Press of America, 2014.

Vatin, M. Nicolas. "Études Ottomanes: Programme de l'année 2008–2009: Traduction et commentaire des *Gazavât de Hayrü-d-dîn Paşa.*" *Annuaire—EPHE*, SHP– 141e année (2008–2009): 42–5.

Vatin, M. Nicolas. *Les Ottomans et l'occident (XVe–XVIe siècles)*. Istanbul: Isis, 2001.

Velupillai, Viveka. *Pidgins, Creoles and Mixed Languages: An Introduction*. Amsterdam: John Benjamins, 2015.

Villanueva, Francisco Márquez. *Santiago: Trayectoria De Un Mito*. Barcelona: Ediciones Bellaterra, 2004.

Vitkus, Daniel. "Barbary Captivity Narratives from Early Modern England: Truth Claims and the (Re)Construction of Authority." In: *La guerre de course en récits: Terrains, corpus, séries*, ed. Anne Duprat, 119–30. 2010. www.oroc-crlc.paris-sorbonne .fr/index.php?/visiteur/Projet-CORSO/Ressources/La-guerre-de-course-en -recits. Accessed March 29, 2020.

Vitkus, Daniel, ed. *Piracy, Slavery, and Redemption: Barbary Captivity Narratives from Early Modern England*. New York: Columbia University Press, 2001.

Vitkus, Daniel. "Unkind Dealings: English Captivity Narratives, Commercial Transformation, and the Economy of Unfree Labor in the Early Modern Period." In *Piracy and Captivity in the Mediterranean: 1550–1800*, ed. Mario Klarer, 56–75. London: Routledge, 2019.

Voigt, Lisa. *Writing Captivity in the Early Modern Atlantic: Circulations of Knowledge and Authority in the Iberian and English Imperial Worlds*. Chapel Hill: University of North Carolina Press, 2012.

Von der fürstlichen Durchlaucht. Vol. 99. Innsbruck, Tiroler Landesarchiv, ff. 252r–254r.

Walton, Timothy R. *The Spanish Treasure Fleets*. Sarasota, FL: Pineapple Press, 1994.

Watzka-Pauli, Elizabeth. *Triumph der Barmherzigkeit: Die Befreiung christlicher Gefangener aus muslimisch dominierten Ländern durch den österreichischen Trinitarierorden 1690–1783*. Göttingen: V&R Unipress, 2016.

Weiss, Gillian L. *Captives and Corsairs: France and Slavery in the Early Modern Mediterranean*. Stanford, CA: Stanford University Press, 2011.

Weiss, Gillian L. "A Huguenot Captive in 'Uthman Dey's Court: *Histoire chronologique du royaume de Tripoly* (1685) and Its Author." In *Piracy and Captivity in the Mediterranean: 1550–1810*, ed. Mario Klarer, 234–57. London: Routledge, 2019.

Weiss, Gillian. "Infidels at the Oar: A Mediterranean Exception to France's Free Soil Principle." *Slavery & Abolition* 32, no. 3 (2011): 397–412.

Wettinger, Godfrey. *Slavery in the Islands of Malta and Gozo, c. 1000–1812*. Valletta: Publishers Enterprises Group, 2002.

White, Joshua M. *Piracy and Law in the Ottoman Mediterranean*. Stanford, CA: Stanford University Press, 2017.

White, Joshua M. "Slavery, Manumission, and Freedom Suits in the Early Modern Ottoman Empire." In *Slaves and Slave Agency in the Ottoman Empire*, ed. Stephan Conermann and Gülşen, 283–318. Göttingen: V&R Unipress for Bonn University Press, 2020.

Wieringa, Wiert Jan. *The Interactions of Amsterdam and Antwerp with the Baltic Region, 1400–1800*. Dordrecht, Netherlands: Springer, 2013.

Wikström, Toby. "Was There a Pan-European Orientalism? Icelandic and Flemish Perspectives on Captivity in Muslim North Africa (1628–1656)." In *The Dialectics of Orientalism in Early Modern Europe*, ed. Marcus Keller and Javier Irigoyen-García, 155–70. London: Palgrave Macmillan, 2018.

Wolf, John B. *The Barbary Coast: Algiers Under the Turks, 1500 to 1830*. New York: Norton, 1979.

Wolff, Larry. *The Singing Turk: Ottoman Power and Operatic Emotions on the European Stage from the Siege of Vienna to the Age of Napoleon*. Stanford, CA: Stanford University Press, 2016.

[Wolffgang, Andreas Matthäus, and Johann Georg]. *Reisen und merkwürdige Schicksale zweyer in die Algierische Leibeigenschaft gerathenen Brüder Andreas Matthäus und Johann Georg Wolffgang, Kupferstecher in Augsburg, samt einer Nachricht von der Wolfgangischen Künstler-Familie.* 2nd ed. Augsburg: Conrad Heinrich Stage, 1769.

[Wolffgang, Andreas Matthäus and Johann Georg Wolffgang]. *Reisen und wunderbare Schicksale zweyer in die Algierische Leibeigenschaft gerathenen Brüder Andreas Matthaeus und Johann Georg Wolffgang, Kupferstecher in Augsburg.* [Augsburg], 1767.

Zook, Melinda S. *Radical Whigs and Conspiratorial Politics in Late Stuart England.* University Park: Pennsylvania State Press, 2010.

Index of Persons and Locations

For ease of reference, the index indicates in which chapter the entries occur. The following abbreviations in brackets identify the relevant chapter. Names of authors of secondary literature are not included.

(A) = d'Aranda
(Be) = Berg
(Br) = Brassard
(C) = Caronni
(DS) = de Sosa
(E) = Egilsson
(I) = Introduction
(M) = Marsh
(O) = Olufs
(P) = Pellow
(Q) = Quartier
(S) = Sturmer
(TM) = Ter Meetelen
(W) = Wolffgang

Abdelkader Peres/Elhash Abaulcodah Perez (ambassador) (P), 229
Abderrahman el-Mediouni/Elhash Abdrahaman Medune (admiral) (P), 216
Abu Djamal Youssef Pasha (ruler) (A), 125
Agadir, Morocco (TM), 277
Ahmed III (ruler) (O), 237
Ala Hacam/Ali Hakem (captain) (P), 216, 218
Alcalá de Henares, Spain (DS), 96
Alexandria, Egypt (Q) (S), 61, 172, 175
Algiers (A) (Be) (Br) (DS) (E) (I) (O) (Q) (W), 1, 4–5, 9–10, 13, 15, 17, 22, 24, 28–29, 32, 36, 47, 49, 91, 94–98, 101–4, 108, 111–15, 117–18, 123–25, 128–47, 152, 156, 158, 161–62, 166, 175, 184–85, 187–88, 190–98, 201–8, 236–37, 247, 249–53, 256, 259, 282, 290, 295, 354
Al-Ḥusayn ibn ʿAlī (ruler) (O), 243
Ali Boffoun/le Bouffon (Br), 204
Ali Goje (O), 251
Ali Hakem/Ala Hacam (captain) (P), 216, 218

[389]

Alli Pegelin (slave owner) (A), 125, 127–29, 134–37, 143
Alli Tagarino (captive) (A), 155
Alli Tagarino (merchant) (A), 152
Alloabenabiz (queen) (P), 218
Amet Arrais (admiral) (A), 146
Amrum (German island) (O) (I), 233–34, 236, 247
Amsterdam, the Netherlands (Br) (S) (TM) (W), 86, 191–93, 204, 209, 279,
Andalusia, Spain (A) (S), 57, 83–84, 131
Annaba/Bone, Algeria (I), 27
Anthonisz, Cornelis (artist) (S), 53
Antwerp, the Netherlands (A) (S), 63, 130–32
Armenia (Q), 168
Arvona, John (slave) (M), 316, 320, 323, 330–31, 333–35
Assin/Kalyan Hasan Bey (ruler) (O), 237
Augsburg, Germany (I) (W), 9, 15, 187, 192, 198–99
Augustus II (king) (O), 246–47
Aydin Reis/Casso Diaboli (captain) (S), 67

Baba Manoly (Q), 178
Babba-Ameth (captain) (C), 345
Balser, Hans (S), 86
Barbeer Assan (A), 134, 141
Bardo, Tunisia (C), 350–51, 354
Barnicoat, George (captive) (P), 216–17
Bascì Amba (C), 346, 348–49, 351–52
Bauer, Wilhelm (W), 192
Bellman, Jacob Martin (consul) (Be), 296, 302
Benali (ruler) (A), 138–39
Benghazi, Libya (Q), 175
Ben Hattar (P), 218
Berg, Marcus (captive and author) (Be) (I), 19, 281–305

Beyram Rais (renegade) (Q), 168–69
Bill of Portland, England (P), 228
Biscay, Spain (A), 121
Bizerte, Tunisia (S), 70, 82–83
Bogart, Humphrey (I), 32
Bone/Annaba, Algeria (I), 27
Bordier (captive) (Q), 181–82
Brandes, Peter (S), 87
Brassard, Isaac (captive and author) (I) (Br), 17, 201–9
Brielle, the Netherlands (Br), 204
Bruges, Belgium (A), 120, 132, 134, 159
Bu Aziz ben Nasser (ruler) (O), 241

Cabo de Tenes/Cap Ténès, Algeria (A), 145
Cádiz, Spain (A) (Be) (S) (TM), 57, 159, 255, 273, 296, 302, 330
Caesar, Julius (E) (I), 21, 105
Cairo, Egypt (Q), 166
Calliou (captain) (Be), 295
Camus, Albert (author) (I), 48–49
Canary Islands (S), 83–85
Candia (historical region) (S) (Q) see also Crete 85, 167, 171
Capati, Franco (merchant) (A), 130
Cape Bon, Tunisia (S), 65, 354
Cape Cornwall, England (P), 228
Cape Finisterre, Spain (A) (P), 124, 215
Capraia Island, Italy (Q), 178
Caprara (cardinal) (C), 355
Capri, Italy (C), 342–43
Captain Delgardenoor/Delgarno, Arthur (captain) (P), 216
Careno, Antonio (C), 354
Careno, Luigi (physician) (C), 355
Carlg (captain) (Br), 204
Carlotti (councillor) (C), 355
Carolina (ruler) (C), 351
Caronni, Felice (captive and author) (C) (I), 20, 27, 339–56

[390] INDEX OF PERSONS AND LOCATIONS

Carono, Giuseppe Antonio (Brother) (C), 354
Cartagena, Spain (Be), 282
Carthage, Tunisia (C), 66, 340, 355
Casso Diaboli/Aydin Reis (captain) (S), 67
Castilla la Vieja (region of Spain) (A), 121
Cataborne Monstafa (A), 137–39
Catallana, Jan (captive) (TM), 261, 263
Cervantes, Miguel/de Cervantes, Miguel (captive and author) (DS) (I) (S), 5, 13, 31, 36, 45, 55, 91, 93, 96–98
Ceuta (Spanish enclave) (A), 138, 140–41, 143, 151–57, 159
Chardin (Sir) (Br), 208
Charles II (king) (W), 192
Charles V (emperor) (A) (I) (S), 12, 22, 24, 53–54, 58, 60, 64, 66–69, 76, 83, 145
Chios, Greece (Q), 171
Christian IV (king) (E), 102, 115
Christian VI (king) (O), 253
Christiensson, Jesper (captive) (E), 114
Clarke, Briant/Clark, Briant (captive) (P), 216–17
Colleti (Be), 302
Cologne, Germany (W), 191
Constantine (I) (O) (S), 18, 32, 74–75, 233–37, 241, 243, 247, 249, 251–52
Copenhagen, Denmark (E), 102, 115
Corfu, Greece (S), 59
Corsica (I), 25
Count of Thurn (C), 347–48
Cremer, Thomas (captive) (P), 217
Crete (Greek island) (Q), 85, 167
Crimes, John (captive) (P), 216
Crisp, James (captive) (M), 307, 309–23, 328–37
Croatia (Q), 391
Crown of Aragon (former monarchy) (DS), 97

Dalmatia (historical region) (Q), 167
Dan, Pierre (author) (I), 43
d'Aranda, Emanuel/d'Aranda, Emmanuel/de Aranda, Emanuel/ de Aranda, Jac Emanuel (captive and author) (A) (I), 4, 14, 17, 20, 29, 31, 36, 103, 117–59
Davies, Lewis (captive) (P), 216–17
de Cervantes, Miguel/Cervantes, Miguel (captive and author) (DS) (I) (S), 5, 13, 31, 36, 45, 55, 91, 93, 96–98
Decius (emperor) (O), 249
Decker, Jan Cornelisz (captive) (TM), 263
de Córdoba y Coalla, Juan Fernández/ Marquess of Miranda (governor) (A), 155
Defoe, Daniel (author) (I) (W), 5, 15, 45, 47, 55, 190
de Haedo, Diego (author) (I) (DS), 91, 93
de la Barre (knight) (Q), 180
Delgarno, Arthur/Captain Delgardenoor (captain) (P), 216
de L'Isle-Adam, Philippe Villiers (S), 62
del Mármol Carvajal, Luis (captive and author) (DS), 91
de Melgaer, Jan (A), 139
Demetrii (Be), 298–99
de Penalosa, Martin (A), 152, 158
de Penaroa, Hieronimo (knight) (A), 153
Derna, Libya (Q), 175
de Saint Maximin, André (knight) (Q), 182
de Sosa, Antonio (captive and author) (DS) *see also* de Haedo, Diego 13, 36, 91–98
Destrée/Jean, Comte d'Estrée (marshal) (Br), 206

de Torres, Diego (captive and author) (DS), 91
Devoize, Jacques-Philippe/De-Voize, Jacques-Philippe (consul) (C), 354–55
Didrichssen, Lars (captain) (Be), 285
di Montalboldo, Settimio (priest) (C), 346
Djerba (Tunisian island) (Q) (S), 64–65, 175
Doria, Andrea/Doria, Andreas (admiral and statesman) (I) (S), 24, 58, 82
Ducaine (Br), 206
Dunnal, John (captive) (P), 216–17

Egilsson, Ólafur (captive and author) (E) (I), 13, 25, 101–14
Egypt (Q), 172–73
Eisenschmied, Leonhard (captive and author) (I), 47
El Dorador (renegade) (DS), 95–96
Elgia (consort) (O), 242
Elhash Abaulcodah Perez/Abdelkader Peres (ambassador) (P), 229
Elhash Abdrahaman Medune/Abderrahman el-Mediouni (admiral) (P), 216
Emhamenet Sageer (P), 220
Enkhuizen, Holland (E), 102
Epirus (historical region) (Q), 167
Erlangen, Germany (Br), 208

Falmouth, England (P), 214–15, 228, 230
Ferdinand I (emperor) (S), 60
Ferdinand the Fourth (ruler) (C), 351
Ferrara (Brother) (C), 353
Ferris, Richard (captain) (P), 215, 217–18
Fesch (cardinal) (C), 354
Fez, Morocco (I) (Be) (Q), 19, 147, 166, 278, 283–92, 295–96, 299–300
Flor, Richard (captive) (O), 236
Fontana, Fulvio (Jesuit scribe) (I), 27
Formentera (Spanish island) (A), 145

Foster, Robert (captain) (P), 215, 217
Fowey, England (P), 214–15
France (A) (Br) (C) (I) (Q) (TM) (W), 4, 14, 17, 83, 122, 123, 140, 151, 159, 161, 163, 164, 166, 169, 173, 179, 182, 193, 194, 201–2, 204–6, 255, 258, 310, 342–43, 352, 355
Francis (captain) (P), 228, 230
Francisco (an Italian) (Br), 207
Francis I (king) (S), 83
Frederick II (emperor) (I), 21–22
Frisch, Johann (author) (I), 29

Gaumont, Jean (Q), 182
Gdańsk, Poland (S), 51, 57, 86
Genoa, Italy (E) (I) (P) (S), 102, 214–15
George I (king) (P), 214, 244
George II (king) (P), 230
Germany (Br) (I) (O) (S) (W), 14, 48, 87, 195, 198, 208, 236, 247
Gibraltar (A) (M) (P), 124, 148, 152, 159, 193, 227–29, 271, 290, 307, 310, 313, 328, 331–32, 335–36, 360
Gil, Juan (friar) (DS), 98
Giraud (banker) (Q), 180
Gloag, Helen (Scottish captive) (I), 40
Gonneau (knight) (Q), 180–81
Goodman, Thomas (captive) (P), 216–17
Granada, Spain (S), 77
Grand Duke of Tuscany (Br), 208
Greece (Q) (S), 58, 60, 61, 167–68, 171
Grimonville (Frenchman) (Q), 169, 180, 182
Grindavík (Icelandic island) (E), 105
Groningen, the Netherlands (Br), 208
Guibaudet of Dijon (Q), 180
Gulf of Venice (Q), 168

Hagy Amour (captain) (C), 350
Halima el-Aziza/Hellema Hazzezas (queen) (P), 220

Hally Rais (renegade) (Q), 168
Hamburg, Germany (I) (O), 36, 252–53
Hamet Ben Ally (P), 224
Hammuda ibn Ali (ruler) (C), 346, 350
Hasleton, Richard (captive and author) (Br), 202
Hassan Veneziano (ruler) (DS), 96–97
Hawk, Edmund/Hawk, Edwd. (admiral) (M), 331, 335
Hayreddin Barbarossa (grand admiral) (I) (S), 22, 52, 58, 64–67, 69–72, 75
Hebenstreit, Johann Ernst (doctor) (O), 247
Heimaey (Icelandic island) (E), 102, 105–6, 108–10
Hellema Hazzezas/Halima el-Aziza (queen) (P), 220
Helm, Cornelius (captive) (Be), 298, 302
Hibraim Arrais (captain) (A), 152, 155
Hogenberg, Frans (copper engraver) (S), 54
Holke (consul) (C), 354
Holland (Br) (I) (Q) (TM) (W), 15, 31, 39, 102, 168, 187, 192, 204, 208, 258, 260, 263, 279, 333
Hungary (C) (S), 60, 67, 351

Ibiza (Spanish island) (A), 145
Ibrahim (dey) (O), 252
Ibrahim (sultan) (A), 135
Ibrahim Kutchuk (A), 251
Ibrahim Pasha (grand vizier) (S), 59
Ibrakim Bahsa (Ottoman commander) (S), 59
Iceland (E) (I) (O), 9, 13–14, 25, 32, 101–11, 234
Iede, Pieter Jansz (captive) (TM), 255, 260–61, 267, 269
Innsbruck, Austria (I), 38
Ireland (E) (I), 14, 32, 103
Isabella of Portugal (empress) (S), 58

Isles of Scilly (English archipelago) (O), 236
Italy (A) (Br) (C) (I) (Q) (S) (W), 20, 57, 60, 61, 68, 83, 128, 132, 167, 197, 208, 339, 342, 349, 353

James II (king) (W), 192
Jansen, Anthony (renegade) (I), 31
Jean, Comte d'Estrée/Destrée (marshal) (Br), 206
Jensen, Oluf (O), 253
Jón the Martyr/Þorsteinsson, Jón (reverend) (E), 109
Jónsson, Jón (E), 110
Jónsson, Margrét (E), 110
Jordan (captive) (Br), 207

Kalmar, Sweden (Be), 289, 296
Kalyan Hasan Bey/Assin (ruler) (O), 237
Kennedy, Jackie (I), 32
Kingdom of Fez (A), 147
Kingdom of Italy (C), 167, 342
Kingdom of Morocco (I) (S), 22, 52, 259
Kingdom of Naples (Q), 167, 178
Kingdom of Tlemcen (A) (DS), 64, 146
Kleubenschedl, Georg (captive) (I), 38
Königsberg (formerly in Prussia) (S), 87
Koroni, Greece (S), 58–60
Księży Dwór, Poland (S), 57
Kühn, Michael (captive and author) (I), 25, 31, 39, 47

La Ciotat, France (Q), 175
La Goulette (fortress) (S), 53, 68–69, 70, 75, 76, 78
La Goulette (port of Tunis) (C) (S), 66, 68–69, 70, 76, 78, 81, 347
Lalla Belkis (queen) (I), 40
Lalla Khenata (queen) (TM), 267
Lambrich, Gustav (captive) (Be), 290
Lambruschini (C), 354

Landcronas, Gustav (Be), 281
La Rochelle, France (A), 121
le Bouffon/Ali Boffoun (Br), 204
Leopold I (emperor) (W), 199
Lepanto, Greece (I), 24
Lisbon, Portugal (Be) (I) (S) (TM), 12, 19, 51, 57, 82, 86, 87, 279, 282, 299, 302
Lison, Frey (S), 60
Livorno, Italy (A) (Br) (C) (E) (I) (S) (W), 2, 10, 29, 37, 57–58, 102, 132–33, 138, 188, 190, 197–99, 203, 208, 247, 353–55
Logie, George (consul) (Be), 290, 295–96
London, England (I) (M) (P) (S) (W), 17, 85, 192–93, 213, 215, 227–228, 307
Lord Salomon (Br), 208
Ludwig II (king) (S), 67
Ludwig, Christian Gottlieb (doctor) (O), 247
Lund, Hans (captive) (Be), 282, 298

Madeira, Portugal (E) (I), 14, 103
Mahomet Celebi Oiga (A), 138–40, 142
Málaga, Spain (A) (I), 2, 10, 37, 131, 147
Malbork, Poland (S), 86
Mallorca, Spain (Br) (DS) (I), 32, 94–96, 144, 202
Malta (A) (I) (Q) (S), 2, 10, 37, 62, 68, 183
Mamora/Mehdya, Morocco (M) (TM), 274, 312
Maplesden, Jervis (captain) (M), 331, 334–36
March of Ancona (historical republic) (Q), 167
Marques de Santa Cruz (A), 148
Marquess of Miranda/de Córdoba y Coalla, Juan Fernández (governor) (A), 155
Marquis of Ruvigny (Br), 208

Marseille, France (I) (Q) (E), 4, 10, 37, 102, 175, 180, 252
Marsh, Elizabeth (I) (M), 19–20, 40, 277, 307–37
Marteilhe, Jean (captive) (I), 31
Master of Rhodes (S), 62
Mauretania (historical region) (C), 353
Maurus, Hans (captive) (A), 149–50
Mecca, Saudi Arabia (Be) (O) (Q) (TM), 173, 176, 248, 267, 297
Medemblik, the Netherlands (TM), 260, 279
Mehdya/Mamora, Morocco (M) (TM), 274, 312
Meknès /Mequinez, Morocco (Be) (M) (P) (TM), 217, 224, 226–27, 230, 255, 259–61, 275, 288, 292, 297, 300–301, 307
Melilla, Spain (DS), 94
Melzi (vice president) (C), 355
Menorca/Minorca, Spain (B) (M), 285, 310
Mequinez/Meknès, Morocco (Be) (M) (P) (TM), 217, 224, 226–27, 230, 255, 259–61, 275, 288, 292, 297, 300–301, 307
Messina, Sicily (C) (S), 58, 60–61, 342
Methoni (former Greek municipality) (S), 59–60
Meyer, Otto (S), 57
Mezzomorto Husayn Pasha (ruler) (W), 194
Milan, Italy (C) (I), 27, 340, 344, 354
Minorca/Menorca, Spain (B) (M), 285, 310
Mirangal (captain) (Q), 180–83
Monstafa Ingles (captive) (A), 134, 136–38, 140, 152, 155
Monstafa Oiga (captive) (A), 155
Morat Rais (Q), 171
Morea (Greek peninsula) (Q), 167

Mörlin, Joachim/Morlinus, Joachim (doctor) (S), 88
Morocco (Be) (C) (I) (M) (P) (Q) (TM), 17–20, 22, 39, 45, 52, 94, 101, 140, 147–48, 155, 161, 166, 211–14, 217, 224, 227, 229, 248, 255–57, 259–60, 265, 268–69, 271, 277–78, 281–84, 294–95, 297, 300, 302–3, 305, 307, 309–21, 323, 328–35, 353
Moulay Abdallah/Mulli Abdulla/Muly Abdela (ruler) (Be) (TM), 259–60, 263, 267–68, 274, 276, 278, 284, 295, 313
Moulay al-Mustadi (ruler) (TM), 274, 276
Moulay Ali al Aredj (ruler) (TM), 267
Moulay Hassan (ruler) (S), 65–66
Moulay Ismail/Moulay Ismaïl Ibn Sharif/Muly Smine (ruler) (B) (M) (P) (TM), 212, 218, 221, 224, 227, 267, 269, 272, 297, 321
Moulay Mohammed ben Arbiya (ruler) (TM), 256, 268–69, 271, 273, 275
Mozart, Wolfgang Amadeus (composer) (I), 40
Muhammad III (ruler) (I), 37
Muley Spha (prince) (P), 218
Muli Dris (M), 328
Mulli Abdulla/Muly Abdela/Moulay Abdallah (ruler) (Be) (TM), 259–60, 263, 267–68, 274, 276, 278, 284, 295, 313
Mulli Gedris (Be), 292
Muly Smine/Moulay Ismaïl Ibn Sharif/Moulay Ismail (ruler) (B) (M) (P) (TM), 212, 218, 221, 224, 227, 267, 269, 272, 297, 321
Muly Zidan (P), 220
Murat Reis/van Haarlem, Jan Janszoon (renegade and admiral) (E) (I), 32, 102
Murate Flamenco (corsair) (E), 102

Naples, Italy (C) (I) (S), 29, 57–58, 60, 83, 167, 178, 340, 342, 343, 348, 351, 353–54
Netherlands, the (Br) (TM), 63, 121, 123, 198, 201, 204, 255, 268, 279
New Sallee/Rabat, Morocco (A) (M) (P) (TM), 217, 313, 315
Newgent, Thomas (captive) (P), 218
Nikelsen, Hark (captive) (O), 236
Nikelsen, Jens (captive) (O), 236
Nombre de Dios, Panama (S), 84
North Africa 1–2, 4–5, 8–13, 15, 17–22, 24–25, 27–32, 36–41, 43, 45, 47–49, 51–52, 54, 62, 75, 77–78, 91–93, 101, 103, 117–18, 121, 125, 132, 134, 137–38, 157, 161, 172, 187–88, 190, 201–4, 211–12, 224, 233–35, 237, 247, 250, 256, 259, 267, 272, 281–82, 290, 292, 307, 309, 339, 340, 353

Okeley, William (captive and author) (I) (TM), 32, 45, 256
Oksen, Jürgen (captive) (O), 236
Olivar, George (friar) (DS), 96
Olufs, Hark (captive and author) (I) (P) (O), 211, 213, 233–53
Oran, Algeria (A) (DS) (I), 27, 48–49, 94, 138, 146
Oruç (brother of Hayreddin Barbarossa) (I), 22
Osmand Rais (Q) 182
'Othman Pasha (ruler) (Q), 171
Ottoman Empire (I), 22, 40, 53, 58–59, 64, 75, 94, 135, 167, 174–75, 178, 199, 226, 236, 250, 253, 348

Palermo, Italy (C) (S), 62, 340, 342, 347, 351, 353
Paolucci (C), 355
Paris, France (O) (Q), 177, 180–81, 183, 185, 252

INDEX OF PERSONS AND LOCATIONS [395]

Parker (captain) (M), 321
Patissiati (Be), 302
Peacock (captain) (P), 227–29
Pellow, John (captain) (P), 214
Pellow, Thomas (captive and author) (I)
    (P), 17–18, 32, 211–31
Peñón de Vélez de la Gomera (Spanish
    enclave) (A) (DS), 95, 155
Penryn, England (P), 214, 230
Perez, Mathias (captive) (A), 131–32
Petersberg, Austria (I), 38
Phillipe (priest) (Q), 179
Piquet, Charles (Reverend Father)
    (Q), 185
Pompeius, Gnaeus (general and
    statesman) (I), 21
Porchera, Giacomo (C), 354
Port Mahón, Menorca (Be), 285, 288
Portsmouth, England (TM), 279
Portugal (DS) (S) (TM) (W), 87, 92–93,
    193, 255

Quartier, Antoine (captive and author)
    (I) (Q), 14–15, 17, 161–85

Rabat/New Sallee, Morocco (P) (M),
    217, 313, 315
Raf Raf (Tunisian commune) (S), 73
Ray (Frenchman) (M), 314–15, 334
Rennes, France (Q), 169, 180, 182
Republic of Ragusa (Q), 167
Republic of Venice (Q), 167
Rhodes (Greek island) (I) (S), 21,
    62, 68
Rodes Monstafa (captive) (A), 155
Rossi (priest) (C), 355
Rousseau, Jean-Jacques (philosopher)
    (I), 47–48

Saban Galan (renegade) (A), 126, 141
Saffee/Safi, Morocco (M), 328

Saldens, Reynier (captive) (A), 126,
    128–34, 136–40, 143, 151–55,
    157–59
Salé, Morocco (A) (Be) (F) (I) (M) (P)
    (TM), 215–16, 255, 259, 260, 267,
    272, 275, 292, 294–95, 297, 300,
    307, 311–12
Salem Chastel (Q), 172, 182
Salimbeni (general) (C), 355
Samois (captive) (A), 135
Sanlúcar de Barrameda, Spain (A) (S)
    (TM), 84, 121, 258
San Sebastián, Spain (A), 121–22,
    159
Sapientza (Greek island) (S), 61
Sardinia (Italian island) (C) (S),
    67, 342
Sels, Joost (captain) (TM), 272
Sicily, Italy (C) (I) (Q) (S), 29, 57–58,
    60–63, 67, 83, 85, 182, 342,
    352–53
Sidi Mahomet/Sidi Muhammad (ruler)
    (I) (M) (TM), 277, 307, 313, 315–16,
    319, 324
Sidi Muhammad/Sidi Mahomet (ruler)
    (I) (M) (TM), 277, 307, 313, 315–16,
    319, 324
Sidim Mahomet, Mula Debbi (ruler)
    (O), 248
Simeon (French agent) (C), 354
South Africa (I) (TM), 39, 257
Spain (A) (Br) (DS) (S) (TM) (W), 57,
    68, 73, 77, 83–84, 92–94, 96, 117,
    121, 124, 131–32, 135, 138, 145,
    154–55, 159, 161, 175, 193, 202,
    255, 257–58, 282, 351
Spener, Philipp Jacob
    (author) (O), 247
Sperea (captain) (S), 81
Staiti (captain) (C), 347–48
Stams, Austria (I), 38

Stewart, Charles (ambassador) (P), 212, 224
Stille, Sven (captive) (Be), 288–89
Strait of Gibraltar (A) (W), 124, 271
Sturmer, Balthasar (captive and author) (I) (S), 9–10, 12–13, 24, 30, 51–89
Sublime Porte (Q), 175
Suleiman I/Suleiman the Magnificent (sultan) (S), 58, 67
Swabia, Germany (W), 195
Sweden (Be), 282, 285, 289, 290, 298, 301–2, 304

Taillerand (C), 355
Tangier, Morocco (A) (TM), 157, 271, 278
Taranto, Italy (S), 61
Tbessa, Algeria (O), 241, 243
ter Meetelen, Jan (TM), 279
ter Meetelen, Maria (captive and author) (I) (TM), 18–19, 39, 255–79
Tetuan/Tétouan, Morocco (A) (Be) (P) (TM) 140–45, 148, 151–52, 154–58, 224, 278, 282, 285, 295–99, 302
Texel, the Netherlands (TM), 279
Thessaloniki, Greece (S), 58
Þorsteinsson, Jón (reverend)/Jón the Martyr (E), 109
Thrann, Christian (horticulturalist) (O), 247
Tønder, Denmark (O), 253
Toulon, France (Q), 175
Towry, Henry (M), 337
Tripoli, Libya (C) (I) (Q) (S), 1, 14–15, 22, 39, 64, 161–62, 166, 169–76, 178, 180–83, 354
Tunis, Tunisia (A) (C) (E) (I) (O) (Q) (S), 1, 12, 15, 22, 24, 27, 38, 51–54, 64–78, 80–82, 112, 147, 161, 166, 172, 175, 243–44, 250, 339–41, 344, 346–48, 352–56
Tunisia (C) (I) (O) (S), 15, 20, 64, 65, 70, 73, 75, 243, 350
Turkey (Q) (S), 58, 166
the Tyrol, Austria (Br) (I), 38, 208

United States (C) (I), 1, 4–5, 8, 20, 28, 41, 339

Valencia, Spain (A), 145
van Caloen, Jean-Baptiste/van Caloen, Jan Baptiste (captive) (A), 120, 126, 133, 136–37, 155
van der Meer, Claas (TM), 255, 258
van Haarlem, Jan Janszoon/Murat Reis (renegade and admiral) (E) (I), 32, 102
van Zevere, Jacques (false name given by Emanuel d'Aranda) (A), 126, 131–32
Venice, Italy (Br) (I) (P) (Q) (S), 38, 61, 167–68, 171, 208, 226
Vermeyen, Jan Cornelisz (artist) (S), 53
Vitoria-Gasteiz, Spain (TM), 258
Vlamertinghe (captive) (A), 125, 130–31, 133–34
von Droste-Hülshoff, Annette (author) (I), 48
von Eckhel, Joseph Hilarius (collector) (C), 353
von Ems, Rudolf (author) (I), 22
Vulcano (Aeolian island) (S), 62

Waller, James (captive) (P), 218
Weilli (captain) (Be), 296, 298
Westman Islands, Iceland (E), 102, 105, 110–11, 114
Westphalia, Germany (I), 48
Witzai (count) (C), 353

Wolffgang, Andreas Matthäus (captive) (I) (W), 15, 187, 191–99
Wolffgang, Georg Andreas (I) (W)
Wolffgang, Johann Georg (captive) (I) (W), 15, 187–88, 191–94, 196–99
Wÿdau, Hans (S), 86

Xalxberner (consul) (Br), 208

Ysarn (Br), 209

Zante (Greek island) (Q), 167
Zappi-Tappa (minister) (C), 351

GPSR Authorized Representative: Easy Access System Europe, Mustamäe tee
50, 10621 Tallinn, Estonia, gpsr.requests@easproject.com

www.ingramcontent.com/pod-product-compliance
Lightning Source LLC
Chambersburg PA
CBHW022025290426
44109CB00014B/746